FAITHSPEAK

OTHER BOOKS
BY THE AUTHOR

For brief synopses of Mark's other books, an author profile, as well as an engaging conversation with Mark about the writing of FAITHSPEAK, please go to the Extras section at the end of this book or visit our website at: www.IFMedia.org/IFBooks.

FAITH SPEAK

READING BETWEEN THE LINES
OF RELIGIOUS LANGUAGE

*A Contemporary Re-thinking of the 300
Most Important Words, Concepts & Personalities
in the World's Languages of Faith*

MARK S HASKETT

IF BOOKS

First Softcover Print Edition, March, 2017.
First Edition Updated, March, 2019.

Copyright © 2017, 2019 by Mark S. Haskett.
Published by IF BOOKS.

All rights reserved. No part of this book may be reproduced in any form—digital, print, audio or otherwise—without written permission from the publisher, except in the case of brief quotations that are part of critical articles or book reviews. For permissions, additional information, or other queries, please write to: IF BOOKS, P.O. Box 3365, Modesto, CA, *or send a message by visiting* www.IFMedia.org/FaithSpeak/Comments.

ISBN 978-0-9971259-7-9 *(print)*
ISBN 978-0-9971259-2-4 *(eBook)*

Printed in the United States of America.

IF Books and IF Media are subdivisions of InnerFaith Resources, Modesto, California.

INTRODUCTION: *Under, Between, and Beyond Words* 1

PART ONE: *The Premise*
    Chapter One: Faith vs. Religion 9
    Chapter Two: Faithspeak Defined 17
    Chapter Three: The Case for Faithspeak 25

PART TWO: *The Lexicon*

A
Absolute	35	Anointed	46
Acts	36	Antidisestablish-	
Adam and Eve	37	mentarianism	47
Addiction	38	Apocalypse	48
Agnostic	40	Apocrypha	49
Allah	40	Apotheosis	50
Allahu Akbar	41	Ascension	51
Amen	42	Atheist	51
Angels	43	Atman	53
Annunciation	44	Atonement	54

B
Baal	59	Bible	66
Bahâ'i	60	Bliss	68
Baptism	61	Body	70
B.C.(E.)	62	Body of Christ	71
Belief	63	Book of the Dead	72
Bhakti	65	Buddhism	73

C
Chakras	77	Communion	94
Channeling	79	Community	96
Charisma	80	Confession	97
Charity	80	Consciousness	98
Chi	82	Conversion	100
Chosen People	83	Covenant	102
Christ	84	Creation	103
Christianity	87	Creator	105
Christian Science	89	Cross	107
Church	90	Cult	108
Clear	92	Culture	110
Collective Unconscious	94	Curse	110

FAITHSPEAK

D
Day of the Lord 113	Devote 123
Death 115	Dharma 124
Demon 116	Disciple 124
Denial 118	Divine 126
Deprogramming 118	Divinity 127
Determinism 119	Dogma 129
Deva 121	Doubt 129
Devil 122	Dysfunction 130

E
Easter 133	Epistles 140
Ecology 135	Eternal 142
Ecstasy 135	Evil 144
Ego 137	Evolution 147
El / Elohim 138	Excommunication 149
Enlightenment 139	Extraterrestrials 150
Entelechy 140	

F
Faith 153	Fool 157
Fall, The 154	Forgiveness 158
Fast 155	Freedom 160
Festival 156	Fundamentalism 161

G
Gaia 165	Golden Rule 177
Gambling 166	Gospel 178
Garden of Eden 167	Grace 179
Glory 169	Gratitude 181
Gnostic 170	Ground 183
God 172	Guilt 183
Goddess 173	Guru 185
Godhead 175	

H
Hallelujah 189	History 202
Healing 190	Holistic 203
Heaven 192	Holy 203
Hell 196	Holy Spirit 205
Heresy 197	Hopi 206
Hero 199	Humanism 207
Higher Self 197	Human Potential 208
Hinduism 200	Hypocrite 210

CONTENTS

I
Idolatry	213	Initiation	225
Image	215	Inner Child	226
Image of God	216	Inspiration	226
Imam	218	Intention	228
Immanence	219	Intercession	228
Immortality	220	Islam	230
Incarnation	222	Israel	233
Infidel	223		

J
Jehovah	237	Judaism	245
Jerusalem	238	Judeo-Christian	247
Jesus	239	Judgment	248
Jihad	242	Justification	250
Joy	243		

K
Kabbalah	253	Kill	259
Kali	255	Kingdom of God	260
Karma	256	Kosher	261
Khalil	258	Krishna	263

L
Law	267	Lord	274
Laying on of Hands	270	Love	275
Liberation	271	Lucifer	277
Light	271	Lust	278
Logos	273		

M
Magic	281	Messiah Complex	298
Mahabharata	283	Metaphysical	298
Mana / Manna	284	Mind	299
Mantra	284	Ministry	300
Marriage	285	Miracle	302
Martyr	287	Mitzvah	304
Mary	288	Mormon(ism)	305
Maya	290	Moses	307
Mazda	292	Muhammad	309
Means	292	Music	310
Meditation	293	Mysticism	312
Messiah	295	Myth	314

N
- Namaste 319
- New Age 320
- Nirvana 322
- Noah 324
- Nostradamus 325

O
- Obedience 329
- Original Sin 331
- Orthodox 333

P
- Pacifism 337
- Pagan 339
- Parable 339
- Path 342
- Peace 343
- Perfect 344
- Philosopy 345
- Pilgrimage 346
- Pluralism 347
- Poor 349
- Power 350
- Praise 351
- Prayer 352
- Priesthood 355
- Programming 356
- Prophet 359
- Proselytize 360
- Protestant 361
- Providence 363
- Psychology 363
- Purgatory 364
- Purification 366
- Purpose 368

Q
- Quest 371
- Quran 372

R
- Rabbi 375
- Rainbow 376
- Ramadan 377
- Rapture 378
- Realization 379
- Reconciliation 380
- Recovery 382
- Redemption 383
- Reincarnation 384
- Relativity 386
- Religion 388
- Repentence 388
- Resurrection 390
- Revelation 391
- Riches 393
- Ritual 394

S
- Sabbath 397
- Sacrament 399
- Sacrifice 401
- Saint 403
- Salvation 404
- Satan 406
- Save 408
- Science 409
- Scripture 411
- Second Coming 413
- Secular 414
- Self-Help 415
- Seminary 416
- Sentience 417
- Service 418
- Sex 418

Contents

S continued

Shamanism	420	Stoicism	434
Sharia	421	Stories	435
Sikh	422	Subliminal	436
Sin	424	Submission	437
Soul	426	Suffering	439
Spirit	428	Superstition	439
Spiritual	431	Swastika	440
Stewardship	432		

T

Tao	443	Tolerance	449
Tarot	444	Tongues	450
Temptation	445	Tradition	452
Test	446	Transcendence	453
Theocracy	447	Trinity	454
Theosophy	447	Truth	456
Time	448		

U

Ultimate Reality	459	Utopia	461
Unity	460		

V

Vidui	463	Vocation	466
Virgin Birth	464	Vodou/Voodoo	468
Visualization	465	Void	469

W

War	471	Word	475
Wicca	473	Worship	475
Witness	474		

X

Xerography	479

Y

Yes	483	Yoga	484

Z

Zeus	487	Zoroastrianism	489
Zodiac	488		

Extras

About the Author	493	Other Books by Mark	497
Author Interview	494	Pages for Notes	498

Under, Between and Beyond Words

During an episode of the iconic television series, *Star Trek: The Next Generation,* one of its more obscure characters, Natira, utters the following line:

"Words are here, on top. What's under them—their meaning—is what's important."

Natira's advice about the hidden subtext beneath the words we use applies not only to our native language, whether written or spoken. It also applies to the world's *religious* languages. Unfortunately, if we are conditioned by social custom and sectarian loyalties to pay attention only to what's "on top," to what our sacred texts and rituals merely look like or sound like, we tend to overlook the fact that "what's under them" are surprisingly similar meanings.

Here's another line, in this case spoken by a friend who helped me put together a year's worth of *Star Trek* quotations for a book of daily readings first published back in the 90s:

"What is it with religious people, anyway?" he complained over coffee one morning. "Half the time you can't understand the point they're trying to make. The other half you *can,* but what they're saying defies logic, or else it's just plain crazy."

The fact that my friend considers himself religious goes to

show just how frustrating this mode of communication can be at times. And it's true: Using religious language does seem to be an increasingly specialized skill. Some people are both adept and comfortable using it—in their own places of worship, at least. But more and more of us won't even bother.

It's not merely atheists who find religious terminology embarrassing or complain that it defies logic. Those who salt their conversations with religious references often come across as spiritual snobs or hypocrites. Or as unquestioning folk who enjoy their microwaves and smartphones, but possess a world-view more consistent with campfires and smoke signals.

And reactions like these often come from people who attend the same church, or share the same tradition. *Outside* that tradition, you'd expect problems with religious language to go from bad to worse. After all, if my friend often fails to understand his fellow Christians, surely the words of Jews, Muslims, Buddhists and Hindus should prove even more perplexing.

Not so fast.

Because one of the primary assumptions of *FaithSpeak* is that getting outside your usual religious environment—or lack of it—is actually the best way to understand it. Author/journalist Ari Goldman, in his best-selling book, *The Search for God at Harvard*, quotes one of his divinity school professors as saying, "If you know only one religion, you don't know *any*."

It's a profound statement. And the implication is, to fully understand your own tradition, you need to study *other* religions and learn what makes them tick. You need to see how other religions do what they do; to hear the words and rituals of your own "native tongue" translated into the words and rituals of someone else's. Only then can you begin to hear and experience the deeper meanings that lie under your particular religious language—the Mother Tongue, so to speak, from which they all derive.

Which is precisely how the process worked for me.

I haven't run across many people who will occasionally visit other religious communities or events in the same way they might catch a show at the local theater. But I do. Or at least did for much of my youth. Not that I'd take in a Sunday worship service as a form of cheap entertainment. For me the habit started as an outgrowth of that great Search for Truth which hits many of us in mid-adolescence, just after you miss the cut for the varsity baseball team, and you discover the girl who's wearing your Key Club pin is secretly seeing someone who didn't.

In my case it also followed the dedicated efforts of a pair of Mormon missionaries to convert me from my lukewarm Methodism to the One True Faith. My own efforts at fighting them off were so effective that I eventually convinced myself that *all* religions were bunk. Their holy scriptures were simply the latest in a long line of fabricated fairy tales, like the book of Genesis or the collected mythology of the ancient Greeks. I found it no more difficult to reject God than deny the existence of Zeus or Eden's talking snake or—sorry, Virginia—Santa Claus.

But I also had nagging doubts. Maybe I was missing something. I soon began to visit churches and temples and fellowships with funny names in an attempt to find out if, as the saying goes, I'd tossed the baby out with the bath water.

I *had*. And what I eventually came to realize was that all the babies and all the bathwater—and all the mothers and fathers up to their elbows in soapsuds—were signs that something deeper was going on. Something was happening in those congregations I visited, something below the level of what I was seeing or hearing, something hidden between the lines. All the rituals and the music and the words of scripture pointed to it, even if most of the people in the pews mistook the pointers for what was being pointed *at*.

In tasting the wafer pushed onto my tongue at Mass, in smelling the sweet incense from a Buddhist altar, in looking through the forest of uplifted arms at a Pentecostal tent meeting... in the rhythmic chanting of the Kaddish or the gentle pressure on my forehead as I bowed with believers toward Mecca... in all these rituals I found an increasingly familiar dynamic. It tasted, smelled, looked, sounded, and felt different in each case. It *was* different.

And utterly, inexplicably, *the same*.

It was as if each religious tradition was speaking in its own private language, while secretly sharing the same meanings. We know, for example, that English, Hebrew, Arabic and Cambodian have their own word for "tree." Each sounds different. Each looks so unlike the others on a printed page you'd swear they came from different planets. Yet all of them point to that object with a trunk and branches and fan-like appendages that blow in the breeze and provide shade from the sun.

Could religions operate like that, I wondered? Could it be that religions were more like dialects, all of which had descended from a common Mother Tongue? Some of these dialects might share many of their words, or sound similar enough that translating them into one another would be relatively easy. Others would look and sound so distinctive that their common linguistic heritage might be harder to trace. But they *could* be traced.

The analogy grew on me. I became even more convinced after I started working for an organization that ran the local food bank. A coalition of some fifty religious congregations, Inter-Faith Ministries not only gave out bags of groceries to the hungry, but clothing and household goods — all with no spiritual strings attached. And they were always looking for fresh recruits.

I volunteered, ended up on its board of directors and twelve years later as an interim president. And what continually amazed me was that the people who volunteered to help, coming as they did from a wide variety of backgrounds, still managed to share a similar concern for people in need. Their religions had apparently produced in them the same desire to serve the less fortunate. So maybe, I thought, it wasn't so much their particular "dialect" that shaped their concern, but the Mother Tongue speaking *through* it.

If only it were that simple.

Trouble is, many of Inter-Faith's volunteers no longer identified themselves as religious. Others, who appeared as devoted to helping the hungry and homeless as the most Bible-believing Baptist, weren't even raised in a religious environment. Perhaps the Mother Tongue I'd heard behind all those dialects could be communicated in ways that aren't necessarily religious at all. Maybe the benevolent faith I'd witnessed in my fellow volunteers could be produced outside of religion.

Or maybe faith and religion are two different things.

Which is where Chapter One starts.

Before *you* start, however, let me provide a few caveats on how this book works. And the operative word here is "works."

Because *FaithSpeak* is a kind of workbook. A primer. Not only for people who already consider themselves religious, but for those who don't. In keeping with that theme, the book doesn't pretend to offer any final answers or universally accepted definitions like some theological *Webster's Dictionary*. It simply draws out the meanings of some of the most important words and concepts found in various religious traditions, then treats them as broadly and inclusively as possible, from both inside and outside those traditions.

Especially outside. In fact, you should understand from the start that individual members of these religions—or at least their spiritual leadership—may not agree with many of the definitions and commentaries that make up the *FaithSpeak* Lexicon. I have made every effort to build bridges from one religion to another, knowing that some people prefer their well-defined boundaries and exclusive claim to The Truth. I have pressed spokespersons from each tradition to find words and concepts in their own religion that express the spirit of words and concepts in other religions. And many *did* find them, again and again, even while disagreeing with my notion of the Mother Tongue that is "under" them.

Deciding whether or not you agree with me is part of the work I hope you'll engage in as you read this book.

To make your work easier, I'll try to keep things simple and accessible. Not that there aren't some overlong sentences here and there. (Along with a few incomplete or grammatically incorrect sentences. Like *this* one.) A few words with more than four syllables may even creep in occasionally. ("Occasionally," for instance.) Still, this is no scholarly treatise for post-graduate divinity students. There is no Ph.D. behind my name, no academic craving for footnotes, no laundry list of professional credits to convince readers of my expertise. Personally, I lean more toward humor than scholarship. A belly-laugh is often more convincing than a footnote. And religion is much too important to leave in the hands of thin-lipped theologians or somber ecclesiastical councils.

On the other hand, the alphabetical gleanings in Part Two of this book weren't designed primarily for amusement, nor were they written without a scholarly respect for objectivity. The three chapters in Part One are an attempt to build a critical framework to justify them. This framework may even come across as the product of somber study and research. But mostly it's been distilled, like the Lexicon itself, from hundreds of contacts and conversations with religious leaders all across the spectrum of tradition and practice. *And* with the ordinary believers and non-believers who accept or reject them.

Though it might be tempting to dive into the Lexicon and start picking out the words that interest you (or puzzle you) the most, you'll be better prepared if you read the chapters in Part One first. The distinction between "faith" and "religion," for example, can change the way you approach the entire subject, if only because it clarifies what the bottom line for religion really *is*. As a result, religious languages and institutions become more accountable for the jobs they do. Which should make even card-carrying skeptics happy.

Understanding how religious language "works," on the other hand, may suggest a different standard for that very accountability. And with it, we can begin to look past the various dialects to their deeper meanings. We can begin translating them from one dialect to another, and back into ordinary language where they can help enrich our daily lives.

By the end of Part One, the groundwork should be in place for a more inclusive and universalizing interpretation of the religious words we encounter. This is no small thing. As societies grow more diverse and the world grows smaller and more dangerous, it's all the more essential we outgrow the notion that religions are incompatible or in competition with one another. If anything, these traditions must not only become more tolerant of their fellow workers in the spiritual vineyard, but actively and mutually supportive.

To accept the premise of *FaithSpeak* is to become part of this movement toward greater understanding and harmony. You'll be able to hear the Mother Tongue whether it's spoken in the practical language of secular society, or the eloquent, poetic cadences of centuries past and cultures apart.

It wouldn't be the first time walls have come a-tumblin' down.

Mark S. Haskett
Modesto, California
January, 2019

PART ONE
The Premise

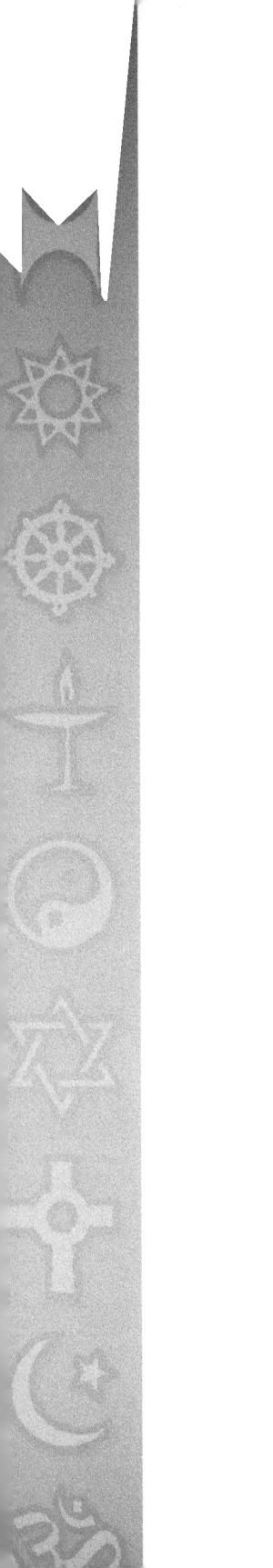

The Difference Between Faith and Religion

The words "faith" and "religion" are two of the most commonly misunderstood words in the English language. Despite what many people think, they are *not* interchangeable. They do not mean the same thing. Misuse of them is not only dangerous in today's world of sectarian infighting, it takes our focus away from what is arguably the most important distinction we can make before setting off on, or continuing on, our own spiritual journeys.

So, allow me to argue. Or at least let me attempt to convince you that labeling those two words as "misused" goes beyond mere personal opinion. To do that, ironically, I'll need to get personal.

Way back in the 1980s, a good part of my life (beyond running a small graphics business) was spent volunteering at our local emergency food bank. The board members and grocery-baggers with whom I worked were, for the most part, a sincere and outgoing bunch. Handing out food to the unemployed cannery worker, or stuffing several bags for the single mother and her three grade-school children—then waving a cheerful good-bye even when no gratitude was shown—was a natural expression of their faith.

There were personality differences, of course. But all shared the same desire to be of service, along with a similar sympathy for the misfortunes and challenges faced by the people who came to us for help.

What we *didn't* share was the same religious background that presumably made us that way. Catholics and Presbyterians, Baptists and United Methodists and practically every other Christian denomination were all represented on our crew. There were reform and conservative Jews, and a Hindu obstetrics intern who recently immigrated from India. A Muslim refugee from Palestine volunteered for a time, as did a whole family of Buddhists from Cambodia.

There were also Sikhs, a handful of closet atheists, and a New Age feminist who put her crystal pendant away whenever she'd show up for her half-day stint, not wanting to offend anyone. All these and more would gladly slip on their aprons and roll up their sleeves to sort canned goods and re-stock shelves, sometimes sweeping floors and doing the necessary grunt work so that hundreds of local families, and pieces of broken families, wouldn't go hungry for the next week or two.

And yet the same religions that produced all these Good Samaritans have also turned out equal numbers who *aren't* so compassionate. You've met these folks, too—the ones who can quote chapter-and-verse but squint with suspicion when you first meet, or ignore you outright if you look different or "foreign." They're the ones who sing and pray as loudly as anybody else in the pew, then go home and yell at their kids and kick the dog when things don't go right. They're the ones who step over the wino on the sidewalk with barely a break in stride, or turn away from the vet with the hand-scrawled cardboard sign begging for food at the entrance to the Walmart parking lot.

How could all these generous and not-so-generous types, some of whom sit next you every Sunday, claim to be of the same faith?

The answer is... *they can't.*

And it's not because one is a good Catholic or Presbyterian and the other isn't. Or because one is a Sunni Muslim, and the other's a Hasidic Jew, for that matter. It's because each person's religion and each person's faith are two separate things.

You've probably attended a dinner or some other social gathering where a nosey new acquaintance will inquire, if only to spike the conversation, "What's your faith?" or "What faith do you belong to?" The expectation, of course, is that you'll respond by naming your religious affiliation. But the correct answer isn't "Buddhist" or "Baptist" or whatever religion you may identify with. Nor is it an affirmation of faith or a personal testimony such as "I believe in the Holy Bible as the literal Word of God, and in the Lord Jesus Christ as my personal Savior."

A truly honest response to *What faith are you?* would be far more revealing, an exposé of sorts, a personal inventory... more like this:

"I am a hard-working, single professional woman who believes in teamwork (but is suspicious of my male co-workers and most younger women since my husband left me for one)... and a caring, devoted mother (even if I do get angry at my kids when they don't behave, but then I didn't exactly respect *my* parents either after they divorced)... who is struggling to find purpose in my life (although a good sale at Macy's or a brief affair with no strings attached can sometimes be an acceptable substitute)... and who is basically optimistic about the future (although, truth be told, I feel like I have absolutely no control over it)."

Faith, in other words, is a characteristic of *people,* not institutions. It's how you as an individual feel about the world and interact with it. It's the sum total of your internal attitudes and outward behavior, your tendency to think and act in certain ways based on both subjective experience and objective factors like genetics and environment. It's what personality tests try to measure and many of us would prefer to avoid: An unblinking assessment of our strengths and weaknesses, dreams and nightmares, joys and sorrows, including all the conflicting emotions and cerebral cross-currents, known and unknown. In short, it's a complete, up-to-the-minute status report on *Who We Are,* from what is observable to what's not, from the masks we wear in public to the secrets we harbor deep down in our innermost heart-of-hearts.

And that leads to some interesting conclusions. The most obvious one is that, even if you don't consider yourself religious, *you already have a faith.* If you're breathing, conscious, and able to express yourself in word and deed, you are living out your faith every waking minute of every day. And sometimes you are the last to know what that faith *is.*

Religion, on the other hand, is part of what *shapes* your faith.

Notice I said *part.* Because there are many factors that combine to create Who We Are, some of which may have far more impact than religion. The physical equipment we're born with, for instance. Or the big, gut-wrenching events that can change us forever. Even small, seemingly unimportant incidents can coalesce to affect us over time. Add to these the expectations and lessons you absorbed from your experiences in pre-school and grade school, and from watching five or ten thousand hours of TV before you ever stepped into a classroom. Not to mention the crucial influence of parents and other childhood role models.

The title of the early pop-psychology classic, *All I Really Needed to Know I Learned in Kindergarten,* by Robert Fulghum, is more than catchy and endearing. It's pretty much spot on. It also has a sobering corollary: The attitudes we've developed by the time we're five or six years old are basically the attitudes we're likely to carry with us for the rest of our lives. And the fact is, organized religion will probably have played only a minor role in forming them.

Which reminds me of a package my wife and I received in the mail shortly after our first child was born. Enclosed with a free sample of baby formula was a poem entitled, "Children Learn What They Live," based on the poem by Dorothy Law Nolte. The poetry turned out to be more nourishing than the pabulum. What it was, actually, was another dose of pop psychology, a litany of the kinds of experiences that shape young minds.

> *If a child lives with criticism,*
> *he learns to condemn.*
> *If a child lives with hostility,*
> *he learns to fight.*
> *If a child lives with fear,*
> *he learns to be apprehensive.*
> *If a child lives with pity,*
> *he learns to feel sorry for himself.*
> *If a child lives with jealousy,*
> *he learns to feel guilty. But...*
> *If a child lives with encouragement,*
> *he learns to be confident.*
> *If a child lives with tolerance,*
> *he learns to be patient.*
> *If a child lives with praise,*
> *he learns to be appreciative.*
> *If a child lives with acceptance,*
> *he learns to love.*
> *If a child lives with fairness,*
> *he learns what justice is.*
> *If a child lives with honesty,*
> *he learns what truth is.*
> *If a child lives with friendliness,*
> *he learns that the world is a*
> *nice place in which to live.*

The poem is as much a description of how we've become Who We

Are as a prescription for raising the next generation. The fact that it doesn't come from the lips of Moses or Jesus, Muhammad or Buddha, makes it no less true. And if we commit ourselves to following its guidance, then not only does *our* behavior change, the faith (and fate) of a child may also be shaped in a positive, lasting way.

And that brings us back to religion. Because religion, like the poem, is a kind of institutional prescription whose overall purpose is to shape our faith. That collection of ideas and recommended behaviors may be more or less *comprehensive,* in that it offers guidance for everything we do, not just for responsible parenting. It may be more or less *rigid,* by insisting that there is only one right way to do things. And it may be more or less *absolute,* in that the "right way" is considered permanent and unchanging, usually because some higher authority said so. But we nevertheless label it as "religion" because its function is to enlist our allegiance, affect our faith, and shape Who We Are.

Ideally, if you're happy with Who You Are, your religion should help you maintain your personal status quo. If you're mostly satisfied, but admit there's room for improvement, your religion should assist you in fine-tuning your faith. On the other hand, if your attitudes and actions have pretty much sent your life spiraling down the porcelain passageway, your religion should provide the transformative tools to stop the downward slide and help you crawl back up from the sewer.

This transformational element is a special hallmark of religion. For it acknowledges the fact that many of us have grown up more in keeping with the first half of the preceding poem than the second. Our religion should therefore incorporate a realistic standard for measuring ourselves against some better, brighter vision of Who We Ought to Be; and it should offer us proven methods for achieving that vision. In fact, *without* a vision and methodology, religion isn't truly religion.

How those tools work will be the subject of our next chapter. Along with a definition of the term "Faithspeak." As for a working definition of "religion," let's try this one on for size:

Religion is the accumulated treasury of tools and resources you use to maintain, fine-tune or transform your faith.

Those tools and resources might consist entirely of some form of Christianity, or some other comprehensive tradition we normally think of as a religion. Or they may involve certain elements of Christianity (on Sunday mornings at least), combined with a set of commercial ethics (which on weekdays must regrettably overrule some of Jesus' more unrealistic teachings because, after all, he couldn't possibly know what it's like to run a business in today's dog-eat-dog marketplace). Both of these components may be supplemented by a code of patriotic conduct embodied in our national folklore (since all that poppycock about "turning the other cheek" is no way to run a *country,* either).

Okay, so I kid. The point is, mere "lip-service"—naming a particular religion as your own—isn't a valid criterion for identifying one's religion any more than words can substitute for action. Instead, your religion consists of the collected resources you draw from and adhere to, whether from a single source or from several different (and sometimes incompatible) sources, including secular ones.

To repeat, the way we're using "faith" and "religion" in this book isn't how people normally brandish these terms in ordinary conversation. But it's not as if I've arbitrarily decided to use them this way. In his early-80s book, *Stages of Faith,* Harvard psychologist James W. Fowler argues for much the same approach, basing his terminology on the work of even earlier authors. Faith, as Fowler described it, involves an "alignment of an individual's heart or will." It is a personal quality, whereas religion is the objective, "cumulative tradition" that exists apart from individuals, and which people draw from and interact with in order to affect those personal qualities.

Other commentators make a similar distinction. Some point out that common usages such as "acting in good faith" or "being faithful" or simply "Have faith!" carry the original sense of the word—the notion that our outward behavior is an expression of interior attitudes. Still others remind us that the Latin root for our word "religion" means *to bind.* Religion is therefore understood as something exterior to us, something to which we bind ourselves. And what we bind ourselves *to* are those same kinds of accumulated resources for shaping faith we've been talking about here.

But even if using "faith" and "religion" in this way were simply a matter of choice, that decision would still make the most sense. Because it is essential to separate Who We Are from *what makes us* Who We Are. We must learn to see ourselves as a kind of "product" in order to focus more attention on the process, on the tools best suited to shaping and re-shaping that product. This is the first, crucial step toward gaining more control of our lives.

It is also the first step toward the kind of expanded awareness required for a better appreciation of the FaithSpeak Lexicon. For example, when you come across the word "salvation," I hope you'll be able to look beyond the definition offered by any single religion and understand it as a process of faith-shaping in which all human beings are engaged—even those who reject traditional forms of religion. And since no religion has a monopoly on faith, or any one type of faith, you'll be better able to consider the full range of tools available for shaping your own.

When you encounter "Jesus" or "Buddha" in the Lexicon—knowing what you now know about faith and religion—you'll be looking not so much for the strictly Christian or Buddhist perspective as for how the story and the person *function* in shaping adherents' faith. As a result you'll be more likely to see parallels in other religions, and even recognize the same dynamic of faith-shaping in non-religious contexts.

If that sounds crazy, just remember: The rabbi and the priest, the fundamentalist and humanist, the Muslim and the atheist, are either alike—or *not* alike—depending on the way they interact with the world and with each other. That's our standard. What they do to *make* themselves that way is another story.

In fact, it's the next chapter.

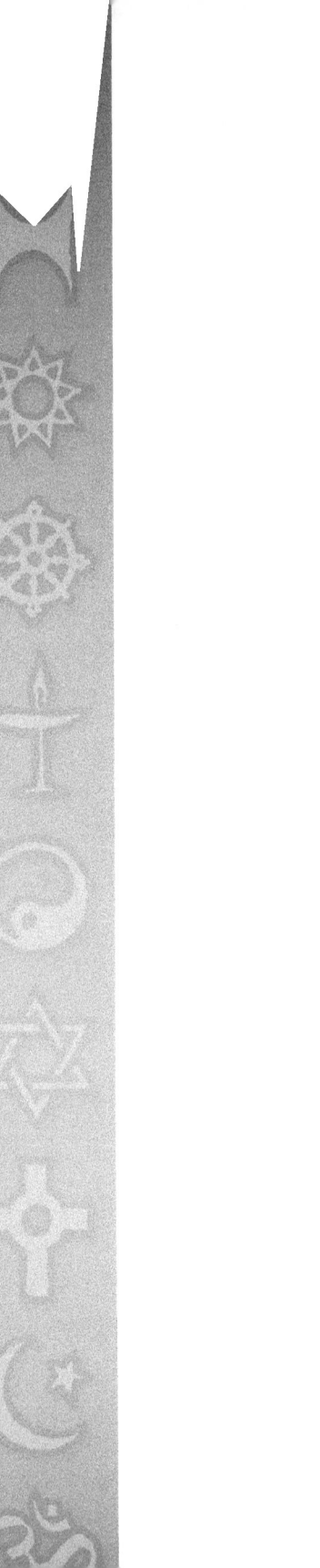

Faithspeak Defined

If we look at "faith" as the sum total of attitudes and behaviors that make up Who We Are, and if "religion" is one of the primary ways by which those attitudes and behaviors are shaped, then the *methods* used by a particular religion become the primary criterion for its success.

Because those methods will determine its overall effectiveness. Those methods will either leave your faith unchallenged and unaltered, or they will reach down into that core of Who You Are, into that heart-of-hearts protected by all those layers of emotional and intellectual insulation... into that Holy of Holies hidden behind the veil of public personae and false fronts... and *transform it.*

The world's major religions, as if you couldn't guess, have been specifically designed to communicate with that core self deep within each of us. The words, the rituals, the music—the whole *aura* surrounding each religion—have all been consciously and unconsciously contrived to break through our personal defenses and speak to our hearts in a way we can relate to and, more importantly, respond to. And that "way," as if you *also* couldn't guess, is not exactly The King's English.

It's another language altogether. In a word, it's Faithspeak.

Faithspeak consists of those communications that are directed primarily *at our faith.* Many of the things we say or do, of course, are not intended to affect us at that level. "I'll have the soup instead of salad, please," or "Sweetheart, could you pick up my poodle skirt at the dry cleaners on your way home?" probably won't change anyone's fundamental attitudes toward life.

But some of our communications *are* potentially faith-affecting. They can take place through spoken language by targeting the intellect, or by aiming directly for our emotional hot-buttons. They can also speak to us in subtler, more indirect ways. In last Sunday's four-part choral arrangement, for example, that subliminally suggests the harmony of life under the baton of a supreme Director. Or in the act of believers kneeling in unison, subconsciously binding themselves to each other and to the divinity they serve. Or in the sun-streaked majesty of stained-glass windows towering overhead, visually celebrating the Light that shines down on our lives. Or in the reverent touching of the Torah scrolls as they're carried up and down the sanctuary aisles, essentially confirming one's submission to the Law bound up within them.

Faithspeak is a language of all five senses, sometimes addressing us at a conscious level, but more often delivering its message without our being particularly aware of it. And its truth lies not in some rational meaning we might objectively ascribe to the words we hear or the rituals we participate in. Its truth for us lies in how well it performs its job—*in its success at shaping our faith,* in the progressive transformation of Who We Are into Who We Ought to Be.

Sadly, we often make the mistake of analyzing religions for their compatibility with scientific or historical fact. (That is, unless the clergy of a particular religion *claim* scientific accuracy, in which case they open those claims to critical analysis.) Instead, what we ought to be asking of religion is: How effective is it at transforming or refining the faiths of its individual adherents? Does it produce in them some ideal expression of attitude and behavior that promotes not only personal fulfillment, but justice and harmony in their relationships with others?

And about *that*—about its effectiveness in doing its job—we *can* be scientific. Because the ability of Faithspeak to communicate with our heart-of-hearts depends on four very objective components.

First of all, to the extent that it has linguistic content, *Faithspeak must be in our own spoken language.*

Using the full range of senses is important, yes; but humans are still uniquely defined by speech. Our very thoughts depend on words. Language is especially important for receiving and processing complex or abstract information, and for transferring thoughts and experiences from one person to another. Unfortunately, if the only language I happen to understand is English, and Brother Devananda delivers this evening's devotional in Hindi, that information simply won't come across.

Secondly, *Faithspeak must take into consideration our level of scientific sophistication.*

Another fact about human beings is that we grasp new data by making analogies, by comparing new ideas with what we're already familiar with. Later in the Lexicon, we'll use the idea of a remotely-controlled robot to help make sense of the words "soul" and "spirit." Unfortunately, if you have no concept corresponding to the word "robot," and no experience controlling something "remotely," this science-based analogy will only leave you scratching your head.

Which is why, in pre-technological societies, the soul was compared with respiration or "the breath." Breathing was something everyone had experience with; a degree from MIT wasn't required. Later, the word "ghost" became the more sophisticated analogy for "soul," which, following the Industrial Revolution, evolved into "the ghost in the machine."

In short, Faithspeak tends to select from whatever conceptual models are available within the current body of knowledge, so long as they're not too technical for ordinary people to understand. The more scientifically-advanced the culture, the more scientific the analogy.

And that brings us to one very important corollary: The more *archaic* those models appear in relation to current technology, the more difficult it is to continue using them to explain religious concepts. Maintaining outdated models may be justified for other reasons—for their poetic beauty, say, or for a sense of connection to the past. But either way, their continued use does create challenges.

Thirdly, *Faithspeak must reflect our social and political environment.*

If everyone lives in a nuclear family where the father is head of the household—and where most fathers are loving and fair and respected—our relationship with a benevolent higher power is likely to be described in fatherly terms. (But note the corollary here, too: In societies or subcultures where many children are born out of wedlock, and mothers end up raising them on their own, the "father figure" might create more atheists than believers.) Likewise, in societies where kings and princes rule, or where masters and servants are commonplace, personal relationships tend to be symbolized along those lines. Words like "command" and "duty" and "obedience" are employed because they are appropriate to that model. They're familiar. They convey meaning.

The fourth requirement for Faithspeak is probably more controversial. Many so-called progressive denominations will find it especially distasteful because fundamentalists often use it so shamelessly, and intellectuals point to it as proof that religion is hopelessly primitive. But here it is, warts and all:

Faithspeak must carry an emotional charge.

As Olivia Newton John put it decades ago, we need to "get physical." The more intense the emotional content, the better. The more inclusive of all five senses, the better. With apologies to scientists and computer geeks, professors of mathematics and students of philosophy, it is nonetheless true that human beings can*not* be defined as The Rational Animal. People can *be* rational on occasion, yes. They can rigorously apply logic to certain tasks. Some individuals may even demonstrate that sought-after quality of having "a mind like a trap." But the human animal is not consistently, not even for the most part, rational.

Maybe it's because the human animal is, after all, an *animal*. From infancy onward, our natural learning process depends on sensory stimuli, to which we react with various pre-programmed motor responses. Those responses are reinforced through reward or punishment, usually by physical means, making them more or less likely to occur in the future. It's the same stimulus-response-reinforcement pattern by which every member of the Animal Kingdom learns. And even as humans add language and other symbolic tools for rational thought—our vaunted "left brain functions"—those new capabilities are inevitably interwoven with sensory data and emotional content.

For Faithspeak, then, intellect alone isn't enough, even when the appropriate language and all the right scientific/cultural models are brought into play. The most effective learning involves *both* sides of the brain. Linking feelings, visual images, sounds and tastes with written or spoken information makes it more memorable. And that data, in turn, becomes connected to our motor functions—in essence, to our behavior. If that linkage is subconscious, Faithspeak becomes all the more effective because it avoids having to be evaluated consciously. After all, our conscious minds have a nasty habit of trying to apply logic to everything, including things that aren't meant to be logical. As a result, psychologists tell us, the needed behavioral transformation doesn't become "habitualized."

Not that this great, logical, conscious mind of ours can always overrule the emotions, even when the facts are plainly on its side. Take, for instance, the experience of watching a movie. We're fully aware that film is a kind of virtual reality. We know the actors are role-playing, that the blood is only red dye #2 mixed with chicken gravy, that the airplane being shot down is only a miniature or digital replica.

We can even watch a documentary about the making of the film we're going to see, before we actually see it. We'll learn how the special effects are created; we'll watch the actors blowing their lines until they get them right; we'll see the camera and the boom mike and the thirty-odd technicians going about their jobs just off-screen. Yet when we finally pay our twelve bucks and sit down in the theater, we can still laugh and cry and hurt and hope everything turns out in the end, because a good simulation of reality can be just as convincing as reality itself—even when we *know* it's a simulation.

And if the film happens to contain a message—like a parable from the Bible or Bhagavad Gita, or like Uncle Scrooge waking up a new man on Christmas morning—that message can reach into our heart-of-hearts and grab us like nothing else can. Because it impacts *all* our senses, consciously and subconsciously, providing analogies with our own experience, using models we can relate to, involving our "whole brain."

Whole brain... heart-of-hearts. One is the more scientific term, one poetic. Take your pick. The bottom line is that your faith—the way you interact with the world—can be changed for the better.

If this is beginning to sound like some sort of apology for why religions are the way they are, well... it *is*. It is also an explanation for why religions are changing, and *must* change. Because for Faithspeak to continue to transform lives, it must employ whatever current resources and models best illumine its message—without, of course, compromising the Mother Tongue and the meanings those words point *at*.

"We all know that Art is not truth," Picasso said. "Art is a lie that makes us *realize* truth." Substitute the word "Religion" for "Art" in that statement and you'll have a handy, one-line summary for the role religion plays. *And* for the methodology by which Faithspeak has worked for the last five thousand years.

Which may remind you of that nagging suspicion you've had since the title of this book first caught your eye. Faithspeak... *hmmm*... sounds vaguely familiar, doesn't it? In fact, didn't some British author invent a similar word a few decades ago? And wasn't it a *bad* word...?

Bingo on both counts: 1) George Orwell, and 2) Newspeak.

In the oppressive society envisioned in Orwell's novel, *1984,* "Newspeak" was the manner by which the government overhauled language for the purpose of manipulating the minds of its citizens. Not only were old words given new meanings, they were purged of any implications that might conflict with government policy. The range of individual and social thought was thus narrowed to what was officially acceptable. Ideally, the language not only warned you when a certain thought was heretical, it prevented you from having heretical thoughts to begin with. Newspeak was therefore a language of suppression, subterfuge, and the well-crafted euphemism.

Ring a bell? Because the same kind of thought-manipulation goes on today. If our own government deems it necessary to wage war, soldiers' deaths are reported as "KIA's," civilian deaths as "collateral damage"—neither of which conveys the terror of what's really happening on the ground. Opponents are dehumanized with generic references to "the enemy," or scriptural labels like The Great Satan. And the latest weapon isn't named for the killing machine it is, but proudly introduced as The Peacemaker.

In the sense that language can be a tool for manipulation, Newspeak and Faithspeak are distant cousins. Faithspeak, admittedly, is designed to change Who You Are, even if it must circumvent your conscious mind and slip in its message while you're looking the other way. The shared methodology can seem sinister and sneaky, like brainwashing. Or at least it feels uncomfortable, like being put under a hypnotic spell and no longer being in control.

But that's where the two methods of manipulation part company. Because, like the techniques of hypnotism or "suggestion" employed to help people quit smoking, Faithspeak is a tool you ultimately control. *You* evaluate your behavior/faith and decide if it's as healthy and productive as you'd like it to be. *You* analyze the available tools and resources for modifying your faith, knowing your heart-of-hearts is an elusive son-of-a-gun that sometimes requires manipulation and subterfuge. And finally, taking into account your culture and experience—and what may or may not have worked in the past—*you* prescribe the methods for shaping your faith. Like a physician prescribes medicine, say, or a physical therapist recommends certain exercises. Except that you're the doctor and the patient, and how or why it works is the legacy of some greater power.

For the time being, let's consider that greater power as the universal truths behind Faithspeak. They're the truths shared by virtually all religious traditions, and described in a different way by science. They're also capable of being known through ordinary experience by ordinary people outside of any religious or scientific framework.

But if that's so, you might ask, why bother with religion at all? Why not simply translate Faithspeak into everyday run-of-the-mill slang and shut down all the sacred temples and neighborhood churches? What difference would it make?

We'll tackle that question in the next chapter, before moving on to the Lexicon. In the meantime, just remember the word "slang."

The Case for Faithspeak

In his classic song, "Imagine," John Lennon asked us to visualize a utopian future in which the entire world would "live as one." Without greed or hunger or borders.

Or religion.

If I read Lennon correctly, we would still have "faith" as this book defines it. The very process of living as one—in fact, the whole outlook envisioned in Lennon's song—*is* a faith. It's just that we would no longer need the help of religion (as previously understood) to artificially shape it. In this imagined, ideal world, we would simply grow up with that faith. Expressing it in our lives would be as natural as breathing in and breathing out.

In their own visions of the future, most religious traditions also embrace this ideal. Some Jewish, Hindu and Islamic theologians will even admit that all the rituals and external trappings which seem so fundamental to their religion are only a kind of scaffolding to support a deeper truth. And if we weren't so dense, if we didn't need all the constant reminders to do the right thing, to act with justice and mercy and love your neighbor as yourself—in short, if our behavior were already as it *should* be, then God couldn't care less if we tore down the temple at Tenth & Main and built another Kentucky Fried Chicken in its place.

Except that it's *not* an ideal world, and we're not ideal people. We desperately need to change our faiths and be changed *by* them. And because many people grow up in religious traditions, those traditions still offer some of the most effective tools for shaping Who We Are.

During my first year in college I worked as Youth Director for a group cleverly dubbed "CommunicaTeen," whose membership was composed mainly of teenagers considered at-risk for drug abuse. The program was sponsored by a pastoral counseling center affiliated with a major hospital in my hometown of Long Beach; and I had numerous occasions to rub elbows with the Christian clergy and interns who worked there with both kids and adults. To my surprise, several of them admitted they didn't believe in the divinity of Jesus, or in dozens of other doctrines supposedly required of committed Christians.

I couldn't help asking: "How can you remain in the Church and continue to do what you're doing?"

Because, they all replied, that was the only way they *could* do what they were doing.

And what *were* they doing? They were preventing people from committing suicide. They were helping people cope with the death of a loved one, or empowering them to abandon some destructive behavior like gambling or alcoholism or child abuse. They were nurturing their patients' self-forgiveness and self-acceptance, while giving them tools for happier, more productive lives. And the people they were dealing with, for the most part, grew up as Christians and were therefore familiar with that religious landscape.

These were pastors who sincerely wanted to help people, to reshape their behavior, to mend broken lives. They were simply using the most powerful tools within the context of their patients' own experience to affect them. "To have any chance of reaching the guy on the street," one of them explained, "you find out what's important to him, what his triggers are, how he talks. You learn his slang."

His slang.

"But isn't there something dishonest about that?" I pressed.

"If you spoke German," he pushed back, "and you had a very important message for someone who could only understand French, would it be dishonest to learn his language so you could communicate with him?" That answer, for me, was the earliest confirmation of what I eventually came to look upon as The Mother Tongue.

Which brings me to the first of three points I want to make in defense of Faithspeak.

By now I hope you'll agree that the walls of separation between religions are often as artificial as the differences between languages. After all, the same dynamic for shaping faith, the same "pointing" at ultimate meanings, is going on in each one. And if that's true, you might be tempted to conclude that one single religion is all this world really needs. Either we could simply decide which one to follow by holding some kind of global referendum, or, like fanatics of all stripes throughout history, we'd have ourselves a rousing, world-wide Holy War to settle the issue. Then again, maybe we could simply create a new religion by combining the best elements of each, in the same way Esperanto was constructed from several spoken languages.

I hope you'll also agree by now that a single religion wouldn't work— even if the global referendum or Holy War produced a clear winner. And why not? Because *people are different.*

Not in any fundamental way, of course. The Operator's Manual for being human is essentially the same everywhere. But the fact is, people develop different response patterns as they grow up, different sensitivities and quirks and idiosyncrasies—in other words, their own unique keys for unlocking that heart-of-hearts where attitude and behavior are shaped. And until people are raised in the same culture, until they share the same linguistic and behavioral symbols for communication, until their early childhood experiences and educations are identical, until they all have the same mothers and fathers and I.Q. and sex and hair color...

You get the point.

We need to *maintain* religious differences, not eliminate them, as long as those differences provide the variety of raw materials necessary for transforming people's faiths; as long as one individual's heart can be opened up by one combination of words and rituals but not another.

The Search for Truth, after all, is not so much a quest for the facts or for some set of Absolutes to believe in. It's a search for the environment in which What's True can most efficiently be understood and translated into one's life. And the right environment (read: "religious tradition" or "support group" or "community") will be more or less different for each person.

Within Christianity alone there are hundreds of variations on the basic theme, each with its own special emphasis or slang for making its point. And if the language of Christianity doesn't work for you, maybe the tools and resources of Judaism or Islam or Unitarian Universalism will. If Western religion in general can no longer animate one's attitudes and behavior, there's always Buddhism, Hinduism or Taoism. Or a synergy of them all.

It's important to preserve the options, just as it's important to recognize that each of these options expresses truth in its own distinctive fashion. During my contacts with various religious traditions, I've witnessed the way people continually gravitate toward the spiritual environment that's best suited for them—given time, given their readiness to take that next step in refining their faith. Even if that step may look like going backward to somebody else.

And that leads to my second point. Which is really a reaffirmation of the first: Namely, that *people need options because they're going to change.* Inevitably. Every last one of us. And we need either a supportive religious environment where change can be accommodated from within, or we need a wholly new environment where that change is already an accepted part of the status quo.

In my own spiritual journey, I went through a phase where I not only rejected the basic precepts of my childhood Christianity, but pretty much lost any connection with a religious tradition or even a generic belief in God. (This, soon after being accepted into a Methodist seminary!) I felt like a fool for swallowing all those "lies" and fairytales for so many years. Unfortunately, there was no support group at the time for ex-believers, so I floundered.

Eventually, after admitting that I may have thrown out the proverbial baby with the bathwater, I found a supportive environment in the Jewish tradition. Among other things, Judaism was a legacy of falling in and out with God. Its history felt like *my* history. And the ironic thing is, I developed a greater appreciation for Christianity within the Jewish community than I ever did within my childhood church.

But, early on, there was also a residue of anger and resentment for what I'd gone through. And it taught me a bittersweet lesson.

A local, Amish-like congregation known as Old German Baptists had developed an interesting relationship with the synagogue my wife and I joined after moving from Long Beach. Many of its women routinely helped cater Shabbat dinners and Bar Mitzvah luncheons at the synagogue, since Jews are forbidden to do such work on the Sabbath. After one such event, a young woman who'd heard whispers about our conversion to Judaism asked to speak privately with my wife and me. She was a sweet, gentle woman, in her mid-twenties, a natural beauty reminiscent of Kelly McGillis in the movie *Witness.*

It turned out that witnessing was precisely what she had in mind. Out of her heartfelt Christian concern for our souls, she'd been praying for us. It was bad enough that my wife and I had become Jews, she told us in so many words. But by converting *after* being brought up in The Church, we'd mocked Jesus and were now on the fast track to eternal damnation. Thank goodness the Savior had died for our sins. Even ours. God had sacrificed his only Son in our place, she assured us, and we might still be saved if we would simply acknowledge His gift.

Acknowledge *what?* I answered almost angrily. Jesus didn't die for our sins because he didn't *die.* In only three days he was back in the saddle, sitting at the Right Hand of God. For a few hours of no greater pain than what hundreds of other mortals suffered on the Roman cross, he not only saved the entire world but his own skin to boot!

What kind of sacrifice was that? I asked. Maybe if Jesus had *really* died, if he was gone for good, if God had permanently given up his Son's life in exchange for ours—that might be a different story.

It wasn't the most tactful response. Nor was it all that original. It wasn't even said out of personal conviction, because I'd already begun to view the gospel narrative about Jesus' sacrifice as more of a parable than a historical event like the assassination of President Kennedy or the destruction of the Twin Towers.

And maybe it *was* out of anger, out of my own sense of betrayal at having been lied to over and over again… by my parents, my church, by the government. (This was the era of Vietnam and Watergate, after all.)

Whatever the reason, for this young woman it was also devastating. This kind of cutting counter-argument had apparently never crossed her mind. I could see that blank, blind-sided look in her eyes, as if the rug had been pulled out, as if everything she'd been brought up to believe was now without foundation. She quietly excused herself and never returned to the synagogue again.

I hoped, for her sake, it was only because she'd decided our poor souls were now utterly lost, and there was no longer any upside in trying to save us. But what I feared was that *she* might've become lost and unsaved; that I'd shattered the simple faith of a kind, considerate young woman who was only trying to help, and now she couldn't believe in anything else because for her, raised as she was, there *was* nothing else. There were no other options.

Of course, there were—and *are*—other options. And my consolation was that she would eventually find a supportive environment in which all the deeper meanings behind her unquestioned beliefs could still be affirmed and nurtured, and her beautiful, caring faith could find a new and even deeper form of expression.

It was a harsh lesson for both of us. And the point of it is, not only should we preserve different religions as options, those religions should *recognize themselves as options*—as different ways of expressing the same Mother Tongue.

Each one might still regard itself as the *best* expression. Each might very well promote itself as the most effective way to transform the faiths of its adherents, or for having a range of built-in options so people wouldn't be forced to go shopping for another religion at the first sign of doubt, or after every new scientific discovery. There's certainly nothing wrong with a little healthy competition in the spiritual marketplace. But if my young Kelly McGillis had understood her religion as one way of expressing the deeper truths, as only *one method among many* that could speak to one's heart-of-hearts, coming face-to-face with an alternate view might not have brought on such a terrible crisis. It is, after all, only a language.

In fact, because it *is* only language, even people who don't consider themselves religious might be more encouraged to explore the various spiritual dialects out there. When religious traditions are understood as languages for shaping faith, and that everybody *has* a faith (whether they work at it or not), religion suddenly doesn't seem so irrelevant or weird or threatening. And the seemingly crazy things religious people say really do make sense, if only we make an effort to learn their slang.

Which brings us to point number three.

Not only do the things religious people say ultimately make sense, their slang turns out to have certain very specific advantages.

Having said that religion is only a kind of language is not therefore to minimize it. To say that Faithspeak can be translated into ordinary language is not to allege that it has no special power of its own. We've already defined Faithspeak as those communications that are specifically designed to reach down into our guts, to affect our attitudes and behavior when logic alone can't seem to do the job. That power or ability is, in itself, an advantage. But I want to go further. I want to say that, without Faithspeak, we are poorer. Without Faithspeak, we are less conscious. Without Faithspeak we don't have as much control over our lives.

The fact is, the words and concepts of Faithspeak, simply because they exist, make us aware of things we might not otherwise see, things that would probably go unnoticed if we limited ourselves to the world of ordinary language. And these aren't just trivial details. They're things that can make a real difference, that have cash value, that enrich our experience and expand our ability to cope with the world around us.

A professor of linguistics made the case for me in a college course called The Philosophy of Perception. He used, as an example, the word "snow."

Our very perception of those tiny frozen crystals, he began, is limited by the single word we have for it. For most of us who live in temperate zones like California, snow is, well... *snow*. We might get a little more definitive once in a while—if we're about to go skiing, say—by using terms like "soft powder" or "hard pack." But that's about as far as our language will carry us.

For the Eskimo such primitive descriptions amount to baby talk. Their language offers some three dozen words for "snow," depending not only on its hardness, but on its moisture content, whether it has a thick or thin crust (as determined by thawing and refreezing, or from a change in air temperature as it fell). There are specific words for snow that floats straight down and snow that blows sideways; for snow that has uniform density and snow that settles in uneven layers; for snow that falls at zero degrees versus snow that fell at minus fifty.

Someone who grew up in California probably wouldn't notice the differences between these types of snow. And not just because he or she is unobservant. The reason is, *we don't have the words for them.* There are no mental files, so to speak, into which the specific characteristics for each type of snow can be stored. That's one of the amazing things about words: They act like mnemonic devices for storing data— in this case, data about the way a particular kind of snow glistens in sunlight, or crunches underfoot, or stings the face, or can't even be felt because it's so powdery.

What's *more* amazing is that, if you don't have a word for the data, chances are you won't even perceive that data to begin with. Even when it's right there in front of you. So the Eskimo will perceive three dozen very different commodities when he steps outside. All you and I will see is... snow.

And the bottom line is that it's not just semantics. It's *survival*. Having the words, and therefore perceiving the differences, provides a significant advantage for someone living under those harsh conditions. Because even though sixty degrees below zero doesn't feel any different than ten below, the air will freeze a person's lungs several times faster. The Eskimo looks at the snow and knows he'd better not stay out long.

Another kind of snow may clue him that certain game animals will be out today; it's a good time to go out hunting. Or it indicates that snowshoes will be needed, or that the ice bridge over that fifty-foot crevasse might not hold his weight. Without the words, and the expanded awareness they afford, a sunny Californian wouldn't last ten minutes.

But life can be harsh even in the temperate zones. People need every advantage they can get in order to survive, or to reach their full potential. Faithspeak is a kind of repository for special words and concepts not generally found in ordinary language, some of which just might provide a life-enhancing advantage. Simply by the fact that they exist, those words give us a mental file in which to store ideas and realities we might not notice otherwise. They allow us to perceive data others might miss. They raise our consciousness of the wider world and its possibilities, and our *own* possibilities. And even if they don't produce an immediate effect, they hang on the pegboard above our spiritual workbenches like tools for future use, shaped to fit our hands as we give them meaning, ready to shape *us* if and when we need them.

The Lexicon that begins on the following pages includes the basic vocabulary that runs through most religious/spiritual traditions. (Or at least the words/names you're likely to encounter in a diverse, predominantly Western culture.) Some of these words will be more important than others. Some are more universal and thus more easily translated from one religion to the next. Some of the words I've included, frankly, are linguistic excuses to talk about *other* words or religious issues.

I can't claim to deal with each of them in great depth. There are books on religious topics that spend a full chapter on words I've parsed in only a few paragraphs, and entire books devoted to a single concept or religious figure.

What I *do* claim, however, is to treat these words in a different way, because I'm not trying to make a case for any single religion. On the contrary, I'm looking for the common ground between them and the shared meanings "under" their words, as Natira put it. I'm trying to explain religious terms outside of a narrowly sectarian context, to recast them in ordinary language that can be plugged back into any particular religion to find their functional equivalents.

Of course, I'll also be attempting to observe the principles of Faithspeak. Which means looking for appropriate models, presenting unfamiliar concepts in terms you're already familiar with, and phrasing it in such a way that it cuts through all the clutter and stands a chance of making a real difference in your life. That, after all, is what faith is about. That's what we both want.

And we've got three hundred chances to try.

PART TWO
The Lexicon

ABSOLUTE

Christianity's *Holy Bible* doesn't have much use for the word, if only because it wasn't part of our spiritual vocabulary when the King James edition first hit the bookshelves. It *does* appear in translations of Hindu scripture, however, usually as another name for God, or as a synonym for those permanent, unchanging principles that lie behind our material world.

The search for what is permanent and unchanging has motivated human beings throughout history, both inside and outside religious circles. In science the goal is often referred to as the "Unified Field Theory," the quest for which has taken on almost mythic proportions, like the Search for the Holy Grail or Golden Fleece or the Fountain of Youth. At the end of this quest are no less than the ultimate laws governing the universe. Things like the Law of Gravity, the behavior of atomic particles and electrical forces, or the seeming contradictions of quantum physics—all of these are thought to be specific "manifestations" of this one, Unified Field.

Applied to the field of religion, the concept often gets bad press largely as a result of people who think they already know what the Absolutes *are,* and who proceed to self-righteously beat the rest of us over the head with them. It's absolutely shameful.

Our own Search for Absolutes—which may explain why our Lexicon starts here—should be somewhat less self-righteous. Because, while granting that there may be some Absolute Truths out there, the reason for our search is The Search Itself. After all, there's usually far more to learn in *looking* for answers than from having found them.

Along the way you'll probably want to try out some new ideas and re-evaluate others, in the same way a scientist would test his theories. And, like the scientist, you may find it necessary to settle for something less than The Absolute Truth and learn to get by for a while on Whatever Works.

Although, from at least one point of view, Whatever Works *is* an Absolute.

ACTS

Frankly, the second word in the Lexicon was also a premeditated choice, if not a somewhat sneaky one.

True, *Acts* is the name of a book in the New Testament that recounts what the followers of Jesus did after he was no longer present in the flesh. But more importantly, it's what we *all* do when we're left to ourselves, when no one is there to nag us into doing what we otherwise wouldn't do. That's because an "act," by definition, is the free, unforced expression of Who We Are. It's the "visible" aspect of our faith, the behavioral by-product of the religion or rituals or collective resources to which we bind ourselves.

If that definition sounds odd, chances are you skipped Part One of this book and the discussion of "Faith vs. Religion," and now you've been caught with your hand in the cookie jar. So before you get in any deeper, please go back and read Part One, do not pass "Go," and do not collect $200 until you discover what faith really is and how it works.

Once you've learned *that,* you'll be able to appreciate one other important thing about "acts"—namely, that acts are not only products of Who We Are, they *produce* Who We Are. Actions are themselves tools of Faithspeak. They are rituals we use, consciously or not, to communicate with our own heart-of-hearts. Like self-fulfilling prophecies, our attempts to act in new and better ways—however unnatural or "phony" they may feel at first—eventually turn us into new and better people. As the Buddhist/New Age proverb puts it, "Act the role of the master and you will *become* the master."

Or, as the Nike shoe commercial advised us years ago: *Just do it.*

ADAM AND EVE

Assuming you're reading the Lexicon from A to Z—which happens to be the way most of it was written—you might wonder if it isn't a little premature to be grappling with the sensitive issues raised by these two scriptural figures. Christian and Islamic fundamentalists, for example, practically live or die by the story of Adam and Eve, the supposition being that if we can't believe the First Couple were historical figures who shared a rib and conversed with a snake, there's no reason to believe anything *else* the Bible or the Qur'an (Koran) says either.

Not to mention that their case against "godless evolution" hinges on it. As does the Christian concept of Original Sin developed by Saint Augustine and heavily promoted in both Catholic and evangelical Protestant theology. Are we really prepared, so early in this Lexicon, to take sides on whether the Bible is literally true, word for word, exactly as written? Or, more to the point, as we *think* it's written?

Because there are dozens of versions around, with slightly different shades of meaning depending on who does the translating. And even where the translators agree, there are some passages that flatly contradict others. Quite a few passages simply *can't* be interpreted literally. "In the beginning was the Word," the New Testament says, "and the Word was with God, and the Word *was* God... And the Word was made flesh, and dwelt among us." Try interpreting *that* literally.

In the case of the "Old" Testament's Adam and Eve, here's the first clue that we're dealing with something equally non-literal: The name "Adam" comes from the Hebrew *adhamah,* meaning "from the dust" or "of the earth." It is also the generic word for "man" (human being).

The ancient Hebrews knew what was going on here, as did other cultures with rich folk traditions. So rather than giving a character some meaningless name, "Adam" pointed symbolically to humankind's genesis through a process firmly rooted in the material world. It's the same process that earlier formed the plants and animals (depending on whether you're reading chapter one or two of *Genesis*), and left an imprint on our natures we must all come to grips with sooner or later.

Except for one small difference. There was something "extra" about Adam's creation (read: *our* creation)... something that raised him a cut above the animal kingdom. We already know this instinctively, if you'll pardon the expression; but the Biblical story dramatizes the idea by showing us that Adam wasn't truly alive as a human being until "God"—if you'll pardon *that* expression for now—breathed into him the *nefesh hayah,* the "breath of life." Which is figurative language for "the soul."

What therefore becomes most important about Adam and Eve is not their historical reality, but the messages being delivered through their story—about humanity's relationship with creation and a Creator; about a world that should be seen as "very good"; about the fact that male and female are inter-dependent; about the fundamental premise that our choices and our actions can have life-changing consequences.

Virtually every culture tells its own story of the first human beings, many of which use equally fascinating symbolism. The Hindu *Rg-Veda,* for example, talks about an immortal Purusa/Man whose sacrificial offering of himself produced everything in the world. The Blackfeet Indians' "Old Man" fashions a woman and boy child, while giving creation a more feminine twist. The African Maori/God creates Mwuetsi, the first man, who together with Massassi and Morongo populate the world, eventually bringing sorrow into it (much like Adam and Eve) through disobedience. The Qur'an's first man is basically the same character that stars in the Biblical role, except that Adam's disobedience is considered an "error in judgment," not a sin that stains the human race for all time.

In these and dozens of other "First Stories," we find cultures trying to grapple with their place in the overall Scheme of Things, showing how human beings are special in some sense, how we are both created and agents of creation. The Adams and Eves who populate these stories are the opening statements religious traditions make about Who We Are. If certain religious authorities insist that we must subscribe only to their party-line version, or that we must attribute historical reality to certain characters else those "opening statements" can't have any meaning, then such views also say much about who those authorities are.

ADDICTION

Psychologists and social statisticians have long known that traditional religions can provide a powerful antidote to addictions of all kinds. The dynamic of accepting oneself as a sinner in the company of other sinners, where weaknesses of the flesh are understood as common and integral to human nature, can provide a strong foundation for recovery. Especially where those other sinners offer mutual support, unconditional acceptance, and examples of positive change that inspire ongoing efforts to improve.

One of the attractions of America's mega-churches, and even the small, unaffiliated congregations that spring up in otherwise vacant strip-malls these days, are their specialized ministries that reach out to people battling drugs or pornography, co-dependency or gambling. Religion is worse than useless if it does not connect with the challenges of daily life, if it cannot provide strategies for coping with the primal urges and destructive habits that often conflict with our social responsibilities and highest aspirations. The customs and rituals offered by traditional religions, not to mention their fostering of community, provide an environment that can literally turn lives around.

But there is also the danger that religious environments can help create the very addict whose addictions the religion is designed to "treat." It's like the advertiser who assaults us with slick messages convincing us we desperately need a certain product... and then offers to sell us that product. A bit self-serving, right? So if we accept the premise that we're "fallen" creatures from the get-go, we are pre-programmed to require a savior to get us back on our feet, whether in the form of a divinity or an all-inclusive set of do's-and-don'ts. Or both.

Which is why Karl Marx called religion "The opiate of the masses." Not that comrade Karl's paint brush wasn't a bit too broad here. Or that replacing religion with The State produces any fewer addicts. It's just that religion (as well as The State) can produce behavioral effects in some people not unlike excessive alcohol or over-eating, with similarly unhealthy consequences for both oneself and one's relationships.

Perhaps we need to ask ourselves: Is the religion we currently identify with—whether understood in the traditional sense, or as a set of personal rituals and habits to which we've bound ourselves—something we've *chosen?* Could you leave it behind, convert to another religion, or adopt a new set of personal do's-and-don'ts to live by, if you were convinced that radical change was needed in your life?

If the very idea of this terrifies you, if what's familiar has a greater hold on you than your need for change and personal growth, chances are you have more experience with addiction than you think.

AGNOSTIC

During Jewish High Holy Day services, some of that tradition's more liberal congregations recite a responsive reading entitled, "If You Look at the Stars and Yawn." Poetically speaking, the reading suggests that God would rather someone yell at Him in anger, or even curse Him, than turn a cold shoulder as if He didn't matter. The deeper message is that struggling with the concept of God—that is, questioning one's relationship to whatever ultimate powers there are—is healthier for one's personal development than not even asking the question to begin with.

To be "agnostic" means that you've struggled with some religious issue—usually concerning the existence of God, but technically *any* spiritual issue will do—and you've failed to reach a conclusion one way or the other. As the saying goes, "The jury's still out." You're simply not ready to decide, either because you don't have enough evidence yet, or you see no compelling reason to reach a verdict to begin with. Maybe when you do, you'll make a decision.

Of course, there's often a deeper reason for not deciding: Because you're afraid. Consciously or unconsciously, you realize your decision might require you to change your behavior, and you're not prepared to give up Who You Are. After all, that would mean risking someone you already know for someone you *don't* know. Change is a scary business.

If we're truly honest with ourselves, chances are we're "agnostic" about more issues than we'd like to admit. Which is nothing to be ashamed of, really. "I don't know" allows that you're still open to the truth, that you're willing to let the evidence take you where it will. Some religious writers celebrate this as "the faith to doubt." Agnosticism admits that an issue is important enough to *want* to take sides, but the moment of decision hasn't arrived. You still have, well... *doubts.*

In the meantime you go on living and acting. That's something you can't avoid. Just don't be surprised if, in the middle of all that living and acting, you suddenly realize the decision has already been made.

ALLAH

Allah is another word for "God"—or literally "*The* God"—used primarily in the Islamic tradition (i.e. by Muslims), although Arab-speaking Christians often use the very same word. It is no more a proper name—like

"Allen," say, or "Elaine"—than the Semitic/Hebrew *El,* which is an even more ancient word for God.

While Allah is described in the Qur'an as having many human qualities, and is usually referred to with a masculine pronoun, no studious Muslim thinks of Allah in such highly personalized terms. Allah is simply the word that represents the Everlasting Unity, the all-knowing, all-forgiving, all-powerful Creator of everything. Just like the word "God" for Christians and Jews—at least theoretically—Allah is utterly beyond human comprehension, while at the same time "nearer to man than his jugular vein."

No culture or tradition owns God, or the concept of God. And sometimes it's refreshing to see or hear the word in another language, if only to remind ourselves of that.

ALLAHU AKBAR

It's the traditional Arabic affirmation meaning "God is Great." And contrary to the book *God is Not Great,* by celebrated atheist Christopher Hutchins, it's also an arguably accurate sentiment voiced by the adherents of most world religions. And by many people who *aren't* religious.

Christians and Jews have intoned the very same affirmation for millennia, repeating it in countless communal prayers and blessings before meals. Sikhs and Bahá'i scatter the phrase throughout their liturgies. The Hindu word *Maha* (great) is affixed to any number of gods, not to mention holy books and revered public figures, to the point that it's become an innocuous and nearly meaningless adjective. Something like saying, "Wow, that's great!"

But there is also this: *Allahu Akbar* has more recently taken on an overtone of ugliness because of its well-publicized usage by terrorists and Islamist fighters who chant the slogan as they launch an attack or witness an explosion that blows up a bus filled with innocent civilians. Or a mosque filled with unsuspecting worshippers of a rival sect whose members chant "God is great" with equal fervor.

And the upshot here isn't that God must therefore *not* be so great, but that it's so easy to hijack a word or phrase revered by the majority and co-opt it for a minority. That's the thing about human language. Repeated by people who no longer use certain words for their intended or customary meanings, those words can be re-purposed.

Which is not necessarily bad. Language evolves as our understanding changes, grows, deepens. That's one of the goals in this book—to look "behind" what's vocalized or printed on a page and discover the underlying meaning that affirms the shared beliefs and universal values which may have previously appeared to us as differences.

Then again, shouting "God is great" while detonating a suicide vest in the midst of a crowded marketplace is hardly a way to build bridges. If anything, it only confirms in its speakers a stunted understanding of God as little more than a tribal deity, and a so-called greatness reduced to the level of humanity's basest impulses.

And that understanding of God is *not* great. By definition.

AMEN

Decades ago, when Walter Cronkite anchored the CBS Evening News, he would sign off each broadcast with the line, "And that's the way it is for this Thursday, April 22" (or whatever the date happened to be). Concluding a prayer with the word "Amen"—or shouting *Amen!* in response to what someone has just said—is essentially the same thing. It's saying, *And that's the way it is.*

But unlike Cronkite's famous tag-line, "Amen" carries with it a note of personal conviction. To *Amen!* something is to affirm its truth and openly align yourself with it. If the prayer or statement happened to come from your own lips, "Amen" would be shorthand for: *There. That came from my heart. That's how I truly feel.* If the prayer is offered by someone else, "Amen" says, *I agree. That person is speaking for me, too.* It's as if you'd said it yourself.

In the latter example, "Amen" represents the aligning of one's heart-of-hearts with something external to you. This kind of "Amen" doesn't necessarily close a prayer, but opens it. And here's where things get interesting.

The Hebrew pronunciation of "Amen" sounds more like *Oh-maine* or *Au-main.* Hindu and Buddhist meditation practices often open with the chanting of *Om* or *Aum*—which some consider the forerunner of "Amen" and therefore shows that Judaism and Eastern religions are distant cousins. This connection becomes even more compelling when you consider that, in Hinduism, *nirgun* is the divine energy associated with chanting the Om, and a *niggun,* in Jewish mysticism, is the repetition of a syllable or phrase designed to manifest divine energy.

In any case, Om/Aum is a sound which, if repeated for several minutes, has the peculiar ability to shut out the hundred-and-one thoughts that seem to play tag inside our skulls much of the time. Shutting out those mental distractions—or "centering yourself," as newer traditions describe it—allows one's mind to focus on that Something Beyond (or Within) that is true and unchanging and might very well transform our lives if only we'd sit still and listen.

Om. Oh-maine. Amen. These and all the other words that open and close our meditations are affirmations to help us align ourselves with the deeper dimensions of existence. There is the universe, and there is me. For the next few minutes at least, let it, and I, be One.

ANGELS

Divine beings with wings and diaphanous gowns who float among the clouds like the cherubs on a Valentine's Day card are not uncommon in ancient literature. Babylonian mythology, especially, was big on angels, and probably embellished the Jewish/Christian concept as the two cultures mingled. Or clashed. Or exchanged Valentine's cards.

But what the word "angel" meant in the oldest Hebrew texts was simply "messenger." (Certain Hindu gods, by the way, were also called messengers. Muhammad was *The* Messenger, or, in Arabic, *Al Mustafa*.) Most angels were understood as beings who were on a mission from God, but they generally looked like humans and were even capable of making dumb, human mistakes. Not to mention that the people who were supposed to *receive* the message could also be mistaken, either by misinterpreting the words or simply failing to hear them.

So what should *we* hear, today, when someone says "angel"?

Notwithstanding the beings of light that have become so popular in books over the past few decades, let's stick with the concept of "messenger." An angel is someone, or some *thing,* that carries a message with important implications for one's faith. In scriptural references, all those trumpets and flapping wings and comings-in-the-clouds are simply dramatic flourishes to grab the reader's attention. "Get ready," these angelic visions are saying, "'cause some Breaking News is coming down the pipe. In fact, maybe you'd better sit down since it might pull the rug out from under your comfy little lives. It may sound foolish, even crazy—

but it's The God's Truth."

And then comes the message. "God loves you," for example. Or "Cheer up, you're about to be saved." There may be instructions attached, or an answer to one of The Big Questions. Or perhaps a bit of unsolicited advice, like the passing stranger who told Abraham's ninety-year-old wife not to put away the diaper pail just yet. "Don't laugh," he seemed to be telling her. "Miracles happen."

But miracles and fanfare aren't required. A good friend or your worst enemy can say something (or *do* something) that hits you like a bolt of lightning. It may be something you needed to hear, or some event that had to happen for your own good—usually right when you needed it. The message might be something earth-shattering, or so small you may not even notice at first, like the lost key to that secret room where you finally find out Who You Are. But somebody points, and there it is.

It's almost as if those people or events have been specifically sent with a message for you and you alone—from somewhere beyond your normal range of experience, sent to break a logjam in your life. Whoever or whatever connects you with that flash of insight is your angel.

Maybe "beings of light" isn't such a bad description after all.

ANNUNCIATION

In orthodox Christian tradition, The Annunciation refers to a specific event—namely, the angel Gabriel's announcement to the Virgin Mary that she was carrying the Savior of the World in her womb. And that's all "annunciation" means: *Announcement.*

Not that this was the run-of-the-mill variety like the opening of another Starbucks, or the latest Twitter response from a thin-skinned politician. Christians place "The" (with a capital "T") ahead of it to emphasize its singular importance, the same way Muslims elevate Muhammad's prophetic role with the title *The* Prophet, or Buddhists recognize one specific teacher of enlightenment as *The* Buddha. Or like pundits distinguish an explosive device that uses nuclear material instead of TNT by calling it *The* Bomb.

Aside from The Annunciation, then, there were dozens of other singularly important announcements in religious history—or at least in religious lore. Like the voice emerging from the burning bush announcing to Moses (and his fellow Hebrews) that "I am the Lord thy God." Or

Jesus' announcement that "The Kingdom of Heaven is at hand." Or Buddha announcing (albeit more quietly) his own enlightenment and his awakening to The Four Noble Truths.

In all these cases something momentous was being broadcast. If the medium for the message had been a newspaper instead of an angel, the headline would've been set in six-inch letters and taken up most of the front page. But there are many more announcements in our spiritual lives that are set in small type, on the page with the marriage licenses or business start-ups or farm reports. And whether big or small, the printed words are only half the story. The announcement is only the spark, the opening line of a dialog, the question that calls for discussion.

An annunciation, in Faithspeak, is more like a challenge. "Here's what's happening," the announcement begins. The next line, "So what're you gonna *do* about it?" is never spoken aloud, never accompanied by fanfare, but whispered into our ears like Elijah's still small voice.

"The Savior is born," is the six-inch type in the Christian media. "Do you accept him as your redeemer or not?" is the unspoken rejoinder, the challenge. Or more to the point: "Are you prepared to worship him through gifts of gold and frankincense and myrrh or by putting a few dollars in the collection plate? Or will you worship him by loving your neighbor as yourself, and by binding up the wounds of the stranger who gets beaten up on the road to Jericho?"

Or take a more recent news flash: "There's another riot on the streets of Baltimore." And then comes the kicker: "Are you gonna just sit there on your sofa and sip your Coors Light? Or will you write to your Congressman demanding that something be done about all the blight and poverty in our inner cities, or the unequal treatment of minorities by law enforcement? And will you, at long last, stand up to the companies that hawk hand guns and assault rifles like tackle and fishing rods?"

Of course, annunciations don't always make the headlines. They can be almost as quiet as the whispered rejoinder. Nor are they always meant for the masses. More often than not they're personal, meant for your ears alone. They're the sudden realizations that something in your life is out of whack, or that the opportunity you've been waiting for has now arrived, or that a friend needs to be stopped before she does something really stupid. Or maybe *you're* the one who needs to be stopped, and it's up to you to stop it. In fact, you're the only one who *can* stop it.

To accept responsibility (i.e. your ability to respond) is an aspect of faith. So is the view that life itself is an Annunciation, and a continuum of annunciations. Mary's was just one example.

ANOINTED

Angels are anointed. Kings are anointed. Messiah, in Hebrew, *means* "Anointed One."

In dozens of cultures, anointing was a ritual during which someone was identified and publicly "set apart" to receive God's healing, or to perform a special service or task. Since substances like Frankincense and Myrrh were rare and valuable, daubing them on someone was perceived as a very powerful symbol denoting that honor.

The Gold Medal, the Nobel Prize, a Master's Degree—or maybe a few sprinkles of holy water—are symbols used today to publicly honor someone for their special qualities. The particular symbol used is not what actually *confers* those qualities, of course. It merely acknowledges what is already a fact.

On the other hand, recognizing what already exists *does* have power. When the Wizard of Oz gave the Tin Man his heart and the Cowardly Lion his courage, he was only acknowledging something they'd had all along. But the public ceremony helped them *realize* it in a compelling way that changed their lives. It elevated them above their own self-doubt. It encouraged them to use the special talent they already possessed, to release its full potential, to let it transform them and, by example, to transform others.

Religion, at its best, functions to point out the powers we have *if only we would recognize them.* All religions know that in addition to our built-in weaknesses, the strengths to overcome them are also in some sense hidden within us waiting to be discovered. They're *given.* Christianity describes that "given" in terms of a blood sacrifice already made on our behalf, that now frees us to embody our divinity. Judaism calls it The Law, given to Moses on Sinai but also built into us like the 613 statutes and rules that mirror the number of bones, muscles and organs in the human body. For Islam it's the new life conferred the moment one submits totally to God/Allah. For Eastern religion it's acknowledging the *Tao* (Way) already present throughout nature, and then living in accordance with it.

We are *all* anointed insofar as we recognize these inner resources for ourselves, and as we make them public through our interactions with each other, and with the world.

ANTIDISESTABLISH-MENTARIANISM

No, this particular word wasn't added to the Lexicon for its amusement value. Even though it *is* rather amusing to see it in print. Again. Because in the 1950s it was the word every third-grader dutifully memorized as "the longest word in the English language." No one really knew what it meant, but it was always fun to say it, and even more fun when someone would get stuck with it during the weekly spelling bee.

What the word means, it turns out, is important because it relates directly to what this book promotes: An appreciation for what religion does, and for all the traditions that struggle to do it. Here's why:

In the United States Constitution, there is a passage known as the Establishment Clause. It's the section that recognizes the grave danger in "establishing" a religion—that is, in giving any one religion the same police powers the civil government would normally exercise. Because, throughout history, whenever the power of the State teams up with religious authority, the worst atrocities against individual liberty have occurred. And still do. Which is why, in the U.S. (and in most progressive democracies), the *dis*-establishmentarians came along to insure that a "wall of separation" between Church and State should always be maintained, and that no religion would ever tyrannize the masses again.

The effort has been largely successful. Despite the fact that some Christian leaders continue to proclaim the United States a "Christian nation," other religions flourish. People of every creed openly practice their traditions in an atmosphere of tolerance rarely enjoyed elsewhere. No single religion dominates. Or at least none does as a result of government influence.

Unfortunately, the Wall of Separation hasn't worked flawlessly. Applied too strictly, *dis*-establishing religion may not only prevent one religion from becoming too powerful, it can prevent religious expression of *any* kind in public life. The unintended effect has been not only to suppress religion, but to teach citizens that "being religious" is something to be avoided. Or worse, that it's irrelevant.

So along come the *anti*-disestablishmentarians, who scramble for every legal means to insure that religion doesn't fade from public awareness or otherwise become invisible. Their goal is to demonstrate that religion has a moralizing, elevating affect this nation needs more than ever; and that, if anything, religion should play an even bigger role in public decision-making.

But now we're back to the earlier problem: *Which* religion? All of them? Only certain ones? And who's to decide?

Can Jews display a giant menorah outside City Hall, next to the Nativity scene of Joseph, Mary and baby Jesus? Can Islamic voices find their way into a U.S. foreign policy that seems overly protective of Israel? Should Catholics and evangelicals impose their religious views about abortion onto the rest of society? How can all these conflicting traditions yield the consensus necessary for public life?

And here's where Faithspeak comes in. Because all these conflicting traditions don't conflict nearly as much as people think they do once they're understood as dialects carrying essentially the same meaning. At the very least, the menorah and the crèche outside City Hall won't be seen as symbols of two different religions competing for influence, but as two different expressions of the Higher Influence that seeks to transform all of us for the better. Faithspeak, then, becomes a tool or model for the process of political/religious consensus.

In fact, politics itself takes on new meaning. As faith is to the individual, political activity is to the State. Politics can now be thought of as the "public faith" because it's what we do as a citizens of a country. It's how we as a country interact with the world.

And religion, as always, remains one of the resources for shaping that faith.

APOCALYPSE

Most of us assume this word refers to The End of the World, or at least to "end times." But what the Latin word actually means is: *Revelation.*

Throughout sacred history, prophets and visionaries have had revelations (i.e. apocalypses) about all sorts of subjects. The ones experienced by John of Patmos, however, concerned the end of an especially significant era and the hoped-for beginning of another. The word's fate was ultimately sealed when church authorities decided John's revelations made a fitting conclusion to the New Testament, even though other books in that collection were written decades after his.

More recently, hundreds of commentaries about John's apocalypse have been published, if only because visions in general are so malleable, and John's in particular can be interpreted to mean almost anything.

Throwing Biblical literalism out the window (since Jesus didn't return "soon," as John had predicted), recent interpreters have made John into a Nostradamus-like character writing for our times, for *us,* rather than for the seven early churches he specifically names as his audience.

Fire-and-brimstone preachers and best-selling authors notwithstanding, scholars are virtually united in identifying the Roman Empire of John's time as the subject of his fantastic visions. The "Beast," as decoded by the Hebrew numerology (*gematria*) John was conversant with, is almost certainly Emperor Nero. And the assurance that Good will triumph over Evil is probably the oldest story in religious literature, going back over 4,000 years to ancient Sumeria's *Enuma Elish* and beyond.

John's version is simply the barn-burner that gets all the attention.

APOCRYPHA

From a Greek word meaning "to hide away," apocryphal writings are texts considered to be heretical by the "orthodoxy" or institutional powers-that-be. Or at least considered of dubious value or authorship.

The Apocrypha, in Christian tradition, is a collection of additional writings sometimes placed between the sanctioned books of the Old and New Testaments. These "extra" books are considered useful in one way or another, but aren't given the same level of authority. Many were written during the inter-testament period, others over the same decades as the Gospels themselves.

Since the modern-day discovery of still more books written before and after the New Testament—the Dead Sea Scrolls, for example, or the Gospels of Thomas, Judas, and Mary Magdalene—it's become clear that many more sacred texts were circulating in the first centuries than the early Church wanted its followers to know about. In fact, that's why many texts were buried or otherwise hidden away only to be found centuries later: Because they were judged heretical, and those who read them as heretics.

Other traditions, too, have their "suspect" or disapproved writings. As Biblical scholars began to realize in the nineteenth century, the Hebrew Bible (*Tanach*) was culled from numerous sources that no longer exist. Transcriptions of several other prophets and sages came and went, based on their ultimate irrelevance or inaccuracy, just as they did in Hindu and Buddhist annuls. In Islamic tradition, it is probable (though heretical to suggest) that whole sections of the Qur'an went through a period of compilation, review and revision. It is *not* heretical to note that stories of the events and sayings of both Muhammad and his companions were rated for their reliability before being assembled into the *Hadith,* some versions of which are deemed apocryphal depending on whom you ask, and who happens to be in power.

All of which is simply to suggest that the word "Apocrypha" stands for the fact that there have always been, and still are, authorities who claim the right to tell us what we may and may not read. Their judgments aren't self-serving in every case, and may in fact arise from a genuine concern that people may not be intellectually or educationally equipped to understand certain documents. Or out of the fear that people's faith might falter if they knew their most revered writings didn't descend in whole cloth from the heavens, but were cobbled together by mere humans.

In contemporary times, however, we are individually accountable for our own faiths. And it is not only our right, but our responsibility, to decide which written and spoken resources we will use to refine our own character and behavior. And to decide for ourselves their relevance and accuracy.

Including this book.

APOTHEOSIS

Another multi-syllabic Greek word, this one means "deification" or "to deify." In essence, it's the process of raising a mere mortal to the level of a god.

That, of course, was the goal of the Mystery religions popular in the Greco-Roman world before and during the early Christian era. Critics both at that time and in recent centuries have dismissed this goal as absurd on the face of it, or at least counter-productive.

Still, the idea survives today in Scientology and the deeper levels of Mormon theology, as well as what's called Theogenic Philosophy. It's also central to various forms of the New Spirituality, most of which hold that human beings possess an innate potential for god-like qualities, if they are carefully nurtured or otherwise released. These can range from psychic abilities to cosmic consciousness, or simply increased compassion and loving-kindness, which together can bring physical and emotional healing to one's life, and to others' lives.

Few of us take deification literally. But insofar as we believe people can (and *should*) be transformed into better, more fulfilled individuals in harmony with other human beings and with all of creation, we are engaged in apotheosis.

ASCENSION

This one's short and sweet. Short enough merely to point out that the prophets Elijah, Jesus and Muhammad (among others) were reported to have "ascended" directly into heaven at the end of their lives. As beloved as these people were, dying a normal death and being buried in the cold, hard ground was simply not good enough. Stories of ascension were the badges of literary respect our ancestors bestowed upon these especially gifted people—*divinely* gifted people. Surely we can appreciate that respect for what it is.

But we can also see it as a kind of theological statement that the more divinity we express in our own lives, the less of a hold the material world has on us. As we overcome our physical limitations, we too can ascend to greater heights.

And that's sweet.

ATHEIST

Let's start with the word's opposite. Technically, a "theist" (from the Greek *theos,* god) is anyone who believes in the existence of God or a Supreme Being. But the term eventually came to be reserved for those who believe in a supreme being *only,* and who reject most of the other trappings of religion. That was the first indication this perfectly good word was headed south. When the letter "A" was affixed to the front end, the term finally hit bottom.

A-theism, however, is not *anti*-theism. Genuine atheists are not necessarily against God, if only because, as they see it, there is no God to be against. "God is dead," the philosopher Nietzsche wrote. "Not exactly," the atheist would add, "because there was no God who died in the first place." No one has ever proven the existence of God to begin with, right?

On the other hand, no one has ever proven that God *doesn't* exist either. So what is the atheist really saying?

Ask one. Chances are the atheist rejects one or more of the versions of "God" we've all come across in religious literature, or in the movies, or we've been taught as children. Maybe they're the same ones *you* reject. But the atheist assumes there are no other alternatives. It's as if the world's religious traditions have given us the only possible choices, and the atheist has checked off the "No" column for each one and that's the end of it.

Or maybe the atheist is just asking for some breathing room. "Stop trying to draw me a picture of God, or limit how God can be conceived." And if *that's* what the atheist is saying to organized religion, there are plenty of other voices who'll gladly join the chorus. One of those voices, in fact, belongs to... well, *God.*

Take the Biblical account during which Moses encounters God on Mount Sinai and is promptly rebuffed after he tries to wheedle God into revealing his personal I.D. "But who shall I say sent me?" Moses asks in response to God's command to return to Egypt to save the Hebrews. The reply, in so many words, was: *Don't fence me in, Moe. A name might give you the idea that you can know me like that portly guy who just moved into the tent next door. Which you can't. Not by a long shot.*

The whole Jewish/Islamic notion that no one can "look on the face of God and live" acknowledges our inability as finite beings to conceive The Infinite, much less to reduce God to some kind of dictionary definition. And if the most brilliant physicists and astronomers are practically speechless when it comes to describing the ultimate building blocks of the universe, how can we expect to do any better in describing whatever lies behind *that?* The most we can do is point in the general direction, or write a little poetry and admit to ourselves what we're doing.

So maybe the atheist is just trying to keep us intellectually honest.

Then again, maybe there *are* no atheists. Or, as the Reverend Lieutenant likes to say, "There are no atheists in foxholes." After all, in the middle of those long, scary, sleepless nights when life seems to pound us with its heavy artillery, doesn't everybody deep down believe in Something Out There, even if it can't be named or described?

Sorry. We need to give the atheist more credit. For, unlike the agnostic who leaves the question open, the atheist says flatly and finally, *No.* Not because he can disprove God, but because deep down he's convinced the idea of God doesn't make any difference. Belief in God doesn't really change anything.

And once again the evidence all-too-often seems to be on his side. Because some people who supposedly believe in God turn out to be liars, thieves and murderers, just as some atheists are. Some "believers" do wonderful things for other people, but so do many atheists. Some believers on their best days aren't half the human beings some atheists are on their worst—and vice versa. In short, people who don't believe in God express the same range of "faiths" as those who do. It's *behavior* that counts, not what someone merely says.

So for all practical purposes you may be sitting next to a hard-core atheist at your next Wednesday-night prayer meeting or Sabbath morning service. An atheist could be occupying the chair you're sitting in right now, though you might not care to admit it as readily as you'd admit to being an agnostic.

Then again, maybe the atheist and the agnostic are really in the same boat. The agnostic admits that the existence of God is still an open question. But the question remains open even for the atheist because it is only through the unfolding of one's entire life that any final answer can be formulated. And life has a way of changing people as they grow in experience, as if all things work slowly but inevitably toward the same conclusion.

Faithspeak has a few words for that process, too.

ATMAN

Although it's a Hindu term, *atman* has a familiar, almost Western ring to it. No wonder: Linguistic analysis has shown Indian Sanskrit to be much more closely related to European languages than geography would suggest. Hindu equivalents for "mother," "father," "brother," "me" and "deity" are strikingly similar. So perhaps Hinduism is not as foreign and different to the Western mind as it might appear.

Atman, for instance, refers to a person's "innermost self," as opposed to our physical body and its mental states. Like our ordinary understanding of "soul" or "spirit," atman is the *You* in Who You Are. It is the personal identity that remains untouched by the particular *Who* that you *Are* right now, by virtue of the behaviors you currently exhibit. It's the self that is "incarnated" in Western religion, and *re-*incarnated in Eastern religion.

Making this distinction turns out to be a crucial step in our personal growth, because seeing an aspect of yourself that is somehow separate from your bodily functions and mental states can give you precisely the leverage you need for controlling them. Your behavior becomes more like a role your self has taken on. Not that you're no longer responsible for it; you must still "own" your actions and live with their consequences. But if and when you realize that Who You Are might benefit from a good overhaul, you needn't feel chained to your present role, or so guilty for something in the past that you can't get on with your life. In other words, *you are not your behavior.*

There is incredible power in this realization. You now have options. You can use the material world of action/reaction to shape your behavior, like a mechanic might rebuild an engine. You put in new pistons and valves, give it a test run, tinker some more and adjust the fuel mixture until it purrs at idle and sings on the open road.

Then again, you might also look for another resource to help shape your behavior, perhaps from the same non-material world where this "innermost self" resides. For whatever this atman is made of, the same stuff probably underlies *all* of life, all matter, all existence. Connecting with that deeper source, through the self, is a primary goal of most religions. And of science. It is the foundation and the motive for what religious people—from Taoists to Christians to New Agers—call "the spiritual life."

Or, as some anonymous flower child said back in the Sixties when he first discovered Hinduism, "That's where it's *at,* man."

ATONEMENT

Here's one of those major-league concepts that can easily come off as formal and lifeless, like the Second Law of Thermodynamics in science. And like good students of religion, we are forced to memorize a twenty-five word definition in catechism class, or read twenty-five pages in Saint Augustine's *Summa Theologica* in order to pass the exam.

The basic premise for orthodox Christians is simply that Jesus died on the cross to "atone" for our sins. And now, as the big bully down the block says, What'cha gonna *do* about it, huh?

The spiritual precedent for atonement was set long ago when the priests of most religions slaughtered livestock on their altars to settle a debt or buy their gods' favor. Back then, the act of ritual sacrifice was common practice and therefore ripe for Christian Faithspeak. Jesus on the cross was like the lamb on the altar, a blood offering to pay a debt. For Christianity, that debt was our separation from God caused by disobedience and sin.

Christianity is only dramatizing the same dynamic that's present in every religion: Sin leads to separation; separation requires "atonement."

Still don't buy it? Let's start over with a little word game many other writers have employed. Unfortunately, the game doesn't work well in any language but English; but here goes anyway.

"Atonement" is *at-one-ment.* It is the method by which something divided can be united, made whole, made one. Made *at* one.

Clever, no?

And it just so happens that one of the central assumptions for all religions, no matter what spiritual language they employ, is that *people are divided.* We're divided from each other into nations and competing interest groups. Divided from our own families—parents from children, husbands from wives, brothers from sisters. Not to mention that we're divided from our *selves.* On a personal level, we seem continually torn between our emotions and intellect, between our careers and relationships, between the spiritual and material, between what we want and what's really good for us. It's no wonder most people are unfocused, unfulfilled, unhappy.

But another assumption for all religions is that each of these communal or personal divisions is the inevitable outcome of one *prior* division: Our separation from the knowledge of Ultimate Reality, from the Way Things Are. Or, in Faithspeak, from God.

And whether we're separated from God by our very nature as human beings, or we get that way through the dumb choices we make—or maybe human nature "inclines" us to make dumb choices, which amounts to the same thing—the result is as unavoidable as gravity. At some point we realize we're standing on the brink of a huge, yawning Chasm that threatens to swallow us up, that separates us from something we need on The Other Side. We can only dimly see what's over there, but we know it's somehow essential to our lives, something by which all those divisions can be healed, by which all the fractured pieces can be brought back into wholeness.

What gets us across that Chasm, or else fills it in so we can walk right over it, has been described in various ways. The particular brand of Faithspeak is what defines one religious tradition from another. For now it's enough to say that the process of getting across the Chasm is what's usually called "salvation"; and the *being* across is atonement—the being "at one" with what's on the other side.

A final point: With its usual emphasis on high drama, Christianity spells out the fact that atonement isn't something we must somehow qualify for, that it's only available to certain people. "Jesus died for your sins" is written in the past tense. The ritual sacrifice, figuratively speaking, was already made for you. It's another "given." If you simply acknowledge it, you can have it—whether you're president of the local Mensa chapter or you sign your name with an "X." Whether you're a Christian or Hindu or, yes, even an atheist.

Which is simply to say that everyone can experience at-one-ment, regardless of their religion (and sometimes in spite of it), and that the mechanism is as universal and rock-solid reliable as, well, the Second Law of Thermodynamics.

Notes

BAAL

It's all well and good to promote understanding and tolerance by interpreting religious words as broadly as possible, based on shared meanings and universal truths. But every so often the line must be drawn. "Baal" represents one of those lines.

Baal was the ancient god of Philistia/Palestine in whose honor adults and newborns alike were sacrificed on blood-stained altars; in whose service women were turned into temple prostitutes; and in whose name all of humanity's crudest instincts were not only excused but commended. No wonder the Hebrew prophet Elijah went ballistic over Baal. For him, God was a supreme being whose "image" was meant to elevate human life above the level of animals. If humans were made in the "image of Baal," however, they were nothing but a more cunning and devious *kind* of animal.

Of course, there is something to be said for the acceptance of our own animal instincts and even the pleasures associated with them. It is one of the jobs of religious traditions (as well as philosophy and psychology) to put those parts of ourselves in perspective and, in some way, to label them as "good." Declaring marriage and sex "sacred," or institutionalizing the ingestion of food with dietary laws and blessings before meals, are two of the more obvious examples. The point is, accepting our own physical natures is as necessary to becoming whole as accepting our innate potential for expressing our divinity or "higher selves."

But if a religion doesn't help us connect with that higher aspect—if it tells us that we don't even *have* a higher nature because its rituals reinforce only our lowest instincts—then that religion is ultimately destructive. That religion stifles our growth. That religion sacrifices *us* on its altar.

In the Biblical story, Baalism was therefore singled out for total annihilation. And yet today that religion is still very much alive: In pornography that idolizes sex without any connection to love; in a work ethic that idolizes money and material things while ignoring our need to work on our*selves*; and in the policies of nations that can't seem to solve disputes without resorting to violence and destruction. Wherever our traditions appeal to animal instinct rather than insight, Baal is resurrected. And whenever we give in to that appeal, we become its disciples.

But as soon as we *realize* that, we can still draw the line. And that act, in itself, becomes an act of worship to another god. Maybe the one Elijah worshipped.

BAHÁ'I

Based on raw numbers, the young religion of the Bahá'i can hardly be considered a major player on the world scene. Then again, Jews comprise something like one-half of one percent of the world's population, yet their religion remains highly influential. So maybe influence is related more to active participation in community affairs than the number of adherents. The Bahá'i, for example, are recognized as a "significant minority" (read: *active* minority) in more countries than any other religious tradition with the exception of Christianity.

And what's attractive about this tradition is that it embraces all *previous* traditions. The Bahá'i adhere to what is called "progressive revelation," in which God/Ultimate Reality has made Himself/Itself known through a succession of prophets from Abraham to Muhammad—and continued with the Bahá'i's own messenger, Baha'u'llah, who lived in the mid-1800s. Echoing Muhammad, Baha'u'llah taught that other religions were all true in their own fashion, but none contained The Full Truth. And one of the reasons they *didn't* was because followers inevitably became fixated on the *person* who delivered the truth, rather than on The Truth Itself. Including the followers of Muhammad.

Bahá'i therefore recognizes truth in whatever form humans have preserved and practiced it. Passages from the Bible and the Vedas are quoted right alongside the Qur'an. Rituals are adopted, adapted and reinvented. There is also an admirable tendency among the Bahá'i to promote the equality of men and women, to work toward the elimination of racial prejudice and the disparity between rich and poor, to find the essential harmony between science and religion, to foster world peace and celebrate the unity of all life.

In the United States, many progressive denominations profess these same admirable goals as part of their own "social gospel." But modern religions often disavow the history that brought them to this point. The Bahá'i, meanwhile, steadfastly maintain their roots in the ancient—even primitive—soil of Faithspeak. After all, the best soil is usually full of the decay and decomposition of what has lived and died before, not the sterilized stuff with the Styrofoam pellets you buy in plastic bags at Wal-Mart and use for your nursery-grown house plants.

Sometimes the only way to grow a faith is to get down and dirty.

BAPTISM

Nearly all religions do it. Nearly always have.

John the Baptist, for whom a denomination of Christianity was named, didn't invent anything new. He was a Jew—a slightly crazy one, by some accounts—doing what Jews had institutionalized a thousand years earlier and countless pagans had practiced long before that.

Ever since somebody first jumped in the river to wash the mud off.

It doesn't take an IQ of 150 to make the connection between cleansing one's body and purifying oneself on some deeper level. Just as people become physically dirty by working all day in the cabbage patch, there are things we do (or merely *think*) that can make us feel dirty or stained "on the inside." Using water as a sign for washing away that inner grime is one of the most universal examples of Faithspeak, if only because bathing is common to every culture on earth. Which means there is no subconscious mind incapable of giving symbolic meaning to that act.

The Shinto penitent sitting under the waterfall; the Jew taking a dip in the *Mikvah* after he's become "unclean" through sin; the Hindu who makes an annual trek to bathe in the Ganges; the Muslim who washes his feet, forearms and hands, then rinses both his mouth and nose before entering the mosque; the Christian who gets dunked in the river or sprinkled with water—all of these people are responding to the same need to feel clean in mind and spirit as well as body.

Not that the water *makes* one's spirit clean in the same way it physically washes away dirt. It only *symbolizes* the inner cleansing. It mirrors the invisible force or spiritual process that clears away the guilt, the "sins," the mental bonds enslaving oneself to the past.

And the fact that it *is* only a symbol can be demonstrated by showing just how dissimilar the ritual can look from the ordinary act of bathing. Take the Protestant practice where the minister does little more than draw his moistened thumb or fingertips across a child's forehead. Or the Catholic priest who sprinkles an infant with "holy water" from a sacred chalice. Or the Muslim who may not even *have* access to water, and is therefore permitted to wash himself with sand or "wholesome soil" instead. The significance of baptism doesn't lie in *what* purifies you, but *that* you've been purified.

On the other hand, John the Baptist did come up with a slightly new wrinkle. Or at least his followers did. Because there is now a version of baptism that's considered a One-Time-Only Event. This narrower definition refers to the ritual that initiates or acknowledges a major, life-changing shift in one's faith, an act denoting that the participant has not merely purified himself from a few miscellaneous sins, but from a *whole lifestyle,* from an outlook now understood as sinful and self-defeating. With this baptism, the person involved says to everyone present—and more importantly to his or her own heart-of-hearts—that the entire slate is wiped clean. From this point on, the rules have changed. It's a second chance, day one of a whole new life.

So what crazy John was doing, basically, was shoving one person under the water and bringing up somebody else. When things are so bad they can't seem to get any worse, drown the sucker and start over. Sometimes nothing less will do.

B.C. / BCE

A brief comment about dating. Not the inter-personal kind as in courtship, but the kind that involves calendars.

The system of dating currently used in the West was built on an assumption that now seems narrow and (pun intended) outdated. That is, "B.C." stands for *Before Christ*, while "A.D." represents the Latin words *Anno Domini* or, in English, "The Year of Our Lord."

Jews have always cringed a bit when reading passages like "Solomon's Temple was destroyed in 586 B.C." because, for them, the "C" in B.C. represents another tradition's Anointed One; and even if it didn't, the guy hasn't arrived yet. Technically, as their tradition sees it, it's *still* "B.C."

Muslims have likewise been uncomfortable hearing that "Muhammad was born in 570 A.D." since Jesus was, for them, a highly respected prophet but certainly not "Our Lord." Not to mention that Hindus and Buddhists and atheists don't see why the birthday of one particular religious figure should be the focal point for everyone else's calendar—even if they've quietly gone along with the system because *some* reference point is needed to keep our dates straight the world over.

But wouldn't it be nice to share a datebook that recognized the existence of more than one religion? A calendar that gave us *all* a common reference point?

Common... now *there's* a concept.

A few decades ago somebody figured out that, without scrapping the entire system, people could simply adjust the abbreviations a bit. For "The Year of Our Lord" one could substitute "Common Era." A.D. thus becomes CE. In place of "Before Christ" you simply use "Before the Common Era," or BCE for short. (And while we're at it, let's dispense with all those periods after the letters.)

Which is exactly what *we'll* do when a historical date is referenced.

After all, the period that began around the time of Jesus can still be recognized as an important watershed. It was an era of significant religious and cultural interaction leading eventually—or at least hopefully—to the mutual realization that we all live on the same planet, and that, as different as we may be, we nevertheless hold the most important things in common.

And, at least for starters, a common calendar.

BELIEF

Along with the words "religion" and "faith," "belief" is one of those misunderstood terms that could easily fill a chapter or two, if not an entire book. Not so much because believing things is what religion is about, but because so many people don't know what it means to "believe" something in the first place.

What a belief is *not,* is a proposition or affirmation like "God exists." Or some written "article of faith" to which you pledge your loyalty.

What a belief is *not,* is an assertion you realize can't be proven, or that may even contradict science or common sense, but you proclaim as true in spite of all that.

Instead, when used as a noun, a belief is *something you willingly demonstrate by acting as if it's true.* Beliefs are individual elements of your overall faith, your outlook on life divided into verifiable, bite-sized chunks.

A few examples:

1) In theory, the sun could explode tonight; but your belief that the sun will rise tomorrow is demonstrated by planning your next day's activities without so much as a trace of doubt. 2) It's possible your husband is cheating on you, but your belief in his fidelity is confirmed by the fact that you haven't hired a private eye to follow him around lately, and he just bought plane tickets for that second honeymoon you've been dreaming about. 3) "Love your neighbor as yourself" is something you believe not merely because it's embroidered on the cross-stitch sampler hanging above your fireplace, but because you've demonstrated it through daily acts of kindness, and by sending off that generous donation to United Way every month.

In short, to act *as if* something is true, intentionally and without being compelled by someone else, is to believe it.

Which means, first of all, that you don't believe much of what you *say* you do because your behavior doesn't confirm it. And you *do* believe some things you didn't think you did, because it's demonstrated by the way you act. Breaking down your faith into observable behaviors like this can be a valuable exercise for just that reason. It's a good way to take an inventory of your faith.

But it will also show, secondly, that some of your so-called beliefs aren't worth the breath it takes to say them out loud. That is, *they have no behavioral corollary.* How, for example, do you "believe" in the Virgin Birth? How do you act as if it's true? So much of what religions ask us to believe doesn't make the slightest practical difference, except as a kind of litmus test for our loyalty to one denomination or another. Such beliefs have no power to affect us positively, and more often end up dividing us from one another, forcing us to focus on artificial differences.

But there is another form of belief that *can* be positive: The verb form. Because belief is not only something that's confirmed by one's actions; it is something one can actually *do*. "I believe" can be a verbal act whereby a person intentionally commits to certain other acts, to the kinds of behavior required by that belief. Saying "I believe in the Ten Commandments" expresses your intention to act *as if* the Ten Commandments are valid and binding for you. It may turn out that you *don't* act that way, in which case you don't actually hold that belief since you haven't demonstrated it. But saying "I believe"—to yourself or preferably in public where friends and other witnesses can provide a little extra incentive—at least puts your heart-of-hearts on notice. It's an act of Faithspeak, from your conscious mind to your subconscious. It's an affirmation in which the very act of saying it makes *doing* it more likely.

Self-help programs and what New-Agers call "guided meditations" use this principle to great effect. Because words have power. Repeat over and over that you're going to act a certain way or break that nasty habit or "feel good about yourself," and in time the corresponding behaviors will begin to emerge. "I believe" or "I will" are assertions of leadership over your self. Repeated regularly and *with emotion,* they can shape your attitudes and actions for the better.

Like when you were a kid and you felt sad about something, and your granny would come over and force you to smile. Funny thing is, it still works. Go ahead: Force yourself to smile right now and see what happens.

BHAKTI

From a Sanskrit word meaning "to revere or honor," *bhakti* is the demonstration of one's devotion to a guru or a god through various rituals, acts of kindness, and personal demeanor.

Devotion, of course, is common to every religious tradition, whether exemplified by the lighting of candles and prayers to specific saints, or by the creation of an altar or memorial in one's home to help center one's thoughts on an ancestor or a spiritual teacher. Or simply by the intense feelings that arise when one thinks about or sees the image of a sacred site or beloved deity.

It is all too common, however, to let our inner devotion to symbols, rituals and images substitute for our social responsibilities, for the outward acts that repair and strengthen our relationships to others and our world. As pundits have long noted, it's easier to love God than other people. Which is why the prophet Isaiah railed against ritual that took the place of service to one's fellow human beings; why Jesus suggested that acts of love "for the least of these" was devotion to him; why Muhammad pronounced on his deathbed that followers should not worship or honor him but continue to devote themselves to each other.

How we practice our devotions is a reflection of our faith. The more we see our divinities as the focus of our time and attention, the less we are inclined to spend it on those who truly need it.

BIBLE

In some circles, "Bible" is shorthand for "The Word of God." Technically, however, the word simply means "books." *Which* books depends on whom you ask. And in what century.

Jews regard the first five books as a fully self-contained, self-sufficient revelation of God's Word called The Torah. The rest of what eventually became the Old Testament is seen as an appendix of historical and inspirational commentaries. Of course, Jews don't recognize an Old Testament to begin with, because "Old" implies that it's now outdated and superseded by a *New* Testament.

For Christians, the New Testament *does* supersede the Old. In fact, the Old is sometimes looked upon as a rather long and boring "Preface" to the *real* Word of God, namely the account of the life/death/life of Jesus Christ and his early followers.

For Islam, the entire Bible is acknowledged as the Word of God, though over time followers have altered and even corrupted it. (Which, ironically, happens to be the view of many Biblical scholars today.) Surprisingly, Islamic scripture imports a large portion of both the Old and New Testaments, but only after purportedly cleansing the passages of any errors.

And so it's been for thousands years. One culture appropriates the words and truths of an earlier tradition, giving them a new and distinctive spin, while eliminating whatever seems contradictory to its own home-grown version of The Truth. Islam was only doing to both Judaism and Christianity what Christianity had previously done to Judaism. Except that Christians were less inclined to change the words in the Old Testament than re-interpret them.

Which they *did*. Liberally. Sometimes vastly changing the meaning from what was originally intended.

But having done so, many Christians also decided that their interpretations were the only ones possible. After all, it was clear enough to *them*, wasn't it? In fact, the whole Bible should be clear because it simply means what it says. Exactly. Literally. If a snake and a donkey are said to have spoken, they spoke. If the sun reportedly stopped in the sky for a few hours, it stopped. If the Red Sea parted to let the Hebrews cross it, it parted. And if the Book of John says Jesus walked on water, well, no wonder he never bothered with swimming lessons.

Trouble is, even for literalists, the Bible is ultimately *not* simple and not exact. Otherwise why would there be so many millions of sermons by thousands of evangelists over hundreds of years trying to make sense of it, trying to continually explain it? No one has ever read the Bible cover to cover and understood its entire contents the first time through. Or the second. Or the tenth.

Because the Bible is a vastly *un*clear collection of books, written in unfamiliar language in an unfamiliar era by unfamiliar people. To truly understand it requires a knowledge of the original languages, and especially the context in which each book was written. Failing that, the Bible can be as obscure and inscrutable as the *I Ching,* as boring as Intermediate Algebra class on a hot afternoon, and as unintentionally funny as *Death of a Salesman* performed by third-graders.

"Cast your bread upon the waters," the book of Ecclesiastes says, "and you will find it after many days." What's *that* supposed to mean? For most people visions of soggy bread are all that come to mind.

It might help to know that the fishermen of Galilee sprinkled bread onto the water to attract fish. The more bread, the better one's chances for a sizeable catch, often for several days running. The author, identified as The Preacher, was merely using an analogy familiar to people of his day. To our generation he might've said, "To make the really big bucks, first you've got to *spend* some." Or "Take a risk and you'll be rewarded many times over."

Or maybe he meant something else entirely. Like "Before you reel in people's souls, give them something to eat." In other words, you can't address people's spiritual concerns without solving their physical needs first. Someone who's hungry can't hear the sermon if his stomach is growling.

Or perhaps The Preacher meant to say *all* of these things. Perhaps the truth of the words depends on who's reading them and what else is going on in their lives at the moment.

Which is simply to say that one's *interaction* with the Bible is what's important, not some textbook-style truth supposedly contained in each word. The reason the Holy Bible continues to be one of the most important written documents in human history is because it *can* mean different things to different people. Like all the world's great scriptures, the Bible is a two-way communications device. The receiver is as important to the message as the transmitter. What you bring to the reading—not only in terms of knowledge and experience, but in what you hope (or need) to get out of it—greatly affects what message comes through. In fact, if you *believe* the Bible has answers, you tend to find them.

And it *does* have answers. Because, taken as a whole, the Bible is the story of humankind in parable form. It speaks of man's coming-to-be and his repeated self-destruction; of his deepening awareness of the world and who/what created it, and his "whoring" after false gods in spite of that awareness; of his longing to know the truth and his constant inability to face it; of his belief and unbelief, and the difference it made or didn't make. There is almost no story that can be told today that wasn't first told in the Bible. Even if it was clothed in different language.

It's the story of *us*. And sometimes, in holding up a mirror, we see truths about ourselves that can set us free. That's about as good a definition of "Word of God" as you can get.

BLISS

For most Westerners, the word rarely appears outside of conjugal relations. As in, "Following their week-long honeymoon in Niagara Falls, the newlyweds are now enjoying a life of wedded bliss in their beachfront Malibu home." Bliss is therefore understood as some kind of ideal state in which the pieces of one's life have finally fallen into place, where some preparatory period—usually courtship—has finally paid off and you've finally begun to live out your dreams.

Actually, the "bliss" in marital bliss is not all that different from the religious understanding. For Eastern religion, where the equivalent word most commonly appears, bliss is also a kind of ideal state. And it *is* a pay-off of sorts, following a period of planning and preparation in which one's dream comes true. But that dream, religiously speaking, is the condition of "wholeness" achieved by having studied and meditated and finally integrated one's life into a unified, purposeful force. It is the *commitment* of that force to Something Higher that binds the separate pieces of your self into a spiritual marriage. A marital bliss of The Spirit.

But there are a few notable exceptions to this analogy. First, although the state of bliss implies an attitude of easy-going fulfillment, it does not imply that life has lost its hard edges. Bliss doesn't make problems vanish. In fact, life can be tougher than ever—if only to test you. Bliss simply supplies a new perspective on those problems. It's an attitude whereby most problems lose their life-and-death urgency and are now seen as the dues one inevitably pays for the privilege of living; or better, as opportunities to grow and improve one's abilities to deal with *future* problems. In short, bliss is a *faith*—one that allows you to face whatever comes along with calm acceptance, that allows *you* to control the situation instead of the other way around.

As the New Spirituality frames it, "The problem out there isn't really the problem. It's the way you *react* to the problem." As the Hindu Yogi puts it, "The world is only as you see it." And when that world is seen as good, the most aggravating problems tend to lose their sting. You begin to live in what Christians refer to as a "state of grace." There's no objective reason for you to be so calm and collected; nor do you question it. You simply *have* it. Like a gift from heaven.

Which leads to the second religious connotation for "bliss." This version is best summarized in Joseph Campbell's slogan, likewise derived from Eastern philosophy, to "Follow your bliss."

Here, too, bliss is something you simply *have,* or you receive like a gift. But in this case it's a kind of carrot-on-a-stick, leading you forward, smoothing out a "path of least resistance" that guides you toward your personal destiny.

Should you finish college or have the baby now? Should you accept a position with that high-paying marketing firm, or work for yourself so you can free up a little more time for your family? What is it you *really* want to do with your life? Your "bliss" will tell you—by subtly warning you not to go in certain directions while gently nudging you in another. And if we would only stop fighting it, if we would simply "follow our bliss," we'd finally find out what was meant for us, what "God's will" is for our lives.

Bliss can therefore be described not only as a state in which the world—both the good and bad—somehow feels like the right place to be, but where the rightness of one's actions can be measured by a kind of intuitive compass.

You can probably guess what magnetic field moves the needle.

BODY

Have you ever wondered where—or *what*—you'd be without your body? The question isn't as crazy as you might think. The fact that we can even conceive it suggests at least some awareness of an identity separate from our bodies, a self that somehow transcends the physical characteristics which supposedly define us.

"Amanda has long, glorious red hair" implies that glorious red hair is a thing the person named Amanda *possesses.* There's Amanda, and there's her long, red hair. If she cut her hair and dyed it black she would still be the same person. That much we can swallow.

But how far can we stretch the distinction and still swallow it? If the Amanda we know served in Iraq and lost both legs from an IED, or she suddenly gained 200 pounds—or if an undiagnosed brain tumor radically altered her behavior—would Amanda thereby become a different person? Or would she be the same person, but is now expressing different character traits?

Obviously, it's hard to separate how we think of ourselves (and others) from what we think of our bodies. Early Biblical writings implied a distinction between our created bodies and the spirit that animated it. And yet, according to Jewish Law, we *are* our bodies for all practical purposes. If someone commits a crime, justice must be meted out to that individual without regard for any subtle considerations of identity.

Babylonian, Egyptian and early Christian theology carried this body-as-person concept to the extreme. But Western religion eventually turned to the kind of body/soul distinction Eastern traditions have always taken for granted. And ironically, support for this view came from the same sources that were used to justify the previous concept.

The New Testament proclivity for "casting out demons," for example, is a wonderful Faithspeak dramatization that we can be "possessed" by alien forces or strange behaviors—or, as some prefer, *psychoses*—without changing or destroying our core identity. And what about Jesus' statement that there is "no male nor female" in heaven? Either there is a resurrected body that possesses no sexual characteristics, or what's resurrected simply isn't a body as we normally think of it.

Other statements like "Your body is the temple of the holy spirit," or "The spirit is willing but the flesh is weak," also imply a clear distinction between a spirit/soul and the body it somehow "inhabits." Or that it learns to cooperate with.

And it is this latter view that corresponds so well with Eastern philosophy. The Hindu practice of Yoga is not so much a set of stretching and breathing exercises as a spiritual lifestyle designed to unify body and soul (or "mind") into a cooperative partnership. The same goes for Buddhist meditation. Body and soul are still essentially divisible. But in this lifetime, at least, it is necessary to meld the two into an integrated whole. Or, in the words of computer-speak, to rewrite the program so the two "operating systems" can be made compatible.

From East to West, the level of spiritual mastery over one's body is one of the primary standards by which one's salvation is measured. Full mastery becomes our ticket to heaven or nirvana; failure is the cause for damnation or re-incarnation.

If nothing else, the concept of "body" can spark some of our most searching thoughts about Who We Are and what we're here for. It can also be instructive to imagine, if only as an after-dinner parlor game, what you might be like with someone else's body. Or even as a member of the opposite sex.

Meditate on it for a while. You just might meet your soul.

BODY OF CHRIST

There's at least one other way of looking at the word "body." As in "body of knowledge" or "governing body." Or as suggested by the word "corporation," from the Latin *corpus* which—surprise!—means "body." Here the word stands for a single entity composed of smaller parts, all of which are united by a common character or purpose. It thus symbolizes "unity in diversity."

Body of Christ is a similar concept—and one of the most beautiful in the annuls of religious thought. Narrowly defined, Body of Christ stands for the entire Christian Church. Although separated into denominations and factions and individuals who may or may not even *belong* to a church, the sum total is said to be acting "on Christ's behalf." The Savior's physical presence on earth, so the teaching goes, has now been replaced by the body of his followers.

If we interpret "Body of Christ" as broadly as possible, however, the title can also signify the saving principle that serves to unite our individual, finite selves to the infinite powers and resources that are the foundation of the universe. This Body is implicit in virtually every religion. And this more generically-defined Christ not only acts on us individually, but acts *through* us to save others. So insofar as we participate in this ongoing activity of saving ourselves and others, we can be considered members of the same corporation—whether we identify as Christians, Jews, Hindus or atheists.

But the symbol also has some very practical implications that Christian writers have done well to point out. Because, like various parts of the human anatomy, all of us have different functions despite our working toward the same ultimate goal. Paul's letter to the Corinthians described it this way:

> *The body is a unit, though it is made up of many parts... The eye cannot say to the hand, I have no need of you, nor the head to the feet, I have no need of you. On the contrary, the parts of the body which seem to be weaker are indispensible, and those parts of the body which we think less honorable we invest with the greater honor...*

The description is true of any working organization. Or any religion. Or the whole *body* of Religion. Many different parts are needed to accomplish its mission. All contribute to its success through a working partnership of distinct skills and activities, some of which only seem unimportant, and some of which appear to be in opposition only because we have such a limited view.

The slogan on U.S. coinage is *E Pluribus Unum.* In religious lingo, the same sentiment might come out as "Christ, Incorporated" or Enlightened One Enterprises, or maybe The Tao-Jones Index. The bottom line is, there are many different jobs to be done. Positions are being filled without regard to race, creed or religion. The universe is an equal opportunity employer.

Apply now.

BOOK OF THE DEAD

Ancient Egypt had one. So does Tibetan Buddhism. And while both were intended to make death less scary by connecting our current lives to a vibrant afterlife (or subsequent incarnation), keeping our "eyes on the prize" can often make the destination more important than the journey.

Of this misplaced emphasis a certain itinerant preacher was reported to have said, "Let the dead bury their dead." And the rather shocking message was simply this: Our present lives should be our one-and-only concern, not the past, and not someone's speculations about an unknowable future. Or, in the immortal words of Star Trek's Captain Picard, "Live for now."

One's reading material can be important, informative... inspirational. But only insofar as it prepares us to *act*, as it provides guidance for *life*.

BUDDHISM

As the story goes, a spoiled young Hindu prince realizes how empty his self-described "life of excess" has become, forswears both his riches and his family, and goes off to seek The Truth. After six years of fruitless searching, he plunks himself down beneath a banyan tree, refuses to eat and, weeks later, now on the verge of starvation, finally experiences a transforming vision of The Way of Salvation. He promptly gets up and begins teaching a new lifestyle based on that vision. For all his efforts the young man, Siddhartha Gautama, is renamed "The Buddha"— the Awakened One, or Enlightened One—and his Way ends up becoming a world-class religion.

While it relies on many of the same scriptures as Hinduism, pure Buddhism leaves no room for gods, priests, prayers, temples or rituals—at least not as they're normally defined. The Buddha's mission, after all, was to free people from the kind of formal dogma and dependence on the supernatural that can become mechanical and destructive of one's innate spirituality. The same disdain probably fueled Jesus' later distinction between the "spirit of the law" and the rigid interpretation of that law. In fact, like Jesus' "Kingdom Within," Buddhism declares that humans have *within themselves* the strength and virtue to lead disciplined, morally satisfying lives.

Not that those strengths and virtues are automatic. We must learn how to access them, and to unlearn some of the habits and superstitions that interfere with that process. Spiritual self-control is required, a discipline best developed through what Buddhists call the Eightfold Noble Path. We must learn to practice and possess right understanding, right goals, right speech, right action, right livelihood, right effort, right mindfulness, and right contemplation.

Al*right?*

Obviously there's a chapter or two that could be written about each of those "rights." And there's also the argument that what makes these rights *right* is the Power or organizing principle behind the universe. Or, in a word, "God." But the point is, an individual needn't concern himself with elaborate theories about God or creation or whether so-and-so said thus-and-thus. After all, what makes something right is not the fact that someone said so, but because it simply *is* so.

Religion, for the Buddhist, therefore consists of learning what is right and doing it. It is behaviorally oriented. Human salvation doesn't depend on what we are, or what we say or think, but *what we do.*

Five hundred years before Jesus, this was pretty revolutionary stuff. The founders of most religions, it turns out, have been motivated by a desire to incite a revolution in people's behavior. Moses didn't set up a system of beliefs (as commonly understood) so much as a code of behavior. Thirteen centuries later, Jesus complained that people's lives had become so constricted around this code that they'd forgotten what it was *for;* and by placing the emphasis on one's inner resources—that same "Kingdom Within"—Jesus hoped to revitalize the basis for behavior. Martin Luther's revolution against the legalism of the Roman Church was a virtual replay. And Muhammad, who reacted to the rampant paganism of his culture, developed yet another system whose primary goal, again, was to *change people's behavior.*

Changing one's behavior from wrong to right is the "enlightenment" or Way of Salvation for Buddhism. Just as it is, essentially, for every other religious tradition. And the fact that it clearly improved his disciples' lives inspired Buddha to offer one more challenge: "Go now out of compassion for the world," he said, "and preach the doctrine which is glorious." Whereupon Buddhism became the first great missionary religion, second only to the Jewish sect whose teacher would offer his own disciples the same challenge, in much the same fashion: "Go ye into the world and preach the gospel."

What Jesus and Buddha were *both* saying was simply that they'd stumbled onto something that could change people's lives for the better—and thereby change the world. Let us show you, they said. Try it for yourself. If it works, that'd be really good news, wouldn't it?

Unfortunately, the simplest message often gets distorted in the retelling. Buddhism lost its original purity; gods and rituals and superstition eventually seeped back in. Some would accuse Christianity of the same thing. Maybe it's because people can't get motivated to change their behavior otherwise. Or because we can't accept enlightenment unless it's laced with a little divine imagery.

Which is not necessarily bad. Adding the supernatural element only reflects the fact that we're dealing with strong medicine here. And putting a human face on it has always made it go down a little easier.

CHAKRAS

Already two decades into the New Millennium and over half a century into the New Age—or at least *a* new age—if you haven't learned to talk about power points, life forces and energy centers, it's high time you did.

The concept of *Chakras* is as good a place as any to get your feet wet. And it's really not all that New Age-y. In fact it's four thousand years old. As conceived by the Hindu Yogis, the chakras are seven "energy centers" within the human body, symbolizing the seven levels of human awareness. Without bothering you with their Hindu/Sanskrit names—after all, you're not being tested on this—let's work up through the seven levels to see what they mean.

The "lowest" energy center or chakra is located around the base of the spine, and represents the kind of awareness that's based solely on animal instinct and physical survival. There is nothing wrong with this sort of primal energy; self-preservation is necessary before the higher levels can be achieved. It's just that, without those other levels, there's nothing particularly *human* about human existence. It's the body running on auto-pilot. Nobody's home.

The second level, centered around the spleen, adds the dimension of human sexuality. While this energy might appear to be just one more primal instinct, this one at least seeks preservation of the species, not merely of the individual. It is the level that provides the first glimmer of something beyond one's self, the first clue that something "other" is required for genuine fulfillment.

The third chakra, associated with the solar plexus, advances into the "life force" or mystic energies of the body, whereby each of us develops a purpose and ambition beyond individual or family survival. The fourth level, or "heart chakra," represents the energy of love, binding the self not only to family or mate, but to all creatures and to the environment. The fifth or "throat" chakra represents the power of creativity, by which one's love for the world is deepened into a dynamic force for the ongoing work of creation.

Located in the forehead, the sixth chakra is associated with the psychic powers that allow us to transcend space and time, not only to "see" things at a distance, but to experience the past and future as well. (If this sounds weird or occult to you, just remember that the holy men and prophets of most religious traditions were said to demonstrate these very powers.) And the seventh, or "crown chakra," represents the highest form of consciousness and spiritual enlightenment, wherein personal identity finally merges with the Universal and Absolute.

It's logical to ask, of course, whether all these energy centers are actually *real*—whether they exist in some objective, scientifically-verifiable way. Let's not be too quick to say "no." Because this objective, Western mind-set of ours has overlooked a lot of good stuff by dismissing such purportedly-unscientific Eastern concepts as body energies and "auras." (Auras, by the way—especially the one emanating from the crown chakra—are pictured in much the same fashion as halos in early Christian art.) Only in recent decades have physicians and scientists acknowledged that the body *does* generate many unseen properties and energies. Acupuncture, biofeedback, mental states that induce physical changes—all of these are finally being recognized, explored and used in exciting, productive ways.

And there is something to be said about a religion that acknowledges the very existence of these energies to begin with. We're not talking about demons or spirits with minds of their own who possess our bodies (although that's another way to dramatize it). The concept of a generic energy coursing through us, capable of being used for evil or good, for lower or higher purposes, is pretty advanced thinking for any era. And the idea that each energy level can be transformed into successively higher levels of awareness is as modern—and as religious—a view of "salvation" as you can find. The fact that people often become stunted or obsessed at lower levels is as good a description of "sin" as you'll find, too.

So whether or not some scientist can hold up a measuring device next to our heart chakra and watch a needle move on his Hewlett-Packard Z-2000 Chakra-meter is beside the point. Chakras are Faithspeak. They are mental/emotional tools to help focus our thoughts and efforts on our own body/soul development. They're rungs on a spiritual Jacob's Ladder connecting our earth-bound selves to the full resources of heaven, or whatever deeper dimensions of reality there may be.

And making it to the top is strictly a one-step-at-a-time process.

CHANNELING

Those celebrated "mediums" of the 1880s supposedly did it. A century later, the author of the *Seth Speaks* books claimed to do it. It's also an article of faith for Christians and Muslims that the authors and prophets of their holy books did it, although most of them would bristle at the use of this particular New Age term.

And yet the process is similar in each case: The mind, voice, or writing hand of a specially-selected human being is essentially hijacked by a higher being—an angel, spirit, alien entity or God Himself—for the purpose of transmitting a message from another dimension to ours. In most cases the human participant is reluctant at first, if not entirely unwilling. After all, being taken over in this way can be disorienting and exhausting. Still, according to the rules, the person being employed has little choice and, more importantly, no editorial discretion over the content of the message. The words spoken or written are entirely those of the higher entity. The message flows more like water running freely through a channel than an interpreter consciously translating Arabic into English. Hence the name.

To imagine that this process is even possible requires a certain, well, "suspension of disbelief." Or, some might say, gullibility. On the other hand, the human mind is one amazing instrument. Mediumship and channeling symbolize the likelihood that our minds have a far greater reach than the sensory world of which we are consciously aware. It's been a genuine disservice that past abuses and self-serving claims of divine authorship have made many of us skeptical of any mental capabilities that might lie outside our ordinary experience. That understandable suspicion and cynicism can limit us, and not just spiritually.

Fortunately, scientific research hasn't been entirely cynical. In recent decades numerous studies have begun to document what religious traditions (and folklore) have contended all along. Admittedly, most of these claims have been for self-serving reasons; and yes, hearing God's voice or writing down words spoken by an angel can seem rather primitive methods for channeling truth. Then again, dismissing them outright can be equally self-serving, and just as primitive.

CHARISMA

A few of us have it. Most of us don't.

From the same Greek word that gives us "charity," *charisma* denotes the qualities of grace, beauty and kindness a person projects. Since we generally admire these qualities, and we're inspired whenever we see them, the word has come to denote a kind of aura certain people have. And because those of us who *don't* have it often prefer to believe that charisma can't be generated by one's own diligent efforts, we therefore assume it must be some kind of natural "gift."

Charisma is not to be confused with "glamour," which is also an aura of sorts. Glamour, however, is the *appearance* of having success or sex appeal, money or power. These are also gifts, but they are not so much earned as bestowed on some people by a public that desires these things for themselves—a public that usually honors material achievements above spiritual qualities... like grace, beauty and kindness.

Glamour or charisma: Which one you admire most says a lot about your personal values, your faith. Whether you regard either one as a gift, or as something you can earn through diligent effort, does likewise.

CHARITY

Assuming the lesson about chakras is still fresh in your mind, you may find that it makes a rather nice introduction to the Western idea of "charity." Because the idea of a personal identity that evolves toward an increasingly higher awareness is precisely what charity is about.

The Me-Generation slogan, "I got mine," represents the lowest level on this scale, even if it *is* only natural. Concern for one's family and its future is the next step up, and equally natural. Most religions will admit, however, that it's *not* as natural to treat people outside your immediate circle—much less total strangers—with similar concern, and to provide for their needs should they be unable to provide for themselves. And yet the homeless and destitute are part of Who We Are, if only because "we" could've been *them* had things been a little different.

Or, to put it in ordinary language, our lot in life often seems a matter of dumb luck. We're born into lives of poverty or wealth without having done anything to deserve it. If the Wheel of Fortune had taken a different spin, the Prince could have been the Pauper, the Pope a produce man. The response to such a realization is usually to thank one's lucky stars. Or thank God. Or to donate generously to the charity of one's choice.

Except that many people never come to such a realization. Many people who enjoy lives of prosperity and material comfort can't imagine themselves in the shoes of someone born on the wrong side of the proverbial tracks. Nor do they see even a theoretical connection between the increasing poverty of others and the deterioration of their own lives.

Which is why most religious traditions, with their longer-term view, came up with the idea of giving to others as an "act of worship." If people won't give willingly, religion *requires* it of them. The Judeo-Christian "tithe," for example—while it now goes mostly to new church facilities and the pastor's salary—was originally a tax to help care for communal needs. The Islamic *zakat,* levied against one's personal wealth every year, is specifically meant to support the less fortunate. Almsgiving in Eastern religions is an acknowledgment that possessions are in some sense loaned to us for our use on earth, and if life has provided us with more than we need, it's our duty to redistribute that wealth. Jesus' statement that there will "always be poor among us" is designed not to make charity seem like a lost cause, but to encourage *continuous giving* throughout our lives—to never give up giving. And not just a coin or two dropped in the Salvation Army kettle at Christmas.

The Jewish writer Maimonides wrote about the kinds of charity we give, from a begrudging donation of money (the lowest level) to teaching people how to earn a living for themselves (the highest). The latter is also summarized in the saying, "Give someone a fish and he eats for a day. *Teach* someone to fish and he eats for a lifetime." And if you think about it, that's as selfish an act as it is charitable.

There's a tale about Abraham Lincoln being chauffeured down some lonely, rain-soaked road when his carriage suddenly comes upon a donkey struggling neck-deep in a mud hole. Without help, the poor animal was certain to die. Lincoln promptly orders the driver to stop, gets out and wades knee-deep into the sludge, then wears himself ragged (along with his brand-new trousers) yanking the donkey onto dry ground. When Lincoln returns to the carriage, his driver gushes with admiration for for the seemingly unselfish act. "Nonsense," the President replies, "that was pure, unadulterated self-interest." Lincoln goes on to explain that he couldn't have slept that night if he'd ignored the donkey in distress. In coming to its aid he avoided the nightmare of knowing he'd passed by some poor creature it was within his power to help. He was, in effect, rescuing himself.

It just so happens that Lincoln's concept of "self" *included* the other creature. The donkey's problem was also *his* problem.

Which is what charity does for us. In giving of ourselves, charity enlarges our concept of self to include an increasingly wider family of people and animals and the natural environment, to the point where acting in the best interest of any of these things is acting in our *own* best interest. And vice versa.

What a world this would be if we were all so selfish.

CHI

In the book of Genesis, God breathes into Adam's nostrils and the First Man's fully-formed body suddenly springs to life. The Hebrew term for this breath-of-life is *nephesh,* a word that also comes to symbolize each person's "spirit," not so much in the sense of a soul or personal identity, but as the animating force that energizes it.

The Chinese *chi*—or *qi,* or in Japanese, *ki*—is much the same, except that the energy pervades not just every human body, but all of nature. Humans can't claim the copyright, so to speak; they only share it. If they learn how, they can also manipulate it, strengthening and concentrating it through one's daily practices and disciplines like Tai Chi. But *chi* itself is universal. It does not distinguish one human from another, or humans from other animals, or redwood trees from roses.

To see all of nature as participating in and dependent upon this universal life force, this inter-connected energy from which all things flow, is a surprisingly scientific perspective. And for all its mystery, for all its hidden dimensions and implicit rules that we continue to explore and have yet to learn, it's a surprisingly *spiritual* perspective as well.

CHOSEN PEOPLE

The movie camera tracks two disheveled workmen as they trudge along a dirt road, shovels on their shoulders, lost in conversation. Finally they stop. "Well," one sighs, "whatever our fate, at least we Jews are God's chosen people." Suddenly the camera pulls back to reveal the wrought-iron archway over the entrance to Auschwitz with its infamous slogan, "Work Makes You Free." The second Jew nods glumly before replying. "So we are. Only question is, what were we chosen *for?*"

There's a similar line in *Fiddler on the Roof* when, after his community is ravaged by the Russians, Tevye wishes aloud that God would choose someone *else* next time. The prophet Isaiah probably felt the same sentiment twenty-six centuries earlier when he wrote that Israel had been selected to suffer not only for its own sins but the sins of all mankind—most of whom were even worse sinners.

Being the Chosen People, in other words, has never been a terribly cushy career. Contrary to the opinion that "chosen-ness" is an expression of Jewish superiority, selection by God implies grave responsibilities and consequences. In return for the honor of bringing a new vision of The Divine into the world, the Jews made themselves strictly accountable to divine Law. And whereas all the heathen nations could still get away with murder (because they "didn't know God" yet), Israel was now bound to a higher code of behavior. Which meant sacrifice and hardship and being subjected to a process of faith-shaping no less severe than the refinement of gold in a fiery furnace.

Like most stories that survive the centuries, the story of Israel's struggle is really about *our* struggle. For whenever we commit to a higher vision of Who We Can Be—whenever we choose to grow as human beings—life does not automatically become a bed of rose petals. More like rose *thorns*. It's as if we are expected by the Powers-That-Be to live up to standards we could never achieve before, but now we can. Or at least we can try. And just like ancient Israel, when we're successful we become a "light unto the nations," a shining example for others to follow. When we fail—as we all do—we are sacked and humiliated right there in front of the whole world. But always, *always* with the intention of refining us for the task to which we've committed ourselves.

Or to which we *re*-commit ourselves. Because being chosen really amounts to choosing. We must *continually choose* to remain committed to something, or to become committed in the first place. But since each choice inevitably brings about consequences we can't predict in advance, what we choose also ends up choosing *us,* as if our original decision takes on a life of its own. Things snowball; we're no longer in control. There are more blind curves than Space Mountain, and there's no getting off until the ride is over. It's no wonder we forget why we're chosen.

Israel wasn't the only people to envision itself as "chosen." There were the 144,000 "Elect" specified in the New Testament. There were also the early colonial zealots who believed themselves to be selected by God to establish a New Israel on the American continent, from sea to shining sea. Which wasn't exactly welcome news for the Cheyenne Indians who were unlucky enough to be in the way, and whose own name happens to mean "Chosen Ones." What were *they* chosen for?

Maybe what we're *all* chosen for is to be a Choosing People. As members of one human family, we must always be ready to make choices about whatever life throws at us, to allow ourselves to be refined and changed and measured against some higher standard.

Ironically, we must begin by choosing that standard. And then it chooses *us.* And things snowball.

CHRIST

It's not a synonym for the name "Jesus." Nor is it a last name, or a name sometimes used as a swear word, because it's not a name at all. What it *is* is a Greek term meaning "Anointed One." Which is exactly what *Meshiach* (Messiah) means in Hebrew. "Christ," in short, is a *title.*

Centuries before Jesus came along, many others had already held that title. Princes and prophets and just plain folks were occasionally selected for a sacred task, and anointed accordingly. At one point the prophet Isaiah declared the Persian king Cyrus to be a Messiah/Christ, specifically anointed by God to release the Jews from captivity and help them rebuild their Temple in Jerusalem.

But titles are sometimes taken out of general use by figures who epitomize those titles so completely that no one else even comes close. There have been hundreds of messengers throughout history, for instance; but say the word "messenger" around a Muslim and he'll likely assume you're referring to Muhammad. For Jews, the quintessential prophet was Moses. And despite the appearance of numerous "enlightened ones" (or *buddhas*) throughout human history, only one person qualifies for that title in the eyes of a Buddhist.

So it is with Jesus the Christ. That title is now affixed to the person of Jesus so inseparably that most Christians reel off the two components as glibly as they might mention the name "George Washington" or "Michael Jackson." Christian Scientists are among the few who keep things in proper order by saying "Christ Jesus." After all, we don't say "Washington President," do we?

The point of all this word play is simply to extricate "Christ" so we can deal with it as a concept, not someone's last name. Obviously, orthodox Christians recognize Jesus as the penultimate Anointed One. But can we find a more universal meaning that extends *beyond* the Christian tradition?

We can. Because titles are given in recognition of a function, a job, a task to perform. "President" recognizes the function of serving as the highest presiding official in the federal government, not only in the United States but around the globe. Similarly, the function of the Christ can be found all over the religious spectrum. And that function, basically, has something to do with *mediating between the human and the divine.* It is the job of acting as a resource—or more precisely, *the* resource—for connecting our limited, self-centered identities with the limitless, selfless Reality that undergirds the universe.

Whether we think of ourselves as religious or not, most of us have experienced two contrasting modes of behavior in our lives. One is self-centered, focused on our own pleasure, personal needs and success. In this mode other people are little more than objects, and material things our primary sources for satisfaction and fulfillment.

But we've probably also experienced the emptiness and *lack* of fulfillment from living in this mode. Every now and then we glimpse a wider perspective. We long to connect with something larger than ourselves, something that provides more lasting satisfaction. And we can see evidence of this other mode, too: In people who appear serene in the midst of hardship; in lives and faiths transformed from despair to hope, from violence to peace, hate to love, selfishness to service. Perhaps we've even tasted that kind of transformation ourselves, however briefly. And we want more.

Except that something prevents us. Religions have various words for describing what holds us back. Like Original Sin. Or the work of the Devil. Or bad karma from previous actions. Psychology describes the blockage in terms of neuroses or psychoses derived from heredity and environment. New Age borrows computer jargon to label it "bad programming." Dianetics speaks of "engrams." Poets call it "The Chasm."

Regardless of how we characterize it, most of us are finally forced to admit that, without help, we can't get past it, or over it. The gulf between Who We Are and Who We'd Like to Be is too vast to jump across. We need a bridge. We need a "mediator" between the two worlds, the two modes of living.

To use Faithspeak, "Christ is the answer." Just remember that Christ can take any number of forms, and *does* take them. And the fact that some people are so adamant about one particular form is simply to emphasize that only one of those forms was right *for them.*

For others, Christ is the quiet practice of the Eight-fold Path. Or the progressive study of the Law and one's annual repentance/rededication on the Day of Atonement. For some people, a singular gut-wrenching experience of conversion helps bridge the chasm. Such powerful experiences are not unknown in Islam, but probably more common in Christianity. "Giving of one's life to Jesus" casts this universal mediating function in the most compelling, emotional, *human* terms possible.

Which, frankly, is why the Christian model has been so successful. Because it *is* so human. Some theological "function" is no match for the down-to-earth story of a carpenter's life and death on an executioner's cross. Labeling a genuine flesh-and-blood person as "Christ," then challenging people to come into a loving relationship with him gets right to the heart of the matter. Certainly it's easier to conceptualize The Divine with a human face. It's also easier to emulate a living example of how we should conduct ourselves than to "observe Torah" or follow the Tao, or take on the rigorous five-prayers-a-day discipline of Islam.

Of course, the true test of having connected with divinity lies in whether or not our behavior actually *reflects* that connection. And what's easier is not necessarily the best, or the most lasting.

Then again, who's to say it isn't?

CHRISTIANITY

There's Christianity, and there's *Jesus*-anity.

One is based on an understanding of the Christ, and a tradition that provides tools for bridging the gap between humanity and divinity. The other is based on the elevation of a certain historical figure to godhood, and the worship of that figure almost to the exclusion of what he taught.

There is also the Bible Dictionary definition: "Christianity is the religious tradition that proclaims Jesus Christ as the only-begotten Son of God, the Lord and Savior of the World, through whom humanity is reconciled with God the Father." Which for most Christians is a delicate balancing act between an understanding of "Christ," and a celebration of the personhood of Jesus.

Because even the dictionary definition is subject to a wide range of interpretations. And the nagging doubts and questions raised within the family of Christian denominations are no less disturbing than those raised outside it.

Was Jesus a real historical figure? Assuming he *was,* are the written accounts of his life 100% accurate? How much of Christianity was adapted from the other "savior religions" competing for adherents in the Greco-Roman empire of that era? Are there deeper truths embodied in Christianity that go beyond historical accuracy or so-called facts?

While Judaism continues to hold that its tradition is best for Jews, religions like Islam and Christianity have generally maintained that their religion is best *for everyone.* Islam, however, gave up any realistic hope for world conquest when Spain finally handed the Moorish occupiers their exit visas—even if some die-hard "Islamists" continue the fight today. Only in the last half century has Christianity begun to doubt its own destiny for world domination. And while Christian missionaries in Africa and Asia continue to make new converts, the result is often a mutant version, blended with the people's existing language and cultural symbols, incorporating the rituals and practices that were already present before Christianity's arrival.

Which, some scholars would argue, is how Christianity originally evolved when Paul first took his show on the road. That, after all, is how Faithspeak works: Casting the timeless truths in language the local folks can understand and absorb, while retaining the power to transform their lives for the better.

And perhaps that's a better way of approaching what Christianity is about. What *are* those timeless truths that transform Christians' lives?

What is so fundamental to Christianity that, without those elements, the religion would be something else?

One of those fundamentals is the conviction that human beings are in need of being saved. We are all, as tradition puts it, natural-born sinners, always falling short of what we could or *should* be. Secondly, we need divine intervention to overcome our propensity to sin. No strictly human resource will do. That's not to say we must look "outside" of ourselves, to some external source like Church or scripture or some religious leader. Most Christians hold that the source of salvation is literally *inside us.* Jesus himself was quoted as saying, "The Kingdom of God is within you."

Unfortunately none of us is able to connect with God's saving power directly, even if it *is* found within. That poetic Chasm is just too wide. So—thirdly—a Mediator (also called an Intercessor) is needed to bridge the gap. For historical Christianity, there is only one reliable, divinely-approved candidate for that job.

According to the fourth fundamental, however, anyone can bring that Mediator into effect simply by *acknowledging* him—that is, by "accepting Christ." In sincerely asking Jesus to "come into your heart" the gap is filled, the connection between human and divine is made, and the healing, life-changing power of God can pour into one's life. Just that quick and—*halleluyah!*—you're saved.

Astute evangelical readers may recognize these four fundamentals as a homespun version of what are sometimes called The Four Spiritual Laws. As the Eightfold Path is to Buddhism or the Five Pillars to Islam, these four Laws are considered the bottom-line requirements for genuine Christianity.

But take away the Faithspeak and you'll find the same universal theme that's behind the Eightfold Path or the Five Pillars. Or for that matter the Ten Commandments or any *other* attempt to reduce the process of salvation to some user-friendly, step-by-step strategy for salvation. Because the fact is, we *are* weak, puny, pitiful creatures if all we can think about is ourselves and our own selfish needs. And we're destined to remain that way until something comes along and bumps into that self-centeredness and shows us a wider, brighter view of Who We Can Be.

Sooner or later we *do* acknowledge some greater power that seems to hold not only our individual lives in its symbolic hands, but the whole universe. Trouble is, we haven't a clue how to connect with it. We suspect there's a connection somewhere because there are enough people around who demonstrate it in their day-to-day lives. And so we struggle to figure out what it is, or wait until it reveals itself in a flash of insight. Or we finally come to the realization that it's right there inside us and always has been, and that realization changes our lives in a way nothing else could.

According to this broader definition, all religious traditions and spiritual movements are forms of Christianity, and Christianity is one form of *them*.

In which case Christianity might still conquer the world.

CHRISTIAN SCIENCE

The philosopher-scientist (and church bishop) George Berkeley was among the first Westerners to theorize that all of nature, all of reality, was a projection of Mind. A century-and-a-half later, Mary Baker Eddy was the first to successfully build a religion around that hypothesis.

Bishop Berkeley reasoned that all objects could be boiled down to our perceptions, our *thoughts,* of them. So why couldn't those perceptions and thoughts themselves be part of a much larger, purely mental matrix? And why, Eddy chimed in, shouldn't we consider Berkeley's all-pervasive Mind as "God"—or let's call it Divine Mind—and use our own individual, separate minds to connect with, and draw guidance from, that supreme Mind?

Unlike some of her contemporaries who saw this quasi-scientific view as the basis for a brand new religion, Eddy made the politically-savvy decision to enfold this perspective into America's religious majority. So not only was this new Science of Mind (as Ernest Holmes would later name his off-shoot) fully compatible with biblical Christianity, its principles were *already built into it* from page one. Its founder, Christ Jesus, specifically taught Christian Science through his parables and living example. Before the modern era, however, followers didn't have the scientific framework for understanding them. They didn't have the "key" for interpreting the Bible's teachings correctly, or at least fully.

Eddy's book, *Science and Health with Key to the Scriptures,* unlocked the Bible's secrets, interpreting the code hidden in its pages and especially within its ultimate Teacher's words and miracles. Like Hindu sages who claimed that Truth had always lain hidden in the similes of the Vedas and Upanishads, or like Jewish Kabbalists who found multiple levels of esoteric teachings camouflaged in the Torah, Eddy was only following a long tradition of reinterpreting ancient wisdom in light of current thought.

The fact that most Christians were further confused or unconvinced, or simply disheartened by yet another sectarian spin-off, is not as important as the fact that Christianity was able to handle the controversy. Nobody died as a result (as happened to Mormons). Baptists didn't declare holy war. Christian Scientists were not stoned to death for heresy, or otherwise excommunicated from the larger tradition. Indeed, many of Eddy's ideas found their way into contemporary Christianity's vocabulary, if not its theology.

Still more people, religious or not, found yet another example that the prevailing establishment never has the last word, or the only correct interpretation. They also reaffirmed, once more, that the bottom line for a religion isn't its rituals or its trappings, but its effects on a person's life, on the kind of *person* one becomes while following it.

CHURCH

For those who are counting, this makes four in a row. Following all that esoteric discourse on Christ and Christianity and Christian Science, it might be nice to deal with a *non*-Christian topic for a change. Alas, as alphabetical luck would have it, we're stuck with "church."

Which isn't so bad as being stuck *in* church. Because even for many Christians, going to church is the last thing anyone should be doing on a Sunday morning, especially when there's a good football game on TV. Church can be incredibly dull, utterly predictable, and amazingly useless for the nurturing of one's faith. As Eldridge Cleaver once said when leaving a Sambo's restaurant, "No soul food in *there,* brother."

Then again, sometimes there *is* food for the soul. Church can be a place of great inspiration and great learning, because that's what often happens when you assemble with other people who are struggling with the same issues in life. You share stories, you dramatize important life events; you hear how other believers deal with problems and give meaning to their experiences in a way that may help you with yours. You listen to other voices, present and past; and then you listen to the voice of your own heart, and maybe the still small voice from Somewhere Else—all in an atmosphere that allows you to hear what's usually drowned out the other six days of the week. And then, like an old clunker with a tune-up and a full tank of gas, you go back out on the highway of faith and see if you can't get over those blasted mountains this time.

Sometimes that refueling process happens in the steepled building on the corner of Whitmore and Main. Sometimes it happens in a living room with John Coltrane and the stereo up full blast. Or while walking through an almond grove bursting with blossoms and the mantra-like droning of honey bees. Or maybe standing in a grove of sequoias, or at the edge of the River Jordan. Sometimes it's a Sunday morning, or a Thursday afternoon.

Or even Friday night at the synagogue.

Yes, "church" can be for Jews if you're Jewish, or for Muslims or Hindus, or for the Kriyabans of the Self-Realization Fellowship. Because church isn't about the building or the place or the time, or any single religious tradition. It's about *gathering*. It's about people coming together for some common purpose, who expect to draw strength and wisdom from a higher source. Which is sometimes the strength and wisdom of simply assembling in the first place.

In fact the word "church" comes from the Greek *ekklesia,* whose root meaning is "assembly." The Hebrew equivalent is *kahal,* the Islamic synonym *jamaah*—both of which also carry a sense of the wider community of like-minded believers. Some of those believers might not even be assembled "here and now," but are present "in spirit." Or they're out there on that highway, practicing the same faith the church was designed to promote. Maybe they're "graduates" of the assembly, so to speak. Or kindred spirits whose goals and lives are compatible with what the assembly stands for, even if they've never officially joined.

From the beginning, Christianity has recognized this distinction between the "visible" church—the people physically gathered together—and the *in*visible church. The first kind you can see and visit. You can run your finger down its membership roster, admire the brick-and-stained-glass building where they meet, and maybe attend an occasional wedding there. That building may somehow be related to another, larger building (or "Mother Church") in Boston or Salt Lake City or the Vatican, with an organization and corporate network that would make even Big Oil jealous.

The second kind you may or may *not* be able to see because it has no walls. Its pews are our daily lives. Its doors are the opportunities we have to lend a hand or say something encouraging to someone who needs it. Its pulpits are the examples of others whose actions shine and illumine our own path. And its altar is that moment in our lives, if it ever comes, when we finally say "Not mine, but *yours.*"

The membership in that assembly is as inclusive as you want to make it. For some it's no more than the 144,000 Elect who are predestined to enter the Pearly Gates at the end of time. For most Christians it's the Church Universal, which includes all believing Christians everywhere. For still others the number includes all those people who are working toward peace and harmony and wholeness, whatever their religious tradition. Or those whom the divine spirit uses to accomplish its job of personal and communal salvation, throughout the centuries and across the globe. Which can be just about anybody, anytime.

Take a look around you. See who else came to church today.

CLEAR

If we use only the "visible" definition of church, it can often take some serious driving time to find one. (Except in Turlock, California, which reportedly holds the record for most churches per capita.) However, if we broaden the definition to include synagogues, mosques, Hindu temples and Christian Science reading rooms, you'll probably find one around every corner.

And speaking of Christian Science—again—let's take this opportunity to remind ourselves that new churches and movements are still springing up almost monthly. (Maybe even in Turlock, California.) One of the most recent of these movements is Scientology, based on the book (and philosophy) entitled *Dianetics,* authored by erstwhile science-fiction writer L. Ron Hubbard.

The merits and *de*merits of Scientology/Dianetics are beyond the scope of this Lexicon. But one thing can be said: Scientology is an excellent illustration of how the same themes found in ancient religious traditions can be recast in the language of the present. Dianetics represents an effort to extend salvation to its adherents through the tools of technology—represented in the form of an electro-mechanical device that operates much like a lie-detector—and to make of that technology a religious practice by which adherents can shape and re-shape their lives. It is, in this sense, a classic case of Faithspeak.

This is not necessarily to recommend it, of course. People who understand how religion works can use that knowledge for both good and evil. There are the ayatollahs and ISIS fanatics of Islam, the Jim Joneses and David Koreshes of Christianity, and apparently a few shady characters in Scientological circles as well, including L. Ron himself, according to some. Not to mention the genuinely Good Shepherds within these same religions who *aren't* in it for the power or money.

Which is a very roundabout way of introducing, as one example of these more recent incarnations of Faithspeak, the concept of "Clear."

To be clear, Dianetically speaking, is to be free of the debilitating effects of the past. It means to lose the chains of shame and guilt and destructive habits that previous experience has encoded into our mental processes. These mental codes, or "engrams" as they're called, are partly the legacy of misguided parents and unskilled teachers. More specifically they are the result of experiences that have secretly distorted or blocked our brains' normal functioning, altering our natural behavior and stunting our inherent potential for greatness. Cleared of these engrams, our brains can be restored to their original capacity for infallible thinking. (That's right, folks—*infallible.*) We are thereby saved as individuals, and ultimately saved as a planetary race.

In its own technological context, the engram does virtually the same job as "sin" does in most Western religions, "demons" in others. It is the wrong thinking that Buddhism replaces, the bad karma Hinduism hopes to reverse. Engrams are the neuroses and psychoses of Freudian psychology, the bad programming New Age describes, and the addictive behavior to be overcome through Twelve-Step programs.

In everyday lingo we might call it the garbage we've dumped into our minds, or the excess baggage we carry around with us. And, clearly, we *do* need to get rid of it, by whatever means best reaches our heart-of-hearts. Beginning with a good dose of forgiveness that wipes our spiritual slates clean.

"Clear" is a well-chosen, multi-purpose word, really. It describes not only a process and a state-of-being, but the kind of "sailing" one can expect once you've achieved that state. At least for a while. Because, while people may be "saved" at some point in their lives, there are always the new temptations and backsliding into old habits that lead AA troupers to say, "Once an alcoholic, *always* an alcoholic." As long as we're human, we're going to sin and require forgiveness. We need *continual* clearing, and accepting that fact is itself part of being "clear."

Clear?

COLLECTIVE UNCONSCIOUS

The term may have been coined by psychologist Carl Jung in the early Twentieth Century, but the idea behind it is woven into the fabric of spiritual thought from ancient India to New Age. It is understood as the place people go in dreams; the dimension where our minds are linked to one another below the level of ordinary awareness; and the repository where everything that has ever been said or done is permanently recorded. This repository is known only by the gods or God, but may be accessible to anyone with the proper spiritual attunement.

For Jung specifically, the Collective Unconscious is stored in the form of emotionally-charged images and templates called "archetypes." In Jewish lore, it is the written documentation in the Book of Life. For clairvoyants ranging from Hindu seers to Nostradamus and Edgar Cayce, it is essentially an audio-visual library of the world's history known by some as the Akashik Record.

Whatever the verbiage used to name or describe it, the concept represents our efforts to explain some of the deepest mysteries of human existence: How can some people supposedly see events far into the future, or sense when a loved one across the country is in danger? How can we explain our eerie glimmerings that we've lived before, or done things we've never actually done, or come to know things we have no way of knowing? And how can a Supreme Being keep track of billions of human souls in order to judge each one worthy of heaven or hell, much less attend to their daily prayers?

Religious traditions can't be faulted for grappling with the same mysteries and coming up with explanations that use the language and conceptual framework of their times. Neither can psychologists or physicists, whose research may yet provide a more scientific answer.

Stay tuned. Or attuned.

COMMUNION

Generically speaking, communion refers to the condition of being so connected with someone or some*thing* that it approaches at-one-ment. True, an individual may still be aware of the everyday distinction between one's self and the "other"; but there is also a sense of profound unity during which some spiritual essence is shared or some deeper message is communicated.

People can be said to be "in communion" with each other whenever an experience makes their identities somehow overlap, almost in a mystical, words-can't-describe-it sort of way. For however brief a time, personal boundaries are blurred, not only between two people, but with the experience itself. That experience can also connect a person to nature, or an idea, or to some other level of existence mystics variously call The Beyond, or The Spirit, or God. By most accounts, it is an intensely satisfying, growth-inducing event to be treasured and celebrated and, if possible, re-experienced on a regular basis.

And sometimes it *can* be re-experienced, at least in an institutionalized sort of way, during the Christian ritual of Communion.

According to the more technical definition, the term specifically refers to the act of connecting with "the Living Christ." As observed in nearly all Christian denominations, the "elements" of bread and wine (or wafers and grape juice) are consumed by the assembled congregants, symbolizing the flesh and blood of Jesus. By ingesting these elements, Christians take into their bodies the essence of their savior, a physical act which mirrors the absorption of his message on a spiritual level, while also renewing their commitment to conduct their lives according to Jesus' example.

Communion is among the clearest forms of Faithspeak you'll find. *And* among the most primitive. After all, the Catholic Church insisted until only recently that the ritual bread and wine were transformed—literally—into the flesh and blood of Jesus once inside believers' digestive tracts. That insistence can be regarded, cynically, as an attempt to convince gullible participants that something real was going on—as if this symbolic communing of congregant and Christ wouldn't get through to people unless they believed some genuine, supernatural process was taking place.

And there's nothing essentially dishonest about a Church that wants its congregants to feel deeply affected by the ritual. Besides, Church fathers were only following an even more ancient tradition. For thousands of years, members of many cultures slaughtered sacrificial animals and ate their flesh, believing the practice conveyed a very real power to transform their lives and connect them with the divinity symbolized by those animals. And if the Christian "Lamb of God" seems too barbaric a symbol for the process of experiencing unity with whatever higher powers there are, then you have only to choose another ritual. Just make sure it works; that no matter what your rational mind may think, your heart-of-hearts is genuinely touched, and that Who You Are is indeed transformed into a closer approximation of Who You Ought to Be.

Because in the end Communion isn't only about connecting with someone or something *else*. It's about connecting with your inner self, with the wiser, more divine soul that really does exist somewhere deep in your guts, if you could only digest that possibility.

The ritual of Communion proclaims, "It's within you to be great. You can be an individual and at the same time part of something much bigger. Get it together and supernatural things will happen."

And they will. Literally.

COMMUNITY

Most of us in Western culture have inherited a very distorted view of what it means to be an individual. Perhaps it's our legacy from the "rugged individualism" of America's westward expansion, where pioneers were forced to rely on their own ingenuity for survival. Becoming self-sufficient was thus considered the opposite of being a member of a community, where you depended on someone else for your welfare.

Nothing could be further from the truth.

Self-reliance is fine. The resources found "within" are the same powers that maintain the universe. But becoming an individual, by definition, is a process by which a person discovers and develops what makes him or her unique. And it just so happens that uniqueness is possible only insofar as we have certain talents and certain weaknesses in a certain combination possessed by no one else. Like the shapes and colors that make each piece of a jigsaw puzzle fit into one and only one location within the larger picture, those qualities becomes most valuable only when we first accept them, and then find a group of *other* individuals into which we "fit."

Notice what's going on here. Far from being the *opposite* of community, individualism is demanded by it and made whole by it. The community needs *us* because of our uniqueness, which, in conjunction with other individuals' unique qualities, completes the jigsaw that would otherwise be left with gaping holes. And we, in turn, need the community because filling our particular "hole" gives our life the kind of purpose and self-satisfaction no rugged individualism of the Wild West variety— which was an illusion anyway—could ever provide.

CONFESSION

There's a saying that if the Catholics hadn't invented confession, somebody else would've.

The rejoinder to which is: Somebody else *did*. But instead of people going into a confessional booth, you lie down on a couch and pay three hundred clams an hour for the privilege.

Which is simply to illustrate another saying: Confession is good for the soul, whatever it costs.

After all, it's an activity that's much older than monotheism, as universal as religion itself. In fact, *more* universal. Even non-religious people practice it regularly. It's called "getting it off your chest" and begins with "Can we talk?" It's the recognition that holding things inside—especially things you've done that you don't feel particularly good about—can be the first step down a long, rickety stairway into misery and deceit, and unless we tell someone about it we'll end up spending our lives trapped in a moldering basement. Religion only dramatizes the process.

Human nature being fairly open to observation, it was inevitable that somebody would eventually figure out the rules. And the rules go pretty much as follows:

As children grow up—whether in a religious environment or not—they can't help absorbing some concept of "doing what's right." When their behavior generally falls in line with that particular concept, they develop positive feelings about themselves. When it doesn't, there is an inevitable sense of failure and loss of self-respect. Much of the time that failure is right out there in front of everybody, and everybody knows what must be done to make things right. But almost as often nobody knows but you, and if you don't do anything about it (which is all the more likely since it's your secret), that failure becomes an annoying, festering wound in one's self-image. Or maybe there's no way to make things right even if you wanted to.

Fortunately, there is a therapeutic affect in simply talking about our behavioral failures with another person, as if formulating it in words puts it out on the table where you can "own up to it" and begin to deal with it. Accepting an aspect of yourself that is capable of doing the wrong thing—what pop psychologists call our "Shadow" and Luke Skywalker calls The Dark Side—is the threshold to growth and self-mastery. And *that* starts with admitting our failures out loud.

In a word, confession.

Of course, it helps if the person to whom you admit these failures can be trusted not to blab to anyone else, and is absolutely non-judgmental. That way you can be totally honest, because the rules of confession demand full disclosure. There's no holding anything back. You can't expect to come clean if you're still in a state of denial.

It also helps if the person to whom you're confessing has some special insight or track record for dealing with people's failures—both others' and his own. In fact, how the confession is handled after you've spilled the beans is what distinguishes one religious tradition (or self-help program) from another. Affixing some concept of "sin" to these inevitable screw-ups is the way some religions emphasize just how important it is that we overcome them.

And it truly *is* important if we want to grow as human beings. Trouble is, labeling failures as "sins" and people as "sinners" can make us feel much worse about ourselves than we should; and the label often becomes a kind of self-fulfilling prophecy. Sinners have an *excuse* for sinning, if not a reputation to uphold. That's what sinners do, right?

Many religions give people a task of some kind to carry out in order to make up for their failures. A few recitations of Hail Mary might suffice, or doing forty hours of volunteer work at the local food bank. And what's important about these compensatory actions is not so much that they have some innate power to right our wrongs, but that we *feel* like they do. If we believe the priest can forgive our sins, or that volunteering for a charity wipes the slate clean, then we're forgiven. If we don't feel that way, we're *not*. Even when the priest says we are.

The power of confession, in other words, is largely in our own minds, and the final judge is our own inner awareness. After all, the part of us that hears our confession isn't really hearing anything new. Our own subconscious mind, or higher self—or God?—is usually more in touch with our feelings and thoughts (and our idea of Who We Ought to Be) than *we* are, at least on a conscious level.

But when we try to hide those failures and weaknesses, we put up walls and roadblocks we can't seem to get past. When we confess them, they become bridges and highways to a whole new place.

CONSCIOUSNESS

Here's an especially tough nut to crack, with implications that can impact everything from the age-old questions of personal identity and immortality to more contemporary issues like abortion and whether it's morally acceptable to eat animal flesh.

If we understand the subconscious as that which is below the level of our normal awareness, it's logical to define consciousness in terms of what we *are* aware of, or as awareness itself. Or, more specifically, as our awareness *that we are aware*—the inward, primal recognition of our own existence.

Look at it this way: A house cat possesses an awareness of sorts. She sees her surroundings, hears the field mouse hidden in the grass, perhaps even senses that the mouse doesn't realize it's being stalked and is therefore an easy target. But is the cat aware of her *own* existence? Can she reflect on her past, remember the other mice she has encountered, imagine the mice and birds and tomcats she has yet to encounter in the future?

To pose these questions is basically to ask whether the cat possesses consciousness.

All human beings—well, with the possible exception of a few feisty philosophers—would pretty much agree that *we* possess consciousness. Not only are "the house lights on," as the old saying goes, "Somebody's home." Each of us has a sense of personal identity (called the "soul" in some circles), composed of an awareness that we exist in the present, that we have a past which can be recounted not only by ourselves but others, and that we have a future which, if we don't yet know the full extent of it, we can at least imagine and prepare for.

Not that human beings have always been conscious, collectively or individually. In Julian Jaynes' book, *The Origin of Consciousness in the Breakdown of the Bicameral Mind*—best known for its title if not its contents—a convincing argument is made that humans did not become fully conscious until rather recently in our evolutionary history. It was only an organic restructuring of the brain that gave rise to what we now call "mind," allowing for our distinctive ability to reflect on our own thoughts, our own past, our own existence.

By this standard (among others), cats do *not* have consciousness. Nor do cows or chickens or coho salmon. Which means killing them cannot be equated with the killing of a human being. And if vegetarianism has a moral dimension, it's less about taking another creature's life than *how* its life is taken.

So the question is, assuming the human brain is the "seat of consciousness" (as Jaynes and most neurologists agree), is the mere possession of such a brain enough to insure that "somebody's home"? Or does consciousness develop only as certain organic structures have matured in that organ, or as a certain amount of life experience and sensory data are encoded within the brain's neural storage banks?

True, the conscious person each of us is today can be traced back to a fetus in our mother's womb, and even further to the moment when "we" were no more than a newly-fertilized egg not yet attached to her uterine walls. But looking *forward* from that moment of conception, when did our fetal "self" become aware not only of external stimuli (as a cat is), but of our own existence? And if that fertilized egg or three-month old fetus had expired from natural causes, or by what's medically described as a D&C, would anyone have been "home" at the time?

Again, by Jaynes' and others' standards, *No*. So if abortion is wrong on moral grounds, it's less about taking a (potential) human life than how that life is taken.

And what are the ramifications for an afterlife or reincarnation? If physical death ends all brain functions, or diseases like Alzheimers can cause such a deterioration that those functions are reduced to bare subsistence, at what point does "somebody home" leave by the back door and supposedly check in somewhere else? In short, does consciousness, once begun, continue to exist even when the brain doesn't?

We'll dispense with what Jaynes said, and what many neurologists say, and end with this:

The importance of consciousness is less about whether it ceases to exist after the brain dies, than how it's used while it *does* exist.

CONVERSION

In the secular world there are any number of meanings for this word: Like changing U.S. Dollars into British pounds; or renovating three floors of rental apartments into own-your-own condos; or turning that Microsoft Word file into a PDF... or becoming a Giants fan after moving to San Francisco, even though you've been devoted to the Dodgers ever since Koufax pitched his perfect game.

In the world of religion, it's this last example that comes closest in meaning. Conversion is the act of transferring your loyalties and devotion from one theological "team" to another—accepting not only the benefits of that switch, but the possible wrath of your former teammates. Or fellow fans.

Converting from Christianity to Islam may reflect your desire for a "truer" monotheism and a more thorough discipline to help quell those pesky proclivities that infected your previous life. But it will also be judged as a step backward by your church-going friends, and a sure sign of "losing your soul" since you've now "denied Christ." Conversion from Islam to Christianity, on the other hand, may reflect your desire for a more personal, loving connection to God; but in any majority Islamic society you'll become an outcast, and might even earn yourself a formal death sentence as an infidel.

In either case, the move from one religion to another is never taken lightly. Whether symbolized by a formal ceremony or in the simple, inner recognition that one is "changed," it portends a brand new chapter in one's spiritual journey, along with the hope of a transformed faith.

Two other types of religious conversion should be noted here as well. The first is a realignment that takes place *within* the larger tradition—say, from the Sunni to Shi'a sect in Islam (which, sorry to say, can also earn a death sentence); or, in Christianity, from Catholicism to Protestantism (which may have drawn a sentence of burning-at-the-stake centuries ago, but today might generate no more that a regretful sigh from your former priest, along with the consoling thought that at least you're still a Christian).

A third type of conversion is often considered the most momentous. It's the move from atheism or agnosticism (or simply "irreligion") into a formal religion of *any* kind. Where you once professed no religious affiliation, now you do. You've been "converted."

Of course, this meaning of the word reflects the mindset you had *before* reading Part One of this book. Because, as you've now learned, all of us have always *had* a religion. Our lives were already full of influential role models and life-changing events, of daily rituals and special activities that have shaped Who We Are. Some of us simply never acknowledged these factors, or weren't conscious of them. The "convert," in contrast, accepts this earlier stage in his developing self, takes full responsibility for it, and intentionally chooses a new path designed to re-shape him from this day forward.

And that *is* momentous.

COVENANT

In ordinary speech, a covenant is a legally-binding agreement or "deal" between two parties that says something like, *If you do this, I'll do that.*

Religiously speaking, however, the term usually refers to one or two *specific* deals. For Jews, The Covenant is the agreement made between God and Israel. As Leviticus reported it, "I shall be your God, and you shall be my people." Of course, to be God's people and earn the protection and love implied by that, Israel was required not only to obey the Ten Commandments, but to observe all of the six-hundred-plus rules and regulations covering pretty much every facet of life.

It wasn't such a bad deal, either. Since faith involves everything we do, why *not* define the rules as explicitly as possible so there won't be any question whether we're keeping up our end of the bargain? And if we *do* keep it, look! Our enemies will be defeated, we'll get rain in its proper season, and we'll prosper and multiply. God promised.

Christians, however, didn't think the deal was all that great—either because people couldn't be counted on to keep their end of the bargain, or because, even if they *could,* the meaning of their lives was getting lost in all the mechanics. So, conveniently, Christians began to look on the Leviticus agreement as the Old Covenant and proceeded to replace it with the New.

The new deal was now between God (through Jesus) and each person individually, not between God and Israel as a whole. And it was the *spirit* of those countless commandments that was important, not the exact letter of the law. "The Sabbath was made for man," Jesus said, symbolically thumbing his nose at all those rules and regulations, "not man for the Sabbath."

Furthermore, the New Covenant doesn't hold anyone accountable for the sins of someone else. Even if Israel (or the world) goes to hell in a hand-basket, you can always find salvation for yourself if you simply live in the spirit of love Jesus taught. "Do unto others as you would have them do unto you" and "Love one another" were the only commandments that ultimately mattered.

Which happens to be how one of the Jewish sages put it decades before Jesus was born—though he expressed it in the negative. "What is hateful to you, do not do to another," Rabbi Hillel said. "That is the whole of the Law. The rest is commentary." Or, as the prophet Micah wrote centuries earlier: "What does the Lord require of thee? To do justice, and love mercy, and walk humbly with God." End of argument.

So maybe the New Covenant wasn't as new as everybody thought. But it *was* recast in the Faithspeak appropriate to that era. After all, it needed an infusion of new blood, as all religions do from time to time.

Islam represented still another Covenant. To the prophet Muhammad, the paganism of the Arab world was long overdue for an overhaul. New ordinances had to be established. Presumably, neither Jewish nor Christian Faithspeak was strong enough for that culture. Besides which, as Muhammad saw it, both of those earlier traditions had lost their original luster. As all religions do from time to time.

And as Islam itself has done from century to century.

But Islam *did* add an important emphasis to the concept of "covenant": The need for balance. Covenant includes the community *and* the individual. Both—not one or the other.

The Christian emphasis on a personal covenant with God (or with whatever supreme power one conceives) isn't enough. An individual cannot be saved in isolation. Our personal salvation is bound up in our relationships to other people—from those in our particular community to everyone else we encounter. On the other hand, the Jewish emphasis on Israel's covenant puts our responsibilities and benefits in such expansive, communal terms that it sometimes fails to speak to our own private heart-of-hearts. The community's salvation depends on our individual, personal transformation. We must begin with ourselves.

So the bottom line is that both Old and New Covenants are necessary. Individual *and* community. The spirit of the law *and* the letter (in which the spirit is first revealed). And that leads to one more "bottom line"—the one we sign our names on.

Because we must *consent* to the deal. The Covenants of every religious tradition, in fact, express an understanding of what we can expect *if we agree to them*—that is, if we behave in certain ways, both individually and collectively. And the fact that, right now, we *do* behave in certain ways implies that we've consented to some deal already. The question is, what is it? And are we getting what we bargained for?

CREATION

Where did we come from and how did it all begin?

It's so basic a question that second-graders ask it right alongside scientists. And so much seems to hang on the answer that both second-graders and scientists often can't hear one another over the noise and shouting of all the other people who claim to know.

Here's one thing we *do* know: The first chapters of Genesis—in Hebrew *B'reshith,* The Beginning—were never meant to be a scientific or historical account. Nor were the Greek and Roman creation myths. The earlier Epic of Gilgamesh, which has numerous parallels with Genesis, was clearly understood as a literary vehicle (like the *Iliad* and *Odyssey* of Homer) for introducing the major players on the world scene, for developing themes on the human condition, and for exploring our relationships to the higher powers. The universe might have come about this way; but the exact details weren't considered important.

And *that's* important.

Because exactly how things got started is really insignificant next to how we as human beings should see our place in the world. Creation stories are therefore important not as science, but as frameworks for viewing our lives. Or, better yet, for *discussing* how we should view our lives. And since creation implies a creator, the stories also encourage us to discuss how we should relate to that being, or concept, or process.

On the other hand, some ancient mythologies assume that the world has always existed. The question of how the world began never comes up. There are still gods and goddesses populating these stories; and a race of human beings is usually created at some point in time. But the universe itself simply exists, and what's to be gained by asking how it all began?

Even the doctrine that God created it—from *nothing!?*—doesn't really answer the question. It merely pushes it back one step by pointing to some Ultimate Power/Force/Being that was presumably there before the universe. But how that Ultimate Power actually *does* the job of creation is never described in any satisfactory way. Nor do we ever find out how that Power itself was created or came to be or, if it existed eternally, what on earth would make it suddenly decide to create the universe when it did.

Perhaps the best response comes from the Jewish stand-up comedian who shrugs and says, "Don't ask."

But physicists and astronomers and cosmologists *do* ask. Not necessarily because they expect any final answers. (Even the Big Bang only leads to more unanswered questions.) They're asking because, as with most scientific inquiries, there's often more to be learned in the search for an answer than in finding it. And what's learned along the way is not only fascinating stuff; it's stuff that gets turned into new products and time-saving devices that even die-hard fundamentalists will gladly exchange their paychecks for. *And* thank God for.

Besides which, new scientific discoveries about the origins of the universe have really done nothing to disprove the existence of God. *Change* it, perhaps. But not disprove it.

If anything, searching the mysteries of the physical universe has been a net gain for religion. Many astrophysicists view the complexity of matter and its interactions with human consciousness with a mysticism that would make Saint Francis proud.

A few centuries ago, Bishop Usher of Canterbury sharpened his quill pen, did a little calculating from the dates of certain Biblical events, subtracted the "begats" and generations and lives of the patriarchs, and established the date of creation at 4004 BCE. On October 23rd to be exact. Somewhere between 9:00 and 10:30 in the morning.

Seriously.

And seriously, folks, it's almost as easy to believe *that* as the idea of a cataclysmic explosion fifteen or twenty billion years ago, starting with an unimaginable concentration of matter about the size of a beach ball if not smaller, at temperatures that are silly to even mention; and that after a fraction of a second that wouldn't register if you put a billion billion billion of them together, the universe was already a billion billion billion miles across.

It's enough to make you stop and think.

CREATOR

In fact, let's do a little *more* thinking.

Creation, we said, implies a Creator. But even if that's true, it certainly can't be the same Creator we meet in the Bible, or in the Qur'an or the Vedas. The Creator/God of religious traditions is simply not drawn from a scientific study of the origins of the universe.

Not that the religious concept is necessarily incompatible with the scientific view. It's just that religious traditions have obviously fleshed it out a bit. Or, as post-modern theologians would say, we humans have "anthropomorphized" it. We've gone and made the Creator in *our* image, not the other way around.

And that's because the act of creating is a very human experience. It's a concept built around the way humans do things—which may or may not be how the "higher powers" work. For example, a sculptor takes clay from the earth, adds water to soften it, then shapes it into the statue of a horse or the bust of Aristotle. What was once a lump of formless material is now not only an object with a defined shape and texture, it represents another reality. It is now so different from the original clay that it's almost as if, well, something came from nothing.

Or take the screenwriter, who starts with no more than a character or a story idea, then translates that vision into digitized words, which are then transformed by a camera and actors and a projector into an experience the human brain records and reacts to—and stores in its memory banks—as if it were reality.

This is how we understand the act of creation: Transforming raw materials by way of a very human, hands-on process into something totally new and different. That becomes our model for the origin of the universe. In Genesis, so humanized is this process that God is pictured shaping Adam from the earth like a grade-school kid molding a replica of Superman from the mud in his backyard garden.

Which is why later theologians decided to update the model from the God-as-sculptor analogy to a more technological one. Two of these later models envision the Creator as a Grand Designer or as The Divine Watchmaker. The universe, after all, was now being seen through the emerging sciences as a pretty complex enterprise. Creation wasn't merely the product of somebody with a few handfuls of moistened clay. This was a scheme cooked up by a Power of incredible intelligence, and the result was like a finely-tuned timepiece—only bigger and *way* more complicated—with delicate gears and wound-up energies no human-like divinity could fashion.

So let's run with that analogy. As Faithspeak, the Designer/Watchmaker was perfectly suited to the seventeenth century mind-set. But what can we bring to that same analogy through the eyes of the twenty-first century?

Easy: Automation and computerization.

Because nobody creates watches the way they were made in 1688. The design of the latest Timex is done on a computer. Forms are machined, cases stamped out and electroplated. Gears and levers are replaced by circuit boards and memory chips too small to see without a microscope. Hands and dials have given way to digital numbers that float on liquid crystal, generated from magnetic fields powered by a three-year battery instead of a twelve-hour coiled spring. Each of the parts is produced in dustless rooms by machines even more complex than the watches, then joined together and packaged by robotic devices and never, not once, touched by a human hand until someone finally takes the thing off the shelf and slips it on. That's the creative process as it moves into the Third Millennium.

And a worthy model not only for a Creator, but how that Creator creates. Whether or not there actually *is* one is a question for later.

CROSS

This is not so much a chance to discuss one more example of Christian Faithspeak as it is to expand our knowledge of Faithspeak in general. For just as a business may have a trademark or logo, religions also have their corporate symbols. These visual symbols embody what the religious leadership—of the time, at least—consider to be the basic thrust of their movement.

Early Christians, for instance, used the fish symbol rather than the cross. Various explanations are given. The fish symbolized food for the soul. It recalled Jesus' commission to Peter to be a "fisher of men," thereby defining the missionary character of the movement. And it could be unobtrusively scratched in the dirt to show your new Roman cellmate that you too were a disciple of Jesus.

At some point, however, that symbol lost its impact—much as a modern company's visual I.D. might lose meaning for its customers. The economic environment changes, or the company takes on a different product line, which means a new symbol is needed to reposition itself in the marketplace. Perhaps the Christian marketplace required just such a change when converts started becoming menu items in the Roman coliseum. The fish symbol was now too "soft," as the Madison Avenue admen might put it. The cross—which happened to be the Roman Empire's equivalent of the electric chair—seemed to be a more powerful symbol for members of a sect who were now giving their very *lives* for their beliefs, just as Jesus had given his. Using this corporate logo for martyrdom was a stroke of genius.

And just because it was a savvy bit of visual Faithspeak makes it no less meaningful. The cross represented the victory of life over death, the giving up of one's physical life for something more lasting. In later centuries it became synonymous with a more symbolic giving of one's life in service to God. And what's especially handy about such a symbol, if it's really a *good* one, is that it can carry all of these meanings in the blink of an eye. Better yet, it allows still more layers of meaning to be added without ever having to be updated or changed.

Other religions have found similarly useful symbols to express their core meanings. The Jewish Star of David, originally a six-pointed battle shield, came to represent Light. According to a more mystical interpretation, it also symbolizes the unity of physical and spiritual—earth, fire and water (the downward pointing triangle), with word, thought and deed (the upward triangle). And out of that unity comes enlightenment.

Similarly, the Hindu lotus flower symbolizes a gradual opening to the light, a petal-by-petal unfolding of our inner selves as we receive greater illumination. The crescent moon of Islam also signifies light, while conveying our coming-to-be—as when the moon passes through its phases, reflecting more and more light until it becomes "full" or "whole."

Through its divided circle emblem, the yin-yang of Eastern philosophy represents the opposing principles in our lives, as well as the complementary forces that together create wholeness and completion. Or take the concentric circles of Zen Buddhism that suggest not only the harmony of all spiritual powers but the hope that, by reflecting this harmony, we can achieve ever deeper levels of enlightenment.

New Age has also explored appropriate symbols: The triangle to represent the "trinity" of body/mind/spirit; the dove to signify peace, or the freeing of Spirit. Even the cross has been borrowed on occasion, to symbolize the intersection of heaven and earth (or the spiritual and physical planes) represented by the vertical line, with the feminine and masculine (or feeling and thought) of the horizontal line.

At the intersection of those lines, presumably, is *us*. Or maybe we're the cross itself; and at its heart is the ideal balance of opposites we continually strive to achieve: The perfect unity of human and divine.

Sometimes a symbol is so universal, no one can trademark it.

CULT

A cult is any other religion or denomination you happen to dislike. At least, that's how some people use the word.

For many Baptists, Mormonism is a cult. For some Mormons, Jehovah's Witnesses are a cult. For Hindus, Buddhism is a cult—or *was,* at least at first. Likewise Christianity in the eyes of most first-century Jews, including a certain Jew who later changed his name to Paul.

Nearly every religion/denomination has been considered a cult at one time or another. Even Baptists.

In fact, among Baptists themselves, there are subdivisions and sects and off-shoots that are looked upon with the suspicion and distaste usually reserved for the Moonies or Ramakrishnans. Because not only are there ordinary Baptists, we now have Southern Baptists and American Baptists. There are also National Baptists and National *Primitive* Baptists, as well as the Evangelical Baptists and the Predestinarian Baptists, who are opposed by the United Free Will Baptists, who in turn see themselves as superior to the merely United Baptists or the merely Free Will Baptists. There are a dozen more Baptist denominations, too, each of which somehow became convinced that a particular interpretation of scripture or personal revelation from God justified going off on their own. Not the least of which is the National Evangelical Life and Soul-Saving Assembly of U.S.A. Baptists.

No joke.

And maybe that's what a cult is: A religious off-shoot defined by some narrow viewpoint that seems to demand separation from the larger tradition. That demand is usually whipped up by a charismatic leader (or leaders) without whose influence the separation probably would not have occurred.

Cultus, it turns out, is Latin for "adoration." Which follows nicely from the last paragraph since, in a cult, the interpretation given to a specific line or two of scripture is adored more than the scripture as a whole. The leader of the new denomination is also adored more than the original prophet or founder of the religion, or the principles and lifestyle for which he stood. As a result, perspective and balance go out the window. Details and minutiae become more important than the overall theme. Language is more important than meaning.

There are some who think the world's major religions are themselves cults. Because their adherents mistake their particular brand of Faithspeak for the One Truth behind them all. Or because they adore the founders and leaders of their religions more than the Ultimate Power that inspired them. Or because they adore the Torah or Bible or Qur'an or Ramayanas or Tao Te Ching more than the greater Reality to which those sacred texts can only point.

And that, regrettably, is no joke either.

CULTURE

While "cult" is most often used in a religious context, the word "culture" might at first seem entirely unrelated to religion, or even opposed to it. After all, modern culture, and especially Western culture, is characterized by a determination to keep religion out of the public square and especially out of government. And not without reason. Centuries of experience with authoritarian religions, or *competing* religions, have taught us bloody lessons about the abuse of power, and the squashing of human dignity, human rights and human potential.

On the other hand, concepts like human dignity, equality, and the god-like potential we all possess were originally *founded* on religious values. Cultures from East to West are infused with religion—generally to society's benefit where its guiding principals are those shared by the world's traditions, and almost always to society's detriment where its principles are specific to a single religion and forcefully imposed on members of others. People have only to turn on the eleven o'clock news to see where cultures are organized according to shared values, and where they're not.

Which brings up one of the more important meanings of our current selection—the *verb* form.

Because what cultures do is *cultivate* its members, as a farmer tills his crops, or the vintner fertilizes, prunes and otherwise cares for his grape vines—including the harvesting and processing of their yield. The yield of that metaphorical harvest is a faith, even in the absence of traditional religions, and sometimes in spite of them. And when a culture's members go on to take primary responsibility for their own cultivation, and lend a hand in others', the resulting crop can yield even more abundantly, the wine taste even sweeter, our collective cups brimming over.

CURSE

It doesn't mean "to swear." But it's close.

"God damn it," for example, is a phrase most people would identify as swearing or cursing. Technically, that phrase is shorthand for a longer oath or sworn statement along the lines of, "I (whoever is doing the swearing) hereby appeal to God to condemn it (the object he/she wants condemned) to eternal damnation." To curse something or someone is therefore to ask for divine assistance in bringing about misfortune or punishment.

Meet the Dark Side of religion. And what's amazing is that curses are found in virtually all scriptures, even the ones that claim to be full of Love and Light. It's as if once we're on God's side—or God is on *our* side—we suddenly have permission to give the sacred shaft to all our enemies. It's not enough to pray for blessings and prosperity for ourselves and our friends. We must also pray for the downfall of our sworn enemies, and sometimes for those who simply disagree with us.

Even some of our seemingly positive prayers are only curses in disguise. Praying for our own business success when there's only so much business to go around is a backhanded way of cursing our competitors. Praying to win the lottery is cursing everyone else who holds a ticket. Appealing for the Phillies to beat the Blue Jays, or for victory in battle, could hardly be more blatant.

So it was something of a surprise when Jesus said, "Love your enemies. Bless them that curse you." It was a radical, revolutionary approach. It was also absolutely on the money.

Not just because wishing our enemies well is often a practical way to convert them into friends. It's because, as modern psychology has demonstrated, you can't hold negative thoughts about others without that negativity rubbing off on *you*. Hindu tradition holds that wishing bad karma on another person returns three times the amount to you. Buddhists strive to harbor only good thoughts about others, as do Jews, to the point of ignoring faults that are obvious to everyone else.

New Age, perhaps more explicitly than any other movement, recommends that we not only hold positive thoughts, but that we actively project positivity to other people. *Especially* to our enemies. It's as if our very thoughts set up an invisible field of energy that molds people's behavior for the better. And if we visualize them as being friendly and caring and generous, more often than not they will respond to us in exactly that way.

What the New Spirituality teaches is what has been more or less present in all religious traditions, and what science is now confirming: Thoughts *do* have a genuine power to affect reality. Those thoughts can be directed at a target, so to speak; but they also inevitably reflect back on the person who is directing them.

Cursing is like wishing that a tornado would descend from the skies and wipe out your obnoxious next-door neighbor's house. If it does, chances are you're going to feel more than a pleasant breeze yourself.

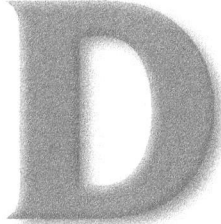

DAY OF THE LORD

This is not to be confused with the Jewish or Christian "Lord's Day" (Sabbath), on which everybody has permission to slack off, put their feet up and relax with a Good Book.

In fact, the Day of the Lord is just about as far from peace and quiet as you can get. The Qur'an envisions it kicking off with a booming trumpet blast, followed by assorted earthquakes and the splitting open of the heavens. On top of that, according to the Bible, we'll witness the assembling of angels and other heavenly hosts (read: "armies of God"). Long story short, this is going to be one heck of a Day to remember.

Actually, from the Faithspeak perspective, it's meant to be a day to look forward to. Or watch out for. Or be prepared for. It's the Day of Reckoning. The Last Day. Judgment Day. It's when everybody's accounts are settled, when the Bad Guys finally get their come-uppance. It's when we all find out who gets the last word, who's really in charge, who's been watching out for us despite our having been food for the lions or fuel for the ovens at Bergen-Belsen.

It's the Day that makes the meek and defenseless take heart;

because whoever's been pushing you around will now be getting a double dose of their own medicine. More important, it's the Day that makes you want to avoid being one of those pushy types to begin with. Or, if you *have* been shoving people around lately, it's the Day that'll make you want to make amends before it's too late. As Islamic tradition puts it, you're going to be sent away with either the Companions of the Right, or the Companions of the Left. Take the Messenger's word for it, you don't want to be caught driving your chariot in the left lane.

Eastern religions, too, have their versions of the Last Day, or at least the end of the present Cycle. These are generally pictured less dramatically, concentrating more on the rewards for being on the side of Light rather than the grisly details of being "cast into outer darkness."

Either way, what the Day of the Lord *stands for* is Justice with a capital "J." It may be true that some people get a raw deal through no fault of their own, while others seem to get all the breaks, or succeed only by trampling over the rest of us. But if mere mortals can't bring the evil ones to justice, Somebody Else *will.* Just you wait, 'Enry 'Iggins.

This heart-felt notion that the world ought to be fair is a remarkably universal human trait. And the fact that things often seem so *un*fair explains much about why we are the way we are. Some people are driven by their sense of justice to help even the score. Prosecuting attorneys and fire-and-brimstone preachers are among the more aggressive and reactionary types. Social workers, physicians, and the humble rabbi represent a more empathetic approach.

Others simply turn away from the world, preferring the physical seclusion of the monk, or, like many Hindus, training oneself to avoid any desire for "things of this world." Still others figure you only go around once, so you'd better grab all the gusto you can. And if the world is unfair anyway, we might as well take advantage of all the breaks that come along, whether or not we deserve them. Maybe even push our luck a little. Hey, why not?

It's the *Why not?* that the Day of the Lord is designed to minimize. Because if you believe it's a real-live Event-to-Come, the thought of it just might scare the hell out of you. Or keep all hell from breaking loose. If nothing else, think of it as a symbol for the notion that somehow, someday, all the good and the bad you've done, or will ever do, is going to come full circle. And all the heavenly hosts and trumpet blasts are simply your wake-up call.

DEATH

More than one anthropologist has theorized that religion began as a way for humans to deal with death.

Much of what we know about ancient cultures and pre-history revolves around burial sites and the way bodies were entombed. From pyramids to peat moss bogs, burial sites are archeologists' first clues that our ancestors lived and died within a framework of belief and ritual we would not hesitate to call religious. Or at least spiritual.

Living and dying, after all, have always been seen as part of a natural continuum. In fact, death was probably far more accepted and better understood back then than it is now—if only because it was more present and less insulated from people's awareness. Even our sacred scriptures don't give us the full picture. There is a huge difference between reading about someone gasping for air on the cross, and watching your own grandmother take her last breath right before your eyes while you hold her gently clutching, then lifeless, hand in yours.

Scripture pales next to the actual experience. But it also lends comfort at a time when people deserve whatever comfort they can find. And it does put things in a certain, well... *perspective.*

Historically speaking, that perspective is some variation on the same universal theme: Namely, that when we die, we are in some sense returned to the realm from which we came. Not merely dust to dust, but to what's behind—or beneath, or beyond—the dust. Where we go is a place that's always been here, the iceberg of Reality whose tip is all we can see because we're still above the waterline. The other ninety percent we can't see until we take The Plunge.

The question is, what is the "we" that finally *takes* that plunge? What exactly *is* it that survives death, if anything?

Do we have the same color hair and sexual organs implied by the Muslim or Christian fundamentalist concept of bodily resurrection? Or will we become a disembodied spirit floating around in some ghostly existence? Will we be, as with the Hindu's *Nirvana,* re-absorbed into the "It," our egos dissipating like buckets of seawater tossed back into the ocean? Should we even bother to think about it before we get there? Or is it enough to know, along with the Amish, that death is being "called home" and whatever that means, there's no reason to be fearful.

Fear, of course, *does* seem to be the emotion death most commonly arouses. Maybe that reaction is a kind of visceral response to how very precious life is, how good it can be sometimes, how lucky most of us feel to be alive right now, regardless of whether there's anything beyond it. Even atheists deal with that fear. Because life is no less precious for the atheist while it lasts. And his response is often no less "religious" either. Quite the contrary. It becomes even *more* important to live life to the fullest, to live abundantly, to find a purpose that makes the fourscore and ten years worthwhile. Because for him, that's all he's going to get. Eternity isn't an option.

And the finality of death, if anything, should be a source of comfort, not fear. As the godless captain of the *Sea Wolf* points out in Jack London's novel, the poor sailor who slips from the mast and falls to his death on the deck below is a goner the instant he hits. There's no longer anyone there to *be* dead, no one left in that stiffening shell to experience what death is like; so it's not worth worrying about.

What *is* worth worrying about—what's worse than death—is a life that lacks meaning, a life spent wallowing like pigs, with all the slop we can eat, maybe, but without friendship, without someone to care for or to care for *us;* without knowing love. And it just might be that whatever lifestyle, whatever activities make life meaningful on its own merits, without any concern for what may come next, are the very things that help one transcend death and actually go on to what's next.

"Whoever loses his life for my sake will gain it," Jesus said. Or, in ordinary language, the person who loses that narrow, self-centered, fear-ridden lifestyle, who joyfully merges his own identity with the lives and concerns and identities of others, is the person who will have truly lived.

Or maybe it comes down to the old joke: Death is the *last* thing to worry about.

DEMON

The ancient world was full of demons. Or at least ancient people must've *thought* so. Because from West to East, there is no religious tradition that does not somehow incorporate them.

In trying to conceptualize how the world worked, our distant ancestors all pretty much belonged to the Church of Animism. Various forces *animated* things, gave them life—from tigers to trees, from volcanoes spewing lava to the sun, moon and planets circling above. What else would you expect? These weren't rocket scientists. They were doing the best they could with the available information and scientific models. Of which there basically weren't any.

And the best they could do without test tubes and telescopes was to make analogies. These people understood that *they* were animated by some kind of unseen, internal spirit who made decisions and motivated them to action. So everything that "acted" was likewise motivated by a similarly unseen entity. There were positive forces that seemed to help people; and there were negative ones that brought harm, or at least thwarted their best efforts. Some of the major players were personified with descriptive names. Others were elevated to godhood. The run-of-the-mill buggers were simply given the generic name "demon."

But now we have test tubes and telescopes, and demons are no longer the model for explaining how the world works, or why people and things behave as they do. Demons are now among the unemployed.

On the other hand, the human psyche doesn't necessarily *know* that, if only because the human psyche is no rocket scientist either. The job that the word "demon" performed, after all, was to take the so-called evil forces in nature and visualize them as nasty little spirit entities. It was a useful way of focusing our attention on the reality that there *are* negative influences in the world, that they often grab hold of us in sometimes inexplicable ways, and it's our job to get rid of them, to exorcise them. Modern science notwithstanding, this is still a useful way to conceptualize a deeper reality that can no doubt be explained by scientific laws and principles of psychology and all—but may not speak to our heart-of-hearts in a way that allows us to actually do anything about it.

Most people who deal with the human mind will admit this. One prominent psychologist has even gone so far as to recommended that participants in his seminars visualize their bad habits as colorful little demons. Like the scary apparitions in horror movies, say, or the devilish little characters in Ghostbusters. Then you simply imagine yourself zapping these evil entities with your own personal laser gun, not merely making them all vanish but preferably blowing them to smithereens.

And you know what? Surprisingly often the problems or bad habits they represent magically vaporize, too. Because demons are closer to the language of our heart-of-hearts than some Freudian analyst's description about how we became addicted to chocolate because Mommy didn't give us enough love but Daddy sure enjoyed the chocolate cream pie she made for him.

So, no—demons don't exist. And of *course* they do.

And that seeming contradiction is one reason why we have science *and* religion, and why there will always be room for both.

DENIAL

We're not referring to the story where Peter denies that he knew Jesus—three times, no less!—after his master was hauled away to his eventual crucifixion. No, we're talking about our own refusal to admit to ourselves what we know on some deeper level to be true. Or how we often continue to do something we know is unhealthy or wrong or likely to end in disaster.

The contemporary phrase for this situation is "living in denial." And all of us do it. We persist in bad habits or bad relationships or bad jobs, all the while denying that they *are* bad. That's because, to repeat the refrain, change is really hard. One of the strengths of traditional religion is that it encourages people to recognize when change is needed, to stop denying that things aren't bad when they really *are*—all within a non-judgmental, supportive community whose members have themselves lived in denial at one time or another.

Regrettably, the explosion of secular recovery groups and 12-step programs is a sign that religious communities are too often the opposite of non-judgmental and supportive. And when the leaders and members in those communities go on pretending to be caring and forgiving and "doing the Lord's work," perhaps it is *they* who are living in denial.

The good news is, there are plenty of religious communities and recovery groups (and now religious-slash-recovery groups) to fill the growing demand. Ain't freedom of religion a wonderful thing?

DEPROGRAMMING

As we're learning, Faithspeak works best when it enlists the language and conceptual framework of a particular time and place to talk about the problems and solutions that have characterized human existence from the beginning. "Deprogramming" is one such example.

Let's begin with the idea that the human brain is much like a computer. It consists of hardware—the physical chassis and built-in operating system that copes with daily life while allowing for software updates and additional programs designed for specific tasks we may want to pursue. Each human being is endowed with similar hardware, but our environment and unique compilation of experiences can program us in strikingly different ways.

Some of these ways are regarded as sinful by religious traditions. Like the tendency to lie or steal, or to treat other people as objects. Or reacting with anger and violence rather than love and compassion, or imposing one's own tradition and laws on others whether or not they agree. To label these negative behaviors as "sin," then calling for our salvation from it, is Faithspeak. And for those who've learned to use this venerable tongue, it can be as evocative and life-changing as ever. But sin and salvation can also be loaded words, heaped with condemnation and suspicion that can never fully separate the sin from the sinner.

"Deprogramming," on the other hand, acknowledges that certain behaviors may be negative and undesirable, but the program that led to them can be updated or removed. More importantly, the offending program is not an essential or defining characteristic of the operating system or the operator himself.

This point of view is closer to what ancient religions originally intended, and were ideally designed to do—to separate the person from the behavior. *Literally.* That's what gave meaning to stories where demons were "cast out" and the person formerly possessed was made whole again. Negative behavior was a matter of being infected with bad programming. So if we scan for viruses and wipe out the malware, wholeness returns.

In the 70s and 80s, and again more recently, deprogramming came to be associated almost exclusively with the effort to re-instill/reinstall wholeness in people who were living under the influence of a cult (as that term is popularly understood). But this more specific definition still carries the more generalized meaning: People are not simply what they do or how they feel, or the "programs" they're running for reasons that are sometimes beyond their control. They, and their lives, can be wiped clean. Their faith can be changed for the better, and through them, the world changed into a better place.

All we need is a good deprogrammer.

DETERMINISM

You won't find this word in the Vedas, or the New Testament or Qur'an. But the philosophical concept is there nevertheless.

In fact, the concept of determinism fueled a huge philosophical debate in the seventeenth and eighteenth centuries, along with a religious doctrine that now goes by the name of its best-known advocate, John Calvin.

Calvinism takes the Biblical passage quite literally that says only 144,000 believers will get to heaven. Out of all the people in history who ever lived, or *will* live, only 12 X 12,000 will end up being saved. And because God already knows who those lucky souls are, one might say they're "pre-destined" to make it. God has foreseen—or *pre-determined*—their ultimate destiny. Anything less would imply that God was not the Absolute, All-Knowing One the Bible (and the Qur'an) tells us He is. God wouldn't be God.

This pre-determinism eventually evolved into the philosophical theory that God—or nature, or whatever it is that has ultimate power—determines not only our final destiny but each and every action (or thought) along the way. The theory seemed only natural in view of the latest scientific models of cause-and-effect. Every aspect of life was presumed to be as mechanical and predictable as billiard balls hitting one another at certain angles and certain speeds. Admittedly there were millions of billiard balls in the game, and maybe they weren't all perfectly round or of equal size, besides which the table might not be exactly level. But if you could somehow *account* for all that, if you knew everything there was to know before each player took a shot, you could predict (determine) with absolute certainty where all the balls would go.

Our success as a human race is based in large part on that presumption of predictability. The more we discover about the laws that govern the universe and ourselves, and the more we know about previous and current conditions, the better we can predict (or manipulate) what's going to happen next.

This isn't just a scientific matter, either. Ancient prophets capitalized on the very same theory. If you keep ignoring God's laws, they would say, the Divine Wrath will come down on you as surely as the sun will rise tomorrow. Or, looking on the brighter side, if you love your neighbor as yourself, your lives will inevitably become richer and more rewarding. And the predictions were true not because Isaiah or Jesus or Muhammad said so, mind you, but because it was built into the nature of things. That's just how the world works.

Actually, this kind of collective wisdom about how the world works is also what religion is about. Religion is the repository of information—in a language that speaks to us on the deepest levels—that reveals us to ourselves, that exposes the world as it really is and tells us what we can expect to happen if we act in certain ways. Calvin was only putting it bluntly: One thing follows another like falling dominoes set in a line, like the movements of a Swiss-made clock, like the ocean tides. Whatever happens was destined to be.

Which isn't to say that things are beyond our control. Even the concept of Free Choice depends on a mechanical/deterministic view of the world. It is predictability, after all, that gives us control, that provides a reason to choose one avenue over another. If we go one direction, *this* is bound to happen. If we go the other way, *that* will happen.

Determinism therefore isn't the opposite of freedom. If anything, it encourages us to expand our knowledge of ourselves and our world, through whatever physical or spiritual resources may be available to us, so we can use that knowledge to our maximum benefit. Because the more we know, the more we're likely to make the right choice or do the right thing.

The catch is, when we reconcile determinism with freedom in this way, we must admit to being all the more responsible for one another's behavior as well as our own. Our words and actions become determining factors in shaping *them,* as their words and actions help shape *us.* And because we are interrelated and interconnected whether we like it or not, "community" is not merely unavoidable, it holds the key to our individual salvation.

So nothing that was true before is any less true now. It's a matter of choosing which brand of Faithspeak you prefer. Or which one seems to give you the most control.

Even if that choice is pre-determined.

DEVA

Nearly half of the listings under "D" in this Lexicon are somehow related to this four-letter beauty, even though it's of Hindu/Sanskrit origin, and even though Western theology prefers to think all the really important religious concepts came from the West.

Deva means "divine." (*Diva* is feminine; *divus,* masculine.) This is the linguistic source for words like "divinity," "devote," "disciple" and "discipline," as well as for "demon" and "devil." It therefore refers not only to the divine powers and gods who eventually came to be recognized as good, but to those who aren't.

The Hindu concept of deva (or "the devas") was originally devoid of value judgment. It simply alluded to the commonly-held belief that beyond this material world is a bustling, behind-the-scenes operation, an unseen level of reality teeming with mysterious powers. And, like the atomic and sub-atomic particles that are hidden from us even as we depend on them for our very existence, we can learn to unlock their secrets and use that knowledge for either good or evil. For atom bombs or nuclear energy. It's our choice; the deva itself is neutral.

It was an astonishingly scientific view of reality, actually. That is, until the devas devolved into petty, human-like gods of the Greek and Roman variety. The ancient Hindus began to populate the universe with thousands of them. *Millions.* When they embodied the divine realm's destructive potential, the devas were turned into "devils." As people were healed and enlightened, those forces were personified and placed in the opposite camp. Maybe this was humankind's earliest recorded effort to create the gods—or God—in their own image.

And it had all started so well.

DEVIL

A devil is a demon who has worked up from lance corporal to first lieutenant. Which is simply to say it's another way of personifying the evil forces in the world, of visualizing what's hostile to our own best interest. Except now we're up against something a bit more dangerous.

In the hierarchy of the Dark Side (to put things in *Star Wars* terms again), demons are the Storm Troopers of the evil Empire. They're nagging and potentially lethal, like a "white lie" or looking at another woman with more than an artist's admiration for beauty; but an occasional zap from the Forces of Light will usually hold them at bay. A devil, however, will zap *you* if you're not careful, sometimes even before you realize he's got you in his cross-hairs.

Not that he's Darth Vader himself. Just a darn good copy. And by personifying him as some kind of Crusader for Evil, we tend to take evil a little more seriously. Because what he represents are the all-too-human character flaws that often *do* end up destroying life: Anger that flares into violence, possessiveness that turns into greed, personal prejudice that boils into hate for a whole class or race. The Devil, ironically, also represents love—the love of money, or of sex, or one's job, or one's *self*—the kind that's so obsessive and all-consuming it forgets balance and wholeness, that desires the things "of this world" rather than the satisfactions of the spirit.

Called "the deceiver of men" or "god of this age," the Devil has one especially sneaky characteristic. Just as a generic angel can be anyone who brings a message you need to hear, the devil may also appear in human guise, and often as someone who only wants to help. But where the angel brings a message you *need* to hear, the devil brings one you *want* to hear. And there's a world of difference.

People sometimes turn over their whole lives to these devils. That's why, to put it figuratively, you can lose your soul even if you gain the whole world. And it's not even the devil's fault. He may have been genuinely concerned for your welfare. He may have been your best friend. Or your mother. Or spouse. It just so happens that the best thing you could have done—if only you'd known—was to turn him down cold. But no, you took the bait, you poor devil.

Fortunately, people can grow even from making the wrong choice. Besides, it's never too late to change course. And that's the Good News.

Or, as every religious tradition says in one way or another, the Devil never gets the final word.

DEVOTE

The common understanding of "devote" revolves around the idea of commitment—the total, unreserved commitment to some purpose or mission, or even to another person. Devotion is therefore an aspect of character, an alignment of your heart-of-hearts, of your *faith*. To be devoted is to be unswervingly loyal, as if you've taken a vow and nothing can change your mind.

The "vow" part, in fact, is of primary importance. And knowing that the root for "devote" is deva, you can guess to whom that vow is made.

Technically, anything which has been devoted has been promised for some purpose to God, or "in the presence of God." It is a vow made binding by divine authority. In the Qur'an and Old Testament, such a promise could never be retracted. Once devoted, *always* devoted. Not only can nothing change your mind, *you* can't change your mind.

There was a time when people took their commitments seriously. *That* seriously.

DHARMA

Now familiar to Western ears as the name of a character in the popular sitcom, "Dharma and Greg," *dharma* is one of the most central concepts to both the Hindu and Buddhist traditions. And, as it happens, the concept has very much to do with "character."

From a Sanskrit word meaning "to establish, or hold steady," dharma refers to the foundational truths supporting the natural universe, including the truths that govern the activities of human beings. Obviously, if we humans could know those truths and live in perfect accordance with them, we would be saved from the suffering and degradation that have characterized our history from Genesis onward.

Dharma therefore became synonymous with the daily practices and observances by which individual Hindus and Buddhists live in accordance with The Truth as they understand it. Back in the Sixties, "doing your own thing" conveyed the same meaning in youthful slang, although that slogan took on a regrettably self-centered emphasis.

Which is why learning what the foundational truths *are* can make all the difference. Since the historical Buddha was considered by his followers as the singular teacher who expounded the essential truths and practices required for righteous living, dharma (for Buddhists) came to mean "the teachings of Buddha." Self-centeredness was specifically *not* among those teachings, the decade of the Sixties notwithstanding. Character-building *was*. In fact the closest Western equivalent to dharma is "service." Presumably the kind focusing not on oneself, but others.

Many Hindus freely admit that Christians, Muslims and Sikhs have a "different dharma"—that is, a different understanding of the truth, as well as different practices and observances (i.e. kinds of service) consistent with it. The core meaning of dharma, however, refers to what is eternal and unchanging, regardless of how anyone understands it or who may have taught it to us.

The Western equivalent of *that* is Ultimate Reality. Or, as some prefer to call it, God.

DISCIPLE

Defining a disciple as someone who follows someone *else* is much too bland. Followers are wishy-washy. Like a herd of cattle migrating to the next pasture because one half-witted Holstein mistakes a patch of oxalis for clover. Or like an unruly mob, in which participants are driven by group dynamics instead of the leader or the idea that initially brought them together.

Again, somewhere in the etymology of this word is the *deva,* the unseen force, the devotion to Something Beyond that provides inspiration and direction. A disciple, in contrast to members of herds or mobs, is motivated by something deeper than a knee-jerk reaction to what the next guy is doing. There must be *commitment.*

The twelve disciples hand-picked by Jesus were presumably chosen for their commitment to his mission. But even Christians admit that the original Dozen Dudes weren't always the most shining examples of discipleship. They certainly weren't the smartest candidates for the job, either. Half the time they weren't sure what their job *was,* or what Jesus' mission was about. (So what else is new?) Judas eventually turned traitor because his own commitment to armed rebellion against the Roman occupation wasn't shared by the others. Simon Peter, the group's supposed Rock of Gibraltar, was also a traitor of sorts, denying that he even *knew* Jesus when the hoped-for Messiah was hung on the cross.

But the moral of the story lies precisely in its banged-up, dirt-encrusted humanity. Discipleship isn't always a pretty sight. It's often confusing and frustrating, especially up front, because committing ourselves to *anything* is difficult in this discard-after-use culture, in this world of microwave meals and debit card convenience. We often make "serious" commitments, then bail out with hardly a second thought when things don't turn out the way we planned. We give up when our initial efforts, sincere as they seem, don't change our lives as quickly as we'd like. The Top Twelve were only showing us how uncommitted we can be, even when we're in the presence of divinity, even when we're close enough to reach out and touch God and we're too dumb to know it.

But the Dirty Dozen also showed that there's compensation for hanging in there. Even as we deny our commitment, our hearts pull us toward an enlightenment that doesn't depend on some mere mortal. The deva, the Ultimate Power, the Holy Spirit, reaches down and teaches us what we most need to know, as long as we keep plugging away and don't throw in the towel. And at some point, what we've learned in spite of all these denials and broken promises—or *because* of them—is a wisdom worth passing on to others. The disciple becomes the teacher or rabbi or guru for still more disciples, either by word or by example, and preferably both.

This continuum is sometimes called "the disciple cycle." It is also the definition of "discipline"—the consistent, patient effort, day after day, that develops character and forges the inner connections to our deepest sources of strength and wisdom. Because it's rarely the big breakthroughs and once-in-a-lifetime conversions that make us Who We Are. It's the patient practice and continuing refinement of our faiths. It's the daily grind.

And whether you're undergoing psychiatric analysis, or medical treatment, or committing yourself to some new religious tradition, the process is bound to be just that: *A grind.* That's why psychology and medicine and religion are called disciplines in the first place. And just as these disciplines seem to blend into one another the deeper you delve into them, most genuine disciples begin to look and act more alike the longer they stick with it—even when they profess different religions.

The ultimate pay-off of discipleship, it's said, is Heaven. Or, as someone else pointed out, no matter which side of Olympus you start from, the hike always leads to the same mountaintop.

DIVINE

What came first—the chicken or the egg? "Divine" or "divinity"?

For purposes of maintaining alphabetical order, we'll start with the first. Besides, before we can imagine gods and goddesses or any single divinity, we need to get a handle on the basic concept of The Divine.

The Hindu notion of *deva* comes close. So does the *Star Wars* movie concept of The Force. It is the idea, increasingly verified in science, that there is another dimension, or realm, or layer of existence somehow beneath or beyond the physical world we experience through our five senses. It is related to this physical world in some essential, inseparable way, running in and through it, providing its laws, and without which we could not exist. It is therefore regarded as superior, in that we depend on *it,* but it doesn't depend on *us.* And it can either work to our benefit, or it can harm us.

We usually conceptualize this dimension as being non-material. Or, in religious terminology, as the "spiritual" or "divine." But these words *point* rather than explain. There is some question, in fact, whether human beings can *ever* explain it, if only because the ways our bodies are constructed won't allow it. We are predisposed to experience physical reality *only,* since our bodies' sense organs are designed to perceive only that reality; which, in turn, is because physical reality is what presents the primary threat to our self-preservation. (Yes, we'll take issue with that statement later. Throughout the Lexicon, in fact.)

But not being able to perceive or explain some theoretical level of reality does not mean it doesn't exist. Imagine, for example, trying to explain "visual reality" to someone who is without sight. Imagine a talking dolphin trying to explain his sonar-sensed reality to us. In other words, do we really think Ultimate Reality is limited to the capabilities of whatever sentient beings there are to perceive it? To coin a phrase, Heck no!

On the other hand, we limited human beings have at least transcended our sense limitations enough to acknowledge that reality is deeper and more complex than we normally perceive. We use electron microscopes and telescopes and super-colliders to extend our vision. We use logic and mathematics to explore the seeming "intelligence" behind the universe in a way that goes beyond routine experience. All of which is a modern-day fulfillment of our remote ancestors' sneaking suspicion that there are controlling influences outside the range of ordinary perception, and we'd be absolute fools if we didn't try to figure out what those influences *were.*

Throughout recorded history, in fact, people have claimed a fleeting glimpse of them. Still others claimed they could perceive their influences by the use of certain techniques, thus enhancing their control over the world and improving their lives.

How these techniques are described and categorized is the jump from "divine" to "divinity."

DIVINITY

There are three primary uses of the word. The first is essentially synonymous with "god." The second, spelled with a capital "D," with God. The third is a kind of personal quality the previous two share.

In mentally picturing the realm of the divine, in trying to imagine how those controlling influences behind the physical universe worked, people have always found it easier to envision human-like entities rather than impersonal forces. As those forces were identified and divided into various job categories (usually along the model of human society), they were given names and histories and thereby made "real" to the people who heard or read about them. All the better to gain their favor, or avoid their wrath.

Describe the sun to an ancient Greek as a huge, spherical cauldron of hydrogen gas condensed by the forces of gravity until its atoms undergo nuclear fusion, and you'd probably be handed a steaming mug of hemlock. Describe it as Apollo taking his flaming chariot for his daily joyride across the heavens and you're finally making some sense.

"Divinity," then, is the term applied to any or all those personified forces that appear to operate and influence our everyday experience. Consolidate those forces into different expressions of a single entity and you've made the jump from gods and goddesses to God, from divinities to The Divine. Dividing them into separate entities again is a move back in the opposite direction—from Allah to a Trinity, say, or from the Greek pantheon to the 330 million gods of Hindu folk religion.

That's right: 330 *million.*

Of course, Hindu scholars will reply that the 330 million divinities merely represent that many "faces" of the *one* Divinity. They are what Divinity looks like when viewed from different angles under different circumstances at different times. And just as Jesus used the term "seven times seventy" to mean "a lot," 330 million was a nice round figure to emphasize the virtually limitless ways divinity can manifest itself.

Notice that the meaning of "divinity" has changed here from a proper noun to a kind of reflective quality. Divinity, used in this third sense, can therefore signify an attribute that something or someone *displays.* A person is said to manifest divinity if he/she performs actions or exhibits qualities that seem god-like. If the realm of the divine is the ultimate source of power and authority—and thus of the confidence and peace which flow from that—then anyone who appears to reflect those qualities possesses divinity.

Most spiritual traditions insist that we can *all* possess divinity. Not in the same way we might possess a shiny new car or a pair of argyle socks, but *as we demonstrate certain personal qualities:* A loving nature or a certain charisma, for instance; or an optimistic, together-we-can-move-mountains attitude. And we reflect this attribute not by buying it or putting it on, but by aligning ourselves with it, by letting it put *us* on.

"Divinity" reminds us that there's a deeper part of our selves and our reality still lying undiscovered, untapped, beyond what our physical senses tell us. And if we can ever get in touch with it, things might be so much more divine.

DOGMA

Using the term "belief" as commonly understood, there are some beliefs we hold or "come around to" based on personal experience or serious reflection. There are also beliefs we *must* come to and agree with and put into practice in order to become, or remain, members of a certain religion or social group. The latter beliefs, together with all the teachings surrounding and supporting them, are what's known as *dogma*.

If you don't believe Muhammad was the last and most authoritative prophet of God/Allah, you can't be a Muslim. If you don't believe in Original Sin and the necessity of being "born again," you can't belong to most evangelical denominations within Christianity. If you don't believe that the Second Amendment to the U.S. Constitution guarantees an individual's right to own an R-15 assault weapon, you don't deserve to be a member of the National Rifle Association. All these mandatory beliefs are examples of dogma.

The problem with dogma is that it's usually enforced in a compulsory way—through public affirmations and loyalty oaths, or assigned tasks designed to prove one's allegiance, or even threats of punishment ranging from the Amish practice of "shunning" or the Spanish Inquisition's tortures to Islam's *fatwahs* authorizing death for designated individuals. The irony is, if the reason you believe something is a result of such punitive measures, you can't, by definition, truly believe it.

And if the tradition or group you belong to *uses* any of these measures, you might want to consider that practice as a strong incentive to resign from it. Or, in keeping with a long line of prophets and other radicals before you, attempt to *reform* it.

DOUBT

Contrary to popular opinion, doubt is not the opposite of belief. It's the opposite of *certainty*.

An individual can act *as if* it's better to "Love your neighbor as yourself"—and can therefore be said to believe it—all the while harboring serious doubts about it.

Your doubt, in fact, can often lead you to believe something you might not otherwise. "Practice silent meditation for twenty minutes a day," a New Age handbook suggests. "Recite the obligatory prayers five times a day," says the Qur'an. The result, both books claim, will be a greater sense of peace and stability in the face of life's problems.

But you doubt that claim. And precisely *because* you doubt it, you try it. You learn meditation, or the five daily prayers, and you start practicing the routine. If it's a fair test, you'll agree to act *as if* the claim is true for a reasonable length of time, until the practice becomes part of your faith. You may even go on practicing it without ever coming to a final conclusion, without ever being 100 percent certain that the claim is true. In fact you may spend a whole lifetime believing it, while doubting it the entire time.

There is a natural dynamic between doubt and certainty, faith and doubt, certainty and faith, running through all living religious traditions. The Christian statement that "Faith overcomes doubt" is not a demand for adherents to suppress their natural instinct to doubt. It's not a requirement to leave one's powers of reason, or one's knowledge about the facts of science, at the sanctuary door. Quite the opposite. "Faith overcomes doubt" is an admonition to put a belief to the test in exactly the experimental mode that science recommends. It asks us to *try* it, to put it on trial. Act *as if* some doctrine is true despite those nagging suspicions. Practice it in your daily life and only then judge the results. See if it hasn't transformed you for the better. *Risk* it.

When religious leaders knock people for having doubts, it's often an admission of their own uncertainty—or even a clue that what they're spouting is balderdash. Because if something is genuinely true, it stands the test. The used car salesman who knows his reduced-price roadster is a lemon wants you to buy it on the strength of his word, or the luster of its fresh coat of paint. Someone who's got a good product just asks you to take out it for a spin.

DYSFUNCTION

Another contemporary word that often substitutes for religious terminology, "dysfunction" is the condition of being out-of-balance in one's personal or communal affairs. It is the opposite of wholeness or at-one-ment, where the various functions of human life—from mental and emotional processing to physical health and gender identity—are working less in cooperation and more at cross-purposes.

Often, to make up for a particular weakness, another aspect of one's life or personality goes into overdrive and imposes itself on the others. Harsh discipline takes over when mercy and compassion can't get the job done. Sex turns into an obsession when love and tenderness aren't returned, or natural urges are repressed. Destructive co-dependencies form when an individual's lack of confidence or suppressed self-hatred devolves into living for, or *through,* someone else. One's career or escapist entertainment becomes a preoccupation when parental or social responsibilities prove too demanding or difficult.

"Living in sin" is Faithspeak for this unbalanced condition, and for one's ongoing failure to deal with it. While religion itself can manifest as a dysfunction, it can also provide the solution for both individuals and communities. The Islamic *Umma* is one vision of it, the Body of Christ another. Then again, so is the parent living across the street who works nine-to-five, meets his or her spouse for a night out once every week or two, and still finds time for the kids' soccer games and science fairs, and makes the necessary adjustments whenever life throws a curve.

Which is something *like* religion, because it's all about identifying one's needs—all of them—making priorities, finding a purpose, looking for help when life gets out of whack and offering help when others face their own dysfunctions... and making a sacred ritual out of the whole bloomin' business.

Because it *is.*

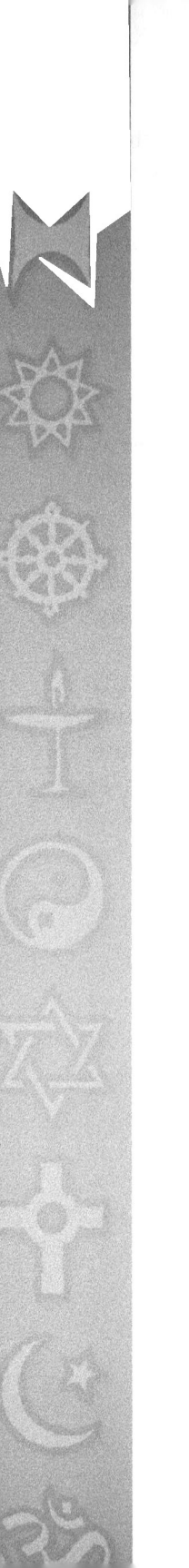

EASTER

It's a shopworn argument to remind everyone that Easter evolved from a pagan rite, just as Christmas did, just as many of the festivals in Jewish, Hindu and Islamic traditions did. So what?

So... what was the theme in the pagan Ostara/Astarte/Oester festival that was so profound, so moving, so fundamentally true that it was transformed into the single most sacred day on the Christian calendar?

Answer: *Death and rebirth.*

Easter is all about the Cycle of Life and victory over death that are celebrated without exception in every culture and tradition. And, quite logically, springtime is the best time to celebrate it. In winter the earth goes dormant, stops producing, all but dies. Even the sun can't seem to warm the cold, hard ground. The very season symbolizes the darker and more depressing times in our lives, the failures, the endings.

Spring, on the other hand, represents beginnings, new opportunities, the promise fulfilled, the hope that's finally rewarded. It proclaims in an explosion of green (and every other color!) that, life is supreme. No matter how hard the winter, how gloomy the predictions, how total the destruction, life goes on. You can't stop progress, can't keep a good man down, can't keep them feet from dancin'.

Or, in other words: Death, where is thy sting?

The Christian celebration had distinct advantages over the earlier pagan rites. It neatly symbolized the resurgence of life and hope in the dramatic death/resurrection of one Jesus of Nazareth. Seasonal renewal is abstract; a man's life is concrete. The image of a tender green shoot bursting up through the decaying leaves from last autumn is an inspiring motif, yes; but the pageantry of an empty tomb, its heavy door rolled aside, is Faithspeak of unsurpassed power.

Of course, the obvious question is: Was the empty tomb—Jesus' resurrection—an actual, historical event?

Clearly, many Christians are counting on it. "If Christ be not raised," Paul wrote in one of his letters, "our preaching is in vain." Which is why so much effort is spent trying to prove it; why the Shroud of Turin that reportedly covered Jesus' body is put on display to show that a supernatural event *did* happen. It's why there are four Gospels, not just one—as if four different witnesses have testified in some international Court of Law and we are now legally obliged to accept their evidence.

Forget the historical fact that other mystery religions also proclaimed savior gods who were raised from the dead long before Jesus. One of these gods, Mithras, was even put to death on Black Friday and resurrected after three days. But those similarities were only part of a conspiracy by Satan to cast doubt on the *real* truth. At least, that's what the Church fathers said.

But the real truth of the Easter story can't be taken away even if the empty tomb is only a rousing good story. The fact remains that life *is* supreme. Death *isn't* the last word. Inherent in even the most rigorous scientific conception of reality is an almost miraculous tendency toward greater complexity, toward life out of non-living matter, toward increasingly autonomous forms that are more and more capable of controlling their own destinies. Decay and destruction only serve to provide nutrients for more growth. The explosions of supernovae only provide star dust for more suns and planets and life and, eventually, intelligence—an intelligence that somehow, to some degree, reflects the Intelligence that lies behind the whole cyclical, super-natural process.

As we celebrate that process, and the Intelligence behind it—by whatever symbols and at whatever season—we celebrate Easter. And we acknowledge that renewal, rebirth and resurrection are not only possible, but programmed into The Way Things Are.

"Christ is risen" is just one way to say it.

ECOLOGY

With all the push-back (or at least indifference) regarding climate change in certain circles, this word has now become almost a litmus test. From the Greek *oikos,* meaning "dwelling" or "habitat," ecology is the science that deals with the relationship between human beings and the environment(s) in which they live, including not only the land and its resources but the other living creatures that share the same space.

In both the Bible and the Qur'an, this environment was originally pictured as a Garden of finite size, which was then scripturally expanded into a vague land mass surrounded by seas and portrayed much like the world still envisioned by the Flat Earth Society. Above this "firmament" was a canopy filled with the sun, moon and stars. Upon it were beasts and other natural resources over which humans were given complete dominion, along with a weather system that could be cajoled into serving their agricultural needs if the people diligently recited their prayers and remained faithful.

So much for science.

Today we don't have a prayer of maintaining a healthy garden without being mindful of everyone *else's* gardens and collective resources and a shared weather system, and where dominion is defined not by our right to exploit the world as we please but a responsibility to manage it for the generations that follow. Of course, rightly read, that's what the scriptures have been saying ever since, well, Day One.

Sometimes it takes a little climate change to figure out that our reading skills could benefit from a refresher course.

ECSTACY

It's as much a spiritual concept as a material (or secular) one.

Ordinary language employs the word to indicate the far end of an emotional spectrum where, for instance, happiness spills over into joy, or commitment turns into obsession, or love boils into passion. The spiritual meaning, however, is anything but ordinary.

Ecstasy is, by definition, outside the norm, or literally "in another place." Some of Israel's prophets were described as "ecstatic," in that they seemed to deliver God's word while in another state of consciousness, as if in a trance. Ancient Greeks saw their Oracle at Delphi in the same way, believing that their reigning oracle's pronouncements came from an other-worldly connection. Her gift was variously explained as a unique ability to communicate with the god Apollo; or, as scientists now contend, an altered mental state induced by the ethylene gases seeping from fractures known to exist beneath Delphi's temple, and which collected in the chamber where the Oracle meditated.

Speaking of which, meditation is the age-old process for inducing a similar altered state, usually *without* the use of ethylene gas—or the Sixties' celebrated hallucinogen, LSD, or yesterday's raft of Ecstasy drugs. Some adherents of Islam's Sufi sect aim for the same trance-like state through such physical practices as chanting or "whirling." Hindus, too, reach higher dimensions through the chanting of mantras or the *asanas* of yoga, where total concentration on repeated vocalizations or bodily poses frees the mind to repair itself, and to work out problems our normal consciousness can't seem to crack.

All these spiritual practices produce measureable changes in brain activity, initially, by lowering our gamma and beta states (ranging from high sensory arousal and normal wakefulness) into the alpha state. There, an induced relaxation response allows our consciousness to connect with our subconscious. Going deeper, meditation can transport us from theta's restorative rhythms into delta, a wave pattern associated with empathy, extra-sensory perception, and out-of-body experiences.

Such changes in our mental patterns can be life-transforming. Not so much in the sense of a one-time event, but like the regular vacations we take from our daily routines, assuring us that how things are today needn't dictate what tomorrow will be. Or like the weekly sabbaths designed to remind us that what we normally think of as important often amounts to small potatoes in the larger scheme of things. Or like the reveries we allow ourselves every now and then... to daydream, say, or simply to pause and take a deep breath, to thereby solve our problems not by dwelling on them, but by putting ourselves *in another place,* where answers emerge in our minds as naturally as new sights appear when we simply, calmly, turn our heads... and *look.*

EGO

This is another term you won't find in the world's sacred texts. But its effects are there on almost every page—in the recurring morality tale about the consequences of putting one's own needs above everyone else's, or in the preoccupation with self (Freud's "ego") that often seems to motivate even our scriptural heroes, much less the evil-doers and run-of-the-mill sinners.

And it's easy to understand why this preoccupation prevails. We see through the eyes in our own skull, not our neighbor's. The hunger we feel comes from our own stomach, not someone else's. We are located in *this* body, not that, *this* time and place, not in some Heaven or Hell that's far in the future and maybe a hoax to begin with.

Taken to an extreme, this self-centered perspective is also depicted as the source of every evil in the book, from personal transgressions to communal disintegration, from tribal feuds to wars between nations. Which is why saving our souls is never defined as a solitary enterprise. When Jews ask for forgiveness and seek renewal on Yom Kippur, the appeal is always phrased in terms of "us" and not "me." St. Paul wasn't handing out advice to the Average Joe in his Epistles, but to whole churches, to the entire community. In the Qur'an and the Granth and countless other sacred texts, the target audience isn't separate individuals, but "Oh ye People."

The current market for self-help books and seminars is typical of a perspective that sees self and ego as the core value. But it's not the self-help movement that created this narrow focus. To a large extent it's the business model that sees each separate individual as its primary target, and uses slick advertising to transform our natural concern for "the necessities" into a vacuum that sucks up every new product regardless of need, that lusts after comfort and pleasure and finally views life not as a quest for spiritual riches but for material ones. Of which there is an endless supply, along with easy financing for those who can't otherwise afford it.

Emotions aren't that difficult to manipulate. The science of psychology isn't just about helping people cope; it's a boon for marketing. It's for discovering what our hot buttons are, and pressing the bejesus out of them for fun and profit.

A recent self-help handbook with the catchy title *Take the 'E' Out of Ego and Go!* suggests that if only we could take charge of our emotions (the "E" in Ego), if only we could guard against their manipulation by others, we might go farther in life than we ever thought possible.

Another self-help book known as the New Testament put it this way: Those who lose themselves, *find* themselves. Buddhism, too, teaches that our true identity is the No Self—the transcendent "person" whose identity merges so seamlessly with everything else that there is no longer any boundary where ego ends and the rest of the universe begins. We are all, quite literally, *One*. Ego, in short, is an illusion.

See if that "self" helps.

EL / ELOHIM

Historically speaking, *El* is an ancient Semitic word meaning "god." Or, to go back a few entries in our Lexicon, "divinity."

Elohim is the plural form of the word and means, literally, "the gods." In the Hebrew Bible, Elohim is used repeatedly in exactly the same way the ancient Greeks spoke of "the gods." Of course, this became rather embarrassing as the Hebrew concept of a single, unified God evolved. But it was already too late to simply exorcise Elohim from wherever it appeared in scripture. These documents were the Word of God, remember. And God must have had good reason, right?

So word got around that Elohim was to be considered a synonym for The Almighty. Using the plural was a kind of royal affectation, in the fashion of the medieval king who might refer to himself as "We" and who might say things like "It pleases *us* to chop off your head, Beckett," or "*We* intend to invade Scotland on the morrow." Except that in Hebrew, the plural Elohim was also to be given a singular verb whenever employed, which would be like saying "We intends to invade Scotland" or "Thus says the gods." It just don't sound right, do it?

Some theologians use this El/Elohim story to show how our concept of divinity changes, even while we try to hold on to the same forms for expressing it. The result is often some fancy linguistic footwork that only confuses the issue. And here's some more fancy footwork that may end up just as confusing:

"El," in modern Latin languages, is what's known as a definite article. It's a so-called *function word* that precedes a noun and specifies it. *El Toro*, for example, means "the bull." Not just *any* bull, mind you, but the specific bull "El" points to in that particular context. The word "the" does the same job in English. It specifies the subject. It *points*.

Combining the Semitic meaning of "El" with the Latin one, we might say that "El" *points to divinity,* but we're not exactly sure who or what that is. For this reason no noun follows it. No concept is definite enough to assign a specific word. There's only a linguistic blank, like the space for your name on a job application. "El" (or "the") just hangs there, so to speak, pointing to that Mystery, preceding the divine blank we fill in with whatever makes sense to us, knowing it's only a function word anyway. By using "El" we affirm that some unchanging divinity exists, but we're admitting that our understanding of it is limited, and can't help but change as *we* change.

Maybe Elohim wasn't such a bad word for it after all.

ENLIGHTENMENT

In the history of Western civilization, *The* Enlightenment was the period during which Europe finally threw off the shackles of a Mother Church that had become corrupt, bloated and repressive. With freedom of thought no longer restrained, reason replaced superstition, science and medicine flourished, and books that were banned could now be read.

And speaking of books, it was no coincidence that the huge library at Toledo, compiled and carefully preserved by the (Muslim) Moors until they were pushed out of Spain, was re-opened to European scholars not long before Europe's Enlightenment finally took off. The library proved to be a treasure trove of lost wisdom, featuring Greek, Roman and Arabic authors deemed heretical by the Church, but whose works the Church could now no longer suppress. Universities—a new concept in Western education—sprang up virtually in the shadow of that great library, disseminating its literary and scientific riches and inspiring whole new fields of study.

The irony with today's so-called Clash of Civilizations between Islam and the West is that Western culture owes its emergence from the Dark Ages, in large part, to the knowledge preserved by the Moors. And yet, ever since that resurgence, much of the Islamic world has retreated into a cultural darkness by repressing what it had once preserved.

In the East, meanwhile, "Enlightenment" had been the operative word for almost two millennia. For Buddhism, especially, Enlightenment is for the individual soul what *The* Enlightenment was for Western Civilization. It is the continuing removal of the shackles of corrupting influences, and the progressive absorption of the Self, through knowledge, reason and right living, into the ultimate reality behind the universe.

How this process is different from the Western concept of salvation, some might say, is mostly a matter of semantics. Or Faithspeak.

ENTELECHY

From the Greek *en* (for "agent" or "being") and *telos* (meaning "aim" or "goal"), entelechy refers to the mechanism by which all things evolve toward the full potential inherent within them.

The entelechy of the acorn gradually produces an oak tree... and not a sunflower. The entelechy of a fertilized human ova develops progressively from a zygote to a fetus to a child to a grown adult... and not into an ape or an alpaca.

Of course, as genetics and physics have enabled us to understand the once-mysterious agent behind these processes, entelechy has taken on a more symbolic meaning. It is now the principle or *process* whereby things evolve toward their built-in goals or ends. Like the inevitable progression of a swirling gas cloud into a star, and finally into a black dwarf. Or the development of elements and molecules into organic compounds, ultimately leading to an endless diversity of life forms.

Or the saving grace that slowly (or sometimes like a lightning strike) transforms selfish individuals into selfless saints.

Entelechy—the word itself—is now rarely used outside of what some call the "esoteric sciences." But the basic concept informs everything from the Human Potential Movement to Yogananda's Self-Realization Fellowship, from the West's notion of salvation to the East's "migration of souls." We can choose to delay this built-in process. Some of us seem to actively work against it. But the universe—or God—is ultimately in control. And He, or It, won't take *No* for an answer.

EPISTLES

The New Testament is probably the only place where you'll find this word anymore. But the practice *behind* it is a time-honored process found across the religious spectrum.

In the narrowest sense, The Epistles are the letters Saint Paul (formerly Saul of Tarsus) sent to reassure and provide counsel for the early Christian churches. In that formative period two decades after Jesus was executed, small communities of Christians were struggling for survival, having the usual growing pains, and confronting the first glimmerings of the persecutions to come. They were also floundering in a sea of conflicting stories and doctrines about who Jesus really was, and what his teachings meant. They were, in short, having a collective identity crisis.

Paul, who was Christianity's hands-down, top-of-the-chart missionary and de facto founder, came to the rescue. He wrote letters. Lots and lots of letters. Some of them while he was in prison for treason against the Roman Empire.

His letters (epistles) covered a wide range of subjects. Some were basically administrative: How the churches should be organized; who gets to speak in church; advice on waiting for Jesus' Second Coming and how to overcome dissent or internal conflict in the meantime. And, since much of that conflict was over theological issues, Paul wrote most of his letters to help the churches get their doctrines in order.

Several early versions of the Gospels were making the rounds, along with numerous less-trustworthy accounts. How were the churches to sort them out? How were they to interpret Jesus' words, especially since he was Jewish and they, increasingly, were converts from backwoods paganism and the Mystery religions of Greece and Rome? A grand theological scheme began to unfold in Paul's letters, most of which were eventually assembled and appended to the Gospels (which themselves weren't assembled until decades later). Eventually Paul's words were declared by the Roman Church to be the Word of God on an equal footing with the authorized biographies of Jesus himself.

It's a long-standing tradition. First comes the life and sayings of some extraordinary spiritual teacher. Then come the Epistles—the written accounts and inevitable editorials by the next generation, drawing out the meanings of the original words to make them more relevant to the times. The same thing happened to Paul's words. Later church fathers added their own refinements, in the form of commentaries and formal creeds, which in turn were reviewed and reinterpreted by still later authorities, all professing the same tradition yet recognizing that no word can ever be The Last Word. There must always be what amounts to a new epistle for each succeeding generation.

Judaism shared the same dynamic. Or more accurately, *started* it.

Even before the proverbial ink was dry on the newly-assembled Five Books of Moses, the collection was further embellished by ongoing oral (Hebrew: *halakic*) traditions that spelled out the meanings of virtually every line of text and often went well beyond them. These oral traditions were eventually assembled and written down in the second and third centuries, CE, and called The Mishnah. Other commentaries from the wisest sages and rabbis of the time reinterpreted *those* interpretations, and the resulting compilation came to be known as The Talmud. Which, for Jews, is something like The Epistles are for Christians, only with multiple authors.

Likewise Islam. The Qur'an, dictated to scribes by Muhammad (since he never learned how to write), was God's/Allah's revelation to pagans of the seventh century Arab world. But it, too, wouldn't be the last word. Oral traditions developed around the daily practices of Muhammad, called his *sunna*. His lifestyle and actions and sayings were eventually compiled in *The Hadith*. As usual, later generations studied these oral and written sources, interpreted them and spelled out their meanings, all of which came into Islamic tradition as the "understanding" or *fiqh*, and were eventually committed to writing in a detailed legal code known as *Shari'a*.

In other words, more Epistles.

The Greek root for "Epistle" is *episteme*, meaning "knowledge." Generically, then, an epistle is something that deepens our knowledge of *previous* knowledge, building on what we're already familiar with.

This book is an Epistle. Every new experience is an Epistle—especially when it's shared with other people who can help you put it in perspective, who can help you give it meaning.

Life is an Epistle.

ETERNAL

As one comedian put it, "Eternity—what a concept!"

If you're not religious, thinking about The Eternal just might change your mind. If you *are* religious, the concept can stretch you, taking you into new and uncharted territory. Because religious traditions *do* have a habit of using this word frequently without really explaining it. Eternal life. Eternal damnation. Eternal bliss. Just plain "eternity."

It would be baffling enough if "eternal" simply meant "never-ending" and eternity was synonymous with "forever," like some historical timeline stretching infinitely back into the past and infinitely forward into the future. Unfortunately this linear, time-based model of eternity, as hard to imagine as it already is, doesn't capture the full mystery of its religious meaning.

Eternity is even more puzzling. Because it is, in some way, *outside of time*. From the perspective of eternity, the Bible says, a thousand years can be like the blink of an eye; a single moment like a thousand years. This is obviously not everyday experience we're talking about here, folks. More like science fiction.

And ironically, it's modern science that provides the most useful models for getting a handle on this ancient concept. Quantum physics, cosmology and theoretical mathematics have confirmed that time as we know it is part of a larger integrated complex called the Space-Time Continuum. Time is as much a component of material objects—and therefore of *you*—as length, width and depth.

In his fascinating book, *Parallel Universes*, Alan Wolf summarizes some of the more recent theories about reality. We're introduced to a ten-dimensional universe that somehow imploded to our current four; to the parallel anti-matter universes residing on the other side of black holes; and to the mirror universes into which electrons disappear, then re-emerge as they dance around an atomic nucleus. Time and physical reality are not only "weird," as physicist Richard Feynman cheerfully described them, but "weirder than you can possibly imagine."

But let's go back to the time-line model of eternity for the sake of familiarity. Picture an endless pipeline through which we are all being pumped by some mysterious power. Let's call that pipe "Time," and the markings on its cylindrical walls the "minutes" and "hours" we pass as we move along. Let's say that beyond the cylinder's walls, *outside* the pipeline, is Eternity. For those who reside there—let's call them Residents of Eternity, or R.E.'s for short—no time is kept and movement in all directions is permitted. Theoretically, R.E.'s could enter the pipeline of Time ahead of where we are now, or at some point behind us. An R.E. might thereby enter our future, and then our past, in what would seem only a moment to us, compressing time into "the blink of an eye." Or he might repeatedly enter the same moment in Time, expanding it into "a thousand years."

This might explain the Biblical description of eternity. It is also the kind of mental construct scientists invent in order to understand inter-relationships between time and matter. Such constructs are admittedly artificial, resulting in some utterly eye-rolling notions like "curved space" and "wormholes in time." But they are helpful tools for talking about things that can't be directly experienced by human beings, using the ordinary language of human beings. That's why they often come out sounding so weird.

Then again, religious traditions know about "weird," too. Try reading the visions of the Prophet Ezekiel or Daniel. Or the Revelations of Saint John the Divine (who was clearly in some other dimension when he took up his career as an author). Or take the Vedas of Hindu tradition. Written 2,000 years before the New Testament, these poetic verses also happen to be humankind's earliest examples of what we'd call "science fiction," with stories of time-traveling and jet airplanes and weapons of mass destruction that almost convince you somebody was hooked into eternity in a big way.

In fact, it is this effort to hook into eternity that motivates a good deal of religious activity. It's not out of the question, even scientifically speaking, that the human mind can somehow connect with—or *may already be connected with*—resources of power and insight that lie outside of time, or in some other dimension. Religious traditions, in this view, may be understood as the collected efforts of various groups to create mental constructs that represent this other dimension; and in that way they help their adherents access it using the language and models that make the most sense to them.

Those efforts haven't stopped, even though the various groups involved—along with their research and development staffs—may change. In fact it looks like things will *continue* that way. Maybe eternally.

EVIL

Just when you thought it was safe to go back into the water, along comes *Jaws*. Just when you thought it was safe to fly again, there's news of another jet airliner going down. Just when the economy seems to be back on track, and your home loan is approved, and a week goes by without a terrorist attack, something else comes along to remind us that life is not only full of surprises, it can be downright dangerous.

Which gives rise to the question human beings have asked since God declared that creation was "good"; namely, *What's so good about it?*

When two hundred people perish in a plane crash, what's so good? Or when 200,000 perish in a famine or a tsunami or a civil war in Syria? What's so good when one pig-tailed little girl clutching her Raggedy Ann while she's asleep on the living room sofa (because Mommy and Daddy can't afford a bed) is shot in the head by a crack addict who fires a few rounds of his handgun in no particular direction just for the hell of it?

Maybe the pagans of 10,000 BCE had it easier. They figured the cards were stacked against them from the start. They knew the evil spirits were out to skin their hides and that there was a better than even chance they wouldn't live past thirty. Nobody ever tried to sell them the absolutely crazy, irreconcilable notion that there was not only a single, all-powerful God, but that this God was all good.

If that's so, our prehistoric friend might ask, why is there evil in the world? Why do bad things happen? Why do the good die young? Why can't everybody have three squares a day and nobody ever dies of lung cancer or the latest mass shooting or even dies in the first place?

It's the same question every religious tradition and every student of philosophy has asked from Day One. In both philosophy and religion, it's called The Problem of Evil.

Because the problem is, there's no fully satisfying answer. And since many people are convinced that no religion or philosophy is worth the parchment it's written on unless it can resolve this issue, religion and philosophy keep on trying.

Buddhism and Hinduism, for example, suggest that evil is the karma of past lives coming full circle. How else can you explain the pig-tailed girl's death? Maybe she was a drug dealer in her last incarnation. Or a guard in a Nazi concentration camp.

Maybe.

Or maybe, like the view of Christian Science and Zen and a few New Age authors, evil is either an illusion of mortal mind or a condition we attract to ourselves by negative thinking.

Maybe.

Or maybe, along with a few Stoics and plenty of Christians, we should simply view evil as God's will and leave things at that. Which, it turns out, is the condensed version of the message in the Biblical book of Job (pronounced like "Joe" with a "b" at the end).

Job, it so happens, was a blamelessly good man who one day finds all his servants dead and his cattle stolen, then promptly loses his house and his children in a freak storm. On top of that, he gets a case of boils bad enough to shake anyone's faith in the power of penicillin, not to mention a bunch of so-called friends who come around and dole out dumb advice that would send any man to the funny farm.

So Job finally pops the question to God: Why? And, why *me?*

God's response, in so many words, was that trying to explain evil, even to a fairly smart cookie like Job, would be like trying to explain the Theory of Relativity to a pre-school kid. In other words, *forget it.*

But the response may also, in so many words, be telling us that trying to figure out an answer to the question for ourselves, at our own level of understanding, is precisely what we're here for. That's your *job,* Job. Solving the question of good and evil is one of the primary purposes for our own existence. Giving us a neat, pre-packaged explanation would be like God passing out all the answers to the final exam before we sat down for the test.

And, as a matter of fact, most religions *do* tend to see our lives as a great cosmic testing ground. Whether evil is real or an illusion (or somehow both), everyone has some concept of what's bad. Evil is a given; it's a fact of life because Adam ate from the Tree of Life or Pandora opened her fabled box, and there's not a damn thing we can do about that now. All we can do is *deal* with it. And how narrowly we define it—whether evil is related strictly to our own selfish interests or it includes other people—becomes a gauge for our growth toward some kind of salvation. That's what the test is *about.*

Of course, there are more philosophical answers to The Problem of Evil, too: The fact that there could never be "good" without some experience of its opposite; the fact that choice would be non-existent if people weren't free to hate each other as well as love one another; the fact that the natural laws governing the universe simply *had* to come out this way or there could *be* no natural law.

All of these attempts at answers are fascinating and worth kicking around over beer and peanuts. But they are really only restatements of what religious traditions have already said. Evil exists because that's the way the cookie crumbles. The only question we can really answer is, What are we going to do about it?

What's reassuring is that none of us faces the question alone. Celebrations like Easter and Chanukah and Holi are there to remind us that we're all in this together, and that nothing that happens is so terrible or so final that it cannot ultimately be turned to good.

EVOLUTION

Funny how some evangelists characterize the Theory of Evolution by spelling the word, "Evil-lution." What's funnier, or else ironic, is that evolution is not only the most potent tool for understanding the physical world, it's the scientific synonym for what is perhaps the evangelist's favorite concept: *Salvation.*

In its most technical sense—though this is hardly a technical discussion—evolution is the fundamental explanatory framework for biology. The theory states that life forms grow into, and become increasingly adapted to, their physical environments through a combination of genetic mutation and natural selection. Obviously the living things we see all around us are too complex and wonderfully constructed to have suddenly come into existence by chance. But a sequence of tiny, accumulated changes that *are* random, and are then rewarded or punished by increasing or decreasing a particular life form's ability to survive—that process *can* explain how those forms came to be.

Other sciences have borrowed the term "evolution" for its generic meaning of coming-to-be through some natural, mechanical process. Astronomers, for example, have shown that stars evolve through a process whereby massive clouds of interstellar gas contract under gravity, their cores eventually igniting according to the laws of nuclear physics, then consume themselves in successive stages until they either explode or shrink into an incomprehensibly dense ball of matter, or both.

Even *non*-physical things are said to evolve—our relationships, our understanding, our personalities—whenever a process of transformation appears to be at work. The main ingredient in each case is the action of *accumulated changes from natural causes,* which in time produce a measurable difference.

This process, however, doesn't exclude sudden or major changes that often seem to come out of the blue. But if we look closely at those sudden changes, we invariably discover some kind of build-up that preceded it. The star that "goes supernova" is only undergoing a natural event predictable from its massive size and remaining elements. The sudden transitions of certain animal species in the fossil record—or the appearance of seemingly *new* species—only testify to some migratory event or environmental cataclysm that brought new selective forces into play, rewarding existing or mutant variants that, until then, were less successful.

And the sudden "conversion" that turns a person's life around is only a natural response to the steady accumulation of conscious and subconscious forces: The external and internal clues that one's life has been going down the proverbial hell-hole, combined with a growing awareness that it doesn't need to be that way, and the fortuitous appearance of an answer that finally breaks through the ego's defenses to one's heart-of-hearts.

Bingo... *Salvation.*

Not that the conversion event is itself salvation. Conversion is simply the heartfelt climax of the process to that point—a process that will no doubt continue by testing one's new faith, by working out the bugs, by adapting the details of that individual's life to its new direction and purpose. Future transformations, or at least further refinements, are a certainty.

In other words, evolution applies to faith, too. Religious traditions of all stripes embrace this as a fundamental precept, however they may phrase it: *Faith evolves.*

The theory of evolution is therefore as religious as it is scientific. That's the main reason it's here in this Lexicon. Evolution is The Living Testament to the fact that, everywhere in the universe, from inanimate matter to the human soul, ongoing transformation is built into the very nature of things. The details of that process may be subject to debate. The mechanics are still being worked out—in both science *and* religion. Which is why people still refer to it as a "theory." But the basic premise of evolution is as close to an Absolute as you're likely to find. It is the process from simple to complex, from dissolution to preservation, from mere survival to abundant life, from the narrow perspective to The Big Picture, from the selfish constraints of our individual ego to the infinite resources of Ultimate Reality.

If there were no evolution, there would be no salvation. Because the same mechanism that transforms the physical universe transforms hearts. The journey from primordial bacteria to human being mirrors the spiritual journey from sinner to saint. The process that rewards life forms for traits better adapted to the environment is the same dynamic that selects human behaviors which contribute to both individual and communal fulfillment.

Salvation. Evolution. One is framed in the language of Faithspeak, the other in the terminology of science. Thank God for both.

EXCOMMUNICATION

From the Latin *ex communicare,* the term essentially means being "outside the communion." In this case, outside of the Roman Church.

More specifically, it's the ecclesiastical act of cutting off someone from having any further relationship (i.e. communion) with their former church. Which happens to include the rite of Communion, as well as all the other sacraments and benefits of church membership. In practical terms, excommunication signaled that a person was headed for Hell, even though the Church insisted the act was not so much a punishment as an incentive to return to its true teachings, and its officials remained hopeful the person in question would do just that.

Being sufficiently perverse or rebellious made you a good candidate for this rather extreme incentive. Someone in the public eye who had a sizeable following made the sentence even more likely. Henry VIII, Elizabeth I, Martin Luther and Joan of Arc had too much influence over others for their heresies to be simply ignored. The Holy Roman Emperor Frederick II was rebellious enough, and influential enough, to be excommunicated three separate times, for three separate reasons.

Galileo, while only *threatened* with excommunication, likewise had too much of a following in social and academic circles for his heresy to go unpunished. Allowing him to openly support Copernicus' notion that our Sun was the center of the solar system would have cast doubt on the inerrancy of the Bible. You might as well deny the reality of Adam and Eve, or Noah's boatload of koalas, Kodiak bears and cockroaches!

Four centuries later, Syria's Maronite Church would excommunicate a poet who had the nerve to pen verses that mirrored the cadences of Biblical scripture, and which suggested that the Church wasn't the only repository of the universal truths. In this case, fortunately, Kahlil Gibran's millions of followers across the globe were enough to convince Maronite authorities that they'd more likely excommunicated *themselves* instead of their heretical poet. The act was quickly rescinded as if the whole thing were merely an unfortunate misunderstanding.

In 1964, Galileo's censure and threatened excommunication were likewise rescinded, but Galileo had long ago caved and confessed that his heliocentric solar system was an affront to Christian teaching. And the irony is, Church authorities knew Galileo was right all along. His unforgivable sin was simply that he'd blindsided them. They hadn't had time to prepare the masses for the coming clash between science and religion. They hadn't yet instructed the faithful that there were alternative ways of reading the Bible, that the Holy Scriptures can still convey essential truths without their words being taken literally.

It was equally ironic that the Church thought it could remove *anyone* from communion with The Divine to begin with, as if mere mortals could render that judgment. Its first missionary, St. Paul, said as much in one of his Epistles. "I am convinced," he wrote to the first-century Romans, "that neither death, nor life, nor angels, nor things present, nor things to come, nor powers, nor height, nor depth, nor anything else in all creation, will be able to separate us from the love of God..."

Too bad the Church didn't take *that* literally.

EXTRA-TERRESTRIALS

From Erich von Daniken's ground-breaking book, *Chariots of the Gods?* to recent TV series like "Ancient Aliens," the notion that our divinities were originally inspired by visits from extra-terrestrials (ETs) continues to grow in popularity. And admittedly, the notion of super-human space travelers coming to Earth serves many of the same functions for the modern mind as "sky gods" did for more primitive societies. The clash of alien beings seeking dominion over the less-advanced inhabitants of the Third Rock from the Sun makes a handy, hi-tech substitute for Lucifer and his fallen angels rebelling against a righteous Jehovah and his heavenly host.

Side-stepping the issue of whether there is good evidence to support either storyline, both of these views can be seen as metaphors for the struggle that remains a reality in either case: Good vs. Evil; morality vs. lawlessness; order vs. chaos; integrating oneself with the wider universe through conscious co-creation vs. egoistic self-absorption and inevitable destruction.

Still, there is something inherently sad and demeaning about a belief that human beings are incapable of finding guidance within their own experience; that they couldn't have invented medicine or technology or self-governance without the benevolent assistance of more advanced off-worlders; or that our chromosomes are the handiwork of alien experiments rather than the product of an ongoing evolution built into the natural order.

ETs are a symbol of the same dismissive perspective some of us continue not only to hold but to foist upon others—that we're just not good enough, that we need saviors from the heavens rather than solutions from within ourselves. Clearly, this top-down perspective represents a certifiable "faith."

Fortunately, it's not the only one.

FAITH

This is what it's all about. Not a compilation of doctrines. Not some collection of definitions in a religious Lexicon. Not the church you belong to, or which religion you identify with. It's not "religion" at all but the *product* of religion.

Faith is how you interact with the world. It's your attitude toward life. Which is what Part One of this book deals with and why we're not about to go over the whole discussion again here.

Except...

Except to remind ourselves that the bottom line for faith is action. All the arguments against evolution, say, or to prove the existence of God—all our going to church or studying the holy books or praying to some Higher Power—are ultimately meaningless unless they result in refining and improving our behavior. And making those improvements part of Who We Are.

In most sacred scriptures, the word "faith" implies a sense of reliability. What can we be *relied on* to do? This is something we can determine in the same way others do: By observing ourselves in action. We must become more conscious of our own behavior, more aware of what we do. Forget all the so-called good intentions and rationalizations that "it's the thought that counts." What have we actually *done?* Or at least *tried* to do, despite our admittedly limited capabilities and imperfect understanding?

This is where the New Testament emphasis on "faith over works" kicks in. Some people continue to insist that Paul's doctrine minimizes the importance of actions. It *is* the thought that counts, they claim. Tender feelings for Jesus are the legal tender for admittance to heaven. But what Paul was really saying about faith is that our attitudes are where it all starts; that action is the result of right thinking; that the proper alignment with Spirit will produce whatever "works" are possible within the context of each person's life.

It is also to say that, even with the very purest of intentions and proper spiritual alignment, we can still manage to screw things up. And we often do, sometimes seriously. Maybe because we didn't know enough, or the outcome was beyond our control.

Which is where yet another sense of the word "faith" kicks in: We must still risk the "work." We are still required to act. To try.

To have faith.

FALL

For the theological underpinnings of what many Christians label as The Fall, feel free to skip ahead to Original Sin. In the meantime, suffice it to say that "the fall of man"—understood to be humanity's inherent sinfulness or inability to live up to his divine potential—is a common theme from Hindu literature to Jewish Kabbalah, from Christian theology to Islamic tradition. And the inspiration for that theme, which continues to this day, is simply our collective exasperation that this world of ours is really, *really* screwed up.

Look around. For all the good there may be in this life, human beings still wage war, use violence to solve disputes, spew hatred. Immorality is as widespread as ever, seen by liberals in the form of corporate greed and economic injustice, by conservatives in abortion and gay marriage. Or maybe it's not the world that's screwed up, it's us.

So how the hell did we get here? A rousing good story might help.

There's the one set in The Garden, of course, where Adam falls for Eve, who fell for the Snake, after which both eat the forbidden fruit and fall ill with some kind of virus that resulted in the pain of childbirth and the formation of sweat whenever their descendants got down to work.

There's also the story of Lucifer and his conspiracy to grab the royal reins in Heaven, aided by one-third of his fellow angels. When the plot was foiled, the whole contingent of rebels fell to Earth—hence the title of that particular story—where they've been surreptitiously infecting us earth-bound beings with the same virus Eve must've caught.

While there's no single event in Hindu or Buddhist tradition that compares to Adam and Eve's garden party or Lucifer's downfall, there are plenty of other characters, both gods and men, whose personal stories illustrate how we all seem to stumble down the road of life, trying our best, but something about our humanity keeps tripping us up.

And it's this inherently human flaw, this Fall, that requires some sort of divine disinfectant to save us. Who or what that disinfectant may be calls for another rousing good story, or stories. And in the same sense that the earlier stories were true, so are these.

FAST

This isn't the fast that's synonymous with "speedy" or "quick." We're talking about the fast in breakfast, the period between your midnight snack and morning coffee when you stop feeding your face.

Actually, this archaic-sounding term refers to any extended period when you purposely don't eat. It might be from dawn to sunset, as observed in the Islamic fast of Ramadan. Or from one sunset to the next, like the Jewish fast of Yom Kippur. It might be the fast of Buddha under the Banyan tree, when he swore off all food until he experienced Enlightenment. Or Gandhi, refusing to eat until his fellow Indians stopped rioting in the streets.

Fasting, in other words, boasts a long tradition of communal and personal practice that can be found all across the spiritual smorgasbord. The question is, what is it spiritually *practicing?* And does it have any value for us today?

What fasting represents, historically, is the assertion of internal self-discipline in the face of external conditions. True, some observers suggest the practice originated because food supplies were often marginal, and religious authorities made it a virtue to regularly abstain from eating in order to stretch reserves. Others suggest that religious mystics began the practice when they discovered that not eating for extended periods brought on visions from the gods or God—which physicians today might call "deprivation-induced hallucinations."

Still others point out that fasting has always been known to have a beneficial, purifying effect on the body. Many doctors would also agree that removing all food sources, when medically safe, can detoxify the blood, revitalize the digestive system and make the entire body more receptive to nutrients when consumption of food is eventually resumed.

In any case, what all these fasts have in common is their goal of turning *not eating* into a conscious, positive act. Fasting is therefore a kind of self-directed Faithspeak, asserting control over one's body and external conditions in a way that goes beyond mere words. Faithspeak, you'll remember, is most effective when it's tied to our emotions or bodily functions. Hunger is obviously one of the strongest of these, so exercising deliberate control over it—*defying* it, so to speak—sends an unmistakable message that the body is not supreme. Your mental/spiritual self has something to say about things, too.

Not the least of which is that, ultimately, each of us is responsible for what goes into our bodies. *And* our minds. It's a healthy practice to break out of our normal routines so we can review what we've been feeding ourselves physically and spiritually. That's why fasting was traditionally combined with religious holy days—though you can certainly declare a fast any time you decide to turn inward or focus on your own sources of dietary or spiritual input. As the computer programmer knows only too well, "Garbage in, garbage out." Or, as the culinary equivalent declares, "You are what you eat."

Fasting is simply a time-tested recipe for making sure the main course will lead to one's just desserts.

FESTIVAL

No one said life was easy. Throughout the world's sacred writings and historical records, the depiction of human existence is inscribed with pain and suffering, toil and trouble. Maybe that's only because bad news makes the best headlines. Or the best novels. Maybe it's easier to draw attention by complaining than by pointing out the good things in life.

But every now and then, as the songwriter says, "You gotta *stop...* and smell the roses."

Festivals are the institutionalized smelling of roses that most traditions call for on a regular basis. From the word "feast," the earliest festivals were "people's celebrations" inspired by the natural cycles of planting and harvest, or the annual commemorations of military victories and other significant events. The common folk would throw the equivalent of a modern-day block party and basically eat, drink, and be merry 'til they dropped.

Unfortunately, the party would almost inevitably get out of hand. Especially during hard times when going a little crazy provided a much-needed emotional release.

Revelry is the term that springs to mind. Public drunkenness. Disorderly conduct. So the authorities step in. And they can either quash the celebration entirely—as some denominations still do by outlawing dancing or birthday parties or any public gatherings except on holy days—or they can turn those festivals *into* holy days. In this way they can legitimize the spirit of the celebration while curbing all the revelry because the event now takes on a more sacred purpose.

Judaism, one of humanity's earthiest traditions, is especially conspicuous with its festivals. There are good half-dozen major ones. Passover, for example, celebrates liberation from bondage. Its central rite is a festive meal—one that requires adults to consume at least four cups of wine. Yet the tradition has turned the feast into a very orchestrated procedure which carries solemn meaning, at the same time inspiring all the joyous feelings liberation ought to inspire.

Festivals, whether religious or secular, are the public affirmations of what we consider The Good Life. At a minimum, they are reference points in our annual cycles, a way of recalling the natural seasons in our lives, of establishing a sense of time, of regularity, of connection to the earth, to our past.

They are also psychic rewards that urge us to hang on just a little longer when things are rough. (It's no coincidence that statistics show fewer deaths in the run-ups to major holidays, as if people's anticipation alone is enough to keep them going.) Festivals can help us recognize that life is worth all the trouble, that it's okay sometimes to feel good just for the sake of feeling good. Let's just throw ourselves a party; don't ask why.

But sometimes we *do* ask why. And at their best, festivals point out in visible Faithspeak that physical cycles and physical events are what support our spiritual lives. Our inner journeys, our transformations from sinner to saint—or whatever terminology points to our increasing fulfillment as human beings—are possible only through our outer journeys, our physical survival. One more day, one more harvest, one more year gives us that much more time to get the hang of it all.

So get out the good china. Put on that pot roast and your best dancin' shoes. Life is a special occasion.

FOOL

The more recent understanding of "fool"—someone who can be easily duped, or someone who's simply stupid—isn't the original definition.

A fool, in centuries past, was a person who was pure and innocent, open and trusting and madly in love with life. These are qualities which might explain why fools are so easily duped, certainly. But there was no negative connotation, no dismissive slur intended.

Foolishness was a welcome, even admirable attribute, similar to the simple, child-like faith Jesus regarded as essential for entrance to heaven. St. Paul asked followers to be "fools for Christ"—at least in the King James version of Acts—meaning that we should always face the world with joy and hope, trusting in God and acting with the kind of untarnished love that brings out the same qualities in other people.

In Tarot's deck of cards, the Fool is an image said to portray the highest degree of human potential, if only because openness and trust are prerequisites for finding the solutions that cynical people can't imagine. *And* for accomplishing the tasks no one else would be foolish enough to attempt. Taoism, too, respects the Fool as one who welcomes the possibilities present in the natural Way of things, who succeeds by taking advantage of the unexpected opportunities that mock others' best-laid plans.

Sometimes the stronger faith demands not so much that we stop fooling around, but that we *start*.

FORGIVENESS

There are specific legal remedies in every society for the repaying of debts, or the righting of wrongs. At least to the extent they *can* be repaid or made right. Ensuring that these remedies are enforced, whether you're the one who's been wronged, or you've committed the wrong, is essential not only to civil society but our own sense of justice.

Some wrongs, however, can never be remedied by legal means. "An eye for an eye, and a tooth for a tooth" often won't work because human feelings and faith cannot be measured and restored like a chipped incisor or a dented fender. A broken promise or a trust that's been betrayed, a relationship that corrodes from angry words or a change in direction... the mother whose son dies in a drunk-driving accident... none of these tragic situations are amenable to $50 a month plus ten percent interest.

Repaying hurtful acts with hurtful acts, or hate for hate, is hardly the solution either, if only because these things can never be viewed objectively. Vengeance only precipitates an unwinnable game of one-up-manship, an arms race of negativity that can only end up in mutual destruction.

Which is where forgiveness comes in.

Not just because *some*one must end the emotional arms race. It's because *not* forgiving is an act which hurts you more than it hurts the person who needs to be forgiven.

Every act (and reaction) has consequences. And every religious tradition characterizes this Law in its own Faithspeak. Christians, Jews and Muslims conceive of a divine ledger or Book of Life—figuratively if not literally—in which every one of our actions is recorded, along with an evaluation of its inherent righteousness or sinfulness. Hindu and Buddhist traditions assign karma to every act, a kind of automatic spiritual payoff or ongoing stain that follows the individual soul around, and is either increased or diminished by future actions. New Age suggests that hurtful acts bind us with spiritual cords or chains which restrain our growth until we sever them. Psychology, too, recognizes that actions can affect what's called our "ego balance," subtly altering our behavior and self-image.

The dynamic in all of these characterizations is that actions have their own built-in force, their own "inevitabilities." And unless we control them, they will control us. Unless we break into that dynamic, we will spend most of our time *re*acting rather than acting.

To forgive someone, then, is to first admit that something has taken control of our lives—some event or act for which there is no physical or financial compensation. There is now a debt or chain or negative force field between both parties, and by any conventional standards you could be expected to hold a grudge for the rest of your life. Forgiveness accepts that ugly situation as "given." But then it does what can't be expected, what others may think foolish, what seems to go against human nature precisely because it *does*. It declares that debt or chain or negative force "null and void." It breaks the dynamic.

You may not completely forget what happened. What you've lost may never be replaced. And you're not going to "turn the other cheek" either, as if you enjoy being a martyr and you're practically begging to be victimized again.

What you *are* going to do is act as if the offending act or event never occurred. You're going to take back control of your life, accepting the present situation without regard for how it got that way or who was responsible. Because even though you can rarely control what others do, you can control yourself.

And what's sometimes even more important is this: If we can forgive others, we too can be forgiven. The message to our own heart-of-hearts is that forgiveness is genuinely possible, that the chains of our own negative acts can be released because we've released the chains of others. It's a two-way street and the traffic light just changed to green.

"Forgive us our trespasses," Jesus taught, "as we forgive those who trespass against us." It wasn't the first time anybody said it. In fact, Jesus was only repeating the centuries-old prescription for Jewish atonement. It's just that we still find it so hard to remember both parts.

FREEDOM

Freedom is a word filled almost universally with positive meanings. It is associated with release from bondage; with worshipping (or *not* worshipping) as one chooses; with "life, liberty and the pursuit of happiness." Or simply doing whatever you want, whenever you want.

No one, however, is truly free to do whatever they want. To live as a human person is to live within limits, within a set of certifiable "can't do" propositions. We can't, for example, jump off a ten-story building and simply walk off whistling after our encounter with the pavement. We can't breathe seawater like our friends with fins and gills. We can't survive a direct hit from a 10-megaton nuclear device no matter how thick our bomb shelter.

Humans are therefore *not* free—if only in the sense that we aren't able to do certain things without certain other things happening as a result. What's more, the "certain things" on both ends of that statement are sometimes defined not by physics and certifiable facts, but by social and religious considerations about which we are bound to disagree.

Take a proposition like: "If you speak out against the king, you'll be given fifty lashes." Or "Unless you believe in Jesus you're going to hell." Or "Whoso commits adultery shall be stoned to death."

The fact is, there's serious question as to whether being stoned to death is related to committing adultery in the same way that splatting onto the sidewalk is related to jumping off a ten-story building. In one case we aren't free by virtue of what some authority has artificially (or even arbitrarily) imposed. In the other, there's a natural, demonstrable linkage between cause and effect.

Humankind's quest for freedom, it turns out, is not so much an attempt to escape the natural laws of cause and effect—to do whatever we want, whenever we want. It's an effort to establish social regulations that genuinely reflect our best understanding of those natural laws, rather than the artificial or arbitrary laws of some human authority who seeks to impose his or her will on others.

Freedom of religion is the recognition that religious traditions have their own regulations which may or may not follow from a natural, demonstrable linkage between cause and effect… but we can live within those regulations *if we choose to.*

FUNDAMENTALISM

In a sense, fundamentalism is what this book is about. (And no, I'm *not* kidding.) Because its underlying premise is that the real fundamentals of every religious tradition are substantially the same. Behind them all is one Ultimate Reality, expressed in various dialects of a single Mother Tongue. In different Faithspeak.

Unfortunately, fundamentalism is usually much more narrowly defined. It is also a word which is sometimes spoken with a kind of denigrating sneer by people who consider themselves far better educated (and usually more affluent) than their poor, gullible, simple-minded neighbors. And the fact that those poor, simple-minded folk often enjoy lives of purposeful service and spiritual serenity while their more educated cousins scramble after second mortgages and the latest iPhone or fad diet, or the all-new, redesigned Lexus complete with soft leather seats, pull-down widescreen video and a self-parking option, doesn't seem the least bit ironic.

Then again, life for both groups has gotten a little crazy lately. It's no wonder people start asking whether all this complexity is really necessary. Why can't we all just get back to the basics?

Which is what a sizeable number of Christians started asking in the late nineteenth century—as people do every hundred years or so. The last time around, this group came to the conclusion that there were five (or seven, or eleven) doctrines you simply *had* to believe in before you could qualify as a genuine Christian. The divinity of Jesus, for example. And the literal truth of the Bible, including Adam and Eve and the talking donkey and the sun stopping for a few hours so Joshua could finish slaughtering his enemies. Not to mention the virgin birth. And salvation by the blood of Christ on the cross. If only we truly believed these things, the fundamentalists said, the world wouldn't be in such terrible shape.

In fact, because it *is* in such terrible shape, fundamentalist movements have caught fire all over the world, with advocates of virtually every religion now claiming that salvation depends on a return to "the fundamentals." If Jews everywhere would simply return to Zion and help rebuild the Temple; if Muslims would cast off the Great Satan's materialism and return to Shar'ia; if Christians would only rid themselves of secular humanism and the popular media and return to God's holy Word—then things would be so much better. Trouble is, even within these traditions people rarely agree on what that Word *is* or what the fundamentals are, and every so often they end up killing each other in an attempt to determine who's right.

It might be funny if it weren't so tragic. It's also why the term "fundamentalism" is now applied to a kind of unbending, militant adherence to an unchanging set of doctrines, and where almost no differences of opinion and practice are tolerated.

To be fair, Jewish, Islamic and Christian fundamentalists (as well as Sikhs and others) are often motivated by a sincere conviction that we've all made a wrong turn somewhere, that things have gotten out of hand and it's high time to do something about it. Unfortunately these groups suffer from an inability to conceive of truth outside the very narrowest of contexts—*their* context. And their fanaticism, psychologists tell us, is less an assertion that their doctrines are true than an expression of their own subconscious fears that they *aren't*.

Maybe the problem is that fundamentalists haven't gotten fundamental enough. The fundamental truths claimed by each of these groups are themselves manifestations of even deeper truths. And if only we would realize that religious traditions (along with philosophy and science) are different ways of getting at those deeper truths, maybe the world wouldn't be such a contentious place.

GAIA

It's the Greek name for Mother Earth, conceived as a goddess in whose symbolic body all living things, including human beings, are like the cells that make up any organism.

The same basic idea is preserved in the more generic Mother Nature, commonly used in contemporary Western culture (and old TV commercials) without any religious significance whatsoever. But it is still infused with spiritual meaning by many aboriginal groups, including American Indian tribes whose guiding principle, "the earth does not belong to us; *we* belong to the earth," is especially evocative.

Teilhard de Chardin's 1955 best-seller, *The Phenomenon of Man,* re-imagined Gaia in philosophical/scientific language that proposed a "living, thinking layer" that surrounds our planet. Mediated by a Noosphere, humans are united with both nature and each other through a kind of collective unconscious *a la* Carl Jung. Today's ecology movement echoes a similar concept by reminding us to treat the Earth as if it were a living, sensitive, conscious entity.

Which is what Genesis-like stories have recommended for

millennia: To treat our homeworld as if it were in some sense alive, to see ourselves as its caretakers and guardians. And if we've been dumb or selfish enough to "fall" from our appointed assignment to use and care for it as if the future depended on it, there are ways (in the immortal words of Crosby, Stills and Nash) to "get back to the Garden."

We can interpret the Genesis story as pure mythology. But if we use that as an excuse to plunder the planet, perhaps we *are* "fallen."

GAMBLING

This one isn't about poker or roulette. Or the fact that most religious traditions condemn gambling because it throws away resources that might have been put to better use. Nor is it a critique of the rising tide of lotteries that claim to raise money for schools or social services while brainwashing the public that it's better to *win* a fortune than earn it.

Rather, it's about the fact that our very lives are a form of gambling already. And maybe that's why games of chance are so alluring. They symbolize our own perception that what life throws at us can seem as arbitrary as cards dealt from a deck. It's a crapshoot where somebody else seems to be rolling the dice, and we just happen to be in the right place at the right time, or the wrong place at the wrong time. No wonder the ancient Greeks loved their gods, if only because their unpredictable squabbles on Olympus were thought to affect human events, and thus explained why we might get all the breaks on Monday, and on Tuesday we just can't win.

But sometimes *we* are the ones rolling the dice. We make a career decision, or we put our trust in someone, or we choose some course of action without knowing whether the results are going to turn out in our favor. We take the chance anyway. We go for it.

There are little proverbs and stories in every tradition that urge us to "go for it." Like the Parable of the Talents told by Jesus. Three servants, so the story goes, are entrusted by their master with various amounts of money while he travels to a far country. Two of the servants trade and invest their money and eventually double it. The third buries the money he was given, afraid he might blow it all if he took any chances. And even when the money was safely in the ground, he probably spent every night worrying somebody would dig it up and he'd still lose it.

You can guess which servant gets chewed out when the master returns: The one who played it safe, who was afraid to risk the money ("talents") he was given. Since the others had been faithful with their talents, the master entrusted them with even more. They grew in responsibility and respect, while the third not only didn't grow, he ended up being "cast into outer darkness." Ouch.

You wouldn't be the first to ask what might've happened to the first two servants if they'd lost their investments. But the presumption of the parable is that risking whatever we have *automatically* earns a reward—if not now, then later. Most successful people, it so happens, have a long string of failures behind them. But they learned from those failures. They kept risking. And the one talent that finally hits the jackpot can make up for all the other losses and then some. It becomes the breakthrough to even higher levels of success and learning.

To risk one's life is not to look into the barrel of a gun or fly your Skyhawk through the enemy's triple-A. "Risking your life" simply means to not play it safe. It means to apply your talents and invest your time like an entrepreneur would, as if there were big rewards for doing so.

And what religious traditions are telling us is that there *are* big rewards. That if you risk growing, risk being the fool, risk serving others as you would yourself... if you play out the hand even though it's not a sure bet, the pot's as good as yours.

Which only *seems* like gambling.

GARDEN OF EDEN

Forget about finding its location on that special supplement in last month's National Geographic. Whether you're a Biblical literalist trying to pinpoint a botanist's dream beside some forgotten Iraqi streambed, or an anthropologist searching for the primeval forest where proto-humans first raised Cain, you're barking up the wrong tree.

Despite the fact that "Eden" probably comes from the Babylonian *Edeen,* an actual region of lush grassland between the Tigris and Euphrates rivers, The Garden of Eden is not an actual place. It's a state of existence, a condition. What it symbolized—and continues to symbolize—is a relationship in which humankind lives in ideal harmony with Nature. It is the understanding, stored somewhere in our collective unconscious, that we were created/evolved to live in perfect symbiosis with the earth; that there was once an inherent balance in our way of life; that we took only what was needed and gave back at least as much as we took.

The Babylonian and Hebrew versions of Eden are remarkably similar. *And* insightful. In what might be described as a pre-scientific doctrine of social and biological evolution, humankind was pictured in the Garden as not-quite-human—at least in the way we picture humanity today. There was a kind of animal simplicity to life, where all physical needs were satisfied, and moral judgments about right and wrong were unnecessary. Adam and Eve were viewed as immortal, not necessarily in the sense that they would have lived forever, but that this arrangement could have gone on forever, with no fear of death to sap our energies or turn our attention from the simple pleasures of life while it lasted.

If only they hadn't taken that next step.

Because something clearly tipped the scales. Something kicked us up the evolutionary ladder and out of our primordial Garden. And that "something" is almost universally portrayed in creation stories as humankind's emerging self-consciousness, our growing awareness of our capacity for moral choice. Which implies not only a higher level of thinking, but the necessity of making critical decisions based on intellectual knowledge and personal responsibility rather than animal instinct.

There is also, almost universally, a literary tone of regret which overlays this new capacity for knowing; the sense that we've given up something sweet in order to gain our ability to "be as the gods," and we're not sure the trade-off was such a good deal. After all, the power to make choices also includes the power to make *lousy* choices. And history is a record of some first-class stinkers, right down to the present day.

The Garden of Eden, however, is not only a symbol of what was. It's also a vision of what *can be.* Present-day environmentalists and the Green Movement describe The Garden in terms of our potential for returning to some kind of respectful balance with nature; for eliminating acid rain and polluted rivers; for not only cleaning up the latest oil spill but the need for oil in the first place; of saving the rain forest and the whales and the owls and all those annoying insects most people can't imagine why on earth we need, but we do.

Yet even this is a limited view. Because Eden is a spiritual environment more than a physical one. It is the knowledge that *prevents* acid rain rather than cleans up after it, that preserves rain forests and whales by respecting the Tree of Life rather than cutting it down. It is the wholesale re-ordering of priorities, the regaining of our place in the overall Scheme of Things that once seemed effortless and instinctive.

And if we've been a little distracted by the forbidden fruit lately, maybe that's the price we pay for finally learning what's good for us.

GLORY

"Glory" is one of those terms that's used in so many ways it resists definition. Then again, maybe that's the point.

As a noun, glory refers to a kind of indescribably divine radiance. In the Bible, we read phrases like "the glory of the Lord shone round about" or "...the brightness that was the appearance of the likeness of the glory of the Lord." In the Hindu *Bhagavad-gita,* the Supreme God is said to be manifested "in countless radiant glories" and a "blinding brilliance." Glory therefore points to the presence of The Divine as an awe-inspiring energy and power, without pinning it down to anything physical.

Light was the ideal symbol long before New Age flipped the switch. But not just any light: *Blinding* light. In other words, we can never see the light directly. That's why Ezekiel practically stumbles all over himself with goofy lines like, "the brightness that was the appearance of the likeness..." Talk about smoke and mirrors! But what a wonderful way to say that what we see is only a tantalizing hint, a symbol, an indirect reflection of a reflection of the Ultimate Source.

And it is this reflective quality which gives "glory" one of its other meanings. In the language of many religious traditions, creation is said to "reflect" God's glory. "The whole earth," Isaiah says, "is full of his glory." Here, the word refers to a characteristic of things. But that characteristic is not so much an objective component of the thing as the subjective effect it has on us. Like the majesty of the mountains or the wonder of life, or the radiance of someone's smile. It's the sense we have that describing things in purely physical terms doesn't always convey what's most important.

And not just "things." *People* can reflect glory, too: When our behavior seems to exhibit a power or meaning that goes beyond purely physical explanations. Or when our actions brighten the lives of others. Which is probably closer to the common understanding of glory—as a quality some actions not only reflect, but *earn;* a kind of respect or praiseworthiness people "pay" to those who perform these actions.

And this definition, in turn, points to one last meaning of glory—as a verb. Because in paying our respects to whomever reflects glory, or to the Ultimate Source of glory, we are said to "glorify." Used this way, glorifying can't be separated from the glory. It's part of a continuum. It's something we do by the very act of seeing it. Like the old adage that a tree falling in the forest makes no sound if there's no one around to hear it, we might say that the divine radiance doesn't shine without someone to perceive it.

But some people *do* perceive it. And they do so either because the divinity "out there" is recognized by the divinity within ourselves (i.e. "It takes one to know one"). Or else humans have evolved some kind of spiritual sense as real as our ability to taste, feel, see and hear.

And glory is the term for what it senses.

GNOSTIC

There aren't too many words left in the English language that start with "Gn." It's just about as odd as starting a word with "Kn." As a matter of fact, Gnostic and Gnosticism come from the Greek *gnosis,* usually translated as "knowledge." Why it's not "gnowledge" is anybody's guess.

In addition to implications of heresy attached to the word by the early Christian church, "Gnostic" has a more generic meaning which is revealed in the contrast with its opposite. *A*gnostic, you'll remember, is the word applied to someone for whom the existence of God is still an open question. Or, technically, one who simply doesn't know. The Gnostic, on the other hand, *knows.* Or gnows.

Before the Christian era, Gnosticism was already an established philosophy that regarded individual knowing as the ultimate source of authority. External sources were helpful, of course, by bringing other people's ideas and experience into our awareness. But nothing could be accepted as true unless the individual soul confirmed it through an internal process which was partly rational, but also intuitive.

In principle, this kind of internal assent by the believer is the ideal of all religious traditions. Thoughtless obedience to doctrines is usually characterized as the lowest form of faith. As Islamic tradition has it, Muslims are asked not to believe anything merely on the basis of what another man says. According to the Muslim writer, Al-Ghazali, one must first "...know the truth, and then you will know who are truthful."

But the Greek or Persian Gnostic was even more radical than that. Everything worth knowing, according to the earliest traditions, was already inside oneself. It wasn't necessary to look "outside" for God or Truth, or for the proper rules of behavior. The Gnostic need only look within, to investigate his own inner workings and behavioral patterns. Because there, on a personal scale, lay the entire universe and the Ultimate Reality behind it.

The First-Century stories about Jesus, which circulated in several forms throughout the Roman Empire, were embraced almost immediately by the Gnostics. Based on Jesus' teaching that "The Kingdom of God is within you," together with his reliance on an inner voice rather than external authorities, Jesus came to be regarded as the perfect, divinely-commissioned role model for the Gnostic faith. Indeed, a set of Gnostic gospels that pre-dates the New Testament was found in circumstances not unlike the discovery of the Dead Sea Scrolls. These manuscripts—the most famous of which is The Gospel of Thomas—convey a strikingly different portrait of Jesus than traditional sources paint. We are introduced to a Jesus who speaks of illusion and enlightenment rather than sin and repentance. We meet a Master who play-acts the role of Savior only until adherents learn to drink from the same wellspring of knowledge he does. "Know the truth, and the truth shall make you free," the New Testament says. "If you bring forth what is within you," Jesus says in *Thomas*, "what you bring forth will save you."

In combination, these gospels are an uncanny blend of Eastern and Western philosophy. Gnostics were contemptuous of bodily resurrection, preferring the more Eastern "release" from the body and eventual re-absorption into The Source. There were apparently meditative techniques that involved the intoning of a repeated sound, like the mystical *Om* of Hinduism. Events as well as words held meaning for the enlightenment of one's soul—a recurring theme in both Buddhism and Hindu tradition.

It just so happens that East-West trade and interreligious dialog were not uncommon in the Middle East during the first and second centuries of the Common Era. Buddhist missionaries had long been proselytizing in Alexandria. Roman historical records reveal a detailed knowledge of Brahmin (Hindu) practices. In short, there was far more diversity of thought at the time than most of us have been lead to believe—a widespread and remarkable sharing of cultural and religious ideas that must've been as exciting and potentially universalizing as it is today.

But there were also power struggles of the life-and-death variety. Both Gnosticism and a budding women's movement were increasingly seen as threats to the growing alliance between the Christian priesthood and the Roman government. The crushing of these and other so-called heresies is as shocking an example of Church/State totalitarianism as any on record.

Alas, if only we gnew then what we gnow now.

GOD

This is The Big One. It's the definition that could easily take up the rest of this book. As a matter of fact, it *does* take up the rest of this book. And everything that's come before.

Because there is no subject in this Lexicon which does not have some implications for our understanding of "God." All of these alphabetical entries, in a sense, are attributes of God; or processes by which people communicate with each other (or themselves) *about* God; or biographies of people who were inspired *by* God.

Which is simply to say that these listings are all pieces of a single, complex jigsaw puzzle representing Ultimate Reality. And only as we struggle with them individually and collectively can we begin to form any kind of coherent picture. That composite picture—expressed in whatever language and images help us to grasp it—is the core meaning of what religions call God. And since every religious tradition openly admits that Ultimate Reality is too awesome, too infinite for the human mind to ever fully comprehend, our picture can never be more than a kind of hazy outline, a working definition. In fact that definition is certain to evolve throughout our lifetimes, as it has throughout history. Even if the Ultimate Reality itself does not change.

So you won't find a neatly-packaged definition of God here. What you'll find, instead, are a few more pieces of the puzzle, or at least a few things that bear repeating. Namely:

The kind of God which is understood as Ultimate Reality is no less personal than the one represented by a voice from the Burning Bush or in the face of a Nazarene carpenter. Those are effective ways of symbolizing it, yes. But even without the voice or the human face, we can still have an intimate, one-on-one relationship with it. And by knowing what the principles and processes of that Reality are, we can gain benefits and avoid hardships that affect us specifically and directly. That's about as "personal" as you can get.

Secondly, let's remember that traditional arguments for the existence of God never convinced anybody who wasn't already convinced. Look at them as word games. Some are interesting and fun; some are highly creative, others contorted and circular. But none of these arguments prove anything remotely like the God of scriptural revelation.

Except, perhaps, for the revelation in which God gave Moses the best one-line description of all time: "I Am That I Am."

Which is not really describing so much as pointing. And what it points *to* is the notion of Being or Existence, a concept that's beyond having to be proved because it simply *is*. It points to some core "unity" which may look to us like a personal entity, but whose very ambiguity and lack of detail is a clue that we should spend our time working on our own lives instead of some theological construct. After all, freeing the slaves from bondage, God tells Moses, is far more important than figuring out some handy label for divinity. There'll be plenty of time for word games later. *After* you've figured out a solution to poverty, or how to ensure everyone a decent job. *After* you figure out how to live together in harmony, or get people off drugs, or encourage kids without yelling at them or punishing them. *After* you've learned to appreciate what you have instead of lusting after what you don't.

And maybe, in figuring that out, you'll figure *me* out, says God.

GODDESS

It's almost an Absolute that our working definition of "God"—whatever it happens to be right now—says more about *us* than about Ultimate Reality.

And it's therefore understandable that God has traditionally been conceived in mostly male terms—at least in Western religion—if only because the institutions of human society have, historically, been so dominated by males. They have been organized for the benefit of males, structured for the preservation of male leadership, and designed to pursue goals which males have decided are worth pursuing. The Western God, as our favorite women's libber once quipped, is a rationalization for, and a vindication of, testosterone.

It hasn't always been that way. In Hinduism, female goddesses are among the countless ways in which the forces of nature or the Supreme God are manifested. The *yin-yang* of Chinese spiritual thought, which symbolizes the dynamic qualities of nature and action, contain equal parts masculine and feminine.

Even in the history of Western religion, legions of goddesses once populated the heavens, many of which were at least equal in stature to the male gods. There were Ishtar and Astarte, Hera and Gaia and dozens of others—all of whom symbolized the so-called "feminine qualities" related to family, fertility, nurturing, and the efficacy of the kind word over the strong arm. And since divinities are as much models for future behavior as reflections of current behavior, goddesses were understood as vehicles for female empowerment. Simply by holding primary positions in the heavens, goddesses encouraged their human counterparts to play an active role, to contribute to society right alongside men. Not to mention encouraging men to share the reigns of power, and to remember the nurturing, caring side of themselves.

Archaeology has confirmed that ancient societies whose religions balanced the roles of gods and goddesses—or in which goddesses were *preferred* over male gods—were among the most productive and vigorous in history. Such cultures flourished in every way imaginable: In the arts; in an appreciation for the human body; in the overall standard of living; and in the equal distribution of benefits throughout the community. Life for these societies was good. All the more so for their conspicuous lack of conflict and violence.

That is, until someone came up with the bright idea that the material wealth of those societies, gained through cooperation and harmony, could be taken away by sheer strength. Which almost certainly was a male idea.

Like a sudden, catastrophic pandemic, that idea appears to have swept through the body of Western civilization in a frighteningly short time. It is traceable in the archeological records almost as clearly as the geological layer of iridium that coincides with the death of the dinosaurs. And it meant the death of male/female equality.

Armies were formed to pillage the wealth of other lands—armies of men, because human males, by and large, had evolved to become physically stronger. Since protection was needed, more armies were formed, also composed of men because the only sure defense against a man's brute strength was another man's brute strength. Maleness and power became virtues out of necessity, since the alternative was extinction. The gods subsequently became more muscular and war-like to serve as role models and to provide inspiration. Goddesses, as long as they lasted, became increasingly subservient to male needs, "helpmates" instead of equal partners, encouraging women to keep the home fires burning and bear more children—hopefully males—to fight future wars.

The feminine side of divinity was relegated to the Jewish Queen Esther (Ishtar), or the Virgin Mary and assorted female saints of Christendom. It also degenerated into legendary figures like The Amazons, who symbolized men's worst fears: That women might come back and punish them for what they'd done—while using their own weapons to do it! Even if we recognize that goddesses were real only as vehicles of Faithspeak, their precipitous decline was a sad testament to the fact that humanity had once again fallen from Grace.

The recent re-invention of "goddess religion" is nothing but an assertion of the rightful place of the feminine role in history and culture. The seeming stridency of some advocates is only the shouting that is sometimes necessary to be heard these days, and a useful reminder that God can just as logically be envisioned as Her than Him.

On the other hand, I Am That I Am has no gender.

GODHEAD

This is one of those weird theological contrivances to which the most common response is, "Huh?" Or else a good laugh at the thought of what the divine cranium must look like.

Actually "Godhead" is more like a theological shrugging of the shoulders. It's an admission that even folks who think about God on a professional basis can't come up with a decent definition either, but here are the major elements, the chief components, the items at the top of your laundry list of divine attributes.

The problem for the professionals, historically speaking, is that every religious tradition has served up a host of names and conceptions for the Head Honcho. And at some point all these concepts need to be cleaned up and made mutually consistent—as if people have been talking about the same God all along even when they haven't. The Jewish sages and rabbis probably had it easiest, having inherited El Shaddai and Elohim, Adonai and Yahweh. These were names with slightly differing traditions and concepts behind them, but could be explained away as localized utterances pointing to the same universal God.

In fact, the *Sh'ma,* the Jewish affirmation that comes closest to a formal Article of Faith, represents a consolidation of all these concepts into a strict monotheism. Usually translated as "Hear O Israel, the Lord your God, the Lord is One," the Sh'ma may actually mean something more like: "Hear O Israel, the Lord previously known to you as many gods, that Lord is a Unity." As evidence of this, scholars point out that the final Hebrew word, *echod,* implies the action of bringing together.

Christians had a tougher road to hoe. Spreading from its Jewish roots into the polytheistic environment of Greece and Rome, early Christianity inherited several concepts of the divine. Some had such a life of their own that they couldn't easily be reconciled. There was the Jewish God, now viewed as Father to the divine Son, Jesus, whose fully human character simply wouldn't go away. And there were dozens of terms for the "Presence" of God—those divine, behind-the-scenes characteristics that seemed to imply separate identities but were finally boiled down to a Holy Spirit or Holy Ghost. And while attempts were made to boil the three major elements back into one, each was too well entrenched.

The early Church fathers found themselves between granite and galvanized steel. They heaved one big, theological shrug, gathered all three entities into a more or less tidy package called The Trinity, and proclaimed that somehow, in some mysterious manner the poor padres couldn't explain and mere mortals could never hope to comprehend, the three were One. The term "Godhead" was sent up the flagpole, formally, for the first time.

But the term also applies in Hinduism, which has perhaps the most difficult job with its divinities. There are, of course, the 330 million faces of God; but there are also, once again, three major players at the head of the class. Brahma, the Creator, is remarkably similar to the omnipotent Creator in Judaism. (And likewise too abstract to loved by the common folk.) Vishnu, originally a sun god who took the role of Preserver, incarnated in a series of "avatars," the most popular of which was the Christ-like Lord Krishna. The third member of the Hindu triad is Shiva. Known as both Destroyer and Rebuilder, he is the god of lifecycles and passion and the basest of human emotions—any of which can produce evil as well as good.

A long history of separate traditions kept these three concepts from being absorbed into a single entity, even as more intellectual Hindus spoke of the divine Oneness. And so the theologians shrugged again. The three are one. Don't lose any sleep over it, okay?

"Godhead" is thus a mental construct invented to keep believers from losing sleep. Unity in plurality; all for one and one for all. So what if we can't really understand it? Who can grasp the mysteries of Ultimate Reality anyway? Is a Trinity any less incredible than a unified set of physical laws that manifest themselves in things as different as stars and starfish? Or hantavirus and human beings?

Divinity manifests in countless ways. If we'd rather not count, we can use our heads and try to package all these manifestations into a single theological concept. The worst that can happen is that people go "Huh?" Or have a good laugh.

GOLDEN RULE

Just a quick lesson on the underlying unity of religions...

Fifty years before Jesus, a Roman soldier reportedly asked another famous Jewish rabbi (by the name of Hillel) to explain all of God's laws while standing on one foot. Hillel accepted the challenge without missing a beat. "What is hateful to you," he replied, "do not do to another. This is the entire Torah. The rest is commentary."

Centuries earlier Confucius had already come to the same conclusion. "Is there one maxim which ought to be acted upon throughout one's life?" he wondered aloud. "Surely it is the maxim of loving-kindness: Do not to others what you would not have them do to you."

A quote from Hinduism's epic tale, the *Mahabharata,* put it in almost identical terms: "This is the sum of duty. Do nothing to others which would cause pain if done to you."

Likewise Muhammad, who would later say, "Let none of you treat his brother in a way he himself would not like to be treated."

Taoism brought in a positive affirmation alongside the negative. "Regard your neighbor's gain as your gain," said Lao-tzu, "and your neighbor's loss as your own loss."

Buddha preferred the strictly positive slant when he said, "One should seek for others the happiness one desires for one's self."

Which is closer to the pro-active form Westerners are most familiar with. "Do unto others," Jesus taught, "as you would have them do unto you."

Any way you slice it, it's the same Rule. And if the common meanings shared by all religious traditions are sometimes difficult to demonstrate, here's one case where it's open and shut.

GOSPEL

Literally the "Good News." Everybody knows that.

What everybody *doesn't* seem to know is, exactly what *is* the News? And what's so Good about it?

"Gospel" is the technical term applied to any one of the first four books of the New Testament—The Gospel of John, for instance—as well as the basic message implied by the entire collection. Some Christian theologians would like to distill that message to a single scriptural passage. "For God so loved the world," John 3:16 says, "that He gave his only begotten Son, that whosoever believes in Him should not perish but have everlasting life." Or, in an even more condensed form, "Believe in Jesus and you'll live forever."

That's the news, pure and simple. And for the majority of folks for whom dying is not a happy thought, the news is good.

On the other hand, *how* to "believe in Jesus"—how that belief translates into a way of behaving toward other people and the world—can't be condensed into a single sound bite on the Six O'clock News. It takes some serious, documentary-length explaining. Maybe a *lifetime* of explaining. And if that's so, chances are there's a deeper truth here that the New Testament text may express, but isn't the only way to do so.

There does, in fact, appear to be a common Gospel underlying all religious traditions. Implicit in Hindu scriptures is the love of the Absolute (pictured as Krishna or Rama) for humankind, and the promise that every soul will eventually be liberated from the suffering of physical life. The Qur'an points to the unceasing mercy of God/Allah, and the "revelation" of a lifestyle designed for man's redemption and heavenly reward. The *Ahavah Rabah* blessing of Jewish tradition says, "So deep is your love for us, Lord our God, so boundless your tender compassion that you taught our ancestors life-giving laws."

Quotes like this may not be as compact or dramatic as John 3:16; but concise one-liners are meant more to capture our attention than explain anything. The full meaning exists in the totality of the writings, in the daily practices of the tradition, and more importantly in the effect that particular brand of Faithspeak has on the individual. And the Gospel that all this Faithspeak seems to be getting at is simply this:

Every individual has infinite value in the Scheme of Things. You— that's right, *you*, dear reader—are important. You matter. Imagine yourself as a child whose father and mother want to provide for your every need, who love you so much they would sacrifice everything they have in order to insure your success. That's how much you matter.

Now, regardless of how poorly you've done so far—yes, *you* again; regardless of how much you've let people down or what trouble you've gotten yourself into, or what kind of miserable (expletive deleted) you can be sometimes, you are no less valuable now than if you'd grown up to become Martin Luther King or Florence Nightingale. So even if you feel in your guts that you're a miserable failure, (or maybe there's just no joy left in living), turning your life around is still important. In fact, it's in the very scheme of things that your life *will* turn around.

Unfortunately, you're probably not aware of all the resources available to help you. If you were, you wouldn't be in the pickle you're in, would you? True, you may stumble onto some of these resources on your own... eventually. Or someone might point them out to you. Other resources, it so happens, are practically right under your nose, or even "within you." But none of them can be used until you first acknowledge that they're there, until you open yourself to new levels of Reality you never knew existed before, ones you may even have denied. Or perhaps you simply ignored them because, well, you figured you could get along just fine without them.

Trouble is, you can't. Not really. And if you think you can, either you're deluding yourself or you're already using those resources without knowing it. Maybe because you happen to call them by another name.

And that's the point. The "good news" isn't about names. It's about resources for transforming your life. From the Five Pillars to the Eightfold Path, from the Law to the Logos, from becoming "clear" to becoming "centered"—The Gospel is simply the universal truth that every one of us is being driven toward a life of wholeness and meaning, and that no wrong turn is ever final. It's the proclamation that Ultimate Reality is working inexorably toward this goal, and all the resources we need are just waiting to be discovered and put to use.

For a struggling, divided world, a story like that is not only Good News, it deserves a banner headline.

GRACE

The good news, we just said, is that humans are being driven toward lives of wholeness and meaning. *Driven*—whether any of us likes it or not. Another word for that driving force is "grace."

Our ancestors, it turns out, were being quite scientific in their efforts to conceptualize the mechanics by which God/divinity/nature operates in the world. It's one thing to say that some people are inspired by God or "divinely anointed." This implies a personal motivation, like a King commands his servant, and the servant obeys. However, it's pretty advanced thinking to recognize that a more mysterious force is at work in people's lives, shaping them without their being aware of it, without necessarily having any conscious relationship to it—sometimes without even deserving it.

In fact some of the *least* deserving people are often the ones who seem to attract this divine energy. The ordinary believer can work diligently to develop a relationship with God or The Truth, patiently studying the sacred scriptures or the guru's teachings, obediently following all the rules; and that person may never feel more than a lukewarm faith. Then there are the degenerate scum who prey on others, who lead selfish lives and bring misery to everyone who crosses their path, who would inspire dancing in the streets if they would just curl up and die; and who suddenly, mysteriously, come to realize what degenerate scum they are and are promptly transformed into model human beings filled with a divine spark that the patient disciple could never achieve.

Of course, personal transformation need not be so dramatic. There are the small victories over bad habits, the lucky breaks in our careers or relationships, the "Oh-*now*-I-get-it!" realizations that seem to come out of the blue when we haven't done a thing to earn them, but lead us to richer, more satisfying lives. The weird thing is, there's probably nothing we *could* do to deserve these kinds of experiences. And expecting them might very well prevent them from ever happening to us.

But when those transformative events *do* come—unexpectedly, undeservedly—that's when people are most likely to recognize this strange force. We blurt out dumb things like, "Somebody up there must like me." Or, in keeping with the gospel tune, "I was blind, but now I see." And we might therefore be inclined to believe that this gift is dispensed only on special occasions because it seems so rare. "Grace," after all, literally means *to find favor*. Which suggests that some heavenly King is watching us, and if he likes us enough, maybe he'll do us a favor once in a while.

The deeper meaning of Grace, however, is that it operates *continuously*, that it is more like a natural law than some capricious decision of His Royal Highness. It's just that, like the Law of Gravity, we generally don't see that force clearly until somebody does a half-gainer off the high dive. We often don't even witness the dive itself, or the fact that somebody was climbing up the tower to begin with, even when the person who's about to take the leap happens to be us. All we know is, we're plunged into a new environment, flailing, struggling to find the surface, and when we finally come up for air, our first breath is like the one we took just out of our mother's womb, the very Breath of Life.

And it dawns on us that something pushed us upward, and buoys us up still. And even if we can explain all of this in terms of scientific principles and natural laws, it is nevertheless true that those laws work to our benefit and are built into the very nature of things; that they're constantly pushing us up toward the life-giving air, toward the light, in spite of how we struggle, or maybe because of it.

As if somebody up there *does* like us.

GRATITUDE

Along with prayer, the ritualized expression of gratitude is probably the most universal practice among the world's religious traditions, if only because it's the most universal of sentiments. Even confirmed atheists will acknowledge an occasional urge to express thanks to someone or some*thing* for the goodness in their lives.

Sometimes the source of that good fortune is obvious: A parent or spouse; a friend or fellow employee; a government program like Social Security or Workman's Comp; or previous generations who had the foresight to engineer those social programs and fight for the freedom to enjoy them. We know whom to thank in these cases, even if we may do so begrudgingly. Maybe we don't like the feeling of being in someone's debt, or we don't like being on the public dole (especially if we're opposed to big government). But in most cases our response is positive and affirming.

And there is growing evidence to suggest that this natural welling up of thankfulness is actually genetic, designed by evolution to reward group cooperation and to strengthen our relationships. Which is why the benefits that come our way without an obvious gift-tag can leave our instinctive "gratitude response" unsatisfied. After all, to whom or to what can we give thanks for the perfectly timed rains that provided such a bountiful crop this season? Or for the successful buffalo hunt that will see us through the winter with plenty of jerky and fresh hides for clothing and blankets and tepees? Or for the gift of a clear blue sky and enough of a breeze to fill our sails and bring us that much closer to the New World?

We can thank our own efforts and inherent inventiveness for well-plowed fields, and the bows and arrows and sailing ships that take advantage of nature's laws. But all of us know that our best efforts don't always make up for the monkey-wrenches Mother Nature can also throw our way. And when, despite that, our efforts turn out well—or we're saved from disaster after they *don't*—we can't help being overcome with a need to express our gratitude. If there are cynics who claim that God (or at least religion) was a response to the mystery of death, a more convincing argument can be made that God was invented to provide Someone on whom to lavish our otherwise undirected thanks.

But gratitude is more than a response from one person to another. Or from lots of people to An Other. Gratitude is a *faith*. It's a way of looking at the world, an acknowledgement of our inter-dependence with others and with the environment. It's a preference for optimism over pessimism, a point of view that focuses on what's good in our lives and actually prepares us to receive more of it.

And prepares us to *create* even more of it.

Because words are not enough. A simple "thank you" may suffice for the parent who puts food on a child's plate, or the firefighter who stops the forest's flames before they reach your cabin in the woods. For the recipient, however, action is the only appropriate response. Not in the *quid pro quo* fashion where I buy you a Christmas present this year since you gave me one last year. It's where my joy at receiving a Christmas bonus from the boss inspires me to make a healthy donation to the homeless shelter, or to volunteer my time for a couple of hours on Saturday morning flipping pancakes for its residents. It's where I'm blessed (undeservedly in many cases), and I respond by blessing someone else, without looking for accolades or seeking repayment.

Gratitude shapes reality by creating a kind of vacuum that draws goodness into our lives, while seeking to fill the vacuums in others' lives. Maybe it *is* genetic. It is also profoundly spiritual, and its regular practice a religion unto itself.

GROUND

There are two important spiritual connotations of the word: The first is the "Ground (of Being)" that underlies all existence, especially all life. This is essentially what religious philosopher Martin Buber equated with God, and others call Ultimate Reality—the deeper dimension or foundation that exists whether we acknowledge it or not, whether we see it as something to be worshipped or investigated with the tools of science. Or both.

A second connotation of "ground" is that which gives meaning to the concept of "grounding oneself" or "being grounded." Because sometimes in our self-guided spiritual journeys, it's all-too-easy to indulge in fantasies about ancient aliens or spirit mediums, guardian angels or magical powers... or even saints and saviors who have nothing better to do than extricate us from repeated crises and cater to our personal whims and wishes.

Grounding is the antidote to our flights of fancy, to our tendency to place ourselves at the center of the universe, to make religion a kind of escapist entertainment or spiritual insurance policy. To be grounded is to be focused on practical issues and "real life," to understand that there are more important issues than our own individual desires, and to acknowledge that the Earth will manage to survive quite nicely after we're gone, thank you very much.

Our spiritual practice should, ideally, keep us mindful of this wider perspective, even as it opens us to realities that are unseen and potentially beneficial to us. And when we realize that, chances are we've reached higher ground.

GUILT

One kind is generic, the other religious.

The generic version of guilt refers to those pangs of conscience we sometimes feel when we act contrary to our mental programming. Psychologists can describe this process with some precision. Just as our fingertips can send a message of pain when we touch a red-hot stove, our subconscious gives us sensations of mental discomfort when we do something wrong. Both are very natural processes which, in either case, say to us: "Don't do that again." It's a kind of negative reinforcement intended to make such behavior less likely to happen in the future. Ideally we won't even think about it next time; we'll already know better. But if we *do* do it the next time—or do it repeatedly—chances are we'll eventually reach some point where those persistent pangs of guilt become even more painful than having to change our behavior.

Unfortunately, as psychologists also tell us, what causes sensations of guilt for one person won't give another person so much as a twinge of regret. It may even produce the opposite reaction. One soldier may experience an overwhelming sense of self-loathing and loss after killing another human being in combat. His fellow soldier may feel a sense of accomplishment and even elation in performing the same act, and a profound guilt if he *hadn't* killed his enemy.

Which means two things:

First, there is no Universal Conscience hidden inside us, with some common standard of right and wrong. And it's not that some people simply don't *have* one. It's that everyone's conscience gets programmed more or less differently, in the same way our faiths can vary depending on the effects of our role models and childhood experiences.

And this means, secondly, that we have all the more responsibility to help shape those faiths—and the conscience that triggers guilt—in accordance with our best understanding of what "right" and "wrong" are. Children don't make those distinctions by some process of careful reflection. They learn it as if by osmosis, by behavioral reinforcement and example. Which, after all, becomes the Faithspeak of childhood.

It is later, in adulthood, that Faithspeak puts a religious spin on the concept of guilt. This kind isn't the mental discomfort we get when we do wrong, but rather the *condition* we find ourselves in as a result of having done it.

Religiously speaking, guilt is the condition of deserving punishment—whether we feel guilty or not, or whether that punishment has actually been meted out. In the Hebrew Bible guilt is usually the result of disobeying (or "transgressing") a law or communal regulation. Fortunately there was always a prescribed punishment or method of atoning for every such act. Being punished not only maintained a sense of justice within the community, but allowed transgressors to free themselves from the condition of guilt and get on with their lives without being enslaved by their past.

This sense of enslavement is even more heightened in other religions. In Hinduism, the karma of previous wrongdoing is said to follow us around—even from one incarnation to the next—like a magnetic field, attracting more and more evil until we overcome it with positive actions and good karma.

Christianity pictures it in equally stark terms. We are shackled by our past wrongdoings, many fundamentalists claim, like guilty criminals dragging their chains around the way Marley's ghost does in Dickens' *A Christmas Carol*. What's worse, we inherit enough chain-link to keep us permanently guilt-ridden simply by being born. The newborn's reassuring wail after childbirth is really the cry of its soul recognizing the shackles it now wears merely by "entering the flesh."

Talk about depressing.

On the other hand, perhaps this grim picture can be seen as an effort to emphasize the importance of doing right, no matter how difficult it may be. Because doing "wrong" often *does* have lasting consequences: In broken hearts and damaged relationships; in the tendency of lies and deceit to suck us down into a whirlpool of still more lies and deceit; in the festering wounds of our own self-image. Genuine wholeness and happiness can never be achieved when we're in this condition.

Religions have admittedly misused guilt to manipulate people and exert power over them. As a result, the word "guilt" probably suffers from one of the worst reputations in this entire Lexicon.

But as Faithspeak, guilt can be what finally forces us to recognize our own wrongdoing, to deal with the causes of it, to free ourselves before it destroys us. And if that's a crime, religion is guilty as charged.

GURU

Here's one more Hindu word that's found its way into our everyday language. Unfortunately, with something *less* than its original meaning.

Technically, guru simply means "spiritual teacher." Buddha was a guru. Socrates was a guru. Jesus was a guru. So were the rabbis of the Jewish schools around the same time, like Hillel and Gamaliel. Similarly St. Paul, Muhammad, Maimonides, Luther, Paramahansa Yogananda, Billy Graham, and thousands of other teachers who never made the headlines and never will.

The greatest gurus, of course, did more than transmit a set of spiritual truths to the next generation: They presented truth *in a novel way*. It was inevitable that some people would perceive this novelty as an entirely new Truth, mistaking the words and rituals for the meanings behind them. But eternal truths don't change; and the most a guru can hope for is to cast them in a new form that will be understood in the language and socio-scientific models of their day.

Today "guru" is often associated with a certain lack of substance, or even flakiness. The word often suggests someone who takes advantage of the fact that so many people today are searching desperately for answers. And since almost anything sounds like The Answer to somebody, almost anyone who proclaims himself/herself a spiritual teacher is bound to attract a few poor souls to sit at his or her feet, while paying dearly for the privilege.

Such gurus can still be positive influence for their students—at least as stepping stones along their spiritual journeys. They can also teach the rest of us how crucial our spiritual life is, and how easily some people will fall in behind any leader who appears to fulfill their needs, if only for a while.

Which brings up another implication of "guru." Because the true guru is a spiritual teacher *only for a while*.

Hindu tradition presupposes a spiritual evolution in which we all progress toward enlightenment in stages, when we're sufficiently ready. We must periodically consolidate what we've learned at each stage by somehow proving ourselves. Only then we can look forward to the next step, the next level of consciousness.

It's said that we are attracted to a new guru at each successive stage, to someone who helps us learn and consolidate our evolving awareness of Truth before preparing us to move on. This guru may be a friend who is going through (or has just gone through) a similar spiritual journey; or perhaps a leader or hero we admire, or an elder who advises us either by direct teaching or by example. Our job is to gain all we can from him or her, learning from our mistakes and failures as well as our successes. And then we move on.

"Guru" is a reminder that most of us have yet to graduate from grade school. We may've gotten past old Miss Healy. But next semester it's Mr. Kim.

Rumor has it he's even tougher.

Notes

HALLELUJAH

Literally, in Hebrew: "Praise God."

Hallel is the verb form of "praise," which means to honor some person or some act; to show gratitude or devotion. *Jah* (yah) is the first syllable of the too-holy-to-say-out-loud word for "God," which is also variously applied as a suffix in many Hebrew names. Like Elijah (meaning "My God is Jahweh") or Jeremiah ("Appointed by God") or Yehoshuah ("God will save").

Of course, since the Hebrew word/name for God is actually a statement about "being"—remember "I Am That I Am"?—Hallelujah can also mean, simply, "Praise *be*." In this sense, it is a call for the existence of praise, or more importantly, a recommendation that we ourselves should join in, or *be* in, an attitude of praising God.

Most of the time, frankly, we aren't in such an attitude. It's so much easier to gripe about conditions and find fault in everyone. Our very faith is distorted by this tendency to dwell on the negative. If we're not careful, *we* become negative.

Saying "Hallelujah," on the other hand, acts as a mnemonic device to help us develop a positive mental attitude: To praise people when they do well, (which encourages them to do well more often); to acknowledge the inherent goodness in things; to actively look for the positive in our lives and affirm it wherever and whenever it's found. By doing this we create a subconscious balance sheet that reverses the red ink and adds to our spiritual income. The world becomes less threatening, less evil, filled with riches we might otherwise overlook, primed with possibilities even if things aren't exactly ideal at the moment.

The New Spirituality isn't all that new in saying that "Our thoughts create our own reality." Hallelujah is precisely the age-old assertion that Ultimate Reality is basically good, and that by emphasizing goodness we can bring even more of it into existence. For real. It's as if our karma shifts from bad to good; as if we become better attuned, vibrating in harmony with the Tao, The Light, with Universal Mind.

Everybody has a word for it, from *Pooja* in Hindi to the Arabic *Na'-abdu Allah*. Norman Vincent Peale secularized it as The Power of Positive Thinking. Catalogs are filled with audio CDs and videos that instruct people to ignore the bad and emphasize (praise) the good. None of which would be effective unless there was an actual mechanism built into the nature of things that made it all possible.

And how do we respond to that fact?

With one simple word. Go ahead, say it... *Say* it...

HEALING

There are dozens of words in the world's sacred texts that are translated as "healing" or "health." Some imply deliverance from a physical illness, or from the condition that produces illness. Other words clearly indicate a recognition of mental problems and the spiritual salvation necessary to restore serenity and well-being. In New Testament Greek, the words for "heal" and "save" are identical.

The supposition behind all these words is the recognition that mind and body are inseparably linked, that there is an optimum condition wherein this psychosomatic unity may be considered "whole," or at least normal. Healing is the process of returning to this optimum wholeness, to this comfortable condition of "being normal."

Every religious tradition promotes healing in some fashion, if only because without it, as the old adage goes, "You ain't got nothin'." One's health limits or expands the possibilities for life. It colors the glasses through which we see it. Or, literally, *if* we see it. And it is the purpose of religion, as much as medicine or science, to enhance our ability to see.

Which is why miraculous healings are such big stuff in scriptures. The Bible, the Qur'an and the Vedas—as well as folk legends from virtually every culture—all contain stories in which holy people heal others of their physical ailments and even bring the dead back to life. Often these healings are intended primarily to convince witnesses (and readers) of the authority or anointing of a particular person. Someone who makes the lame cast off their crutches must have a special relationship with God, right? Therefore what he says must be true.

But helping people cast off their crutches, or enabling the blind to see, is also powerful Faithspeak symbolizing the *inner* healing that can take place as a result of a prophetic message. To "love your neighbor as yourself" or "beat your swords into plowshares" is to return to a lifestyle that heals individuals and communities just as dramatically as the leper who is cleansed, or Lazarus leaping from his deathbed. In this sense, miraculous healings are symbolic affirmations that no matter how diseased we've become, no matter how unbalanced or decadent or lost we may be, we *can* regain wholeness, both personally and communally. Whether or not the healings recorded in ancient texts were factual events is irrelevant.

Of course the organic causes of illness and mental dysfunction weren't well known when those scriptures were written. People who either knowingly or accidentally contributed to someone's healing were automatically presumed to be miracle workers. For that reason alone we have a right to be skeptical. Still, to deny the possibility of miraculous healings in ancient times would be to deny them today. And some of today's most skeptical physicians can testify to recoveries that defy medical explanation. At the very least we must admit that the impulse toward healing and wholeness is not fully understood, and that it must be as strong as any impulse in the opposite direction. If not stronger.

Physicians and psychologists will also testify that a person's mind (read: attitude or "faith") can be of paramount importance in the healing process. New Thought techniques of visualizing the body fighting off disease, or picturing one's white cells zapping cancerous intruders with biological ray guns, are merely variations on earlier Christian Science principles of mentally imagining "perfect health." And those, in turn, are only extensions of health affirmations taught by every religious tradition.

None of these techniques works by some kind of white magic or black magic or by making a deal with The Devil. The dynamic of achieving wholeness and healing is an aspect of reality available to anyone. A doctor, after all, doesn't actually cure anybody or anything. The E.R. physician doesn't heal a gunshot wound by stitching up the hole. All he or she can do is enhance the conditions in which the body *naturally mends itself.* Digging out the bullet and stopping the bleeding with a row of stitches may save the victim from dying outright. But the damaged muscles and skin will eventually knit themselves together through a process the physician can only stand back and watch. In fact, further tampering with that process will often retard rather than help healing.

Likewise psychological and communal healing. We can remove the immediate causes of damage and maximize the conditions for recovery. But ultimately, the healing must be allowed to happen through a mechanism built into the very scheme of things.

No wonder "heal" and "save" share the same root word. The process of healing is parallel to that of salvation, if not identical. We can't do either one by ourselves. It *happens* to us under the right conditions; the mechanism is already in place. Nor can we be healed alone. To become fully whole, we must create the same conditions for others; because what's making them sick is the same thing that makes *us* sick. Our recovery depends on theirs. And just like a Blue Cross policy, the longer we put off our return to wholeness, the more we *all* end up paying.

HEAVEN

It's only coincidence that the next two words in the Lexicon are usually paired together like day and night, good and bad, hot and cold.

As a matter of fact, hot and cold are exactly how Hell is pictured—depending on whether the prospect of searing heat or freezing cold was thought to be the better deterrent to evil. Desert societies preferred visions of fire-and-brimstone. More northerly tribes, insofar as they envisioned Hell at all, saw it as a place of endless grey cold just this side of nothingness.

And of course the opposite notion was also held by these groups. Heaven was pictured by desert dwellers as an endless oasis of lush greenery, abundant fruit trees and cool, crystal-clear wellsprings. Arctic nomads envisioned a secure shelter from the biting storms, with a blazing fire pit and all the smoked halibut you could eat. Whatever wonderful, positive images could be cooked up as a reward for having lived a good life was Heaven. Whatever terrifying, negative images could be conjured up to frighten someone out of doing evil—or to repay evildoers for what they'd already done—that was Hell.

Religious traditions, however, have not always supported this classic vision of heaven and hell. In fact heaven and hell simply didn't exist before twenty-five centuries ago. Not that an afterlife wasn't in the cards. Primitive burial sites suggest a widespread belief that the dead went on to some kind of other-worldly existence. Gardening tools and seeds for planting were placed in the humble graves of agricultural people along the Seine River. Native Americans were supplied with canoes and spears for the next life. Not to mention the fully-outfitted tombs of the Egyptian Pharaohs, complete with mummified concubines and slaves and a gold-encrusted raft for their re-animated excursion to the other side.

And the "other side" was simply the place you went when you died. There were legends and vague scriptural references to hint at what that mysterious place might be like. But it was generally viewed as some netherworld that would remain cloaked in shadows until you actually got there and saw it for yourself.

Shadows, in fact, are pretty much what the Hebrew concept of Sheol was about. This poorly-illuminated underworld was not a precursor for Hell by any means, but a rather hazy, purposely ill-defined notion that stood for whatever might become of human beings after death. And how could it be anything *but* hazy and ill-defined? There weren't a whole lot of eyewitness accounts to rely on.

So where did the "classic" concept of heaven and hell come from?

Credit the evolving notion of Justice. Judaism, especially, had developed a strong sense of communal law, according to which those who were obedient and disobedient received specific rewards and punishments. This, after all, is the technical meaning of "justice." But reward and punishment weren't merely a function of some legal code; there was also a kind of divine justice. The righteous were expected to reap more blessings during their natural lifetimes—in terms of wealth, children, longer lives and communal honors. Sinners or wrongdoers, in contrast, would not only suffer the long arm of the law, but feelings of guilt, mental instability, and shorter life spans.

That is, most of the time. Or at least enough to make righteous living the better gamble.

Unfortunately, by the time the Assyrians, Greeks and Romans had turned Israel on its ear a few times, the justice-in-one's-lifetime idea was wearing thin. Worse, the people who were most obedient to God's laws seemed to be the ones most often selected for torture and death by the invaders. Since righteousness didn't seem all that profitable, some people figured, why go to all the trouble? If the bad guys prosper, how can there be any Justice with a capital "J"?

It's been one of humankind's most troubling questions ever since. And the answer, to use legal jargon, is that the statute of limitations was extended... beyond the grave. If good people weren't rewarded in this life for meritorious acts, they would be rewarded in the next. If evil-doers seemed to be living in the lap of luxury and dying in their feather-beds at a ripe old age, they will surely catch hell in the World-to-Come. If justice has any ultimate meaning, so the argument went, death can't be final.

Christianity and Islam, likewise justice-oriented traditions, came up with basically the same solution: Heaven and Hell, or Paradise and Hades. Hinduism, too, had its concept of justice. Karma, the positive or negative energy from one's actions, could be affixed to the soul/atman through many incarnations or lifetimes. If a good act could not be rewarded in one's present life, the karma would be carried into the next, like the balance in your checking account might be transferred from one bank branch to another. The same for punishment. If you didn't pay the mortgage this month, it'll definitely come due later. Along with late penalties and compounded interest.

Of course, there's the old saying that "Goodness is its own reward." In this view, also embraced to some extent in most traditions, heaven and hell are created anew each day. The balance sheet is adjusted with every new act and every thought. Reward and punishment are immediately woven into the fabric of our lives, changing our faiths, improving or damaging the way we relate to others and to the world. And if we think evil-doers often seem to get away with murder, it's only because we can't get inside their heads to experience their pain and self-loathing. If we witness good people who die without apparently getting what they deserve, maybe it's because our own standards for justice are too materialistic. Maybe the good people who supposedly died without their reward were themselves looking for something tangible, when the real blessing was in some other form and they simply failed to realize it.

After all, who's to say what the spiritual reward of a righteous act should be? Are we looking for a two-bucks-an-hour hour pay-raise because we donated a bag of groceries to the emergency food bank? Does helping a blind lady cross the street after work make up for yelling at the kids over breakfast? Is telling the truth worthwhile only because that's how we get to walk on the streets paved with gold?

Concepts of heaven and hell often say more about the people who formulate them than about some real or imagined afterlife. This is not to *deny* an afterlife, but to acknowledge that how we envision it is shaped by our spiritual development and level of understanding. Many agnostics, as well as some Christians and Jews, simply shrug their shoulders at the notion of heaven. If it truly exists, and if a positive balance on Life's Ledger is the price of admission, that's all fine and dandy. But the acts that create the positive balance already have enough value in this life to make them worth doing.

What's more, doing something charitable only because it gets you past the Pearly Gates is the epitome of selfishness. It's not even charity. Committing action "X" as a way of getting to heaven means that, as far as you're concerned, the only value in X is the stake it buys in Paradise. Theoretically, X could be *any* act. And the problem is, someone else will always be happy to define X for you. Killing the infidels, say. Or reporting the infractions of your neighbor to Big Brother. Or performing whatever services benefit whoever happens to be holding the reins of power at the moment.

So maybe "getting to heaven" and "going to hell" have a more symbolic meaning instead. Heaven, for example, is sometimes defined as "a deeper relationship with God," or "becoming increasingly conscious of the What Is." And actions *do* have a way of getting you there, even if that's not their primary purpose. Your faith, after all, involves your whole attitude and tendency to behave in certain ways. As your personality grows and your behavior tends to be less self-absorbed, you become more enriched by the lives of others, more involved in your community, more open to new learning through both physical and spiritual means. This broadening of one's spiritual self in this way can be understood as "coming to know God" or Ultimate Reality more fully. And that, for many, constitutes the experience of heaven.

Conversely, pursuing only selfish goals, ignoring others (or even trampling over them), is "going to hell." It's the condition of being cut off from the deepest levels of meaning and purpose, to have lost all but the tiniest sliver of connection to Ultimate Reality.

The bottom line is, heaven and hell are not beyond our ability to perceive in this physical existence. As we live our earthly lives, we can sense ourselves moving between two poles of a spiritual continuum, sometimes more connected to the highest levels of reality, sometimes less. Judging where we are on that continuum is a way of holding ourselves accountable—not to some heavenly gatekeeper, but to our own highest potential. And in a way that motivates us to achieve a richer, more meaningful, more satisfying life *now*.

Thank heaven for that.

HELL

Assuming you just finished "Heaven," you may be wondering if there's anything left to say about Hell. Half of the previous discourse, after all, covered the lower end of the heaven/hell spectrum.

Unfortunately, Hell can't be disposed of quite so easily. If only because we humans—at least in the West—have such a fascination with it. Hell is part of our culture. Demons and devils inhabit our psyches whether we consider ourselves religious or not. The books and movies of today are full of evil beings that hide in our attics or rise from the grave, as well as aliens from space that make the old, pointy-tailed caricature of Satan look more like Mickey Mouse. In their own way, such images perform the same job as those gargoyles on the cathedral parapets, reminding us that even when we're in the presence of God some little bloodsucker might be out there in the shadows just waiting.

But concentrating on hell rather than heaven can be self-defeating. The fire-and-brimstone preachers of the past (and present) may perform a valid service in convincing their flocks that evil exists, and that it has the power to ruin people's lives. Hell gives a kind of "graphic reality" to evil. And for those people teetering on the brink, a good old-fashioned scare-fest can sometimes be the only thing that keeps them from falling in.

Unfortunately, that's like fighting fire with fire. The concept of Hell feeds on the very same animal emotions it seeks to destroy. And if an angry God can condemn a living soul to eternal torture as just punishment for a few years of wrongdoing, why shouldn't we put heathens in stocks, or burn witches at the stake, or stretch non-believers on the racks where they can be drawn and quartered for their own good?

In other words, Hell can be a kind of self-fulfilling prophecy. As New Age puts it, whatever you spend most of your time thinking about—even if they're the things you don't want—is precisely what you're most likely to attract.

Which is why Hinduism, Taoism and Buddhism prefer to concentrate on the good, the truth, The Light. There's no place called Hell. Even bad karma is intended only to chastise one into turning toward the good. And if a person doesn't learn righteousness this time around, he or she will inevitably be sent back to earth again and again, as long as it takes, until the message sinks in. God is too loving, too powerful, to allow even one soul to be lost forever.

Read that last sentence a few times, for that too is The Good News.

Of course, this sentiment is not exactly foreign to Jewish or Christian tradition. For most Christians and Jews, Hell is more of a symbol anyway. Which doesn't mean the existence of evil should be taken any less seriously. It merely affirms that, for a God of Love, Hell cannot exist as a real place of endless punishment.

And maybe that's the kernel of truth behind even the most gruesome vision of Hell. If there's enough of an individual left to suffer in flames, there must be enough left to save. Where there is life, so the proverb goes, there's hope. It may be true that the *kind* of person who lands at the bottom of the heaven/hell continuum is eternally damned and destined for the scrap heap. But the person's soul or atman is always capable of being transformed. Hell is simply the junkyard or toxic waste dump for all those self-limiting characteristics we must cast off in order to achieve our full potential.

In the end, Hell isn't for people, it's for *faiths*. It's for attitudes and lifestyles that ultimately don't work, that disconnect us from other people, from love, from the resources that give our lives meaning and purpose and power. Hell is a way of saying, "That's where I've been, not where I'm going." It's The Past, the molted skin, the discarded chaff. It's the lesson finally learned, the chains of bondage broken and piled in the corner of an empty cell.

Or maybe... an empty tomb.

HERESY

The original meaning of the Greek word heresy was simply "sect" or "party" (as in "political party"). It was a kind of sub-group within the larger group, loyal to its broader goals and traditions, though emphasizing certain distinctive elements.

The Pharisees, Sadducees and Zealots were heresies, or parties, within Judaism. The early church was also a Jewish heresy or sect—at least until Paul took the helm and James gave his approval. There are two main heresies, or sects, within Islam: Shiite and Sunni. And there are literally dozens of heresies within Hinduism, each focusing on its own practices within the larger tradition, worshipping certain "faces" of God rather than others.

The downhill slide from this neutral definition of heresy to a term with a decidedly negative connotation followed from the power struggles within early Christianity. It is almost inevitable that any single sect which garners the most followers (or the most power) will begin to look on competing sects as somehow mistaken or less genuine, or even in direct opposition to what that larger sect stands for. The history of early Christianity is a lesson in how religious diversity can be brow-beaten into a single party line, where heresy starts as a different way of conceptualizing deeper truths and ends up being vilified as the incarnation of evil. At least in the minds of those who have the Emperor on their side.

Admittedly, not all heresies are constructive or merely harmless. The tendency for sects to break off from the larger tradition is often associated with a narrow-mindedness that turns a single line of scripture or one interpretation of reality into an idol, a "false god" that ends up harming adherents even more than the punishments meted out by the larger tradition.

And of course there are heresies that truly *are* destructive to the larger tradition, or to humanity in general, that deserve to be rooted out like cancer because they have betrayed some essential spiritual truth. But deciding what that truth *is* has always been a tough job, subject to selfish motives or the common mistake of confusing form with substance.

Maybe the problem is one of methodology. Genuine truth proves itself not in some outward power struggle or doctrinal debate but in the lives of those who embrace it. Which is what Jesus meant when he said "Each tree is known by its fruit... No good tree bears bad fruit, nor does a bad tree bear good fruit."

And many a heresy has gone on to bear the best apples in the whole bloomin' orchard.

HERO

There's an old saying that "We all need heroes." Today that tidbit of wisdom has a mostly secular ring, especially in view of the fact that so many of us seem to prefer rock stars, basketball players, movie actors and even comic book characters as our heroes.

But the original understanding of "hero" carries a more profound meaning. A shortened version of *heirophant*—combining the Greek words for "sacred" (*heiros*) and "to manifest" (*phanein*)—the hero is a person in whom the sacred or divine is manifested. The father who jumps into a raging river to save another family's tot who wanders out too far; the secretary who confronts a newly-fired employee after he storms back into the office with a gun, then talks him out of a killing spree; the nun who works tirelessly to heal the bodies and minds of lepers and social outcasts—all of these people manifest a kind of divine self-sacrifice, empathy and love that surpasses human understanding.

It's one thing to want to reel off riffs like Jimi Hendrix, execute a lay-up like Kobe Bryant, or mow down your adversaries like fictional super-spy Ethan Hunt. It is quite another to be inspired by the examples of ordinary people whose actions demonstrate the potential we all have within us to manifest greatness, to prove that divinity isn't something beyond our capabilities. That's why heroic stories about real people, or the real life role models we are lucky enough to witness for ourselves, are the most compelling.

But fictional accounts of heroes can work just as effectively. If a story reaches into our hearts, if it powerfully affects our emotions, if it can inspire us to connect with our own inner strength or some deeper level of compassion or forgiveness or love that ends up saving someone's life—not the least of which is our own—then that story is as true as any real life example.

And that's why sacred scriptures can still convey truth, regardless of whether the events recounted on their pages ever really happened.

HIGHER SELF

In three words, it's the *hero in us.*

In a wider sense, the Higher Self is the divine component or "spark" within each human being. It is the soul that's not limited by our mortal (or moral) weaknesses, or even by our current location in time and space. It's our own facility for connecting with the universe or Gaia or God—or at least with the dimensions beyond our normal human senses—which, if only we could connect with them, would guide us progressively toward our own highest potential.

Or, to use Faithspeak, would "save" us.

HINDUISM

More than any other religious tradition, the incredible diversity of forms (or heresies) within Hinduism make a one-line, textbook-style definition virtually impossible. Then again, maybe that very diversity is what best defines it.

No prophet or messenger or divinity founded it. No central dogma summarizes its beliefs. No great reform movements wrestled for control over its adherents or distilled its practices into a specific institution. In fact, new traditions and writings and mythologies have been added continuously to Hinduism from at least two thousand years BCE to the present, stirring themselves into its spiritual cauldron like ingredients in a rich stew. As a result, adherents can pick out only certain elements for their nourishment, or ladle out whole bowlfuls.

Interestingly, there is no Hindu concept which corresponds to the Western word, "religion." The closest term translates as "approaches"—that is, paths or ways of approaching the Ultimate in order to enhance one's life. Another useful term is *dharma,* which refers to the collective behaviors that keep one on the proper path or "approach." These are viewed as ritual observances or moral laws, almost in the sense of Islamic or Jewish Law.

Primary among these collective behaviors is the practice of renunciation. Like the ascetics found in most religious traditions, devout Hindus deny the importance of material things or bodily pleasures. Which is not to say we can't have these things. It simply means we shouldn't live as if new cars, fancy clothes and creature comforts are what The Good Life is about. If we have them, fine; if not, it's no big deal. What *is* a big deal is when cars and clothes and comforts take our eyes off the real prize: The salvation and liberation of our souls. *That's* what counts.

Which sounds rather Christian, doesn't it? And Jewish. And Islamic. And New Age. It especially sounds like Buddhism—which, as a matter of fact, got its start as a heresy of Hinduism.

Of course, since humans seem to require personifications of the many forces that help or hinder us in our struggle to achieve liberation, Hinduism offers up a list of divinities as thick as a New Delhi phone book. Hindu philosophers and intellectuals can look past all these to one Supreme God or Lord, of whom the others are only partial manifestations. But it would be misleading to say that all Hindus are aware of this God-behind-the-gods.

Most deities are worshipped in their own right: Brahma, Vishnu and Shiva, in a sort of primal Trinity... or the avatars (incarnations of Vishnu on earth) who appear in the form of both humans and animals... or the Mother Goddesses and village goddesses, the legendary heroes, the guardians of the world and genies of the heavens. All of these divinities personify the forces found in nature, or within ourselves. They can be as wonderful and beneficial and inspiring as the gods worshipped in other traditions, or uniquely terrifying and destructive.

As in other traditions, there are sacred scriptures to support them. Hinduism, however, doesn't insist that these scriptures be taken literally or considered infallible because truth, like the Absolute God, appears only in bits and pieces and is always clouded by human limitations. In fact The Upanishads, writings which can be traced to the fourth and fifth centuries BCE, were an effort to explain how earlier texts and rituals, once taken literally by the masses, were really allegories or "equivalences" for deeper truths. Upanishads *means* "equivalences."

Which is also what this Lexicon is about. Equivalences between, say, the Hindu practices of purification and similar rites in both Judaism and Islam. Equivalences between the recitation of Hindu sacred formulas (mantras) and Catholic or Greek Orthodox chants. Or between the initiation of the "twice-born" in Hinduism and being "born again" for Protestants. There is, in short, hardly a practice in any other religion or denomination for which some parallel cannot be found in Hinduism.

Because, ultimately, Hinduism recognizes that a diversity of people requires a diversity of approaches. None is exclusive. All can be useful, depending on our spiritual development, our soul's stage in its journey toward salvation. As long as we remain enslaved by strictly human motives, addicted to "the things of this world" for our fulfillment, the karma of our actions will follow us "as the calf follows its mother." But if we seek the Absolute, unite with the divine, we break those bonds.

And the result can be liberating.

HISTORY

Historians have long acknowledged that there are two basic versions of history. There is outer or *objective* history; that is, the events as they actually happened. And there is inner or *subjective* history, which is how humans interpret or experience those same events based on their limited understanding, and viewed through their specific biases and conceptual models. This may include the outright fabrication of events that never really happened, but might as well have happened if enough people believe they did. After all, popular belief in an event that never really happened is also an historical event of sorts.

So the crazy thing about history is that what actually happened is only rarely what matters most. It's what people *think* happened.

And what people think happened not only depends on who won the last war, or who has the power to write the history books, but what people *wish* had happened. History therefore becomes a repository of so-called facts and events which are paraded as proof of whatever the historians want us to believe. Depending on whom you ask, history conclusively shows that God deeded a certain piece of real estate for all time to a certain people—or didn't. Or that a certain person from Nazareth rose from the dead—or that it was only a Passover Plot. There are claims and counterclaims and so many inconsistencies in the record that all we can ever really prove is this: Someone isn't telling the truth.

Or *none* of them are. Which is no great crime because it's a mistake to assume religious accounts are meant to be history books.

The real question about history concerns how our individual faiths ought to be related to the past. It is a peculiar notion that the way we behave or how we face the world should depend on whether purported events of two or three thousand years ago did or didn't really happen. Certainly history is a kind of "experience" which instructs us about human behavior: Like how far we've come or haven't come as a species; or what our capabilities are in terms of physical limitations and possibilities; or what consequences might arise from behaving in certain ways. Surely we would be much poorer without some form of access to the Wisdom of the Ages, if only because it prevents each new generation from having to re-invent the wheel.

And that's where history gives us all something to believe in. History, in this sense, is not so much an objective chronology of events, but a treasure chest brimming with the ideas and resources by which our ancestors struggled to understand themselves and find their place in the world... and whether or not they succeeded. History is an Old-Times Testament to the proposition that what transforms the world isn't found in such events as the discovery of fire or the invention of the telephone, but in the example of a carpenter to "Love one another" or the act of turning inward and listening for one's "still, small voice."

Or there's this: History doesn't prove anything. It just gives us a place to prove our*selves*.

HOLISTIC

Occasionally spelled with a "w" to remind us that it derives from the word "whole," (w)holistic refers to the cooperative unity that governs a functioning society, organization or person... or the rituals and practices which act together to *unify* that society, organization or person.

Used mostly as an adjective, holistic describes the state in which all things are working together for good, in a balanced way that allows no single part to dominate the others. It's where tradition and folkways play a role right alongside social engineering; where massage and acupuncture and bedside manner are as important as pharmaceuticals and surgery; where emotions and dreams are enlisted in our personal development as much as logic and utility and hard work.

This kind of old/new, left brain/right brain, everything-has-its-place perspective also forms the basis for concepts like The Body of Christ, the Islamic Umma and the United Nations. It's the notion that working together is better than going it alone or fighting amongst ourselves, that each of us is an essential part in a greater whole, and that the whole is greater than the sum of its parts.

The achievement of this condition, described in scientific circles as "synergy," is known in Western spirituality as "at-one-ment" or salvation, and in Eastern tradition as *samadhi* or Enlightenment. The opposite is chaos. Or, to go back a few listings, Hell.

HOLY

Many of us encounter this word in situations that suggest almost the opposite of what it really means. As in "That kid's a holy terror" or

"Holy (four-letter word)!" Antiquated titles like "His Holiness, the King" don't help either, since "Your holiness" has become the tongue-in-cheek appellation for people who regard themselves as holier-than-thou.

Even to the average churchgoer, "holy" is attached to so many words—Holy Spirit, Holy Bible, Holy Communion—that it's now little more than a generic prefix implying some vague connection to religion. The word lacks any separate identity of its own.

And yet "holy" is precisely about separate-*ness.* The meaning behind the word—*kadosh* in Hebrew—refers to being "set apart." Someone or something, for example, might be set apart for a special purpose, and thus be made holy. God reportedly asks us to make our*selves* holy. Which simply means to not allow ourselves to be swept up in the world's busyness or madness, to avoid going along with things just because that's the way everybody else does it. Instead we are called to stand apart or to stand *out* from the crowd, to remember Who We Are and not give a rip if people label us as "different." Holiness is therefore an attitude.

Holiness is also a condition. Something may be perceived as holy because it already possesses a quality that sets it apart, that makes it stand out. And that quality, the *way* it stands out, has something to do with God or Ultimate Reality or whatever lies below the surface of our mundane existence. It might simply be a place that has some special or inspirational meaning for us. Not necessarily a towering cathedral, but a mountain stream, or a spot in the woods where the light filters through the trees just so. Maybe it's an "energy vortex" around the red-rock cliffs of Sedona. Or the back porch at grandma's house where she used to sit in her rocker and darn socks. Or your own four-poster bed where little Sarah climbed up alongside you when the sky opened and the thunder let loose and she learned the difference between fear and awe. Wherever it may be, when you're in the presence of holiness, you just know it.

People, too, can possess this quality. It's easy enough to spot in a spiritual advisor or your favorite college professor. But it's just as likely to be found in the old man shuffling with determination down the hall of the rest home, or a baby fast asleep, lips intermittently pursing as if to suck from a breast that isn't there. It might be visible in the face of a friend or a lover or, for a few fleeting seconds, in a father's glance that says "I understand, and I still love you."

Actions, in particular, can be holy. Sometimes even our religious acts—if we aren't merely going through the motions. Dropping your last few coins into the Salvation Army bucket surely qualifies, or sharing half your peanut-butter-and-jelly sandwich when your school chum forgets his lunch bag. Not to mention those rare, heroic acts like pulling an accident victim out of a burning car, or admitting when you're wrong despite your god-awful pride.

Holiness is an awareness of something going on that transcends what's "only human," that's not just mechanical, that's beyond appearances. It's the hint of a deeper reality, the presence of something that reaches down into our hearts and has the ability to profoundly affect Who We Are for the better. And the experience of that moment, that place or person, stands out in our awareness, separate, like a light glowing in the darkness, undimmed by the workaday world, the crowded freeway, the kids fighting again, the rent payment due tomorrow, the headlines on tonight's news.

Nothing can ruin it. Nobody can take it away. It's holy.

HOLY SPIRIT

To treat this as simply a name is a mistake.

For Christians, of course, "Holy Spirit" *does* happen to name the third person in the Godhead, that mysterious unity which also characterizes God as "Father" and "Son." As part of this conceptual tri-unity, Holy Spirit is meant to point to the Godhead's activity in the natural world, and in the hearts and minds of people.

According to Christian theology, when God (the Father) says "Let there be light," it is the Holy Spirit that actually flips the switch. If God (the Son) redeems our sinful souls through his sacrificial death, it is the Holy Spirit that actually enters our hearts and minds and thereby makes us whole.

On the other hand, this kind of divine activity can be alluded to without presupposing a distinct entity that's responsible for it. Judaism and Islam ascribe both the creative and redemptive power directly to God/Allah. The Hebrew Bible and the Qur'an use the very words "Holy Spirit" (as well as "Holy One" or just plain "Spirit") when speaking about God's activity in the world. But the words don't thereby function as a proper noun identifying a separate being.

A good analogy might be found in the Native American term, "Great Spirit." In the tradition of giving people names that describe something about them—like "Strong-as-a-Bear" or "Dances-with-Wolves"—Great Spirit is not so much a name as a uniquely descriptive activity. It's like saying "Exalted Animator-Within-All-Things" or "Supreme Mover-of-Man's-Heart" or "Chief Breath-of-Life."

That is the sense of Holy Spirit: Active, working in the world and within us; the cosmic process or principle or natural law that infuses everything with energy and life while somehow remaining separate and unsoiled by contact with the imperfect creatures it deals with. Which is something like digging around in a garden without getting any dirt under your fingernails.

And which is no less difficult to conceive than some "third person" in a Godhead.

HOPI

Let this be a respectful nod toward some of the world's smaller, aboriginal peoples who exist outside the larger religious traditions that have spread across the globe, but who nevertheless embody a spiritual wisdom equal to, or sometimes surpassing, their more famous cousins.

Take, for example, the tiny band of Pueblo Indians living in America's arid Southwest. From a native word translated as "peace" or "harmony"—or today, "holistic"—the Hopi are known for their concept of a Great Spirit, and especially for their conviction that all of us have a sacred relationship with the Earth that ought to guide our daily practices.

Also known for their Kachina dolls and once-outlawed Rain Dance, the Hopi have inherited a treasure-trove of divine prophesies passed down by their elders, much as Hebrews heard the voice of Yahweh in the words of select spokespersons (prophets) throughout their history. Among the Hopi's more noteworthy prophecies is a prediction that a "Gourd of Ashes" must come to pass—understood by present-day Hopi to mean nuclear war!—before humanity's current disharmony with the Earth can be overcome and proper balance restored.

As with certain Hebrew and Hindu prophecies, it is unclear whether this prediction foretells an event certain to happen, or an event that's inevitable only if we fail to change our current practices. Since the Hopi are by and large an optimistic people, let's assume the latter. And let's start changing things before it's too late.

HUMANISM

As your favorite on-line dictionary would have it, "Humanism" refers to the philosophy that asserts the fundamental dignity and equal worth of all human beings, and that promotes a way of life centered on human interests and human values.

Nothing controversial so far. But wait: Those values, according to Humanism, can be determined and refined through human reason, observation and experience alone. No appeal to divine revelation or supernatural intervention is required. In fact, revelation and belief in the supernatural are precisely what's been holding humans back for the last thirty-plus centuries.

Aye, there's the rub. At least for adherents of traditional religion.

And yet, as a philosophy, Humanism was largely responsible for the resurgence of Western culture, science and democracy. Based on the writings of Petrarch, Erasmus and other "free-thinkers," it fueled the industrial revolution and instilled society with a respect for the common man that produced such egalitarian documents as Paine's *Rights of Man* and the Declaration of Independence. In many ways it was the logical extension of the Protestant Reformation. Because, in freeing the masses from the mind-numbing authoritarianism of the Roman Church, Protestant leaders set the world on a course where no artificially imposed authority could limit the capabilities and potential of human achievement.

And aye, there's the *bigger* rub.

Because Humanism has also seemingly freed people from having to obey *any* limits, even those limits that might be good for them. Since the birth of Humanism, history has served up such notions as "survival of the fittest," Western imperialism, godless Communism, rock n' roll—or worse, rap music—as well as crack cocaine and Big Pharma's opioid crisis. If that's what free-thinking Humanism is about, say our fundamentalist friends, bring back That Old-Time Religion *now!*

Of course, that's *not* what Humanism is about. The caricature of the "secular humanist" as someone who is anti-religious and either amoral or immoral is flat-out false. If Humanism holds that our concepts of right and wrong are discernable through reason, observation and experience, that's not to say the "right and wrong" handed down through religious tradition is therefore mistaken. And it certainly doesn't imply that values are arbitrary inventions.

Humanism merely points out that rules for conduct are, after all, for the benefit and improvement of *humans*. If lying and stealing and murder are bad, it isn't because a Supreme Being says so. It's because of something inherently damaging and self-destructive about those behaviors. And if we would only stop "taking God's word for it" and find out exactly *why,* maybe we could become more autonomous and creative in meeting the problems of the future. Like a child learning to take more responsibility for his life as he grows into adulthood.

As it turns out, Humanism professes the same basic goals as religious traditions do, including the eventual salvation of both the human individual and human race. The attack by Christian fundamentalists and others is therefore largely misdirected. If anything, Humanists say, it's Christianity that should be criticized for an even more bizarre form of "humanism": Reducing the infinite power behind the cosmos, the Ultimate Reality which cannot be confined by time or space, into the finite shape and fragile form of a single human being born of a human mother just like the rest of us.

Then again, the birth, death and resurrection of Jesus is Faithspeak. That's Christianity's language and methodology for personal transformation. It's also what Humanism could use more of. Because the ranks of card-carrying Humanists will remain limited insofar as the lofty language of reason and experience and self-autonomy fails to reach down into the hearts of ordinary people with enough emotion to deeply affect and transform them. It's like the smoker who knows his habit is filling his lungs with soot, tripling his chances for getting cancer, but can't quite kick the habit without electroshock treatment or hypnotism or some other program that literally side-steps his rational mind and does whatever Pavlov did to make his dogs salivate on command.

Humanism is an ongoing testament to the human intellect. But the human being, for better or worse, is more than that. And in some ways, less.

HUMAN POTENTIAL

Over recent decades the Human Potential movement (by whatever name) has become an increasingly important component of The New Spirituality. More to the point, it's a more recent incarnation of what Humanism aspires to be but too often fails to achieve because it lacks, well... *heart.* Or as our Madison Avenue ad man calls it, "sex appeal."

For all the reasons outlined in Part One of this book, the human intellect is not always the best means for changing people's behavior, even when they desperately *want* to change. Nor is logic the best teaching tool for the very young. Learning is a body/mind/spirit process—often more body and spirit than mind. Research should've made that clear by now.

Research has also proven that when all three of these components are fully engaged, the human being is capable of some utterly astounding achievements—from feats of physical prowess to mental agility, from transformations of behavior to remarkable cases of self-healing. In fact the Human Potential movement claims that many (or even most) of the miraculous healings, visions, and out-of-body experiences recorded in religious literature are based in reality. They're the natural outcome of our endowment as humans.

Jesus' prediction that "Greater things than I do, you will do" was more than a parting word of encouragement before he walked off into the sunset. Now that we can systematically study ourselves and the natural world and begin to apply all that knowledge in a scientific way, the time is ripe for doing those greater things.

Or at least ripe for perfecting our golf swings.

Because, so far, the Human Potential movement has failed to live up to *its* potential. That is, unless you're referring to the commercial kind. What the movement is mostly known for is an array of flashy websites and mail-order catalogs offering instructional videos or smartphone apps teaching us how to get a dimpled ball out of a sand trap, or how to lose those ugly dimples on our thighs, or how to keep your brain cells from dying off by playing games on your laptop.

But what we really need are flashy new apps for kicking addictions or stopping child abuse. What we really need is an effective body/mind technology for insuring satisfying human relationships, for teaching us how to live wholesome, productive lives without falling into sand traps or any other traps.

And in all fairness, that's where Human Potential wants to take us. Perfecting your golf swing is only the prelude to perfecting more important abilities. Not the least of which is the ability to transform Who You Are—in keeping with the same spiritual truths religious traditions have espoused.

The problem with Human Potential is that, as we slip in our smartphone earbuds or hunker behind our laptops, we too-easily retreat into our own little world. Our goal should not be to enter some private reality apart from everyone else, but to build a personal platform for more realistic interactions with others. Especially with those who are trying to accomplish the same goal of personal transformation.

Having other people around while we try to improve ourselves can be extremely helpful. Let's face it: The idea of "church" or "religious community" is a response to a need that no biofeedback device or guided meditation app can ever satisfy. The "human" in Human Potential must allow for the fact that we are not merely individual souls but social animals. More than reassuring voices in our ears, or how-to videos on our computers or big-screen TVs, we need *each other.*

HYPOCRITE

Phony. Fake. Fraud. Rhinestone Cowboy. Pecksniff. Lip-server. Charlatan. Quack.

There are plenty of words to describe people who pretend to be something they're not. Hypocrite, from the Greek word for "actor," is the term reserved for people who pretend to be morally or religiously superior to others, but whose feet are made of the same crumbly clay as everybody else's. Or worse.

An evangelist who preaches chastity and stewardship but has sex with his church secretary and lives in a mansion with gold-plated faucets is a hypocrite. A guru who promotes a communal, spiritually-oriented lifestyle while indulging himself with a fleet of personal Rolls Royces is a hypocrite. And the individual—or author of spiritual handbooks—who finds fault with the phony morality of people in high places, then fails to see the corruption and fakery in his own life is, you guessed it... a hypocrite.

We are *all* hypocrites, more or less. We all pretend to be better than we are, to be farther along on our paths toward perfection. We present false fronts to others at least on occasion, if not most of the time. And of course there's the false front we present to ourselves.

Some of which really isn't all that bad. Psychologically speaking, those air-brushed, spit-shined images we see in our mental mirrors are a kind of self-preservation mechanism, to keep us from wilting in the face of our own failures and weaknesses. The cards are often so stacked against us that we must sometimes construct a fantasy of Who We Are or else we might never make it through the day. Not to mention the fact that pretending can be a way of growing into the kind of person you want to be. Fantasies can set the stage for genuine self-improvement.

But they can also *substitute* for self-improvement. We may easily lose sight of the reality behind the public image. We become blind to Who We Really Are; and without that knowledge we can never get a handle on how to effectively become Who We Ought to Be. In our self-deception, we lose touch with the deepest resources inside and outside of us. And if we can't know ourselves, warts and all, we don't stand a chance of ever knowing Ultimate Reality.

Which is closer to the Islamic and Jewish understanding of "hypocrite." It's not just that we're all fakes; that's a given. It's that in being fake we thereby turn away from God. We reject that spark of divinity within us, on which our evolution into better people must be founded.

Others will eventually see through our hypocrisy. The sad thing is, *we* often can't see through it, or don't want to. And as much as it hurts, we sometimes need others to point it out. To hold up a *real* mirror so we can finally see ourselves.

Fortunately, like the backside of that mirror, there's a silver lining.

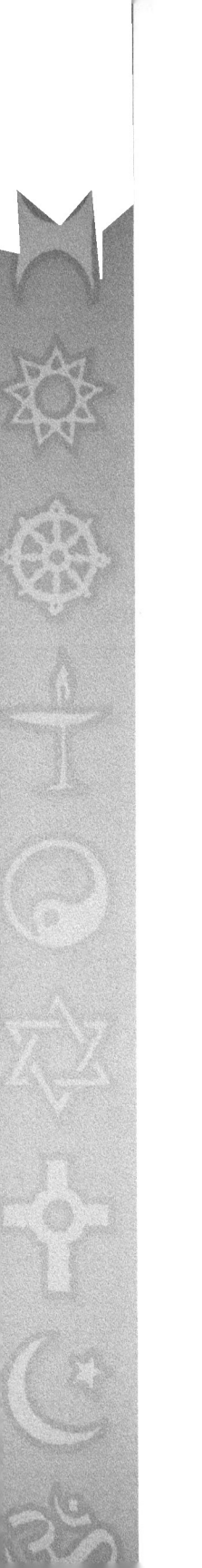

IDOLATRY

A story is told about Abraham, the ancestral father/patriarch to Jews, Christians and Muslims. Abraham's father, according to tradition, was a maker of idols for his fellow pagans in Chaldea. With the flair of an accomplished artist, he would carve fierce-looking creatures and delicate fertility goddesses out of wood or stone, or cast them in clay. People would come from all over the region to buy them, believing the idols to be inhabited by spirits or gods. And then they would cajole, bribe or otherwise worship those idols, hoping to receive some benefit from their magical powers.

    Watching his father make these "gods" with his bare hands, Abraham realized at an early age how foolish it was for people to fall down on their knees before these man-made creations. Even if the idol was meant only to represent some deity, people rarely treated them that way. They related to their idols as if they really *did* have some inherent power, as if the wood or stone or oven-fired clay could by itself determine their fates… as if the success of this year's crop, or how many lambs would be born this year, revolved around their new owners' "service" to these inanimate objects. Young Abraham understood that the idols were therefore a trap, that they turned people away from the truth and focused their attentions on things that had no real power to benefit them, much less save them.

Which is the case today as much as in Abraham's time.

Except that now, instead of worshipping a block of wood carved into the shape of an eagle, we worship pieces of paper etched with eagles. Instead of bowing down to a golden calf, we make ourselves subservient to a gold-toned BMW or a six-bedroom house on Goldenrod Avenue, or the gold watch at the end of forty years' worth of sixty-hour workweeks during which our children never went hungry but hardly got to know us between our commuting to the office and our nighttime stops at the bar or bowling alley so we could blow off enough steam to do it all over again the next day.

In other words, our priorities often get mixed up because we fail to understand what's ultimately important in our lives. "Idolatry" is the misplaced focusing of our efforts and energies on things which cannot ultimately help us achieve life's most important goals. Idolatry is looking at our car, or our house or career or body, as if each of these is an end in itself rather than a means or a tool to assist us in achieving our higher purposes. Idolatry is making things of only relative importance into the supreme standard against which everything else is measured. Idolatry is allowing what should be our servants to become our masters.

And it isn't just material things that end up ruling our lives. Our idols can just as easily be our country or religion, or the Torah or Qur'an or Holy Bible when their forms become more important than the messages they contain. Our idol can also be unrestrained science or Reason or "progress," or whatever else masquerades as Ultimate Reality but is only one facet of it.

Chances are we've all been guilty of idolatry at one time or another. Likewise every religion and denomination. So much so that merely reorganizing our priorities isn't enough. Occasionally we must clean house from stem to stern and throw the bastards out: Dump that collection of Hustler magazines, flush the valium down the john, find a new church or mosque or 12-step group that doesn't just pump us up with hot air but actually transforms our faith for the better.

Like Abraham did. One day when his father was out taking new orders for his latest line of magical figurines, little Abe sneaked into the workshop and beat the hell out of the previous week's handiwork. Just plain smashed the deaf-and-dumb idols to smithereens. And you know what happened? *Nothing.* Even his father couldn't lift a finger to punish the future patriarch. He too realized it was time to move to the next stage of theological evolution. Because the idols, reduced to wood splinters and shards of burnt clay, spoke louder from his workshop floor than they ever did from the altars people erected for them.

And a little idol-bashing might do *us* some good now and then.

IMAGE

The word is often used in scripture to mean the same thing as "idol." It usually referred to the likeness of an animal or fantastical creature believed to have magical or divine powers. Image carries a negative connotation when it becomes confused with the reality behind it, or when there's nothing real behind it to begin with.

We often use the word with the same negative twist today. A political candidate might be described as "all image and no substance." For some movie stars, media personalities, luxury cars and corporations, image is all they've got. Or all that's necessary, anyway. And if people aren't patient enough or savvy enough to look below the surface, why not ignore the corrosion and just spray on another coat of glossy, quick-dry enamel?

On the other hand, "image" can be a positive thing if it's the product of substance and not a mere substitute for it. Just as a good reputation derives from a record of praiseworthy actions, a good image can flow from the beneficial way an organization or a person relates to other people or to society. Here "image" is not based on surface-level appearances, or cooked up in a brainstorming session on Madison Avenue. It's the good feeling we get when we think about that organization or person. The image becomes a kind of shorthand for everything we know about him, her or it. The image acts as a mnemonic device.

The image of the lotus can stand for the unfolding of one's life and eventual opening to ultimate reality. An image or photograph of the Capitol Building can stand for the ideals of democracy. The portrait of the Good Shepherd carrying a baby lamb on his shoulders—used for King David and other religious figures long before Jesus—stands for the idea of a watchful, caring God.

Such images are Faithspeak of the visual variety. They are pictorial reminders about what we believe, or *want* to believe. Or what we want to *become.*

The photograph of Einstein on the professor's desk; the portrait of Jesus in the pastor's study; the poster of Martin Luther King above the school kid's bed—all of these images can instantly connect a person to ideas or feelings or dreams that may play an important role in personal growth. Countless self-help programs have demonstrated that carefully selected images, from pictures to cut-out news articles, can help build a visual environment to motivate and inspire us. They aid in affirming our principles and self-worth, spiritually connecting us to sources of wisdom that can make measurable improvements in our lives.

It is in this sense that images *do* have great power. Seeing a likeness can make us *like* it. Our faith is literally shaped—positively or negatively—by the likenesses we surround ourselves with.

Which, of course, is why the use of images is sometimes forbidden outright, as in some Islamic communities, since people can't always be trusted to pick out the right ones. Or else their use is severely restricted, in the sense that only certain images can be displayed, and then only after all the evil ones are torn down.

In the Ten Commandments, we are told not to make images and "bow down to them." Which is simply to say that whatever power images may have over us does not come from the images themselves. It comes from the "I Am That I Am" that underlies reality, and according to whose rules images can work to the benefit, or to the harm, of the people who gaze upon them.

IMAGE OF GOD

And one of the images or "likenesses" that can work to our benefit (see above) is this one.

The phrase "image of God" comes from the Hebrew Bible where, after creating heaven and earth, God reportedly announces: "Let us make man in our image, after our likeness…" For now, let's ignore what is implied by "us" and "our." The point is, as Genesis goes on, "God created man in his own image; in the image of God he created him."

The Latter-Day Saints' (Mormon) view probably represents the most literal reading of this passage. Reasoning backwards, church founders concluded that human beings must be the semblance of God Himself. After all, if we are made in God's likeness, then God must look like us, right? Grey hair and a beard, maybe. A handsome, Schwarzenegger-like muscular build. A rich, stentorian voice like John Huston or Charlton Heston. And let's not forget eyes to see with, ears to hear with, and even—don't get squeamish here, folks—male sexual organs. Why else call God "Father"? And because God *is* literally a father, a Son of God suddenly makes all the more sense.

And if you wanted to know what the word "anthropomorphism" means, now you know.

On the other hand, what lies behind this straightforward "image of God" is a more symbolic understanding that humans are, in some sense, the offspring of divinity. A young girl, for example, is said to resemble her parents not merely because she might look like one or the other, but because she shares important personality traits: The same confident manner her mother has; or maybe, like her father, a facility for fixing things; or a generous nature that seems inherited rather than learned.

And that, in fact, is the core meaning of "image of God": Our *inheritance.* What aspects of divinity do we inherit simply by being born? In what ways might we resemble a Supreme Being? Skip the human frailties and evil inclinations and all the rest. What are the positive resources we possess as humans?

"Image of God" is the phrase virtually every religious tradition employs to focus attention on all the good things about us. Like the ability to make choices, to discriminate between what's good and bad. Or the ability to love—certainly that's one of our better traits, along with compassion and forgiveness.

Even more God-like is the power to create, to make things that never existed before from stuff that does. Islam and Judaism suggest that God purposely left Creation incomplete, so we humans could essentially finish it by living up to our innate potential as co-creators. And in co-creating the world, we might thereby create ourselves.

The Mormons, in their supremely literal way, believe we can create ourselves to the point of becoming Sons and Daughters of God, potentially on an equal par with that divine role model, Jesus. More to the point, it is our life's work to do so.

As self-indulgent as that might sound, it is hardly different from the perfection of the soul in Hinduism, which ultimately results in our merging with the Absolute. It's no different from the more traditional Christian view that, in Jesus' own words, we are meant to "become sons and daughters of God, even as I am." Or the New Age practice of affirming our divinity with such chants as "I am God, God I am."

And the fact is, affirming our own divinity is where it all starts. Because if we don't know we already possess it, if no one points it out to us, if we fail to imagine it in other people despite what their lives look like on the surface, we can prevent that divine likeness from ever manifesting itself. Not only in them, but in us.

IMAM

Unlike most religions, Islam has no official priesthood. There is no worldwide, institutional hierarchy, no paid clergy or supreme leader established by scripture, no infallible spokesperson for God.

At least in theory.

Because human beings, being only human, look for guidance wherever they can find it. And they often invest those who guide them with an almost dictatorial power to rule over their lives, even to think for them if they are too timid or ignorant to do so for themselves.

"Imam" is the Islamic equivalent for the *de facto* supreme religious leader. Not to be confused with the more political Caliphate, the "Imamate" (like the Roman Catholic Papacy) was originally established to provide religious guidance for the Community after their founder—in this case, Muhammad—was no longer around.

And like the Papacy, the Imamate hasn't exactly performed without a hitch. There have been disputes about who the leader should be, how much power he should have, where he should rule from, and what qualifications make someone eligible in the first place. (Besides, of course, being male.) The resulting acrimony from these disputes contributed to Islam's first major division into the Shiite and Sunni sects. It also produced numerous wars between lesser sects, a succession of twelve "original" Imams who were all poisoned or otherwise murdered in the course of various power struggles, as well as simultaneous Imamates in Persia, Egypt, Spain and elsewhere.

So much for theory.

Then again, the gaping disparity between theory and practice is the thorn in the side of every religious tradition, and why the universal standard for religion must be *the faith of its adherents.* The Imam or Pope or local pastor—the latter being the Muslim equivalent of how the title is used today—is not finally responsible for Who We Are and how we relate to each other. *We* are.

Not that the concept of the Imam doesn't have its good points. For one thing, an Islamic religious leader—whether supreme or local—need not be a Ph.D. or Doctor of Divinity from the I.M. Religious School of Theology. He can be, like Jesus, a journeyman carpenter who labors for his daily bread, but also knows that man does not live by bread alone. He can be, like Buddha, someone who has a passion for knowledge, as well as the increasing enlightenment which grows out of applying that knowledge to everyday life. Married or unmarried, young or old—and let's pretend: male or female—the Imam is simply the one who embodies the tradition in a way others admire and seek to emulate. He (or someday *she*) becomes a kind of public "image of God"—not to be worshipped, but to provide a living example for us to copy.

Still, for most Muslims, the Imam is no more infallible than the next guy. In fact he can occasionally foul things up just as badly, if not worse, in which case the Imam now has a golden opportunity to demonstrate how to recognize one's own sins and repent of them. If he doesn't, Islamic tradition says, we're no longer bound to use that person as our model, and it's time to start looking for yet another embodiment of The Best We Can Be.

Which, in theory, is exactly how it should work in every tradition.

IMMANENCE

This is one of those twenty-dollar terms bandied about more by theologians than ordinary believers, mostly to distinguish the kind of God who dwells *within* the natural world from the transcendent God who remains outside or above it.

Immanence means seeing the divine in everyday life—in the cycles of birth and death, in the passing seasons, in the holiness of seemingly-ordinary events that connect us to deeper dimensions not accessible to our five senses. Immanence is related to "pantheism" in that God is present throughout the universe, not only in other people and other life forms but in non-living matter as well. God, in short, is everywhere.

We remain connected to this God without the need for a mediator, without uttering a prayer or entering a church. In fact our thoughts and actions *are* our prayers, and our daily lives the sacred spaces where we offer them.

IMMORTALITY

To be immortal is the condition of not being mortal; that is, not subject to the natural cycle of birth, life and death. Or, as traditionally understood, to be "exempt from death."

The concept of immortality embodies the near-universal hope that our physical demise isn't the end. The idea that a human life can suddenly spring into existence and then get snuffed out forever is flat-out intolerable for most religious traditions and more than a few atheists, despite all evidence to the contrary. And if anyone *does* want their life to end, it's probably because they're hoping for better accommodations in the hereafter, or at least in a succeeding lifetime, to make up for the lousy conditions they got stuck with this time around.

So there simply must be some component of Who We Are, something beyond our physical bodies—call it "atman" or "soul"—that survives the inevitable cessation of breath and brainwaves... right?

Unfortunately, an immortal soul has never been captured in a laboratory flask. The atman can't be recorded on a CAT-scan, can't be measured or photographed or otherwise proven to exist beyond a reasonable doubt. It remains conjecture: A fantasy for those who find no meaning in their present lives; a consolation for people who can't get their minds around the fact that they didn't exist for the fifteen or twenty billion years it took the universe to prepare for their arrival, and now they can't imagine the universe going on for another fifteen or twenty *minutes* without them. Alas, how foolish and egotistical is this species that refuses to accept its own place in the natural order of things—that can't accept the brevity of their lives and the finality of their deaths.

Then again, there is something to be said for the caterpillar and the chrysalis and the butterfly.

Here is this wormy little creature who lives and eats and grows, and then goes off to die in its own self-fabricated coffin, having no notion of what lies beyond, but finally emerges transformed into something so different and free from the limitations of its earlier existence that it might as well be an entirely new creation.

This, some would suggest, is the scientific precedent for immortality. We are all, according to this quaint analogy, little buggers who know all about being little buggers, but whose buggerish limitations keep us totally in the dark about a future stage in which our little bugger-ness literally dies in order to give birth to a new creature that defies the gravity of earth and drinks the nectar of the gods. And maybe what's *un*scientific is precisely to close our minds to the idea of immortality just because we can't picture exactly what it might be, or because we haven't built a device capable of recording it.

Or maybe we *have* recorded it. And the device we've used is the human mind.

Prophetic visions in virtually all scriptures have reported glimpses of a Beyond that may connect with our present physical lives as naturally as digestion after dinner. But seeing it through our five human senses gives as distorted or ungrounded a view as a Monarch butterfly trying to describe winged flight to a garden-variety caterpillar.

Modern-day accounts of near-death experiences seem equally ungrounded and unreliable. Maybe all these visions involving tunnels of light or encounters with dead relatives or glowing celestial beings are perfectly normal manifestations of human brain activity just before that organ shuts down once and for all. Maybe the reports about people who have clinically died and disconnected from their bodies, only to look down on themselves while the doctors and nurses struggle to revive them—or who can recount the private conversations of people in the next room word-for-word, or who magically appear to a faraway friend at the moment of their death—maybe all these experiences are merely the final synaptic gasps of a dying cerebral cortex.

Maybe. But they are also really, really weird. If nothing else, these experiences show that the brain or mind (or whatever it was that transcended our usual physical limitations) is not exactly the little bugger we figured it was. Evidently our minds are capable of much more amazing flights than we ever dreamed.

And *that* opens up the possibility that reality runs deeper than our limited senses and scientific devices can perceive, that we are connected with more than we know, that our lives aren't defined merely by the time spent between a baby's wail and the final pump of an artificial respirator.

To see whether that possibility really changes anything, try it on for size. Go ahead... imagine that you are immortal. Human life becomes no less precious, maybe even *more* so when measured against eternity. At the same time, death becomes less foreboding, if not less real.

And the reality beyond, if we're even that interested in it anymore, will be revealed in due course.

INCARNATION

Incarnation literally means "to take on a body." Which sounds a lot like science fiction to some people if only because it presumes we have an identity *without* a body.

Hindus believe we do. Most Christians and Muslims and New Agers believe we do. And the very same component of Who We Are that is said to survive death is what first "incarnates" by taking on a body. Or being given a body. Or by coming into existence by means of a body.

And any way you look at it, it does sound a lot like science fiction.

Of course, the Christian use of the word Incarnation (with a capital "I") refers to the mysterious, once-time-only event wherein *God* took on a body, living on planet Earth in the form of Jesus of Nazareth, and as a result of which we are left with another term right out of science fiction: Son of God.

The Son, who presumably had an identity apart from the fully human form that was eventually nailed to a cross—or else the term "incarnation" would make no sense—took on the fleshly clothing of humanity "...and dwelt among us." Whether the Son has retained (or *must* retain) a resurrected body of flesh and bone after concluding his earthly obligations is a matter of theological debate. The fact that similar debates caused splits and heresies and power struggles in the early Church only goes to show how seriously some people took the issue.

The greater issue, perhaps, is the idea of incarnation (with a small "i") itself. Do bodies require souls or spirits to operate them? Do *all* bodies, or only human bodies? What about slugs and snails, or cats and dogs? Do some human bodies run on auto-pilot, so to speak, without a soul sitting in the driver's seat? Does the soul do any driving at all? Maybe it just sits there like a passenger, hooked up to the body's thoughts and sensations like a kid on the Star Tours ride at Disneyland.

In short, if we are all in some sense incarnated, what is the relationship between this non-physical component, and the bodies we inhabit? The answer to this question, or the failure to regard the question as valid to begin with, will become something like your basic World View. Not your faith exactly, but something that greatly affects your faith.

Because seeing your identity as essentially linked to your particular body makes physical life your Number One Priority. It tends to make people more attentive to physical appearance, to tie one's success or failure to bodily characteristics such as intelligence or skill or athletic ability. It can make you more competitive or even aggressive, more sensual and selfish; but also more active, more involved, ready to barrel through life with a gutsy, go-around-only-once passion that inspires you to do everything, see everything, experience everything.

Not that those who make the traditional body/soul distinction have any less lust for life. One's soul is presumably incarnated for a reason or purpose. Searching for that purpose may lead you to become a bit more introspective, yes; but it can also turn life into a kind of giant classroom where the objects and people inhabiting it become crucial to your education, where everything matters, where physical objects become tools not merely to transform other physical objects, but tools for transforming Who You Are.

Physical life is full of rich, sensual experiences and moments of jaw-dropping awe; and religious traditions do well to celebrate its raw beauty and simple pleasures. But the physical world is only part of it. To allow "incarnation" to mean something is to open up another dimension where additional resources are hidden, and a deeper, more exciting sense of self awaits our discovery.

One of the most powerful messages of Christianity, shared equally by Hinduism, revolves around this theme of divinity incarnating "in the flesh." The message is two-fold: First, that if God (or the gods) feel the human body is worth putting on, then having bodies must be a good thing. Secondly, when God (or divinity) is in the driver's seat, the body is capable of extraordinary things.

If only we would embody *that,* we might accomplish extraordinary things, too.

INFIDEL

From the Latin root, *fide,* meaning "fidelity" or "faithfulness," an infidel is a person who is *not* faithful. The word is most often associated with Islam, and is routinely misunderstood not only by members of that tradition, but others as well.

Christians, for example, think they are regarded by Muslims as infidels because they don't accept Muhammad as Prophet or the Qur'an as God's word. Which, as a matter of practice, is indeed how many Muslims view Christians. As a matter of theology, however, both sides are sorely mistaken.

Because an individual's *un*faithfulness presupposes that he or she *was* faithful at some point in the past. Example: My being unfaithful to Elizabeth presumes that I was once devoted and faithful to her. Maybe even madly in love. But if I never truly committed myself to Elizabeth (i.e. we were "just friends," say), or if I didn't even know her to begin with, there are no grounds for accusing me of infidelity.

Technically, the vast majority of Christians—or Jews, Hindus and atheists, for that matter—cannot be unfaithful to Islam simply because they were never faithful to Islam in the first place. Only Muslims who once "knew" and committed themselves to Islam, but then renounced the tradition by converting to another, technically qualify as infidels.

The prescribed punishment for the Muslim infidel is death. This rather extreme measure may have been understandable when the new religion was fighting for its very existence. The surrounding tribes who labeled Muhammad's early followers as traitors for their strict monotheism were reportedly relentless in trying to woo them back to the pagan ways of their fathers. And the possibility that someone who had accepted Islam's revolutionary teachings might later renounce them threatened not only the confidence of the original Muslim converts but the viability of the early Islamic community. Death threats were a convincing antidote. Just as they'd been for the medieval Church when its Inquisition sought to eliminate its own infidels—not merely by putting them to death, but by inflicting the most hideous tortures beforehand.

But that was then. This is now. Which leads to two conclusions:

First, the global community of Islam, with over a billion-and-a-half adherents, is no longer fighting for its existence. "Death to the infidels" is therefore no longer a necessary battle cry. And if there are those who think it is, their extremism speaks volumes about their *own* infidelity... to Muhammad's explicit assurance that "There is no compulsion in religion," for one thing. *And* to the claim that Islam is a tradition worthy of adherence on its own merits, not because unbelievers will be stoned, shot or decapitated.

Secondly, it should be increasingly clear that humankind's sacred texts were meant primarily for, and often *only* for, the communities and the conditions that existed at the time during which they were written. It is our job today to understand the historical context of those scriptures—all of them, from the Qur'an to the Bible, from the I Ching to the Vedas—and to adjust the meanings we draw from them in light of this broader historical perspective.

If we don't, perhaps it is *we* who are being unfaithful... to the truth.

INITIATION

"Beginning"—that's what it means literally.

But even as far back as the Mystery Schools that competed with early Christianity, the term referred to the intensive training and trials an "initiate" had to endure before he could begin his new life, or his new mission. Like the hazing required to join a college fraternity, initiation has always been considered a physical or mental ordeal, a demanding test of one's commitment and worthiness. Because, to put it bluntly, it's not just anybody who has the right stuff.

And that's as it should be. After all, every job demands specific skills and the passion to perform them. Only qualified pilots can fly a 747 and land us safely at our destination. Only seasoned firefighters can face the flames and put them out. Only an ordained minister has the background to weave a compelling sermon, the knowledge of scripture to quote a few relevant verses when a parishioner needs guidance, and the organizational skills to build a thriving spiritual community.

Okay, okay—so the latter example is just the ideal. Every now and then a candidate will pass the initiation, but fail to measure up when the real test comes, when preparation meets practice, when "book larnin'" is applied to the real world.

Or maybe the initiation is too easy, so almost everyone who tries can pass the test. "Accept Jesus as Lord, and be saved." *Really?* "Knock and the door will open." Seriously? It's just that simple—?

Of course not. Initiation into the kind of life we desire is rarely a slam dunk or a walk in the park. We need to work at it. Developing skills, whether physical or spiritual, requires commitment and, most of all, concrete acts that demonstrate our worthiness. Some of us are still trying to pass the test. For many of us, initiation is the whole point. It takes up our whole life, and we never *do* pass the test. Or at least we're never sure we have.

And looking back, that too is as it should be.

INNER CHILD

A concept many people associate with New Age spirituality, Inner Child recalls scriptural passages as ancient as the Old Testament, and as orthodox as, well, Greek Orthodox. "And a child shall lead them," says a verse from Isaiah. "Except ye become as little children, ye shall not enter the kingdom..." proclaims a passage from the New Testament.

Such verses remind us of the pure, wide-eyed innocence of our "lost childhood," the deeply-felt experience that we are born into a world of awesome diversity and endless surprise and, as Genesis says in so many words, "It's all good." In Christian and Islamic doctrine, the loss of this innocence is a symptom of The Fall. In 12-Step recovery programs, restoring and healing this "child" is the paradigm for building a solid foundation for the emotional adult we're meant to be.

In a more symbolic sense, the Inner Child represents the endless potential all humans possess, and why we'll never grow up even when we are adults. Because there will always be more for us to learn. Because the possibilities for what we can do and *be* is an inexhaustible wellspring. Because the universe really is endlessly surprising.

And because, if you've read the previous entry, our initiation is still going on.

INSPIRATION

Two types, religiously speaking, should be noted here. The first is a code word describing how certain sacred scriptures came to be written. The Old and New Testaments, for example, are said to be the "inspired" Word of God. Other sacred texts, including the Qur'an, were similarly written with the guidance or inspiration of their respective divinities.

What that means, for some people, is that God/Allah spoke directly to Moses or Muhammad or Matthew—whether audibly or subconsciously or through an angelic intermediary is beside the point—and out of the writer's crow quill pen came the Divine Words just as surely as if they'd been transcribed in Heaven and delivered in the form of a finished manuscript. For people whose only incentive to obey the Ten Commandments is that God dictated them word for word, belief in this kind of inspiration is at least better than the alternative.

For others, the more common understanding of "inspiration" is sufficient. According to this view, writers of scripture were inspired by God in the same way anyone can be inspired to write about any subject: By their conviction that they have something to say that's important and potentially useful to others; by some insight or vision or passion that simply won't stay bottled up inside.

To be inspired by such a vision, and wish that it be conveyed to others, is a natural human experience. Natural... and human. Does that mean the process of committing it to writing might be tainted by human emotion and human fallibility? And are we therefore to conclude that our scriptures might contain errors?

Whatever errors there may be, an even greater one lies in our own failure to look behind the veil of words and struggle with the underlying message. The greater error is our unwillingness to consider the conditions and context that inspired the message in the first place. Because that kind of gut-wrenching, soul-searching, down-and-dirty inspiration is no less, well, *inspiring* than the kind that funnels God's words through a Prophet's ear and sends them ready-made onto the sacred parchment.

In fact it can be *more* inspiring—if only because, in theory, it can happen to any of us. Like the rush you get standing in Yosemite's Big Meadow, between Half Dome and El Capitan, when the sound of passing cars dissolves into the roar of the surrounding waterfalls and you begin to merge with the majesty and beauty and vastness of it all. Like those peak experiences pop psychologists describe, when you suddenly become what you're doing rather than the person who's doing it. Like the power that comes over an artist or a writer, when nothing else matters but the canvas or the manuscript, when the process seems to take over and you lose consciousness of the bills and the heat and that stupid ring-tone on your iPhone, and you're nothing more than a paint brush or a word processor being guided by someone else's hands.

Which brings us, ironically, back to the first definition of inspiration. The artistic process, it turns out, makes a pretty fair analogy for the method by which scriptures came to be written. Because the artist (or prophet or messenger) may indeed have some artistic talent to get the ball rolling. But the real talent lies in listening to your heart, in hearing one's inner voice, in being receptive to divinity. Then, once the inspiration—literally the *breathing in*—takes effect, you allow your personal identity to fade into the background while the process begins to work through you. Or in spite of you.

It's a magical, mystical thing. A bona fide religious experience. And when it's over, it's as if Ultimate Reality has spoken.

In truth, it *has.*

INTENTION

An especially important concept for Muslims, intention is the Gold Standard for Allah's/God's judgment. If your intention or "will"—defined as your "consciously formulated motive"—is pure and righteous, you earn another ounce or two of precious metal to counter-balance the lead weight of your sins. The *outcome* of your intention, assuming you act on it and don't just think about it, isn't what matters. What makes all the difference is the intention itself. And it just so happens that Allah/God can read our intentions a lot more clearly than we can.

This focus may have been Islam's solution to the Christian/Jewish debate about "faith versus works." Whereas belief in Jesus ("faith" for Christians) was sufficient to earn one's heavenly reward, Jews emphasized works. Action, *behavior,* was the bottom line. It wasn't enough merely to feel pity for the poor, or sorrow for the sinner. Actually feeding and clothing the less fortunate is what Judaism demanded. Making a genuine attempt to change the evil-doer's ways, not just condemning him, was the path toward salvation. Both for his sake and ours.

Muhammad, on the other hand, knew that trying to help the poor can sometimes have the opposite effect, and that our best efforts to turn sinners into saints are unsuccessful more often than not. Which is why our well-intentioned efforts are enough. Act with a pure heart, the Qur'an implies, and leave the outcome to God.

That last sentence is not only crucial to Islamic tradition, but even more so for newer forms of spirituality. Because intention isn't merely a "motive" formulated by our "will." According to New Thought, intention is what literally opens the conduit to Divine Consciousness. As a result, not only do we receive the cosmic energy to act on our intentions, we enlist the cooperative efforts of others who share our goals.

In either case, intention is basic to our humanity. Whether purely personal or linked to the Divine, it's what separates us from all other living things. Handle with care.

INTERCESSION

Whatever the causes of his drinking, the boozer who's about to climb into his coupé and charge out onto the highway needs to be stopped. Someone's got to step between him and his Honda, take away his keys, give him a ride home and put him to bed before he puts someone else in a box. You can worry about his drinking problem later. Right now he needs somebody to do what he's unable or unwilling to do for himself.

The plain truth is, sometimes we just can't seem to do for ourselves what bloody well needs to be done. Or we're too far gone to *know* what needs to be done, and we don't even notice the cliff our Hondas are about to sail off. Maybe we're in the grip of an addiction: Drugs, alcohol, food, sex; the ponies or dice; dead-end relationships or dead-end careers. Or maybe we're simply in one of life's ruts and don't have a clue how to haul ourselves out. Sooner or later virtually everyone comes up against a rock that won't budge, or the nasty little notion that we can't save our own hides. Not without help, anyway.

"Intercession" is a fancy Latin term for getting help. The concept is built around the admittedly archaic model of a king and his subjects, where the subject is too lowly to merit an audience before his highness and therefore requires a third party to represent him. This representative is known as the Intercessor. ("Mediator" has much the same meaning.) Sometimes the subject asks the Intercessor to speak to the king on his behalf. Sometimes the Intercessor takes the initiative without the subject's knowledge or permission, perhaps because he sees a problem the subject doesn't, or can't.

You can create any number of scenarios based on this model, though it's pretty obvious from a religious point of view who the king is and who the subjects are. The identity of the Intercessor/mediator is another matter.

For Protestant Christians, the Intercessor is Jesus, and the intercession has already taken place. By merely accepting him as our representative in the Heavenly Court, we are saved and our sins forgiven. Jesus can then continue to intercede for us through our prayers to him. Roman Catholics also enjoy a whole cadre of lesser intercessors, from the Virgin Mary to various saints, any of whom are authorized to stand in for us. After all, why bother the Son of God with every little problem?

Hinduism and New Age also embrace the concept of intercession. With millions of gods to choose from, Hindus can select whatever conduit to divinity seems most convenient or most effective. (And for some Hindus—who remain loyal Hindus despite this—Jesus is also a viable option.) The ultimate source of power is the same in any case.

A common New Age approach is simply to *invent* an intercessor, at least if none of the traditional candidates seems the right fit. Jesus or Buddha might work for many people; but another figure from history, or a deceased relative—or even a fantasy figure who exists only in one's mind—can also do the job. The key is that the intercessor be perceived as sympathetic and caring, that he or she fully accepts you as you are right now, while representing some higher image of Who You Can Be. In this way, intercession becomes a mechanism of Faithspeak, helping transform you from your old self to new, from sinner to saved, bridging that yawning chasm between humanity and divinity.

Of course, there are many who claim that no third party is necessary. If the human form was good enough for God to incarnate himself in, surely it's good enough to make an appearance before the Divine Tribunal. Besides, we are made in God's image, aren't we? That means we can intercede for ourselves, thank you.

Except for that fallen-down drunk who doesn't know he's a hazard to himself and to everybody else on the road. So if we accept the notion that we can intercede for ourselves, we must also accept the responsibility to intercede for each other.

Which, many people would also claim, is precisely The Message behind the message of every religious tradition.

ISLAM

Over the past few decades, no religion has forced itself into our awareness and our daily headlines with as much drama—and, some would say, as much revulsion—as Islam. In a way, that public notoriety recalls the religion's first few decades.

At a time when the Arab world was still a tangle of feuding, barbaric tribes who worshipped a variety of pagan deities, Islam suddenly appeared with its message of One God, a strict code of moral conduct, and a revitalizing sense of purpose and identity. Since this insurgent monotheism was so different from existing practices, early converts were branded by fellow Arabs as *Muslim,* which literally means "traitors."

Despite being targeted and sometimes slaughtered, these traitors swiftly took over a geographic area larger than all of Christendom, from Northwest Africa across the Mideast to India and Southeast Asia. That effort was accomplished as much by missionary zeal as by sword, which is probably no worse (and no better) than the rise of Christianity through armed crusades and forced conversions. Islam, however, instituted a program of tolerance for other monotheistic religions within its territories, a practice certainly better than the way Christians treated Jews or Muslims under *their* dominion.

Other cultures were likewise tolerated and preserved in those early decades. Muslim authorities, in fact, created vast libraries to house the Greek and Roman writings that fell into their possession, along with other cultural artifacts and treasures. As things turned out, most of the West's inheritance of Greco-Roman philosophy, history and science—otherwise destroyed by the Holy Roman Empire (with the blessing of the Church)—was preserved and reclaimed through Islamic sources. The West owes a huge debt to Islam for that largely unacknowledged act.

The newly-enlightened West also rediscovered its passion for justice and humane treatment of the poor through the example of Islam. It has been said that the ethics of Islam consist of Jesus' Sermon on the Mount translated into daily life. And as much as women are still subjugated under many Islamic cultures today, Islamic law advanced women's rights far beyond the existing Christian world by enforcing a husband's responsibilities and imposing severe penalties for prostitution.

In orthodox Islamic society, there are still no brothels, no taverns for the consumption of alcohol, no gambling houses, as well as a tradition of interpersonal communication that is both respectful and without profanity. If there are Ayatollahs who label the United States and Western culture in general as The Great Satan, it is because the social liberalism of the West openly allows certain kinds of behavior Islam considers immoral and evil. For a religio-centric culture that has had little experience in dealing with female equality, drinking, gambling and other secular freedoms, the influence of the West—despite the many benefits it might bring—is a frightening specter.

And out of that fear has come many of the activities that have given Islam such a poor public image lately: The terrorism ignorantly conceived to purge Western influence; the ongoing conflict with modern Israel, (which is regarded less as a rebirth of the ancient Jewish state than a base for spreading Western ideology); as well as the totalitarian excesses of Islamic overlords and strongmen whom their subjects embraced primarily because they couldn't see any other option.

But the actions of certain Muslims—ISIS, Al Qaida, Boko Haram; take your pick—should not define Islam any more than Jim Jones or Timothy McVeigh can be said to represent Christianity. No individual or group of individuals can stand for an entire religion.

So what does the religion of Islam stand for?

The tradition basically revolves around what's known as the Five

Pillars, which together are designed to uphold the Muslim's faith. The First Pillar represents a belief in the oneness or Unity of The God (in Arabic, "Al Lah"). The words of the "Kalima"—*La ilaha illallah*—are reminiscent of the Jewish *Sh'ma:* "There is no god other than the One God." The opening prayer of the Qur'an is addressed to "The Merciful One, the Compassionate One... Whom alone we serve, to Whom alone we cry for help..." And to whom, according to this basic tenet, the Muslim must submit totally. The word "Islam," in fact, means "submission," or "the peace that flows from submission."

The Second Pillar consists of the five-times-a-day recitation of prayers, called *Salat,* a communal and/or individual practice that not only enforces one's continuing awareness of divinity, but builds a sense of solidarity with fellow Muslims everywhere. No matter what he's doing, or where he's doing it, the devout Muslim kneels, faces the holy city of Mecca and prays at the appointed hour. As in Christianity or Judaism or Hinduism, praying with genuine intention and not merely "going through the motions" is what counts.

The third major element is charity, or *Zakat.* Every Muslim is obligated to donate at least one-fortieth of his annual wealth—which includes not just one's yearly income but the value all one's current possessions. Up to ten percent is not unheard of. And since Islam is not nearly as institutionalized a religion as, say, Christianity, zakat isn't likely to be spent on the mortgage for the new mosque or the imam's salary. It is intended primarily for needy people. That, after all, is what charity and tithing are *for.*

Fasting is the Fourth Pillar. During the holy month of Ramadan, or at other times for one's spiritual cleansing, the Muslim denies himself food, water or sex between dawn and dusk. Ideally, one who fasts also refrains from hearing, seeing or even thinking about anything "unclean." Try *that* sometime. If nothing else, you'll learn a little humility.

The pilgrimage to Mecca, known as the *Hajj,* is the Fifth Pillar, required by all Muslims at least once during their lifetime—assuming they can afford it. Which isn't such a bad idea, either. As with Christians and Jews who visit the Holy Land or Buddhists who visit the monasteries of Tibet—or Americans who visit their national shrines in Washington, D.C.—the act of treading on the same ground as one's ancestors can be an effective way to ground oneself in the tradition. A religion becomes more tangible, more compelling, when the places mentioned in its sacred writings turn out to be real, when its geographic roots (if not its spiritual roots) can be seen and touched and experienced directly.

Not to mention that, as Sufi mystics taught, the pilgrimage to Mecca symbolizes the soul's journey back to its Source. It recalls the journey from the mundane world in which we live and work to the deeper reality from which that world originates, and to which we all return at the end of our physical lives. Pure Faithspeak, that.

As with all traditions that employ Faithspeak, the highest goal is not the outward activity of going to Mecca, or the fasting, or the praying or donating to charity. It is the effect all of these activities have on one's attitude and behavior, on one's faith. To quote from the Qur'an:

> *It is not piety, that you turn your faces*
> * to the East and to the West.*
> *True piety is this:*
> *To believe in God and the Last Day,*
> * the angels, The Book, and the Prophets;*
> *To give of one's substance, however*
> * cherished, to kinsmen and orphans,*
> * the needy, the traveler,*
> *Beggars, and to ransom the slave...*
> *For they who fulfill their agreements...*
> *And endure with fortitude*
> *Misfortune, hardship and peril...*
> *Are they who are true in their faith.*

The Five Pillars are only the outward, physical supports for the Muslim's inner, spiritual foundation. After all, some kind of structural supports—call them pillars or doctrines or traditions—seem to be required to get the Good News through our thick skulls. And Islam continues to be one of the world's primary resources for spreading it.

Despite what recent headlines might say.

ISRAEL

The name first appears in the Biblical account of Abraham's grandson, Jacob, after he spends one momentous night wrestling with "an angel of God." The very next morning Jacob is called by his new Hebrew name, *Yisroel,* which we've anglicized to "Israel." His descendants were thereafter known as Israelites, and the nation they established several hundred years later called Israel. Some decades after the reign of King Solomon, the name would be applied specifically and only to the Hebrews' Northern Kingdom, as opposed to the Southern Kingdom of Judah, from which the term "Jude" or "Jew" derives.

Names, in Hebrew tradition as well as most other ancient cultures, were usually symbolic or descriptive of the person to whom they were given. Here, the suffix *el* refers to God. *Yisro* means something like "to struggle," or "wrestler." Hence the translation of the name as "Struggler-for-God," or "Wrestler-with-God."

Throughout their history, the descendants of Jacob/Israel have certainly struggled with, for, against, and over God. More than the name of a legendary figure or Mideast nation, then, "Israel" represents a three-thousand-year-long tradition of struggling with the concept and implications—and reality—of God.

The Hebrews/Israelites/Jews carried on that struggle by themselves for the first thousand-or-so years, at least as far as Western civilization is concerned. Then Christianity joined the struggle, seeing Jacob/Israel as their ancestor too, but visualizing their divine wrestling partner in a more *human*-ized fashion. Islam jumped into the fray in the seventh century CE, likewise claiming Jacob as a founding member of their wrestling team, while insisting that both the Israelites and the Christians were too pooped to finish the contest. Or words to that effect.

The symbolic banner of "Israel" has also been raised more recently. Some of America's founding fathers, for example, saw themselves as the true inheritors of Jacob's struggle. Brigham Young and his rag-tag band of Latter-Day Saints believed they were founding a "new Israel" in the mountains of Utah. Many other Christians speak the name Israel with their own symbolic overtones, sometimes as a synonym for the Body of Christ. Even for contemporary Jews, Israel is not so much a country as a People bound by God's Covenant, whomever or wherever they might reside on the planet.

What troubles many people today—and Muslims throughout the Mideast are only some of the most outspoken—is that it's difficult to continue using "Israel" in this generic, symbolic sense when there is now a specific geo-political entity by that name with barbed-wire borders and self-defense strategies and settlement policies about which we may or may not agree.

Then again, maybe that's the point: The present state of Israel, for all of us, is an opportunity to test just how far that original struggle-with-God has come in the past three thousand years; to find out if the wisdom we've supposedly gained can be applied to some form of corporate life even in the midst of a hostile environment. That's the real, and ongoing, struggle well into the twenty-first century.

And perhaps the only realistic solution is to recognize that the physical world in which we live is entirely the outcome of our internal wrestling with divinity. The existence of Israel as an independent nation is a now a challenge to "put up or shut up"—to finally confront the deeper, Universal Power and shared themes behind the religions that came out of Jacob's ancient struggle.

Can Judaism really live out the vision of justice and wholeness its prophets proclaimed, and thereby become a "light to the nations"? Can Christianity save humankind from that brutish, selfish side of our species and infuse us instead with redeeming Love? Will Islam live up to the simplistic stereotype of a prideful, saber-rattling code of the desert, or fulfill its destiny as a bestower of mercy and creator of harmony for all?

Now's your chance, people. Show us your stuff. There's lifetimes of study, five prayers a day, sweet hymns to Jesus and all the collective resources that parade as religion. And then there's plain ol' down-to-earth faith: How we act toward one another.

And "Israel" is what it all boils down to.

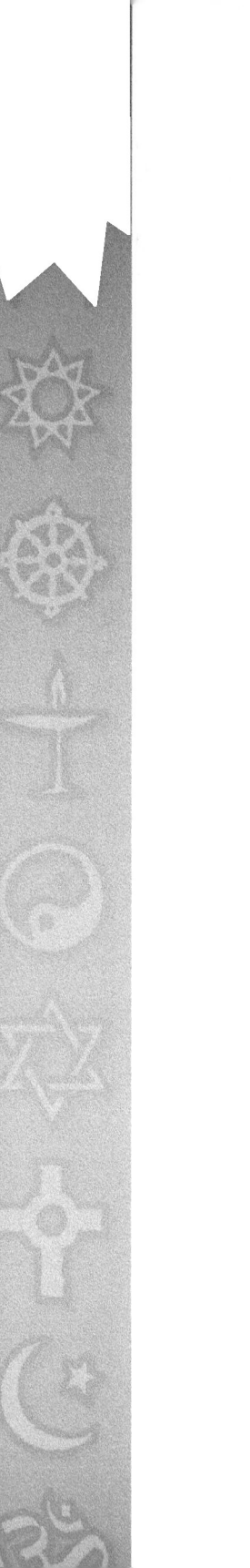

JEHOVAH

This so-called name of God was given to us by the translators of the King James Bible.

By mistake.

Biblical scholars tell us that the oldest manuscripts of the Holy Bible were written without vowels, and often without spaces between words or periods at the ends of sentences. They were, after all, originally intended as a kind of shorthand for priests and cantors who memorized the text by hearing and repeating the spoken word—not by leisurely reading the text as seminarians and church-goers do today. Since parchment was precious and everything was inscribed by hand, it was far more efficient to leave out the spaces and write down only the consonants.

Unfortunately, scholars who weren't part of that priestly circle had a tough job putting the spaces and vowels back in, which has produced numerous mistakes in pronunciation if not meaning. The four-letter word YHWH, by which God revealed himself to Moses as the "I Am That I Am," is one such example.

The problem with this word is all the more understandable since no one was allowed to utter it except the High Priest. And then only a few times during the Day of Atonement, mostly beyond earshot of all but a few penitents standing outside the Jerusalem temple's Holy of Holies. By the sixteenth century CE, the correct pronunciation was known only to a handful of Jews, none of whom happened to be members of King James' royal court.

So the King's translators prayed for divine guidance and took their best linguistic shot. The result was *Jehovah.*

Of course, some bright scholar later thought to ask the folks who carried on the priestly tradition, and who had reason to know how the word was actually pronounced. The proper way to say it, they replied, was "*Yah*-weh." But please *don't* say it, they added. Because some names—or better yet, spiritual concepts—are simply too sacred and too expansive to encase in syllables, or slip into the latest joke about the priest, the evangelist, and the rabbi when they walk into a bar. So you should maybe have a little respect, *nuh?*

Even today, Jews who come across "YHWH" while reading their prayer books will, without so much as an instant's hesitation, substitute the generic word *Adonai,* meaning "Lord." Our own use of words and names can likewise reveal how much, or how little, we respect other people and things. The use of "boy" for a whole class of human beings, for instance; or calling women of all ages "girls"; or the increasing practice of addressing teachers and parents by their first names—these become not merely words and names, but messages. And they not only reflect current attitudes, they teach those attitudes to future generations. In a sense, they help create the world we live in. Words are *that* powerful.

Like God/YHWH/Jehovah speaking the words, "Let there be light."

And suddenly there was light.

JERUSALEM

The Hebrew word for "peace" (or "wholeness") is *shalom.* The Arabic equivalent is *salaam.* The anglicized version, Salem, has become a common name for cities throughout the Western world.

Jerusalem, from the Hebrew *Yerushalayim,* was the Canaanite city chosen by King David around 1,000 BCE to be the capital of Israel. The city fell to conquering armies in later centuries; it was again capital of the Roman territory of Judea when Jesus rode triumphantly through its gates only to drag his cross back out; and it was the site from which the

Messenger Muhammad later ascended into heaven. No wonder Jerusalem continues to be the focus of religious contention, as well as both political and military conflict.

Which is ironic, if not downright depressing. Especially since Jerusalem means City of Peace.

Although not exactly. In delving into the meanings that make up its original Semitic roots—and noting that *shalayim* is the pluralization of the word "shalom"—we come up with a more nuanced translation. The name "Jerusalem" implies something more like "The foundation for the elements of peace," or less literally, "The community that strives to achieve wholeness."

Jerusalem, it so happens, was always meant to be more than a nation's capital, just as "Israel" symbolizes more than a nation. It was designed to showcase the peace and wholeness people can achieve through a faith built on a transformative relationship with divinity. It was meant to demonstrate in blocks of stone, cobbled streets and inspired citizens what the Holy Spirit could do.

Not that Jerusalem has ever fully lived up to that ideal. For that matter, neither has Belfast or Beijing, Berlin or Birmingham.

How's *your* hometown by comparison?

JESUS

Almost from the beginning, the notion of an "historical Jesus" has existed right alongside the Jesus presented in orthodox Christian tradition. Most people, in fact, recognize that there's often a disparity between the plain, unvarnished truth about someone or something, and the version that eventually gets packaged for public consumption. The problem is, what one person believes to be plainly true is pure propaganda to the next guy.

The Jews, for example, couldn't agree whether Jesus was a prophet, a Messiah, or just another rabble-rouser like the dozens of other itinerant preachers of that era. The Greeks and Romans caught wind of the many first- and second-hand accounts circulating after his death, put their own spin on them, all of which were eventually rated as authentic or *not* authentic by the early Church. Various schools of thought sprung up to defend this or that view of Jesus' life-and-death, or to champion one or the other of the Gospels recounting it. An official pronouncement about Jesus wasn't formalized for another three hundred years, and then promulgated by Emperor Constantine largely to stamp out heresies and consolidate his own imperial power base.

Not that the so-called heresies *were* stamped out. Over succeeding centuries the Gnostics, Valentinians, Arians, Cathari and Albigenses resurrected the claim that Jesus was no more than human—or not human at all. Similar post-Reformation heresies evolved into Unitarianism, Christian Science and other spiritual movements, with Jesus ranging from a humble rabbi to a purely mental "image of God" whose flesh and blood were as illusory as our own temporal bodies.

In other words, *Will the real Jesus please stand up?*

Or, as Governor Pilate said to a reportedly blood-thirsty mob after Jesus' trial, "Behold the man!"

The man, first of all, was a Jew. All his life. He was never, not for a nanosecond, a Christian. Jesus—which is Aramaic for the Hebrew name variously rendered as Yehoshua, Y'shua or Issa, or the anglicized Joshua—lived and died in the tradition of his biological father and mother and ancestors before him. And like many of those ancestors, he wasn't about to swallow the tradition whole. Nor was he expected to.

Judaism, in practice, has always embraced an almost democratic willingness to debate and reinterpret the Law (Torah) so that it might never lose touch with daily life. At the time of Jesus there were several factions or sects doing exactly that. Jesus clearly knew about them and actively participated in the public debate. Throw in the fact that Nazareth, his hometown, was situated near the crossing of major caravan routes, and you have a diverse social environment that couldn't help but expose Jesus to a wide variety of ideas and experiences, and almost certainly other religions. Including the European "mysteries" and Eastern philosophies early Christianity came to resemble.

Which is not to say that Jesus was an intellectual sort. If anything he was as down-to-earth as human beings can be: A working carpenter (or better, "craftsman") for over twenty years; eldest brother of perhaps seven children, and probably a whiz at weaving bedtime stories; gifted with a fine sense of humor and a quick wit that could easily turn the tables on those who tried to corner him verbally; and often accused of over-indulging in food, wine and the company of common folk.

In short, Jesus was intimate with life as it was lived in first-century Judea. He knew its simple pleasures as well as its traps—including the glaring disparity between rich and poor, the way people could appear religious without really giving a damn, and the fact that the bottom line was what you did for people and why you did it. Posing for the cameras, so to speak, was the last thing on his agenda.

All of these characteristics can be gleaned from the official, church-approved records of Jesus' life. Apocryphal writings and "heretical" gospels often portray him quite differently, giving Jesus a more mystical or supernatural persona, or making him more akin to a wandering Buddhist monk. These other writings were eventually declared invalid because they purportedly distorted the true picture.

But it would be an act of naiveté, if not sheer blindness, to pretend that the true portrayal of Jesus hadn't already undergone substantial change by the time the Church formalized his identity. The fact that his life and dramatic death meshed almost perfectly with the savior/mystery religions already spreading throughout Europe, combined with the fact that the rampant political corruption and moral decay in society left the masses longing for a fundamental overhaul... and considering the fact that the Jews were *still* clamoring for Messianic rescue from foreign occupation (which became a rallying cry for other oppressed people throughout the Roman Empire)... all of these factors clearly exerted tremendous pressure on what was to become "the truth" about Jesus. Regardless of what actually happened.

It's been said with good reason that if the great religious figures of the past could come back today and read about themselves in the world's sacred texts, chances are they'd either fail to recognize the person those stories were about, or they *would* recognize themselves and then go have a good laugh.

Or maybe a good cry. Because the heart of Jesus' message is no closer to realization now than it was 2,000 years ago. Twisted by what we want to hear, ignoring the call for genuine transformation because it might change our lives too much, we have yet to "Behold the man."

Still, the life of Jesus continues to inspire serious study and speculation for Christians and non-Christians alike. Because whatever the historical truth, it was a life that galvanized hundreds of millions of people and therefore inevitably touches *all* our lives. Indeed, the truth of that single human life is no longer what matters most, much as we might like to know it. What's transmitted *through* his story is what counts: Whether we are inspired to follow his example in our own lives, for one thing; or whether his words motivate us to discover deeper truths; whether they draw us into a relationship with the same Ultimate Reality that spoke to him, a reality that defines us all as "sons and daughters of God" and therefore worthy of equal justice and mutual respect.

Which means that Jesus, or our idea of Jesus, or the ideas inspired by the life of Jesus, can still "save" us. And in that sense the so-called historical Jesus is no less our savior than the authorized version prepackaged for public consumption. Except that the historical Jesus could probably care less about getting all the credit.

JIHAD

Here's one of the most unnecessarily frightening words to enter the religious lexicon in recent years. "Frightening" because jihad raises the specter of Islamic terrorists flying jumbo jets into skyscrapers or beheading helpless captives as fodder for the internet. "Unnecessarily" because that specter has no more connection to mainstream Islam than the Holocaust or the Iron Maiden had to mainstream Christianity.

Let's face it: Some people are fanatic and downright loony, and they often take religious ideas out of context and use them to justify their own fanaticism and lunacy. "Jihad" is an easy target for such misuse.

Which is not to say that jihad is one of the kindest and gentlest ideas, either. After all, the Arabic word does connote the concept of Holy War. And one of the two primary interpretations of that concept does justify the use of armed, even ruthless, violence whenever the practice of Islam is threatened.

A similar understanding of holy war is documented in the first few books of the Hebrew Bible. When faced with a threat to its physical or spiritual survival, the tribe or nation was encouraged—no, *required*—to slaughter its opponents down to the last man. Canaanite cities were "laid waste," their idols and places of worship violently torn down. Even women and children could be put to death to prevent non-believers from staging a chromosomal comeback. Considering seventh-century Arabia, it was something of an innovation that Islam counseled against leveling unbelievers' cities or destroying the land's productive resources. And like the Christian definition of holy war—assuming that's not a contradiction in terms—armed violence was permitted only as a last resort, and only after all other legal measures had been exhausted.

But more importantly, this outward kind of Islamic holy war was clearly understood as "the *Lesser* Jihad." A second type, the "Greater Jihad," refers to the more life-transforming, and ongoing, holy war: The inner battle each individual wages against the evil in his own soul.

The literal meaning of the Arabic *jihad,* in fact, is simply "effort" or "struggle." Overcoming one's weaknesses, bad habits and sins requires effort. Finding a higher purpose in life than the pursuit of pleasure or comfort is a struggle. And winning that inner battle must be our primary goal because, if we can't transform ourselves, we certainly have no right to impose our religious laws and traditions on anyone else.

So the greater struggle is always *within.* Jihad is therefore a call for personal transformation of the same kind every religion encourages. As Sufi Muslims would later contend, even the Lesser Jihad should be understood only as a symbol, a graphic allegory, for this struggle-with-self. The call to arms merely depicts the fervor with which we must root out our own evil inclinations. The practice of killing every last remnant of "the Infidel" illustrates that the job requires more than a quick-fix or half-hearted commitment.

And it's true. The alcoholic mustn't leave even an airline sample of scotch in the kitchen cabinet (or sock drawer). We can't allow ourselves to fudge on our income taxes, even if it's only a few dollars. We can't tell "little white lies," or take something that's not ours "just this once," or commit adultery because "no one will ever find out." Minor dishonesty inevitably breeds the major kind. We must be ruthless with our faults, Islam tells us, in the same way Christianity says to "pluck out your own eye" or "cut off your hand" if those physical features continually lead you astray. Better to lose an eye or a hand than your soul.

Jihad, then, is Faithspeak for the internal struggle we all experience. Its graphic imagery can be useful in convincing our heart-of-hearts that the struggle is crucial, and that it can spiritually (if not literally) make the difference between life and death. Because, in the end, it does.

JOY

Lest anyone assume religious traditions are dour, serious enterprises that dwell on death and discipleship and dull-as-a-doorknob sermons, let me remind you of the three-day-long Buddhist New Year celebrated with holiday lights, sumptuous meals, theatrical presentations symbolizing the victory of good over evil... and a few rounds of *saké* or the warmed alcoholic beverage known as *chang.*

Then there's the *Eid al-Fitr* marking the end of Islam's month-long fast. This is another three-day celebration involving gifts of charity, festive gatherings with a focus on family, games for kids, and more sumptuous meals (but no alcohol, please). And let's not forget the spring celebration of Purim, sometimes called the "Jewish Mardi Gras," which is not only festive but downright raucous, involving silly costumes, noisemakers, mildly bawdy skits, and permission to over-indulge in the fermented juice of the grape—a liquor license that's also extended to one of Judaism's most serious holy days, Passover.

The Hindu Festival of Lights, *Diwali,* features not three, but *five* days of singing, dancing and gift-giving, as well as permission to over-indulge in food if not drink. And, not to be outdone, there's the minor Christian holiday that begins with Advent candles, decorations of fake fir trees and electric lights pretending to be candles, spans the better part of a month while celebrants shop for just the right gift (a candle, maybe?), and concludes with musical performances by carolers holding candles while they sing "Joy to the World!"

There are any number of reasons for joy, and for celebrations that express joy within the context of a spiritual community. True, there are also religious sects that frown on fun, that prohibit dancing and games and sex for anything but procreation. But these are the exceptions. Life is just too full of joyful experiences and joy-inducing events: the new job, new home, the first baby, first words, first steps. It's not just that we're happy about these achievement or events; it's that we can barely contain ourselves.

And maybe that's the point. At certain blessed moments in our lives, it suddenly becomes clear that our Self can't be contained, that Who We Are isn't bounded by our body or separated from others, or disconnected from a universe whose rhythms and energies empower us. We are on this journey together. We are part of a larger community in a wider world. We are linked in time and space, spiritually and physically, maybe *meta-*physically; and the emotion produced by that realization doesn't so much well up within us as shower down on us from above, and onto everybody else in our proximity.

Religious celebrations are opportunities to practice joy, even if they sometimes seem artificial, even if our lives have been filled with sorrow lately. We are not only allowed but obliged to take advantage of them, to at least go through the motions. You'll be surprised at how easily you get caught up. Or showered down on.

And be patient. Because it's only a matter of time before the real thing comes along, maybe with only a few sprinkles at first. And then it's as if the heavens break wide open.

JUDAISM

Your average encyclopedia calls Judaism the "first great monotheistic religion"; that is, the first religion to proclaim a belief in One God. Most historians would agree, despite the short-lived efforts of the Egyptian pharaoh Akhenaton some centuries earlier.

But historic Judaism, in a sense, is not so much a religion proclaiming the Oneness of God, as a tradition of *coming to realize* the Oneness of God. The early Hebrews, precursors to the descendants of Judah—i.e. Jews—were not truly monotheistic. They were what anthropologists call *heno*-theistic. Like most of their neighbors, they acknowledged the existence of several gods, some of whom they even recognized as fairly stiff competition. But they pledged their allegiance to only one god, the "most high" god, the Lord of Lords, the god who was not only the strongest, but the most righteous and most devoted to his earthly children. Let the other nations worship their inferior gods, their ghastly deities who devoured children, the ones who could not ultimately save their people. We've got the King of Kings on our side.

It was hardly unusual for the ancients to brag about their own tribal deity in the same way. Most of them thought their particular god was Number One or they wouldn't have bothered with all those bloody sacrifices. What was unusual about the Hebrews was their growing realization that there really *was* only one God, a single Lord of the Universe who was no less the God of other peoples than he was of them.

Culminating in the era of The Prophets during the seventh and sixth centuries BCE, a whole new mind-set began to sweep through the tradition. And looking back on their own history, the Hebrews/Jews could see this single God revealing Himself little by little—first as a jealous god contending with Baal and Moloch and dozens of other deities, then as "the Almighty" who had appeared to Moses on Sinai, and finally as the divine Unity "beside whom there is no other."

When only partially (or mistakenly) perceived by humans, this Unity appeared as other, lesser gods who demanded obedience to laws that were elitist, even evil. But perceived in all his/its fullness and glory, the Unity could be recognized as the Wonderful, the Counselor, the Mighty God from whom goodness and mercy and justice flowed to all people.

But despite this new, prophetic vision of God, believers weren't exactly rushing to fulfill their destiny as "a Light to the Nations." Those lesser gods were still seducing certain of the Twelve Tribes. Not to mention that the nation as a whole was in dire straights. The Northern Kingdom fell to invading armies in 721 BCE. Judah was defeated a few decades later and its most accomplished citizens carted off to Babylon like booty from the Temple. Then came the continuing occupations of the Greeks and Romans. All of these outward struggles were ascribed to the Jews' falling in and out of their proper relationship with God. (Remember the "wrestling" analogy?)

In a similar way, Jewish history can be looked on as a parable for our own personal struggles to comprehend and "obey" God; or in modern lingo, to transform our faith in accordance with an increasingly accurate view of Ultimate Reality. Because the more our faith is informed and guided by that One Reality, the more our lives become harmonious and productive and blessed. When it's not, our divine potential is taken captive, our lives laid waste like the smoldering cities of Israel.

But monotheism is only part of Judaism's legacy. The fact is, most people simply don't have the kind of prophetic vision that can transform their faiths and give meaning to their lives. The world can't wait for everyone to become an Elijah or Isaiah—or a Buddha or Jesus or Muhammad. Judaism therefore evolved a code of conduct based on their sages' deepest convictions about God. Many of us will never have a direct experience of the Divine Unity, Jewish tradition said in effect; but here's how you'd want to live your life if you *had.* Just follow these 613 regulations and ordinances and you shouldn't get too far off track.

And so, as with Buddhism, the bottom line became an ethical life. A class of Judaic scholars and teachers soon arose to help interpret the regulations and resolve any disputes. Discovering exactly what was required, and then living according to the "letter of the law" was seen as the way to serve God.

Of course, it was this kind of legalism that Jesus took issue with, as did many other Jews before and since. The prophet Micah complained about the same problem hundreds of years earlier. At that time, many people apparently conflated the making of ritual sacrifices with being religious. Offering the burnt flesh of a newborn calf was mistaken for serving God. To which Micah responded (in his best King's English), "...What doth the Lord require of thee? Only to do justly, and to love mercy, and to walk humbly with thy God." Skip the veal flambé, please.

Maybe it was his way of saying that the proverbial lightning bolt wouldn't strike you dead if you ate a ham sandwich once in a while, or forgot to say your morning prayers, or mowed your lawn on the Sabbath. All those sacrificial offerings and laws and regulations were meant only to make you a good person. And if you would only *be* a good person—if you would serve God by caring for your family, dealing honestly with your fellow human beings and helping the needy now and then—then you will have fulfilled all the laws in spirit.

Which doesn't necessarily make things any easier, God knows. The spirit of the law often turns out to be more difficult to obey than the letter. And in trying to find a balance between the two, Judaism was eventually forced to rethink and renew itself, much like Christianity did, through its own Reformation. The grip of strict orthodoxy was finally loosened in the Eighteenth Century. The Reform Movement promptly replaced Hebrew liturgy with "the vernacular," just as Luther insisted on bringing German into the Latin Mass. The movement also eliminated daily practices that no longer seemed relevant to modern life.

A second movement, Conservative Judaism, agreed that orthodoxy had lost much of its relevance, but insisted that many of its seemingly outdated laws and rituals were worth preserving. Since Jews had been dispersed from their homeland to every corner of the planet; since they were continually branded as scapegoats for anything that went wrong; since Jews had survived and even thrived under these conditions by maintaining those supposedly irrelevant traditions, perhaps there was something in them that shouldn't be tossed out so lightly.

A more recent movement, Reconstructionist Judaism, recognizes the preceding three—Orthodox, Reform and Conservative—as valued expressions of the same Spirit and the same People. It now seeks to integrate them all, combining them with the principles of democracy and local autonomy.

Beyond this Reconstructionism, perhaps, is the process of integration that would recognize not just Jewish movements, but different religions as valuable expressions of the same Spirit. And that, it just so happens, is what many Jews believe will bring, or in essence *be,* their long-awaited Messiah.

JUDEO-CHRISTIAN

If we consider this compound word as a noun, there's probably no such animal. Using it as an adjective makes it only slightly less problematic.

Jews, especially, are uncomfortable with its use, in the sense that "Judeo" seems to signify the opening chapters of a story that came to its divinely-appointed climax in the birth, death, and resurrection of

Jesus of Nazareth. The Jewish tradition, of course, sees itself as a complete story in its own right—or rather, as an *ongoing* story—that doesn't need Christianity's help to remain a vital, living tradition which continues to nourish the souls of millions of people. In fact, if it weren't for the centuries-long efforts of its younger spin-off to persecute and preferably stamp it out, Judaism might have gone on to become the globe-spanning religion Christianity became.

Contemporary Christianity, for the most part, now sees its legacy of Jewish persecution as a blood-stain on its history, and an affront to its own highest ideals. On the other hand, many theologians, both Christian and Jewish, admit that the Judaism of the early Common Era had probably spread about as far as it was ever going to, with practices that were designed for a specific time and place, and laws that were too alien and restrictive for the wider world. It is in this sense that some of these same theologians regard Christianity as "what Judaism had to become" in order for the Greco-Roman world to accept its deeper truths... about compassion, social justice, and life-transforming love.

It is also in this sense that "Judeo-Christian" has served as a useful adjective to describe a long tradition of spiritual development connecting humankind's earliest aspirations with today's ongoing quest for justice and peace. Adding Islam to the Judeo-Christian narrative gives us another adjective—as in the three "Abrahamic" traditions—knitting together an even more compelling epic through their common patriarchs and prophetic lineage.

"Unitarian Universalist" is the adjective applied to one of the newer spiritual traditions whose two main components grew out of Protestantism some three centuries ago. This one not only sees its storyline running through the Abrahamic trio, but also finds nourishment in the wisdom of Eastern traditions and earth-centered practices, tempering all of these with the findings of modern science.

What's the adjective—or adjectives—that best describe *your* story? Insofar as you bind yourself to it, or them, you'll begin to understand what your own religion is made from.

JUDGMENT

The word "judgment" is theological shorthand for the proposition that *Everything matters.* Or in other words, that all acts, no matter how seemingly insignificant, affect and contribute to Who We Are.

The Biblical "Day of Judgment," of course, is dramatized in the language of kings and their loyal (or disloyal) subjects. At the end of one's earthly existence, according to this scenario, each person is brought before the Heavenly Court. The Book of Life is opened, and one's good and bad deeds—even one's thoughts—are stacked on the divine scales like some Wells Fargo agent assaying your nuggets. If your good deeds outweigh the bad, you get a Gold Account. If not, prepare to exit through the back door. And bring along some very strong sunscreen.

For a wonderful, lyrical update on this theme, rent or download Albert Brooks' movie, *Defending Your Life*. Here, instead of God or Allah or Christ in the judgment seat, the movie portrays a pair of judges, one male, one female, who appear to be quite human (albeit more advanced), while equally human prosecuting and defense attorneys argue your case. If you win, you graduate to another, more advanced level of existence, or directly to Celestial Retirement. If you lose, you must repeat the same level until certain crucial lessons are learned.

The idea of being evaluated according to your behavior—which is the outward expression of what you've learned—is common to most Western traditions. The aspect of being recycled until you pass some important lesson, however, is very Eastern. Hinduism and New Age embrace the notion that a single, end-of-life Judgment doesn't express the full depth of Love or infinite goodness built into the Scheme of Things. Bad behavior is still judged harshly, and even punished with terrible consequences (i.e. karma). But there is no length to which God will not go to insure that we eventually pass The Final Test, even if it takes a hundred lifetimes, or a thousand. And since "judgment" is derived from the same Hebrew word which means "deliverance," passing that Test implies our being delivered from repeating the cycle, from having to continue learning our life lessons. At that point we've been saved.

But deliverance or salvation is strictly a one-step-at-a-time operation. The concept of judgment is Faithspeak's way of making us pay attention to the individual steps, of forcing us to realize that we are accountable to ourselves and to others with every thought and deed; that we have the responsibility of choosing the low road or the high, Hollywood Boulevard or the Straight and Narrow, or a little of both. And if we fail to take some other path when it might have been better for us, at least we ought to have a good reason.

JUSTIFICATION

Here's another one of those officious-sounding concepts that theologians define and dissect as if they're talking about some natural process like photosynthesis or molecular attraction.

Actually it *is* a natural process, even though Christianity's first theologian, Saint Paul, made it sound as unnatural as a lecture on chewing your food. With the classic Greek affinity for analyzing and categorizing everything, Paul broke up the process of salvation into artificially separate components. "Justification" was submitted as the first step.

Put simply, justification means "finding peace with God." It means discovering your missing link to Ultimate Reality and thereby recovering wholeness. It means being brought into a proper relationship with the Supreme Power and putting your priorities in order. Or perhaps aligning them like your Word doc squares up both margins on a printed page—which, coincidentally, publishers call "full justification." But unlike the typesetters of the past who had to justify lines of type by manually squaring up each end, the process is automatic today. The software does it for you.

And so it is with Paul's version. Justification is not a manual process. It is built into The Program of Life. Once a person fully realizes the existence of a deeper reality—a reality that runs through all things and all people and connects us with some dimension beyond physical space and time—priorities seem to reorder themselves automatically. The rat race loses its exclusive claim on one's energies. Personal development, meaningful relationships, creating harmony and peace begin to take on primary importance.

For Paul, that realization was symbolized in a blinding experience on the road to Damascus, and a voice that seemed to say, "Look, you're a talented guy, you're a hard worker; but you've got things backwards. I want you *with* me, not against me." In Christian Faithspeak, "accepting Christ" thereafter became the outward act that accompanied this realignment of priorities.

But justification is also embodied in the Jew's heartfelt acceptance that the Divine Unity should be the foundation for faith. It is the Muslim's soul-wrenching, eye-opening realization that "God is great" and we are mere flesh, and submission to that Reality is the only proper response. It is the Hindu's willingness to see The Divine everywhere and worship it in all its myriad forms, the Taoist's joyful submersion into the flow of Life, and the Buddhist's conformance to his Path.

It can also be the simple recognition, by anyone at any time, that we don't ultimately make The Rules. They're "given." Facing that fact is the initial alignment of attitude/faith leading to salvation. Fighting against that reality for the rest of our lives is pure hell.

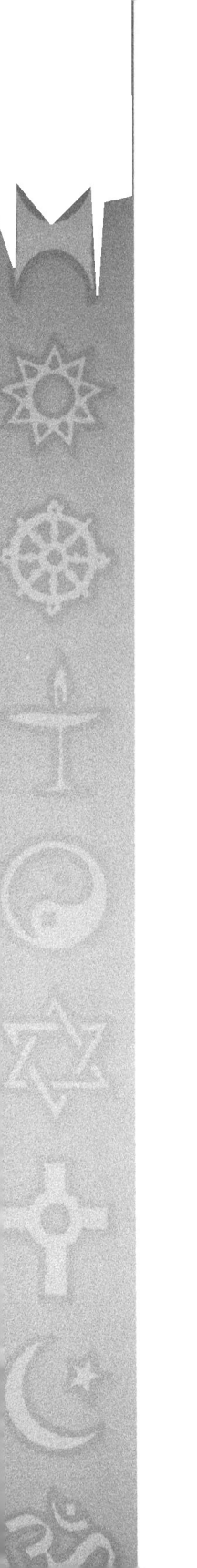

KABBALAH

Leave any religion sitting around long enough and it's bound to happen: Someone will come along, pick it up and infuse it with all sorts of new and creative twists the mainliners and traditionalists could never have imagined. Usually these creative types will look behind every word for hidden meaning, find symbolism where none had been noticed before, even discover common threads that are interwoven with other spiritual traditions and practices.

Let's call these spiritually creative types "mystics."

Kabbalah is the name for the collected works and wisdom of the Jewish mystics. Much of this wisdom was distilled and compiled into a book known as the *Zohar*. But just as it is with most brands of mysticism, the heart of Kabbalah can't be learned from any book.

Derived from the Hebrew word which means "to receive," kabbalah implies a special kind of knowledge that can't be transmitted by written or spoken word—not directly, anyway—or even by ordinary experience. It is the understanding that must be received through an inner illumination from the Divine Presence, similar to the spiritual insight Pentecostals associate with the "baptism of the Holy Spirit." Under the influence of that Spirit, sacred texts can communicate to us on a deeper level. Even routine experiences convey symbolic messages and esoteric information that an outsider simply can't see.

In fact, to an outsider, Kabbalah can look an awful lot like magic. While promoting an awareness of The Divine in one's daily life, many Kabbalists also believe in evil spirits—and therefore in the sacred objects, numbers and magical incantations intended to ward them off. Kabbalah, after all, embraces the notion that life is a battleground for the ongoing struggle between good and evil. And not just between the little devils or guardian angels that whisper in our ears. We're talking about Good and Evil on a cosmic scale, where the Supreme Good Guys might be overthrown if we don't pitch in and give them a hand. It's a world view shared by the Babylonians and the earliest Christians, by the Jewish sect that produced the Dead Sea Scrolls, by millions of Muslims and Hindus throughout history, as well as a few televangelists and present-day statesmen who see Armageddon just over the horizon.

But in waging that larger campaign, we must all keep our eyes on the small details. Recall the morality tale about how Napoleon lost his last great battle because of a nail. One lousy nail! Just before the final assault, so the story goes, a spy discovered a crucial piece of tactical information that, if Napoleon had only known, would have changed his entire strategy. *And* the outcome of the war. But the messenger's horse threw a shoe and no one could find a nail to fasten it back in place. By the time the horse limped through enemy lines with the spy's message, Napoleon had been defeated and the future of the world was changed.

The nails, those little two-penny details, often come in strange places. It pays to actively look for them, Kabbalah suggests, to be spiritually awake at all times so we're able to receive what God or The Universe is trying to tell us.

There's another story that concerns the Torah, spelled with one missing vowel, as per manuscript rules, TORH. Kabbalists have uncovered a very interesting coincidence. In the first book of the Hebrew Bible, the initial letter in TORH happens to be the 49th letter to appear in the text. If you count 49 more letters you'll find an "O." Another 49 letters brings you to the "R," and after 49 more comes the "H." The same pattern is followed in the second book of the Bible: Successive sequences of 49 letters spell out TORH ("Torah").

In the third book, the four-letter word for "God," YHWH, is found in a repeating cycle of every 7th letter. In the fourth and fifth book, the lettering sequence of the first and second books again spells TORH, only this time in reverse. Two mirror images of "Torah" are thus found on either side of "God" in the middle book.

What's it all mean?

Not a dang thing. Or as much as you want to make of it.

Maybe the point is that by looking beyond appearances and first impressions, order and purpose (and sometimes goodness) can be seen all around us. Or that even in the simplest of things there is an awe-inspiring complexity. Or that in the mundane words we speak or read every day, there are deeper levels of extraordinary meaning—clues, hints, crucial bits of tactical information that, if only we knew them, might make the crucial difference between our spiritual victory or defeat.

Life is such a mystery. Kabbalah acknowledges that mystery, celebrates it, asks us to enjoy it and be challenged by it. The answer is there, hidden, waiting to be received. Just look for it. Closer... *closer...*

KALI

One of the many faces of God in Hindu tradition, Kali is also among the most fearful. Portrayed as an ebony goddess with piercing eyes, sharp teeth and a necklace of human skulls, Kali is said to represent Time. Even as she gives birth to all creatures, Kali ends up consuming them in bloody fashion, like a female Grim Reaper who trades her scythe for tiger's fangs. And the grim irony is, Kali remains one of the most beloved divinities among India's masses.

What are we literate readers of religious lexicons to think about such ugly, frightful portraits of the Divine?

Maybe that, for countless millions of human beings, life continues to be ugly and frightful; that even for those whose lives are privileged and pleasurable, it's a scary prospect to realize that we are born, we live, and we end up in the same gaping maw of death as everybody else.

Or maybe that, by facing our worst fears like other cultures do with their Day of the Dead or Halloween, or bloody visions of God nailed to a cross, we receive exactly the motivation we need for concentrating on *life...* for taking full advantage of the span between birth announcements and obituaries... for thumbing our collective noses at our inevitable demise and shouting, "Sorry, pal. I ain't done yet!"

KARMA

What goes around, comes around. You can't reap the corn if you only plant thorns. Someday we'll all pay the piper. It all evens out in the end, or comes out in the wash, or turns out for the best.

There must be fifty ways to say it. Most people, after all, have a built-in sense of fairness, and they sincerely believe—or *want* to believe—that the world will somehow reward good deeds and punish the bad. But most people also know it doesn't always work out that way. Some guys get away with murder. Only the good die young. The sun shines on the wolf as well as the lamb.

So there are probably another fifty sayings to illustrate the fact that life isn't fair much of the time. Everyone has a story. Like old Uncle Benny, poor sap who keeps his nose to the grindstone for forty-six straight years, puts the kids through college, remains faithful to his wife and never misses a mortgage payment. At last he retires so he can finally enjoy life and dies of a brain clot the next day. And then there's that S.O.B. from Barstow who cheats on his wife, never pays his bills, blames everyone but himself when things go wrong, puts two bucks on a Lotto ticket at the Circle K and wins sixty million bucks.

Who's in charge here, anyway?

The most frightening possibility is: *No one.* Because then life wouldn't be, never could be, fair. Even if the good guys win on occasion and the rotten ones get the shaft, it would only be by accident, or maybe because someone changed the outcome artificially. What's "fair" would amount to little more than a set of man-made rules, like those for a game of Billiards. And either we agree to play by those rules, or we go find another pool hall.

But some people believe the rules of fairness are built into the very nature of things. We don't make them up. They just *are*. And if we follow them, if we do what's good and avoid the bad, we will earn more good in return and eventually come out winners. Automatically. Maybe the pay-off won't come right then and there; but the check, theologically speaking, is in the mail. Or the invoice, if you've broken the rules.

Karma is the Hindu equivalent of the check or the invoice being "in the mail." According to this system, everything we do earns a check or requires a payment, no matter how small. Sometimes the check is cashed on the spot, like a kiss on the cheek from the old lady you just helped across the street, or the good feeling you get from doing it. Sometimes it comes later, like when the old lady hits you with her cane instead of kissing you because she suspects you're a mugger; but, looking back on it, you give yourself credit by having a good belly-laugh since, what the hell, you *tried,* right? Which is sometimes the best payoff of all.

Of course, all too often payday never seems to come. The bills never arrive. The Jewish/Christian/Islamic notion of a Book of Life in which one's actions are recorded is Faithspeak for the fact that our accounts may not be settled in this lifetime. The picture of Saint Peter and his staff of angelic record-keepers is just one model.

A more scientific model, perhaps, is the Law of Cause-and-Effect. Admittedly the "effect" may sometimes be separated from the cause by a seemingly endless series of intermediate steps. But it's as natural and mechanical as sinking the 10-ball in the corner pocket, using just the right combination of side cushions and other balls remaining on the table, and maybe a little "English" to get around that menacing 8-ball. The energy of the original shot, like each of our acts, is transferred and eventually dissipated, which in turn leads to the next shot or act.

The problem is, we often make new shots long before the last one has run its course and the balls have stopped moving. Which would be an accounting nightmare for old Saint Pete if something like scientific law and energy transference didn't automate the process.

In other words, the Book of Life is karma. And karma is the Law of Cause-and-Effect applied to human interactions.

But take note: This Law implies one interesting, non-Western corollary. Let's go back to the old lady crossing the street and imagine someone else who only pretends to help her, then suddenly knocks her down when she reaches the other side and runs off with her purse. Karma says not only that the mugger will eventually pay for his devious act, but that the old lady's being mugged was one of *her* "bills" that finally came due. The mugging was a pay-off for something she'd done in the past, a missed cue in her own game on the green felt; and the mugger was simply the 8-ball careening past on its way toward the corner pocket.

Not that we can all go out and steal somebody's purse on the premise that if we succeed they must have deserved it. A mugging will create bad karma for the mugger no matter what. But there is a secret symmetry behind all of these actions and reactions, an undeniable symbiosis of the sort that must've sparked that old aphorism, "God works in mysterious ways."

If nothing else, this karmic corollary encourages us to take responsibility for *all* the events in our lives and not blame others for our misfortune. We create not only Who We Are, but What Happens to Us. Our present is inextricably linked to our past, and sometimes the past catches up even when we thought it was long gone. Karma merely poses the same question every religious tradition must finally ask: "What's done is done, so what're you gonna do now?"

And the Good News is, what we do now will create its own karma, its own energy to change the future, to alter the Great Billiard Game. If we do something good—instead of whining and complaining about how unfair everything is—we may create enough good karma to offset the bad that's still chasing after us. Or maybe even make that connection with Divinity or Christ or the What Is that tips the karmic scale in our favor once and for all.

That's the hope, anyway. That's our goal. It's not what we've done that matters so much as what we *will* do. Starting now.

KHALIL

Arabic for "friend." The Jewish patriarch Abraham, for instance, is known by Muslims as Ibrahim el-Khalil or "Abraham, friend of God."

The anglicized word is also known to many readers as the first name of Kahlil Gibran, a Lebanese Christian artist/author whose vision of an inter-religious spirituality resulted in his excommunication from his native Maronite Church. Gibran's most famous book, *The Prophet,* first published in 1926, is perhaps the most beautiful distillation of universal religion ever written. It is a poetic, scriptural-sounding reflection on what we are about as human beings, as well as the meaning and purpose and inherent goodness of our lives. Its essence is more ancient than the Bible or the Vedas, newer than New Age.

"Your daily life is your temple and your religion," Gibran wrote. "Who can separate his faith from his actions, or his belief from his occupations? Who can spread his hours before him, saying, 'This is for God and this for myself; this for my soul and this other for my body?'"

Lebanon's Maronites, as it happened, generously agreed to accept the renowned poet back into their fold, on the pretext that he was never really excommunicated to begin with. But maybe it was really because, even when a religion or sect claims to speak the language of Divinity, it sometimes requires a Friend to re-phrase it in words we can relate to.

KILL

To kill something means to take away its life. Whether the act is done rightfully or wrongfully is a separate issue involving moral and/or religious considerations.

Which is why the sixth of the "Ten Commandments," usually translated in the King James Bible as "Thou shalt not kill," is more correctly rendered in the Torah as "You shall not murder."

Because the simple fact is, all human beings are killers. Not usually murderers, thankfully; but certainly killers. After all, we sustain our own lives by taking away the lives of other living things. We pull up nets full of fish and dump them into cargo holds to suffocate and die. We clobber emasculated bulls over the head, slit their throats and carve them into pieces. We wring the necks of chickens or steal their unfertilized embryos to fry for breakfast. We pluck fruit from trees that are only trying to propagate, dig up beets and carrots, and chop off heads of cabbage and cauliflower in their prime.

Virtually everything we take from the shelf at the local grocery store was once alive, and someone had to kill it, process it, and package it for sale. And we, in buying and consuming it, are no less responsible for its death than the laborer who hacked it out of the ground or drained its life-blood before it arrived on our table.

Ancient peoples, who were more likely to hack things out of the ground for themselves, or slaughter the very animal whose tenderloins they would be feasting on that night, were much more aware of their own nature as killers. Being human, they knew, involved a daily dance with death. Not that they were any more cold-blooded about it. In fact, in staring into the eyes of the fatted calf they were about to dismember, or in stripping a cluster of grapes from the vine, they probably felt a much closer kinship to other living things than we do—we, who often miss the connection between a brightly labeled can of beef stew and the creatures who once walked the earth or plunged their roots into it, and who have now died so that we might live.

Our ancestors were grateful for the lives of those other creatures, recognizing through daily experience and religious ritual that their deaths promote our survival. And that realization often made them more responsible for using their own lives productively and joyfully, reminded with every bite how precious life is, how truly precious.

KINGDOM OF GOD

Unless you happen to live in Great Britain or Saudi Arabia—or in the distant past—"kingdom" is probably not the most helpful word for discussing God or Ultimate Reality. But let's try.

A kingdom, technically, is the chunk of real estate, together with its people, over which a king rules. Since this was a political entity that commonly existed at the time Jewish, Christian and Islamic scriptures were written, it was a useful model for making analogies about power and conflict and obedience. Or *dis*obedience.

Hindu scriptures talk in terms of "princes" rather than kings, but the model was basically the same. And what that model was *for,* in this case, was to symbolize the struggle between Good and Evil—a struggle which can seem unexciting and abstract until it is redrawn in terms of armies and open combat between competing kingdoms.

As Hebrew (and Babylonian) scriptures portrayed it, the Kingdom of God stood for justice, righteousness and unity, and included all people everywhere who aligned themselves with those ideals. In the opposing camp was the Evil Kingdom, the Kingdom of Baal or Beelzebub, the forces and people who rejected goodness and God. Life was thereby turned into a spiritual battlefield, a campaign for the high moral ground, a war of loyalties that was as real and perilous as the conflict between ancient Israel and Assyria.

But what had once been a convenient model for symbolizing the struggle between Good and Evil became the blueprint for an actual political structure. The Jews—and later, Christians and Muslims—began to envision the Kingdom of God as something with borders and standing armies and a succession of royal monarchs who were hand-picked by God to rule on His behalf. The result was a sometimes oppressive nation-state whose religion was its constitution, the priesthood its political leaders.

Whereupon a certain rabbi from Nazareth objected. "The Kingdom of God is *within* you," Jesus said (according to most translations). It's that small foothold of divine territory which seeks to enlarge its dominion over the rest of your life. It's that "image of God" struggling to break through the bonds of selfishness and suspicion and create a new world of generosity and love.

Other translations render Jesus' famous catch-phrase as "The Kingdom of God is *among* you." In other words, it exists (or can come into existence) *outside* of us, in the community of sharing-and-caring being created and spread through the body of believers. It's what results when we collectively put God/Ultimate Reality at the center of our personal and corporate life.

Either way, the Kingdom was never intended to be a place on the map. More like a space in our hearts. It's the attitude of an individual or group that has discovered a part of himself/herself/itself that reflects the same Force which created the universe; a part that's connected to everyone and everything; a part that works inevitably, mysteriously, toward wholeness and fulfillment. The Kingdom of God is, by the definition in Part One, a faith.

No earthly Kingdom can exist for long unless this interior kingdom (faith) is established first. Every religious tradition acknowledges that the exterior world depends, finally, on what Martin Luther King called "the content of our character"—on Who We Are as individuals and as a community. We can legislate morality all we want; we can try to control people's behavior by laying down the law and patrolling the streets day and night. And sometimes that is necessary. But it's also like treating the effects of a disease rather than its causes.

Change the individual and you change society. Better yet, before you attempt to change society, or any other individual, work on your *own* personal shortcomings. Or, as Jesus put it, remove that two-by-four from your own eye before bothering with the speck of sawdust in your neighbor's.

Look to your own realm first, and the rest of the world will take care of itself.

KOSHER

Every ancient society has had some form of dietary regulation. Most were cooked up after generations of experience, then preserved in tradition. Some were spiced with divine injunction. The body of Jewish dietary laws, called *Kashrut* (Kosher), are probably the most visible in Western culture. But they're hardly the only ones still in use.

Muslims, for example, aren't permitted to eat pork, just like Orthodox Jews. Jews, however, are permitted to drink alcohol while Muslims are not. Seventh-Day Adventists avoid pork *and* alcohol, while Mormons may eat pork, but are advised against alcohol or any drinks that may contain caffeine. Certain Hindus are not only precluded from eating pork but *any* meat. And devout Buddhists won't eat rich or spicy foods whether meat or anything else, because it arouses the desire to consume food "as a sensual experience" rather than a necessary fuel for the proper functioning of one's body/mind.

Religion, in short, has as much to say about what goes in your mouth as what comes out. And not without good reason.

The common prescription against eating pork was probably a preventative measure against trichinosis, a frequent cause of poisoning (if not death) in the ancient Mideast. Even if the risk from spoiled pork was relatively low, the social engineers of the time felt that outlawing it entirely was better than playing the dietary equivalent of Russian Roulette. And putting the decree into holy scripture forestalled further debate on the matter.

But there's more to dietary laws than physical health. Because what people eat can also affect them mentally. Not merely in the sense that caffeine makes you edgy and alcohol causes drowsiness. The fact is, what you eat and *why* you eat it can help shape your attitudes. It can subtly affect your relationships with the world around you, and with your own heart-of-hearts.

Take the kashrut injunction against eating meat and milk products during the same meal—a rule that nixes cheeseburgers, sausage-and-cheese pizzas, or even pie a la mode if the crust contains animal fat. Many centuries ago a panel of rabbis pointed to a passage in the Book of Leviticus that made it unlawful to "boil a baby calf in its mother's milk." As a result of this one statement, the rabbis ruled that meat and milk must never come into contact, whether during preparation of the meal or later, in our digestive tracts.

You might say they went a little overboard. Really, what are the odds the Leviticus casserole conjunction would ever happen? On the other hand, maybe the message the rabbis wanted to bring home was more of a recipe for respect... that human beings have an obligation to honor the other living creatures who provide them with sustenance. And the thought of milking a cow or a female goat, then slaughtering one of her offspring and cooking it in a sauce made from that same milk—which wasn't all that unlikely in ancient times—was not just disrespectful; it was downright barbaric. Anyone who did it knowingly (or even carelessly) stood a good chance of losing touch with the same Source that gave *him* life. If he hadn't lost touch already.

Today, the chances that the hamburger patty on your barbeque is related by birth to the slab of processed cheese on top of it are practically zero. But the meat-and-milk injunction, as well as a slew of other dietary laws from various religions, are still practiced. Why?

Perhaps because religious traditions have a spiritual depth that the latest fad diets don't. Kosher-type regulations are Faithspeak's way of reminding us to think before eating. After all, anything we do three times a day is worth reflecting on—from the health risks of certain foods to their nutritional benefits, from the people who bring food to our tables to the natural Process behind it all.

Not to mention the least appreciated (and most important) aspect of Kosher laws: Sacrifice and self-discipline. If, admittedly, there is no longer any health reason for not eating pork, one can still *choose* to not eat pork as a kind of sacrificial offering signifying one's obedience to God. What's more, a person may have tasted and enjoyed pork—or chocolate cake, or a rum margarita—but abstaining from it now becomes an act of devotion and self-control, like fasting. Not eating or drinking some culinary creation says to one's inner self, "My body, my physical urges, are not in control here. I am. My Higher Self is."

Stopping yourself from doing what you didn't especially want to do in the first place is one thing. Being able to stop doing, or eating, what you *desire* is something else again.

In fact, it's kosher.

KRISHNA

After the fearful depiction of Kali a few listings ago, here's a vision from the Hindu pantheon that's a bit brighter. Perhaps even playful and erotic. Said to be an Avatar (or embodiment) of the supreme god Vishnu who lived sometime around 3,100 BCE, Krishna has more recently been celebrated by some as Hinduism's Christ-figure, even to the point of linking the title "Krishna" to the Greek "Kristos."

Although admittedly, it's a stretch. Whereas Christ/Kristos literally means "anointed one," Krishna is Sanskrit for "black." (Or was Krishna anointed with ashes, which made him *appear* black?) True, the Lord Krishna delivers an inspiring message, recorded in the Bhagavad-Gita, describing the human soul and its purpose as we live out our years on Earth. And likewise the Lord Jesus taught his disciples about a purposeful, love-driven life, as recorded in the New Testament. Moreover, similar to Krishna's portrayal as a flute-playing cowherd, Jesus is pictured as a Good Shepherd, guiding and tending his metaphorical flocks like the boyhood King David.

But the similarities end there. The playful god/man Krishna also happened to be the celebrated lover of Radha, thereby adding a sensual, human dimension the celibate Jesus did not have. Unless you believe all that church-censored gossip about Jesus and Mary Magdalene, or that crazy theory about Jesus' death being faked so he could be spirited away from Palestine to France, along with a wife and child who carried on his bloodline. (*The DiVinci Code*, anyone?)

Whatever your belief, human history demonstrates that we prefer our divinities (and heroes) to reflect our own earthly pursuits and passions as well as their more heavenly qualities. This makes it easier for us to bridge the gap between ourselves and the deeper resources that might yet save us. Some of our sacred stories focus more on the earthly—or better, "earthy"—aspects of those divinities, some less.

Try reading a few tales from other traditions. Then ask yourself which ones inspire your spiritual journey the most?

Then ask yourself why.

Notes

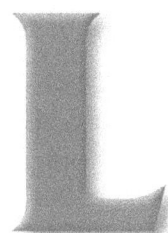

LAW

Most people put laws into either of two categories: Good laws... and bad.

An example of a good law is Social Security—as long as benefits keep up with inflation so your mother-in-law can still afford her own apartment. A bad one might be exemplified by the 25 mph speed zone over on Sylvan Avenue where the road is straight and wide and free of cross-traffic, and a motorcycle cop waits for unwary drivers to yield to temptation.

There are, however, two even more basic categories of law which pertain to religion, and to human society in general. The first category is law that human beings *devise*. The second is law that humans can only *discover*. (Or, using Faithspeak, that "God reveals.")

The good and bad laws described above are two instances of laws that people have devised. They are formulated and imposed in order to regulate human activities, to make the social structure operate more smoothly, and to promote the "greatest good for the greatest number" of citizens. If these laws restrict our freedoms, like the 25 mph speed zone or a prohibition against murder, it is only to prevent what the authorities believe to be disastrous consequences, like traffic accidents and disrupted lives. Of course, what the authorities believe, and why they've devised the laws in just such a way, is always subject to debate and possible revision. It's not uncommon for some laws to be repealed entirely.

But some laws *can't* be repealed. These are the Laws with a capital "L," sometimes called Absolutes, that people can only discover (or have revealed to them). They simply *are*. And insofar as we're aware of them, we have no choice but to accept them and organize our lives accordingly. They can never be "broken" because they do not depend on humans to work or not work.

Take the Law of Gravity. Again. Human beings accepted and understood this Law long before Newton's apple fell and the good professor gave it a name. Neanderthal man knew that jumping off the cliff above his cave was not a good idea. He also knew that whenever he threw his spear into the air, it wouldn't go up indefinitely but would soon arc downward—hopefully into the side of the poor beast he was aiming at. Newton simply discovered the precise physical relationships between mass and acceleration that were already in existence, and described the Law in a way that allowed humans to better conceptualize and take advantage of it. Since then, structural engineering, roller coasters and space flight have resulted from this knowledge. Along with more accurate spear-throwing, which today is represented by pin-point artillery and the Multiple Warhead Re-entry Vehicle.

Which also brings up the fact that Law with a capital "L" tends to be morally neutral. Einstein's discovery of $E = mc^2$, for example, opened up the power of the atom. But it is our job, our responsibility, to use that power constructively or destructively, for good or for evil.

And here's where religion re-enters the picture because, presumably, *its* laws can guide us in making those decisions. Unfortunately, this is also where "law" and "Law" often get confused.

The Torah, with all of its commandments regulating daily life, is frequently referred to by Jews as "The Law." Muslims refer to the "understanding" derived from the Qur'an (called *fiqh*), together with the example set by Muhammad (called *sunna*), as the Shari'a. While that Arabic word literally means "Way," Muslims regard it as synonymous with "Law."

Fundamentalist Christians conceive of the Four Spiritual Laws. The Gospels, along with Paul's Epistles, were taken as "Law" by the early Christian church. The Roman Church has continued to elaborate on divine "Law" throughout history, including more recent papal pronouncements about such issues as birth control, abortion and sexual identity.

The confusion lies in the fact that injunctions against birth control or abortion—as well as the commandments of other religions—are held to be Law as if they were pre-existing Absolutes. But what they really amount to are lower-case laws humans have devised (or would *like* to devise) based on their imperfect understanding of the pre-existing Absolutes. Claiming that God "revealed" them does not make them so. Even the law against murder, which is common to every society and religious tradition, is not on the same par with $E = mc^2$. For one thing, it can be broken; people are murdered every day. Sometimes at elementary schools, peace rallies and synagogs.

What makes "Thou Shalt Not Murder" a valid law (even with a small "l") is not that it was inscribed by the hand of God—though that's a powerful symbol for insisting it be followed. What makes it valid is that it is the corollary to some fundamental, higher, unbreakable Law as it applies to the human condition. In other words, there must be a Law behind the law.

What that Law *is* can only be discovered, then formulated as logically or as scientifically as possible. In the case of murder, it might come out something like, "If any life-form is artificially terminated, the natural harmony between living things will be disrupted in direct proportion to that life-form's capacity for self-consciousness." Or "Ending a sentient life before its naturally-induced expiration impedes the flow of positive energy (or psychic connection or synaptic resonance) throughout the larger social network."

Or maybe it's just this simple: "Kill one, injure all."

However we formulate it, Laws of this type don't depend for their truth on whether human beings accept them or obey them, or even if we understand them. Whenever the first part of the equation is met, the second part follows inevitably.

So yes, people can drive faster than the speed limit. They can scam Social Security, or violate the tax code, or cheat on their wives. But they can't break The Law. And neither can God.

And when that last statement finally sinks in, you may know something about God you never knew before.

LAYING ON OF HANDS

There is something deeply symbolic about body contact. A firm handshake. An arm around your shoulder or a full-on embrace. A pat on the back... or a kick in the butt.

Psychologically speaking, an emotional transfer takes place in these tactile exchanges. An affirmation of friendship. Congratulations. Shared happiness or sympathy. Disappointment or disapproval.

In much the same way, the "laying on of hands" is Faithspeak for publicly transferring spiritual power or some other unseen energy from one person to another. Or at least acknowledging that a transfer has already taken place. Virtually all religious traditions and societies have employed it. The Pope, for example, might lay his hands on a newly-crowned King, signifying the transference of divine blessing or authority. The King, in turn, might lay his hands on his subject, signifying the bestowal of some honor or royal favor. In ancient purification rites, a priest might symbolically collect the sins or guilt or bad karma from the assembled community, then lay his hands on a specially-selected animal, visibly transferring all their negativity to it before it would be sacrificed on the altar or sent off to die in the desert.

More recently, the act of laying on hands has come to be associated with physical healing. Some Pentecostal or New Age faith-healers would have us believe there is some kind of objective life force conveyed by the act. Kirillian photography has captured what appear to be auras of energy emanating not only from our hands, but from all parts of our bodies. Eastern philosophy looks on the whole body as a "responsive field of energy." So why shouldn't certain interactions between these energy fields stimulate physical effects such as healing?

Others believe that touching the head or shoulders or affected body part is a strictly symbolic gesture. It is intended to make visible what can't be seen, to demonstrate to those watching that something *in*visible is happening (or about to happen), and here's the person it's happening *to*.

Or perhaps the gesture is important only to the people directly involved. Because when one person touches another, it tends to capture and focus their attentions. The physical sensation each feels acts as a mental device that says, consciously and subconsciously, "Get ready; there's something stronger than just the two of us at work here. And if only we can release our fears, drop our preconceptions, remove the blockages and restrictions, healing will happen."

When we touch, we remember another reality where we're not alone and separate and helpless, but connected and united and empowered. And once again what is only symbolic can end up making a real, measurable difference in our lives.

High-tech hardware has its place. Chromium steel is bright and shiny and germ-free. The iPhone may be the modern equivalent of reaching out and touching someone. But the "laying on of hands" is a reminder that nothing speaks to one's heart, nothing has the cleansing, affirming, recharging force, of one human palm gently, lovingly pressed against the flesh of another.

LIBERATION

As salvation is to Western theology, liberation is to the East.

The physical/political liberation Jews celebrate while retelling the story of the Exodus is really a symbol for freeing ourselves from *all* the forms of slavery we're bound by. Addictions to drugs or sex or comfort, for example. Over-reliance on others. Worship of the Golden Calf and the money and material possessions it represents. In a famous story retold in three of the four Gospels, Jesus advises a wealthy young man to sell all that he owns and give the proceeds to the poor before he can become a disciple. Essentially, Jesus is asking him to demonstrate his allegiance to the riches of the spirit rather than the material world.

Losing our own attachments to material things, as well as the illusions of self and separateness, is what Hindu, Buddhist and Taoist traditions emphasize. Living in this larger universe where one's identity merges with other beings and with nature, where material possessions are only "on loan" to us, and valued only insofar as they support our spiritual journeys—this is true liberation.

It is also our salvation.

LIGHT

Light has been a symbol for divinity in virtually every culture and every age. Not just because the sun and moon and other luminous objects have been worshipped as gods, but because the very idea of light captures the wonder and mystery of The Divine so beautifully.

Light provides the warmth and energy that fuels the growth of plants and trees, providing not only for the herbivores that live off that vegetative life but the carnivores that prey on *them*. As the singular prerequisite for this living food chain, light therefore symbolizes Life itself.

Light also allows most of these creatures to see, including those who list themselves at the top of this food chain. We stumble along in the dark without it, lose our way, perhaps even fall into The Chasm. Light therefore symbolizes what we must see in order to survive: The way forward, the best Path... The Truth.

And yet light, as common as it is and as dependent as we are on it, is not only strange and mysterious, it is essentially unknowable. Scientists point out that light sometimes behaves like a substance, composed of discrete particles that bounce off objects with a measurable force and whose direction of travel can be bent by the gravity of objects it passes. Other times it behaves like waves, propagating from its source like the concentric circles that spread when you throw a handful of pebbles into a pond, each circle expanding from the point of entry, passing through the waves caused by other pebbles and continuing to ripple outward as if they'd never intersected.

Light is a particle, then a wave, then both, then neither. Physics can describe its behavior, its relationships to other forms of matter and energy, and the conditions under which it is produced. But even the most brilliant physicist cannot tell you what it *is*.

The analogies your high school science teacher might've concocted to explain light are strikingly similar to the way theologians talk about God. First of all, it's almost impossible to separate light from other energy phenomena. What we normally think of as "light," in fact, is only a tiny range of frequencies in a continuous spectrum of electromagnetic phenomena. If we could somehow sense the full spectrum, we could "see" heat and hear radio transmissions without that Blaupunkt in your dashboard, have X-ray vision like Superman and feel the tiny tug of gravity from every object in the room.

(And some theologians talk about God as if He/She/It cannot be separated from the rest of creation.)

Secondly, as your science teacher might go on, you can't actually *see* a ray of light passing by. You can only infer its presence when it bounces off an object and some of it happens to find its way onto your retina. And even then what you see isn't the light itself but the object whose atoms reflect its particles/waves and thus becomes visible.

(And likewise, the theologian says, we don't see God. We only see what God makes or does—that is, what "reflects" divinity.)

But beware, your teacher might add; if you try to look at the source of light directly, chances are you'll end up seeing spots, or even roast your eyeballs. Assuming you *do* catch a glimpse of the source, what you've probably seen is really more like an event—the production of light "happening"—not the substance or object actually producing it.

Ultimately, as science teachers and theologians would both agree, the best we can do is figure out how light/divinity *works,* how we can relate to it, and quit trying to figure out what it is "in essence." And if we're forced to invent analogies to describe those workings and relationships in terms we know aren't literally true, that's okay. After all, that's the only way we can grasp what's beyond our reach, to understand what can't finally be understood.

Which happens to be something else your science teacher probably taught you: To go from specific to general, from the concrete to the abstract. Human beings must put things in human terms, symbolizing what's outside of human experience in the language of what we *have* experienced. Krishna and Christ, Shiva and Satan, the anointed or the apostate—all of these are to God what waves and particles are to Light.

Or as the sages of every religious tradition have said—perhaps after finally throwing up their hands in frustration—"God *is* Light."

LOGOS

The Greek word for "word" is *logos.* The fact that Logos was elevated to the status of divinity is somehow fitting.

The New Testament book of John opens with the phrase, "In the beginning was the Word." While the author is using "the Word" as a synonym for "Christ" here, the original Greek carries with it a colorful history of theological and philosophical interpretation. Many ancient Greeks had long realized that their pantheon of gods and goddesses were only convenient play-actors representing some deeper, more universal Divinity. By the time of Plato and Aristotle, the word "logos" was already being employed as a kind of summation of all divine attributes.

Fifty years before Jesus, a Jewish writer/philosopher by the name of Philo put his own spin on it. A resident of Alexandria, Egypt—then a hotbed of Greek culture and learning—Philo attempted to synthesize

Greek philosophy with Jewish theology. For him the Logos represented an active, divine force that bridged the gap between human beings and the mysterious "other-ness" of the Hebrew God. Philo described the Logos as a mediator who reconciled mortals with the Immortal, connecting our merely human capabilities to Divine Power. Through Logos, mankind could be transformed. Or to use another word, saved.

And it shouldn't come as any great surprise that the Gospel of John, in which the word "Logos" is heavily promoted, was compiled and circulated by the Christian community in—you guessed it—Alexandria, Egypt.

But why should the word *Word* be chosen to represent this grand philosophical/theological concept?

Probably because words are precisely what elevate human beings from a particularly intelligent species of animal to something more like the Image of God. Words allow us to communicate with one another, to bridge the gap between our separateness. Words are the vehicles that transmit meaning, that allow the experience of one person to be conveyed to and incorporated by another, thus building our shared knowledge into what eventually serves as "wisdom."

Even more crucially, words are the substance of our very thoughts, without which we would probably have no self-consciousness. In other words (if you'll pardon the expression), without some form of language based on words, we would not exist as persons.

Let that brew for a few moments...

...And then see if "In the beginning was the Word" doesn't make a whole lot more sense.

LORD

Many people will admit to being uncomfortable with the word "Lord." It seems a bit too quaint and anachronistic, doesn't it? Like "thou" and "thine." We recall late-night movies about twelfth-century England during which lowly serfs kneeled before kings and dukes—or the thieving landowners to whom they were indentured—and said things like, "Yes, my Lord" and "If you wish, my Lord" and "Let me give thee the shirt off my back, my Lord." There's a kind of implied subservience about the word that offends the modern ear.

Actually, the word "Lord" *does* imply subservience simply because it means "Master." Reflecting the Hebrew *Adon* or *Adonai,* a Lord is a person to whom someone owes their allegiance or obedience, who rules over them. "Guru" is the corresponding term for Hindus, *Bhagara* for Buddhists. Whatever language it's in, this is hardly a politically-correct, twenty-first-century, right-to-life-liberty-and-the-pursuit-of-happiness sort of concept.

On the other hand, even if we modern sophisticated types don't recognize any one person to whom we are subservient, we are nevertheless "ruled over" by any number of things. The Law of the Land, for instance. Current economic conditions. Unexpected events in our personal or corporate lives. The weather. Gravity. All these things control *us,* rather than our controlling *them.* They are, even if in a strictly impersonal way, lords over our lives.

But Lord, technically, implies a personal relationship. A lord is not merely something that happens to control us at any given moment. It's what we consciously acknowledge as having legitimate authority over us. Or even *ultimate* authority over us. Phrases like "Jesus is Lord" or "The Lord our God, the Lord is One" or the Islamic equivalent "That then is God your Lord" are all ways of verbally acknowledging one's primary relationship.

Of course, we all know by now that lip-service doesn't cut it. Behavior is the bottom line. So if our top priority is the accumulation of money and material possessions, those things are our real masters. If we are motivated primarily by whatever contributes to our own personal satisfaction, even at the expense of others, our Lord is more likely our own ego, our *self* (as understood in the adjective, "selfish").

Identifying who or what one's Lord is, is another way to characterize one's faith.

LOVE

There are many different words, found in many different scriptures, used in many different religions, spoken in many different languages—all of which are translated as "love." The usual explanation is, there are that many *kinds* of love.

For those who watch a lot of TV, the *eros* variety is what most often springs to mind: The love of lovers, the kind you "make" or are "in" with another person; the kind of animal attraction married and unmarried couples all-too-often start out with but fall "out of," usually in seven years or less, as movies like *The Seven Year Itch* would have it.

Brotherly love is another familiar kind: The caring love between good friends; or, especially in Islam, between "fellow believers"; the non-sexual love between males and males, or females and females. When applied to opposite sex relationships, the usual adjective is "Platonic." (And which, if you'll recall the film *When Harry Met Sally,* is simply not possible!)

There is also, of course, the love of a parent for his/her child, and vice versa. This kind is so universally strong and indestructible that scriptures often use it as an analogy for the love between humanity and divinity. The reassuring ring of "God the Father" and "Mother Earth" depend on our familiarity with this primal relationship.

A particularly Christian variation on the theme is *agape*—the kind of love one extends to everybody, regardless of how friendly or physically attractive they may be, or whether they deserve it or not. This is the love we presumably bestow even on our enemies, an effort that requires an almost superhuman act of will. And since that effort is usually doomed to failure, this love is said to flow only from a complete change of heart, if not a radical transformation of one's faith. Once you have it, *agape* gives you the downright foolish ability to see the essential goodness or Image of God in every human being, even if it's hidden to most. Which it usually is.

This is no "warm and fuzzy" kind of love, either. *Agape* is more an assumed relationship, with strangers as well as friends. It is the tendency to act as if every other person—or animal, or object—is an important thread in what's sometimes called the Interdependent Web of Life. It is the conviction, at the deepest level of one's being, that living in this all-inclusive, inter-connected matrix creates the peace and harmony and mutual well-being that literally saves the world. It is theoretically strong enough to transform a Hitler or Attila the Hun. Or even you and me.

Love, by this definition, is envisioned in virtually every religious tradition as a kind of mechanism built into the very nature of things. We can enter into it, and benefit from it; or we can remain aloof from it, deny it, perhaps even fight against it. If the latter, we'll either live miserable lives separated from others and ourselves, or simply fail to receive the greater blessings we might otherwise have enjoyed.

Christianity has gone so far as to equate love with God. "God is Love," a verse in the New Testament proclaims; and Christians often quote this scriptural slogan from John's Gospel so glibly, so reflexively, that what it means goes right over their collective heads. It is an utterly radical statement, a lesson in de-physicalizing God, implying nothing like the anthropomorphic Almighty or bearded father-figure imagined by some.

What's implied is nothing less than a Law of the universe. Love is a component of The Way Things Are. It's the Tao, the fundamental process whereby chaos is transformed into harmony and unity. Ironically, this Unity is made possible by its very diversity, and strengthened by the fact that participating in it is its own highest reward. And what happens when we *do* participate becomes manifested in one or more of the experiences people normally describe as "love."

Seeing in one other special person the embodiment of this process is what attracts us to a lover or marital partner. Bearing and raising children expresses the very same process within the circle of family. Community is simply a broader expression of that familial love. Environmentalism further widens one's involvement to include other living things and the natural world. All the various kinds of love, in short, are manifestations of this one Law or process—a process of expanding the boundaries of self until it somehow merges with Ultimate Reality.

To "lose yourself" in this way, as another New Testament verse suggests, is really to find yourself. It's a life-long process of re-birthing, of being born again, and again. It's salvation in action. And part of the Good News is, it's what the universe is going to do to us, whatever it takes, whether we like it or not.

The other part of the Good News is, we *do* like it.

LUCIFER

Sometimes word-of-mouth is as important to a religious tradition as what gets written down in scripture. Often, in fact, word-of-mouth is what eventually *becomes* scripture.

Jewish tradition makes no bones about it. Even though the Torah and Prophetic writings were always the official text of Judaism, a body of oral traditions had also been preserved from generation to generation. These word-of-mouth stories included interpretations of written scripture, practical advice, and tales that carried on from where the official text left off, like the sequels to a popular movie. Much of it was no more than back-country folklore, but it was so pervasive and beloved that this too was finally written down and recognized as a kind of second-class scripture.

Christianity's version of second-class scripture consists largely of what is known as The Apocrypha, from a Greek word meaning "to hide away" or "secret." In several Apocryphal stories and other Christian folklore—and also in the Qur'an—we are introduced to a character named Lucifer. While he was later (mistakenly) identified with Satan or The Devil, Lucifer was originally one of God's right-hand men in the angelic domain.

Unfortunately, Lucifer was also a little too big for his britches. Long story short, he didn't think God was handling the day-to-day affairs of Heaven as well as *he* could, and, setting a less-than-shining example for countless human dynasties to follow, Lucifer thereupon staged the first full-scale revolt. Taking a sizeable number of "fallen angels" with him, he started his own *un*heavenly regime, and the competition for new human recruits has been fierce ever since.

As some sort of explanation for the continuing battle between Good and Evil, the story of Lucifer offers a dramatic alternative to the philosopher's theoretical speculations. Certainly it's no less useful a symbol than Freud's struggle between the Id and Superego. And, as an added bonus, there's a moral to the story: Sometimes even people who are close to God can make the wrong decision. The only way to make the *right* decision—consistently—is to know everything, to *be* God. Trouble is, in addition to the fact that we're only human, having a small taste of The Truth occasionally leads some people to think they know it all.

And it's the know-it-all, especially religious ones, that often end up causing the most trouble.

LUST

Except for a few self-destructive cults that promote the practice of indulging in whatever you desire whenever you desire it, lust is soundly rejected by every religious tradition. Which doesn't imply some universal, Puritanical rejection of sexuality, because sex is only one of several zillion things people can lust after.

Lust is the unhealthy, often obsessive, desire for something. It's the kind of desire that throws one's life out of balance, that unfairly disrupts other people's lives, that directly or indirectly breeds disharmony and disunity. One can lust after a job or a new house, or a car or money or knowledge, just as easily as one can lust after another person. Or having sex with another person.

The oft-quoted (and much maligned) statement Jesus reportedly made concerning lust merely uses sex as the most obvious example. He said, first of all, that a married man who has sex with a woman who is not his wife has "committed adultery." Nothing new there. However, the same married man who merely "lusts in his heart" for that woman has committed an equal sin. That was pretty revolutionary, if only because Judaism is so behaviorally oriented. Committing an act is one thing; only thinking about it is a whole different thing, right?

But what Jesus was pointing out—actually quite in keeping with his Jewish tradition—was that "thinking about it" almost invariably leads to the act itself. In New Age terms the rule is, "We are as we *think* we are." How we fantasize about events and relationships, how we imagine and visualize our own behavior, will sooner or later manifest in our outward lives.

So when Jesus talked about someone lusting in his heart, he was really being redundant. Lust is by definition a thing of the heart—an attitude or tendency that involves a person's whole being. Lust is a defect in that attitude which, if not corrected, will almost certainly lead to serious problems. Making it one of the so-called Seven Deadly Sins is just a way of pointing at it and wagging our collective fingers. It's a smoldering ember, a slippery slope. If you don't put it out before it flares, if you don't heed the signs that warn you away, sooner or later you'll get burned or broken.

It's as if every thought is a seed that can someday grow into an action. Some thoughts we water and nurture. Some we'd better not even remove from that colorful little packet.

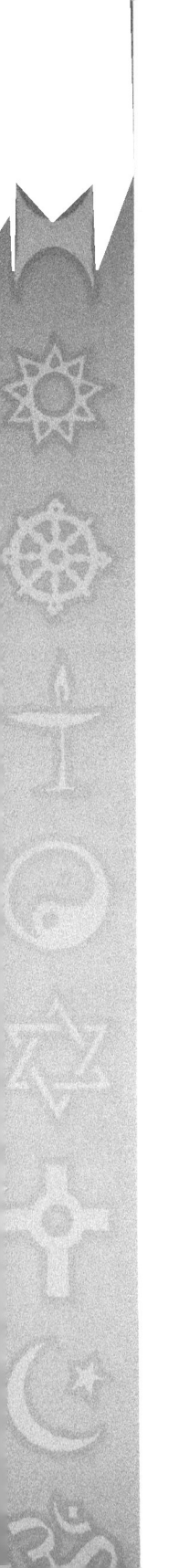

MAGIC

It is virtually impossible to separate religion—*any* religion—from magic. Fortune-telling, sorcery and the casting of spells not only pre-date the world's major religious traditions, but are quietly (and sometimes openly) embraced by them even today.

Technically, "magic" is the use of any special implements or words which, in themselves, are believed to be capable of unleashing supernatural powers or revealing hidden information. Insofar as the spirit world or supernatural beings may be called to action, those beings have no choice but to perform their duty once the magical words are spoken. They are controlled by the inherent power of the "spell"—like the genie in Aladdin's lamp.

Early magicians were thought to have a special relationship with the gods or God, and their stories and practices were often incorporated into their respective religions. Professional soothsayers and oracles were popular in Greek, Persian, Indian and Chinese traditions. The Hebrew High Priest rolled a pair of magical dice called the Urim and Thummim, the outcome of which supposedly provided divine guidance. The Three Kings who greeted the Christ-child in Bethlehem were actually magicians (or "Magi") whose astrological readings convinced them a Savior was about to be born. The *Ka'aba,* Islam's holiest shrine, is considered by many scholars to have originated as a structure built long before Muhammad's birth to house a certain object—a large meteorite—revered for its magical powers.

The use of sacred formula, common in every religion, borders on magic. Made up of specific words spoken in a specific order, and uttered only under specific conditions, these formulas are believed to absolve sins or bring forth blessings. Rosary beads, crosses or crystal pendants around the neck, hex signs on the barn, statues of Jesus on the dashboard—these are hardly different from four-leaf clovers and the neighbor kid's prized rabbit's foot. Except that these "charms" happen to be permitted by a particular tradition while others are not.

Not that any of these expressions of magic are inherently evil. The human mind, to repeat, is a mysterious beastie. And special words or objects can sometimes be used to bridge the real or illusory gap between humanity and divinity. If people sincerely believe they've opened a door to another dimension by reciting some formula, they can and *do* receive extraordinary insights on occasion. If one person casts a spell on another who gives that spell credence, that person's fearful expectations can literally bring about events which might not otherwise happen. Modern psychology has confirmed many of the mental processes that lend magic its purported power, much as a placebo can substitute for actual medicine.

So the problem with magic is not that it exists, or that it can be used for both evil purposes (so-called black magic) as well as good (white magic). Magic becomes a problem when it stifles inquiry, when regarding something as "magical" implies that there is no logical or scientific explanation for it. Computers, laser printers and laxatives seem to work "like magic," but that doesn't mean their technology can't be explained. And if people don't know what the explanation *is* and therefore label it as magic, that label says something about *them,* not about the process to which they're referring.

Magic, in other words, is an indirect way of admitting ignorance. Worse, it can be a way of institutionalizing ignorance. It focuses on the rosary beads or crucifix or Ka'aba—or the church, or the Bible, or Natural Law—as if those things were themselves the power rather than expressions of some Greater Power. Magic mistakes the literary agent for the author, the servant for the king, the smoke for the fire. Magic elevates "the gods" to "God."

Which is good enough for some people if only because it gives them the illusion of control. Rub the lamp and the genie pops out. Recite the Hail Mary ten times and your sins will be forgiven. The world is a giant control panel whose buttons we push to make things happen.

Unfortunately, when we realize that we, too, have buttons, and something larger than ourselves can press *us*, perhaps it's time to look beyond magic and find out what's really going on.

MAHABHARATA

An unrivaled collection of verses dubbed "India's national epic," this text describes events said to have happened during the lifetime of Lord Krishna some three millennia BCE. Like the Jewish compilation known as the Mishnah, the Mahabharata was likely passed down through centuries of oral tradition before it was finally recorded in a more permanent form and gathered into one enormous volume.

The same process has been followed throughout history and across cultures. First, stories are told and retold, often in poetic verse to make them easier to remember, and usually refined for specific audiences, concentrating on the details and issues most important to each. Sooner or later the orally-transmitted accounts are transcribed into the written word, in some cases by merging several versions into a single book—as is evident in the Hebrew Bible—and sometimes by compiling similar accounts side-by-side, as was the case with the Christian Gospels.

A few scriptural texts, however, were compiled long after the scribal arts had already become prevalent, and stories had no chance to pass through a period of refinement over generations of oral transmission. The Qur'an, for example, was written down "in real time," so to speak, from Gabriel's mouth to ink on parchment. Which explains why then-current issues in the life of the growing Islamic community routinely resulted in a new chapter that just happened to provide a timely, divinely-scripted answer.

Whether transmitted in real time or over the centuries, all scriptures emerge from a specific historical context, leaving subsequent generations to re-interpret verses and stretch meanings to keep them relevant. The Mahabharata was simply the one that set the precedent.

MANA / MANNA

A word that appears in various forms in numerous religious traditions, *mana* initially appeared in Polynesian dialects (where it signified "supernatural power") and nearly simultaneously in Indo-European languages (where it meant "mind" or "intelligence"). This is the suffix in the Hindu At*man* and Brah*man,* as well as the *manu* of the Greco-Roman Mystery religions. It is also the mysterious "manna from heaven" that, in the original oral tradition, was probably meant to symbolize what was more important to the Hebrew diet than "bread alone."

That Old Testament story, in fact, is a precursor to the term used in Theosophy, where *manas* indicates the power still unfolding in humanity today—our emerging ability not only to know or imagine what's true, but to mentally *generate* it. In other words, to create reality.

Which isn't so far-fetched if we see *manas* as a contemporary way to conceptualize what religions have taught for centuries. Human beings, after all, have always engaged in practices designed to connect them with deeper dimensions and divine energies for the purpose of changing the world. Or at least the world close to them.

The old-fashioned word for such practices is "prayer."

MANTRA

As an addendum to the recent entry on Magic, some would call this word a prime example of it. Because a mantra (from the Sanskrit *manyate,* "to think") is a sacred formula believed to have the inherent power to center one's attention on The Divine. It's a way, so to speak, of "casting a spell" on oneself. Or on one's mind.

And there's nothing all that magical about it. The idea of mantra simply recognizes that words *do* have a kind of power, and that speaking certain words can affect people in positive ways. The mantra is a carefully chosen word, or series of words, repeated by Hindus or New Age devotees in order to aid mental concentration, or to induce a meditative state wherein that person feels more closely connected to God. It may consist of the simple repetition of the generic *Om,* or the name of a specific divinity, or even a string of nonsense syllables. One of the more classic Tibetan mantras is *Om Mani Padme Hom,* which means something like "Hail to the Jewel in the Lotus."

Studies have demonstrated that a devotee's brainwave patterns can indeed be altered by the recitation of a mantra. The Beta state of active awareness drops to Theta, during which our workaday world fades from consciousness. The mind becomes more restful, less analytical, and thus more receptive to suggestion or divine guidance.

Choosing exactly *which* words or nonsense syllables to use is something of a science. A spiritual advisor or guru is often called upon to prescribe the appropriate words for an individual, and only after careful consideration of his personality and special needs. Of course, no one is prevented from experimenting. Do-it-yourself mantras can work equally well. A name or favorite passage from scripture can do the job, or a line from a cherished hymn. The key is to repeat the words, either aloud or silently, until the mind lets go of the mental baggage we usually carry around: The daily list of things-to-do or bills-to-pay; the nagging pain in your lower back; that self-critical voice whining that you're not good enough or still haven't lost enough weight... all the various grudges and judgments that hold back the divine perspective. Or at least interfere with the mind's natural tendency to heal itself.

Which, by the way, is exactly what is supposed to take place during a typical worship service. The Latin Kyries of the Catholic Mass; the somber, monotone repetition of The Lord's Prayer; the davening of Hebrew prayers so familiar that they're uttered more for atmospherics than for meaning; the joyous chanting of "God is Great!" by Muslims—all these sonic rituals are meant to induce an uncluttered mental state in which healing and communication with Ultimate Reality can more easily occur.

A mantra is simply the device, Faithspeak or otherwise, that pushes everything else out long enough to let renewal *in*.

MARRIAGE

Long-term commitments between opposite-sex couples for the purpose of bearing and nurturing the next generation have been promoted in virtually every society and historical era... except perhaps one.

Marriage was not highly regarded during Christianity's first century or two, primarily because the imminent return of the Christ was expected and there simply wasn't enough time to get caught up in child-rearing. Later, after the Second Coming had to be rescheduled, marriage was frowned upon because the denial of one's sexual needs had become the mark of a virtuous life. In fact men and women who remained single and celibate were looked upon as the tradition's superstars, held in the same high regard as people today might view an Olympic athlete or an Oscar-winning actor.

It was also an aberration that many modern scholars—not to mention feminists—believe to have permanently scarred Western culture and the human psyche. Male and female alike.

For most of history, however, marriage has been a highly revered practice. Religious traditions and scripture generally consider it the fundamental social institution, both for the preservation of the human species and the transmission of values. Not that every tradition or every era has played by the same rules.

Jewish and Islamic practices, for example, have varied widely through the centuries—from marriages made binding merely by a husband's public announcement, to unions in which the duties of each partner (including the frequency of sex) were spelled out in a detailed legal contract known as a *ketubah*. In such contracts, the wife was often accorded so many protections that, should there ever be a divorce, she would almost certainly (you'll pardon the expression) come out on top. At other times the husband could secure a divorce simply by declaring "I divorce you" three times in the presence of witnesses. In such cases the wife might conceivably (again, you'll pardon the expression) get screwed out of all her personal possessions, and even be forced to relinquish her children. In addition to her dignity. And all strictly in accordance with accepted religious policy.

It's hardly surprising, then, that the changing nature of marriage has been the subject of so much recent debate, from polygamy to biracial and same-sex unions. Nor is this kind of periodic re-analysis anything new. What *is* new is the opportunity to bring the full resources of history, biology, psychology and social equality into the discussion.

But part of that discussion must revolve around the functions of marriage that *don't* change. Within this unit, after all, marital partners and their children, if any, role-play their rights and responsibilities in the larger society. The family acts as the basic model for all relationships. It is the classroom in which children (and parents) learn and finetune their faiths—not necessarily in the religious sense, but in terms of developing and confirming fundamental attitudes.

Is life easy or hard, good or bad? Am I basically secure or insecure, loved or unloved? Will events happen in predictable ways, or is there nothing in life I can really count on? The events and personal dynamics that occur within the intimacy of marriage and family determine Who We Are as nothing else can.

Which is why both society and religious traditions have such a big stake in the institution. And why marriages are worth celebrating with such fanfare and hopeful expectation. What comes of it is no less than our first exposure to the Image of God. Mother's milk, father's arms, a warm blanket, a loving smile—all of these are symbols that will speak to our hearts for a lifetime.

The Anglican prayer book states that marriage is not something "to be entered into lightly." No wonder.

MARTYR

What is the one thing now in your possession that, if it were taken away, would make life no longer worth living?

Your home? A child? A job? Your eyesight? That classic '56 T-Bird with the moon windows you've wanted since you were a kid, and now it sits in your garage?

Put it this way: Is there anything without which you simply couldn't face another day? Or for which you might even consider dying?

Take religion. The fact is, hundreds of thousands of human beings throughout history have been forced to choose between life and belief. Threatened with death if they didn't renounce their religion, many people have preferred death. Deserting their tradition, abandoning their particular understanding of God, was simply inconceivable.

Those who give up their lives for this reason are called "martyrs." From the Greek word for "witness," a martyr is a person whose death provides a witness or living testimony to what he or she believes.

Every religious tradition has its share. When the Romans decided someone couldn't be a good citizen of the Empire and a Christian at the same time, the lions beneath Rome's Coliseum never lacked for protein. Many of Muhammad's early converts, who were crazy enough to join him in proclaiming the One God, were attacked and killed by the surrounding pagan tribes. History's longest-running succession of martyrs are arguably the Jews—sometimes as a result of warfare with the more powerful Assyrians, Greeks and Romans; but more often as the result of living among people whose religious sensibilities were outraged by the

Jews' stubborn refusal to be converted, along with their underserved reputation as "Christ-killers."

Of course, Western civilization can't claim the exclusive rights to martyrdom. Disciples of the Buddha, Tibetan monks, Hindu ascetics, Sikhs, practitioners of Native American and African religions—as well as assorted non-believers and free-thinkers—have likewise been slaughtered simply for admitting to beliefs that differed from the person standing over them with an executioner's axe.

It seems incredible to the modern, democratic mind that people should ever have been tortured and killed for their religious beliefs. Even more incredible is that victims *accepted* torture and death rather than change their views. Perhaps most incredible of all is the fact that the people who were doing the torturing and killing felt they were acting in accordance with their own religious beliefs. The Grand Inquisitor who presumed to be representing the Prince of Peace and the Incarnation of Love, even while stretching his victim on the racks and peeling his skin off layer by layer, must be one of history's cruelest jokes.

But the reality of a million martyrs—or *six* million, or perhaps as many as a hundred million over the course of human history—is hardly a joke. And the fortunate fact that most of us will never face The Inquisition shouldn't prevent us from wondering what it is that makes life worth living; what would make us merely turn the other cheek; and what would compel anybody in his right mind to sign up for the cross.

MARY

"Holy Mary, Mother of God..."

A direct quote from the well-known Hail Mary prayer of Roman Catholic tradition. And which, to Jews and Muslims (as well as most Protestants), would be downright blasphemous if it wasn't just plain silly from the start. Because God *has* no parents. The Supreme Being can't be born of a woman like we are. If it could, it wouldn't be "supreme," would it?

Then again, most Catholics already know that. Or at least Catholic theologians and their seminary students do. Insofar as we take "Mother of God" literally, we've missed the point.

To say that Mary formed "out of her own flesh" the body into which God incarnated is still too literal. Perhaps the only way to make sense of the phrase is to understand what "Mary" represents.

Certainly Mary represents, in Faithspeak, far more than the woman who bore the Jewish child eventually proclaimed as The Christ. How else can anyone explain the almost fanatic devotion Mary has inspired through the centuries? Eight hundred years ago, for example, an incredible building program spread across Europe, resulting in hundreds of chapels and churches and glittering cathedrals, all named and dedicated not to Jesus but to Mary. A whole new system of theology called—what else?—"Mariology" was developed, equating Mary with the "new Eve," the mother of redeemed humanity, the Head of the Mystical Body who was nearly as crucial to one's salvation as Jesus Christ.

Which is a pretty amazing jump, actually, given Mary's lightweight treatment in the New Testament. If anything, her son's own words minimize her importance. Jesus practically ignores Mary during his ministry. Worse, he spurns her. "What do I have to do with you?" he says bluntly on one occasion. And apart from the four Gospels she is mentioned only once, in a routine listing of people at a certain prayer meeting. Hardly the stuff rock-stars are made of.

What makes Mary a major actress on the Catholic stage, despite her lack of good written material, is that she brought back the missing element in what had become a stuffy, patriarchal, male-oriented tradition. Quite simply, Mary resurrected "the goddess." Any drama, any tradition that purports to address issues having to do with real life is only half-baked without the feminine ingredient—and feminine symbolism. And not merely in terms of the tenderness, the freedom to express emotion, or the so-called nurturing instincts that are regarded as female qualities. Mary is also The Earth, the Womb, the flesh from which we spring. She is the raw material, the ground-of-being that has its own built-in Way, a more instinctive, more intuitive mode of action.

Mary is the message that we don't necessarily become good people through cold logic and harsh discipline and rule-following. We do so by giving birth to the Image of God already within us. Acknowledging the Holy Spirit in ourselves somehow fertilizes the seed of divinity. And each of us, male or female, becomes mother of a Child of God who can then incarnate in our lives.

Mary's son said as much. Once, at someone's house, Jesus was told that his mother was waiting outside in hopes of speaking with him. "Who is my mother?" Jesus replied before going on to answer his own question: "Anyone who follows the will of my Father in heaven." That person, Jesus implied, is his mother.

So Mary is *us*. By following the "will" of Ultimate Reality, we give birth to the Incarnation and thereby express Divinity. Mother and son, together. Female and male. Spirit and flesh. Yin and Yang. The bitter—for Mary literally means "bitter"—as well as the sweet.

MAYA

So you think that comfortable new Barca-Lounger you're sitting in is *real,* do you? Just because you can see it, feel its leatherette cushions cradling you while built-in rollers gently massage your aching lumbar? Besides which, the little beauty set you back a thousand clams and you're still paying off your Wal-Mart charge card, and if it *weren't* real you sure wouldn't be getting all those infernal monthly statements, right…?

Wrong. It's all an illusion. The Barca-Lounger. The credit card statements. And you. Or at least the "body" part of you.

For thousands of years people have suspected that everything we see, feel, hear, taste and touch—the whole "phenomenal world," as philosophers like to call it—is basically not real. What *is* real, they say, is some Higher Truth, some Ultimate Reality that manifests in these material things we only *think* are real.

In Hinduism, the power that leads us to think those things are real is called *maya.* Maya is the divine mechanism or process that tricks us into accepting the illusion. Like your dad's old Bell & Howell movie projector that flashes a series of still pictures on a screen at 18 frames a second, and you'd swear your Uncle Richard was right there in front of you doing his dumb impression of Humphrey Bogart. Except that *our* view-screen is in three dimensions all around us, and we're hooked up to a "projector" that also delivers the sensations of touch, taste, smell and sound at the same time. If you've watched enough science fiction movies—or at least *The Matrix*—it's not all that hard to imagine.

In fact modern science fully supports the notion that the world as we know it is more illusion than reality. Take the simple act of seeing. What actually happens when we "see"? Science tells us that light floods an object such as a chair, and much (if not most) of it is absorbed by that object. Certain wavelengths, however, are reflected off its surface; and some of these waves enter our eyes and are focused onto our retinas. What we see is not the object itself—the chair—but certain intensities and vibrations of an electromagnetic wave phenomenon that our brains reorganize in a way that creates a mental copy.

But what is actually being "copied"? The chair itself, as science describes it, is a complex matrix of billions upon billions of sub-atomic particles or energy fields, all swirling and vibrating, which consist mostly of empty space. If that chair you're sitting in could somehow be compressed into the amount of solid substance it contains, you'd be perched on the point of a sewing needle.

So maybe all the "chair" can ever really be for us is a mental facsimile. The sheen of its leatherette surface, the faint aroma of Naugahyde, the cushy feel and familiar squeak against your Dockers as you slip into it—all of these are essentially experiences in our minds. Our sense organs merely receive data that's interpreted by our brain and presented to our consciousness as what we call "sensations."

Which gave someone the bright idea that if everything is reducible to mental copies, maybe that's all that exists in the first place. *Everything* is mental. The whole world is "Mind." And we as individuals are merely localized thoughts in some larger, Universal Mind.

Plato toyed with this idea twenty-five hundred years ago. Another philosopher named Berkeley picked it up again in the eighteenth century. A hundred years after that Mary Baker Eddy developed Christian Science based on the same concept. All is Mind—*God's* Mind.

But... back to the chair. And to the question you're about to ask.

Because whatever the chair may be "in reality," what the heck difference does it make? We still "see" it in some sense. We can touch it; we can still sit in it and kick back for an hour or so to get a nice back-rub and our weekly dose of *Mad Men* re-runs. Even if it's an illusion, at least we can *rely* on that illusion. It's as real as anything can be in this life, so why worry about some deeper reality, namely all this maya/mental copy hocus-pocus? Let's be practical here, okay?

Well, Ultimate Reality *is* practical. By discovering that matter was actually composed of invisible particles called atoms, science found new ways of manipulating it and generating energy. By unlocking the mysteries of DNA and the genetic codes that exist beneath the level of our senses, biological science can now help overcome disease, improve food and animal resources, and perhaps repair the environment.

And it all started by imagining that what human beings could normally see, smell, hear, taste and touch was not the whole ball of wax. That was *maya*, illusion, like the way an object seems to grow smaller as we walk away from it. So there just might be a more direct way of manipulating the phenomenal world than the mechanical mode we've employed in the past. And that Way starts by making a more direct link with the Reality behind the illusion. By exploring what some people have referred to as the spiritual realm or The Divine.

Isn't it ironic that science has taken the lead.

MAZDA

You might drive one. Or maybe your neighbor does. *Zoom zoom,* as the TV commercials used to say.

In Persian/Zoroastrian religion, however, Mazda (or sometimes *Ahura* Mazda) was the supreme god of goodness and light. According to the inherent dualism of this tradition (and the many other Mideast traditions it influenced), life was a constant battle between Good and Evil, between light and darkness, between the powers of heaven and the prince of hell. Who, in this case, was named Ahriman. (There's that suffix "man" again). For the Zoroastrian, rising from mankind's original state of darkness into The Light, by aligning oneself with the god Mazda, was life's primary objective. And the faster, the better.

Zoom zoom.

MEANS

As in "The end justifies the means."

Or, to spell it out, "If your goal is a worthy one, any method employed to achieve it is justified."

Which is flatly fallacious.

History is an ongoing lesson demonstrating that "end" and "means" cannot be separated. Moses' advice to treat strangers with kindness, if only because he and his fellow refugees were themselves "strangers in a strange land," must've fallen on deaf ears. Conquering Canaan by wiping out whole cities and exterminating their inhabitants was a means to an end that would come back to haunt Israel more than a few times.

Neither has Christianity lived up to the example set by its namesake, ever since Revelations' imagery of holy warfare began to be taken literally. The resulting bloodshed put a hold on the Second Coming that continues to this day. And the "peace" which is part of the very name "Islam" was likewise corrupted when Muhammad's plea for persuasion (in lieu of compulsion) was set aside in favor of the scimitar.

Modern democracies are no less innocent. President Lincoln said on more than one occasion that founding a new nation on the backs of slaves would someday require payment in blood. If the Civil War was an atonement of sorts, it didn't last long. America's westward expansion at the expense of the land's original inhabitants built up still more bad karma, while proving once again that the means employed to achieve one's goal can taint the outcome, if not render it unattainable.

Clearly, it's better to set goals while also using a means that doesn't compromise those goals (or yourself) in the process. Achieving peace without waging war, for instance. Or detering murder without having to execute people for the crime. Or enriching one class by taxing another.

But sometimes the goal itself is the problem, not the means. Some goals are so far away that the steps to get there can't be seen clearly, or the time required to achieve them allows too many unforeseen events to intervene. Or else the seemingly endless journey and lack of positive reinforcement saps people's resolve so they simply give up.

Which isn't always a bad thing. Because those same people usually learn to re-focus on what they *can* achieve, on shorter-term goals where the path is easier to see and fewer things can go wrong. "Baby steps" replaces the more dramatic strides. Not lighting up a second cigarette or ordering another gin-and-tonic becomes one's goal instead of the longer-term effort to quit smoking or stop drinking. Buying a hoagie for the homeless person you pass on your lunch break, or not telling a lie even though nobody would find out—these concrete actions become your objective rather than "getting to heaven" or "being a good person."

And you know what happens when you concentrate on the small victories?—when you focus on the short-term goals where the steps are clear and reaching them is almost too easy? What happens is that your loftier goals begin to take care of themselves. All those baby steps combine to out-distance the longer strides.

Maybe that's why Micah's humble "walk with God" can end up covering more ground than running with the pack.

MEDITATION

For millions of people across the globe, religion doesn't revolve around a temple or The Church. It's not worship services, not priestly rituals, not the study of scripture that infuses these people with a sense of divine perspective. It is the simple act of meditation.

Not that meditation is all that simple. There are dozens of more or less complex forms: From the "loving-kindness" meditation to the *v'passana* exercises of Buddhism; from Jewish kabbalist meditation to Hindu kama yoga or the repetition of mantra. The whirling dances of the Muslim Sufi, the tribal chanting of African or Polynesian or Native American traditions—even the Christian mystic's "prayer of the heart"—all these can be considered forms of meditation.

Nor is the practice of meditation easy. The most common word associated with it, regardless of the tradition, is "discipline." For meditation to have any positive effect, it must be practiced regularly and often. As a long-distance runner consistently puts in her ten miles first thing in the morning, or a body-builder lifts weights after work to enlarge and tone his muscles, so must those who meditate strive continually to enlarge and tone their mind/body skills.

The results, by most accounts, are worth it. Whether infused with a religious dimension, or promoted as a stress-reduction technique by the latest self-help book, meditation is a powerful technology for transformation. In a very practical sense, meditation can *save* you.

How?

If only because it *does* take practice and discipline, meditation builds character. Trite as that sounds, making a commitment to do something every day can, by itself, have a positive effect on your personality. It's as if you thereby take control of your life, or at least part of it. The "you" in Who You Are begins to assert itself. And that discipline inevitably transfers to other areas of your life.

"Developing concentration" is another cliché, but no less true. Meditation enhances one's ability to focus, like the ability to listen to a single voice when ten other people are yakking away nearby. Concentration doesn't mean forgetting everything else; it simply means prioritizing things, releasing what is irrelevant and giving proper attention to what's important. No one can teach you this. It's like learning to walk, or throwing a ball through a hoop. You just give it a try, keep at it, and eventually your mind and body reorganize their circuits to get the job done.

And because you *can* concentrate, you now acquire certain mental abilities you never knew you had. This is where meditation often starts to take on religious overtones. The fact is, meditation allows one to experience reality on a finer level than before. Just as a deep dish antenna can concentrate the faintest radio signals from space to "hear" reverberations from the edge of the universe, meditation enables you to sense inner signals usually drowned out by the noise of daily life.

Listening for these messages has been described as "looking at one's soul" in the way a scientist might study a specimen under the microscope. The cells of a leaf, the human chromosome, the structure of the atom—these building blocks of reality have been there all along. Similarly, below the surface of our outward selves is a wealth of data about Who We Are and what our lives really mean.

Getting into a state in which we're sensitive to such data is the task of meditation. It is the Biblical equivalent of enabling oneself to hear that "still small voice." It's the New Age practice of "centering" or "entering The Stillness." And unlike the Western concept of prayer—which is ordinarily understood as a kind of human/divine dialog—meditation is more like a monologue. It's the benevolent inflowing of spirit or "grace" or The Logos. It's the opening of one's heart to levels of awareness known more by their effects than as some message reducible to words.

Among those effects is not only a deepening realization of one's true identity, but a release from the chains of negativity. The old fears, the expectations of other people, the self-doubt, the pain and suffering caused by life's unavoidable problems—all the things religious traditions are supposed to relieve (but sometimes end up making worse) are absolved through meditation. There is also an increasing ability to appreciate life's simpler pleasures, to feel compassion for other people, to experience at-one-ment with the universe, and to carry a greater sense of serenity back into one's daily life. Genuine meditation is therefore not a withdrawal. It is the equipping of one's self to better cope with life.

Which is why, for millions of people, meditation *is* religion.

MESSIAH

According to the mainstream definition of "Messiah" during the time he lived, Jesus of Nazareth did not qualify for the position.

Clearly.

He was not "anointed"—Hebrew: *Meshiach*—in the fashion prescribed by his tradition. He was no king or High Priest, no leader of armies. And he obviously did not complete, or even start, the job most Jews expected the Messiah to perform. After eight hundred years of being kicked around by Assyrians, Babylonians, Greeks and Romans; after watching their society's best and brightest carted off to foreign lands; after occupying armies desecrated their Temple and restricted many of their religious practices—after all this seemingly endless humiliation, the Messiah's Job Number One was to throw the rascals out. It was his duty to break the chains of political oppression, rescue the captive Jews in other countries, and generally re-establish Judah/Israel in such a way that King David's glorious reign would seem lackluster by comparison.

In short, the Messiah would save his people in the same way God had always been understood as Savior of the Jews, and in accordance with the requirements for salvation described in the Bible: The twelve tribes would regain their sovereignty, the people would be free to worship in peace, and Israel would again become "a light unto the nations" through their example and fulfillment of the Law. And this time, with the Messiah's help, the change would be permanent.

True, a small percentage of Jews had always maintained that the Messiah was not necessarily a military or political figure. God's Kingdom, after all, wasn't a land with physical borders. A thousand years before Jesus, the prophet Samuel had objected to Israel's becoming a "nation" just like their neighbors, with their own king and standing army and central government. According to Samuel, as well as most of the other prophets, Israel was a People defined only by service to God.

Jesus stood in this same prophetic tradition when he declared that The Kingdom was not an earthly domain but "within you." And he was likely not alone in saying it. Numerous schools of Jewish thought had been established during the so-called Inter-Testament Period, along the same lines as the Greco-Roman schools. These centers of learning often professed divergent interpretations of scripture and practice, some of which were decidedly non-traditional.

Various sects had also formed along party lines—the Scribes, Sadducees and Pharisees being only the most notable. A more mystical sect, the Essenes, virtually withdrew from mainstream Judaism and established the reclusive community that probably produced the Dead Sea Scrolls. These Jews not only awaited their own version of the Messiah—a kind of rabbinical hero who would expound the proper (or "righteous") meaning of the Law—but prepared them for a final battle between Good and Evil described in documents that pre-dated the end-of-the-world writings of later Christians.

The old joke that for every two Jews there are at least three opinions (which Jews tell about themselves), was never more true than during the era Jesus lived. And if Jesus was clearly not the Messiah by the mainstream definition—and no one else seemed to be, either—then maybe it was time to re-evaluate that definition.

Which, for that matter, was already being done. And not necessarily by the Jews.

The fact that Jesus' life was an almost perfect re-enactment of the savior-god legends circulating in the Roman Empire at the time was a stroke of serendipity. These "Mysteries," the most famous of which featured a sun-god named Mithra, told the story of a young demi-god who was sacrificed and resurrected following his visit to the underworld, and in whose blood a believer's sins could be washed away.

How (or whether) these legends cross-pollinated the emerging Christian gospels can be left to your imagination. Or to historical scholars. The bottom line is that the Jewish understanding of "Messiah" became charged with entirely new meanings as stories of Jesus spread from Judah into the Greco-Roman world. The Messiah evolved from a restorer of God's people in some communal/political sense, to a personal Savior whose death atoned for an individual's sins.

Then again, the line between the two isn't that sharp. If enough people can be saved individually, those few can have a transforming effect on the entire community. That's what the saying "salt of the earth" originally referred to: The few grains of seasoning that can enhance and preserve the flavor of the whole stew. So the fact is, personal salvation is where communal salvation starts.

But even *that* is not so cut-and-dried. If people are in bondage, or economically oppressed; if they're sick or starving; if their conditions don't meet some minimal standard of living, then the cultivation of their individual souls is the last thing on their minds. Someone must rescue them collectively and physically—by setting them free, by first meeting their outward needs.

Which brings us back to the Jewish Messiah. Or to the Islamic equivalent, known as the Mahdi, who likewise shepherds the community from oppression to freedom. Or to the Hindu version, called the Avatar, who incarnates on earth whenever evil and tyranny become too widespread.

What's common to all these Messiahs is the notion that salvation usually comes in some sense from the outside. It's like a gift from heaven or God or the What Is. We do nothing to earn it except act like humans do—which often means fouling things up for ourselves. And yet, built into Ultimate Reality is some fail-safe mechanism that kicks in whenever things get really bad.

That force, that person, that set of circumstances which seems to reach into our individual and communal lives, and then decisively turns things around once and for all, no matter how little we may deserve it, is, for us, the Messiah.

MESSIAH COMPLEX

Having just defined "Messiah" as the person, force, or set of circumstances that finally turns things around for us (i.e. "saves" us), let us acknowledge that human history—if not our immediate social circle—is filled with people who seem all-too-willing to take on that assignment. Most of these people aren't so much "anointed" as self-appointed.

The problem isn't that these wannabe Messiahs are necessarily bad, even when their efforts turn out that way. Neither is it a question of their acting rashly or selfishly. Sometimes, in fact, they're not only careful and deliberate, but willing to personally sacrifice everything they own for what they believe is in the best interest of others. Rather, the problem arises because the messianic masqueraders make these sacrifices when no one asked them to. And if they're successful, the rest of us end up feeling indebted to them, and guilty if we don't show our gratitude for all the trouble they've gone to.

Which, it so happens, is a lot like the story about the most famous Messiah. Nobody asked Jesus to die on the cross for humanity's sins. Nobody wants to be put in debt, or forced to express gratitude, for a service they never requested. Not to mention that over half the world's population doesn't believe the story to begin with.

Obviously, being a Messiah is no easy task, and much of Christianity is still trying to figure out if it was meant to be a job for one person, or for all of us together. The issue isn't a simple one. It's, well... *complex.*

METAPHYSICAL

If you drop by your neighborhood metaphysical bookstore—assuming there's still one around—chances are you'll find out why the term "metaphysics" has now become synonymous with all things kooky, spooky, occult or otherwise paranormal. Not that these adjectives automatically disqualify such books or subjects from thoughtful consideration. It's just that a once narrowly-defined concept has now become a catch-all for any and all forms of knowledge that can't stand up to scientific scrutiny or Logic 101, and often don't even *try* to.

From Aristotle to the Enlightenment, however, metaphysics was understood as the rational study of what lies "beyond" (Greek *meta*) the world known through our five senses—with an emphasis on the word "rational." Because if such knowledge wasn't a product of direct observation and experience (i.e. "physics"), it should at least be intellectually coherent and logically constructed. So if none of us can see and touch God physically, we should at least be able to logically deduce His/its existence. If it's impossible to see and touch the atomic world or the building blocks of life—back when Aristotle first proposed their existence—they should at least be conceivable through rational argument.

There are those who view the claims of traditional religion or the New Spirituality as forms of metaphysics in the original sense, as making claims that go beyond scientific verification but are nevertheless defensible through logical argument. There are also those who view those same claims as metaphysical in the more contemporary sense of being kooky and occult, and don't even bother to justify them through science or reason.

In this book, science and reason have their place, especially when such disputes enter the public domain. But the more important proof lies in how people *act* as a consequence of their religious or spiritual practices. It's the faith they reflect in their daily lives that ultimately validates whatever claims may go beyond what's seen and touched.

Because human actions are *not* metaphysical—in either sense.

MIND

According to the dictionary definition, "mind" is the "observing awareness" within each of us that is distinctly our own, while also having the capability of expanding beyond our individual identity to take in the entire universe. Whether this expansive capability is merely a product of human imagination, or an acquired skill for actually merging or connecting with the universe, is a good topic for further study and debate.

It is also the subject of, and primary principle behind, newer forms of spiritual practice from Christian Science to Science of Mind, as well as older forms from Zen Buddhism to Hindu Vedanta. According to the latter two, the human mind (known as *antahkarana*), borrows its individual awareness from an all-pervading Divine Mind. Our minds are therefore more like a process that organizes all things into more or less manageable illusions of reality, but have no separate realities in themselves (Zen's "No Mind"). The Westernized version of this posits that mind derives from God, but "individuates" into the separate human beings we perceive as *us*.

And maybe that's the key. Your conception of Mind depends on your perception of reality. The traditional view, of course, is that an actual physical reality exists "out there," that during our physical lifetimes we perceive it through our senses, and the locus for our individual perceptions is the non-physical entity we call our mind. New Thought—as well as the even-more-recent New Physics—views what we previously labeled "physical reality" as an illusion created by our individual minds within a larger Divine Mind or Universal Mind, in which each of us, in some sense, is an ongoing thought.

Whoa, Nellie.

The irony here is that this new concept is just as unfathomable as traditional concepts like "soul" or "spirit" or "Godhead," and fits into the broader scientific worldview leaving just as many unanswered questions as those concepts do within the context of traditional religion. So the more relevant issue is, which of these perspectives produces a faith you can live with?

Or maybe *expand* with is the right way to put it.

MINISTRY

In ordinary language, to "minister" (or *ad*minister) is simply "to help make something happen." A college exam or an eye test, say. Or in a larger context, a poverty program or the goal of Equal Justice Under the Law. To be a minister is to be in charge of making those things happen. A ministry is the specific field in which making-it-happen *happens*.

Great Britain and other European countries (along with their former colonies) continue to honor the ordinary sense of the word by the use of such titles as Minister of Finance, or Minister of Education, or Prime Minister. The fields of finance, education, and executive government are the title-holders' respective Ministries. In the U.S., the word "Secretary" is the equivalent title—as in Secretary of State, or Secretary of

Health, Education and Welfare—each being responsible for its corresponding Department (rather than "Ministry").

The U.S., in short, pretty much relegates the meaning of "ministry" to its one remaining use. It's still true that a minister is someone who makes things happen, and his/her ministry is still the corresponding field of activity. But that someone and that field are restricted to the province of religion, and usually on the Protestant end of the Christian spectrum.

A minister baptizes, buries the dead, officiates at weddings, teaches adult Sunday school or Wednesday Bible class, leads prayers and preaches sermons, counsels people who are experiencing family problems or crises of faith, and otherwise manages the life of a particular church—all of which is referred to as his or her ministry. Ministers talk about their ministries in terms of how many new members have joined the church, how well collections are keeping up with expenses, how broad a range of in-house activities and community outreach programs are being offered, and how satisfied church members are in general.

If things are going well, the ministry is said to be thriving. If attendance and collections are down and programs are being cut back as a result, the ministry "suffers." In the latter case, the minister can often seek advice and assistance from the larger Church with which the individual church is affiliated, or from the institution or seminary that ordained the minister in the first place.

Either way, restricting the concept of "ministry" to ordained ministers and their churches is much too limiting. Because there's a wider spiritual sense in which we are *all* ministers. We all deal with births and deaths. We're all involved in personal relationships, some of which may lead to weddings. We all teach ourselves (and others) the principles that sustain and improve us. We all endure and support one another through our crises of faith. And we all judge our lives by the people who are attracted to us and the company we keep, by how well our work provides for our needs and theirs, by the ways we reach out to others (or don't), and by our general sense of satisfaction.

If things are going well for us, we thrive. If we've lost friends and aren't making ends meet, or we've withdrawn into ourselves and feel a sense of overall dissatisfaction or even hopelessness, we suffer.

In the latter case, help is at hand. Because there's a larger Web of Existence, a greater Reality to which we're affiliated, even if we seem to have lost touch with it. Bountiful resources are available for advice and assistance. They go by many names and operate under many guises.

Some of them can be found on these pages. The one that's "true" is the one that speaks to you, that resonates, that guides you through your present crisis and helps you thrive once more.

You're already ordained. Go make things happen.

MIRACLE

More than the event itself, it's the way you look at it. Or fail to understand it.

Countless miracles, frankly, have been labeled as such only because of superstition and ignorance. Since most scriptures were written long before the explanatory tools of science were available, divine intervention and supernatural causes seemed the only way to explain certain events. The rainbow was a "miraculous sign" only insofar as people didn't know the laws of light refraction. The origin of life was "supernatural" only when biologists hadn't documented the ability of certain complex acids to replicate themselves. Creation was the handiwork of the gods only until the natural processes of cosmology became known.

And yet...

Do scientific explanations really make things any less miraculous?

Take the miracle of the Hebrews' crossing of the Red Sea (actually *Reed* Sea) while the Egyptian army was in hot pursuit. Let's analyze this Biblical event with a more modern eye and suppose that the fleeing Hebrews found a strip of relatively dry marshland to cross, where the water had retreated with the help of strong winds and a low tide. Let's suppose the Egyptians, who considered taking the long way around, got impatient and tried to follow the Hebrews directly across the marsh.

Now let's imagine the wheels of their chariots and supply wagons getting bogged down in the mushy sand, and that before they could reach the opposite shore, the tide sweeps back in and engulfs them all, drowning many of the Egyptian warriors who were unable to swim because of their heavy armor. Let's say that's how things really happened.

Does the Hebrews' escape seem any less amazing? Coming on the heels of a long series of natural disasters, doesn't it still give you pause to think of the odds against all these events happening in exactly this way? And isn't there still room to wonder whether perfectly natural occurrences somehow work to the advantage of people who are driven by a vision of freedom and a sense of divine purpose? Maybe the miracle is not that some supernatural power caused an event, but that the event happened at all.

Or maybe we fail to see what the miracle really is.

Like the miracle of Jesus "feeding the five thousand." According to the New Testament story, Jesus goes to "a far place" where people from all over the countryside can gather to hear him speak. Problem is, more people begin showing up than originally expected, and Jesus decides to put off his sermon until everybody arrives.

So the day drags on and people start getting hungry. What's worse, some of the early arrivals didn't plan for what is now turning out to be a full day's outing and therefore brought little or nothing to eat. Amidst the increasing complaints, Jesus takes the basket of food he and his disciples prepared—barely enough for themselves—and publicly offers to share it with anybody who's hungry. The few dried fishes and loaves of bread are passed around, everybody gets enough to eat, and the basket eventually returns to the disciples with more food than when it left Jesus' hands!

What's the miracle here? That God somehow refreshes the contents of the basket over and over as people reach in, like a magician's hat with an endless supply of rabbits or plastic daisies? Big deal.

But what if this crowd of grumbling, self-centered human beings, sitting impatiently in the hot sun, their stomachs growling until food is all they can think about—what if they watched Jesus stand up and offer to share his own meager rations with the five thousand of them? What if the assembled people, moved by this one man's selfless, almost laughable display of generosity, now decide to scrape together everything they have—from those who'd brought more than they needed to those who had nothing to bring—and as a result all five thousand ended up pooling their resources and realizing that if someone only showed them how to help each other and act like a community instead of a loose band of selfish whiners, there might actually be more food (and love) to go around than anyone dreamed possible?

Now *that* would be a miracle.

Maybe the miracle is simply an event no one expects to happen, an event that would seem to defy nature—especially human nature—but given just the right combination of conditions or someone's example to follow, it *does* happen.

Despite the inevitability of death, life still flourishes. In the midst of the darkest downpour, there's a ray of sunshine and a rainbow. While the world seems bent on its own destruction, creation still goes on, and each of us somehow manages to find our own small part in that whole, wonderful process.

All of which is only natural. And totally, utterly miraculous.

MITZVAH

Hebrew for "command" or "commandment."

Together, the *mitzvot* (pl.) comprise the divinely-ordained Rules of Conduct concerning virtually every aspect of Jewish life. The equivalent term in Islamic tradition is *fardh* or *farz*, understood as a religious duty assigned by Allah/God. Some duties are obligatory, some merely recommended. Some are described in the form of what adherents should do, others in the form of what *not* to do.

For Jews, ritually accepting these obligations and rules, customarily at the threshold of adulthood, made one a Bar (or Bat) Mitzvah—a "Son (or Daughter) of the Commandment." Which was no small thing, considering that the Hebrew Bible specified 613 of them.

Of course, that daunting number has been debated by various Biblical scholars ever since someone took the trouble to count them up, on the basis that many of those rules overlap, or they're restatements of previous rules, or their performance is simply no longer required now that the Temple in Jerusalem was mostly flattened by the Romans. Other rabbis have gone on to boil the commandments down to as few as ten, or seven or three—or even one!—from which the several hundred others follow as corollaries.

If all of us would simply observe the rule to "Love your neighbor as yourself," for example, or "Do to others as you would have them do to you," we'd pretty much know how to conduct ourselves in virtually any life situation. As one rather famous Jew insisted, that's what was meant by the "spirit of the law"—the more universal obligation at the heart of all our actions, which informs and supersedes the "letter of the law." And it's the latter "letter" that so often divides us. Or enslaves us.

Over recent centuries *mitzvah* has therefore come to signify any good deed performed out of this more universal spirit of love and human compassion. The word thus embodies our shared recognition that some acts have an inherent power to bring healing: to others, to oneself, perhaps even to the world. And whether or not the mitzvah was originally commanded by God or by Jesus, by Muhammad or Buddha—or enacted into law by some religious council or governmental authority—is simply irrelevant.

MORMON(ISM)

If this entry starts to sound more and more autobiographical as it progresses, that's because it *is*. After all, this is where the author's spiritual journey began, where a high school kid with a lukewarm Methodist upbringing discovers what religion is about (or *thinks* he does), then throws it all out the proverbial window, enrolls as a philosophy major in college but soon finds something missing in his life, begins attending worship services the way a foodie tries out different restaurants, and finally rediscovers religious community in the Jewish tradition... all the while continuing to explore the themes and spiritual treasures socked away in all the other repositories of humankind's unending search for truth.

Whew!—some sentence, that. And some journey.

And it all started with a blonde, green-eyed girlfriend who happened to be a Mormon. Or as that tradition prefers, a "Latter-Day Saint."

Her parents, good Latter-Day Saints that they were, wanted to make yours truly worthy to date their only daughter; so I was thereupon "invited" to study LDS history, practices and beliefs under the tutelage of two energetic young missionaries, every Wednesday evening for two hours, six weeks straight. And I was willing enough. It was two more hours on a weekday night when my girl and I could be together—or at least in the same room—and impressing her parents couldn't hurt. My own parents saw nothing wrong with this either. My mother, especially, had been quite taken by the pomp and pageantry of Temple Square during a road trip through Salt Lake City, the Mecca of the LDS world. Guess she thought she might gain something from my lessons, too.

However, by my third or fourth lesson, I began to feel like my childhood religion and I were under assault, which we were. In my defense I reacted with pointed questions and clever arguments that left the missionaries speechless, either because they were deeply offended, or they had no good response.

At the end of my LDS education, while convinced that Mormons were an admirable, industrious people with a proud history and a bright future, my own future with a certain blonde had evaporated. Moreover, an unintended consequence of my mud-fight with the missionaries was to shoot down my own meager Methodism, as well as religion in general. I had argued myself into agnosticism, if not abject atheism.

Ironically, I could probably mount a better defense of Mormon tradition today than the missionaries did decades ago, if only because I would argue in defense of all traditions to the extent that they are dialects of the Mother Tongue. So the storied "golden plates" from which Joseph Smith transcribed The Book of Mormon would now symbolize the illuminating revelations about our own past efforts to discover and embody our spiritual truths. The founding of a new religion on the American continent would represent our collective efforts to connect what happened in Asia or the Middle East two or three thousand years ago with our lives today. And if modern archeology provides no real evidence of the historical accuracy of Mormon scripture, I'd still insist that its stories can enrich and inspire us.

Perhaps more influential than Mormon history and scripture are some of the daily practices encouraged by the church. The focus on family bonds, and the roles and responsibilities of each member, are commendable. The emphasis on a priesthood to which all males are called—and, it's hoped, to which females will be called someday—results in a church hierarchy that works from the ground up as much as the top down. A period of missionary work for Mormon youth, whether by riding bikes through local neighborhoods or flying off to foreign countries, helps refine members' faiths while opening their eyes to other cultures and different lifestyles.

An LDS review process similar to Papal convocations or rabbinic councils, where social change and scientific progress can be debated and eventually accommodated, allows for periodic renewal even as it honors the tradition's past. And a commitment to tithing (i.e. dedicating a tenth of one's wealth to church and charity) would put most other Christian denominations to shame, at the same time developing a strong work ethic, financial discipline, and a sizeable pool of resources to facilitate the community's ongoing growth.

Among many fundamentalist Christians, the Church of Jesus Christ of Latter-Day Saints is considered a cult. My own encounter with it, however, provided my first serious lesson in judging people not by their religious affiliation or their unfamiliar (and sometimes crazy) beliefs, but by their behavior and their character.

If that lesson wasn't exactly what the two missionaries had in mind, it was exactly the religious conversion I needed.

MOSES

If there were a Guinness Book of *Religious* Records, Judaism would no doubt be in the running for top honors in the category of "Having the Oldest Moral Code in Continuous Use." In the category of "Person Most Responsible for the Oldest Moral Code in Continuous Use," the hands-down winner would be Moses. So pervasive was his influence that this code is referred to even today as The Law of Moses.

Essentially unchanged for three thousand years, Mosaic Law is basically a collection of rules and regulations—with the Ten Commandments as its centerpiece—designed for the optimum functioning of human society. At its core is the conviction that moral behavior must ultimately be founded on What Is, or the I Am That I Am. In short, *God*. And whether the Ten Commandments were actually carved into those stone tablets by God's fiery finger, or somebody was using a little literary license to inscribe them onto our hearts, is irrelevant.

Whether Moses brought down the Ten Commandments from Sinai and wrote the entire Torah himself—as Orthodox Jews like to think and fundamentalist Christians insist—is also beside the point. What matters is that under Moses' guidance a sizeable band of Hebrews escaped from their servitude in Egypt, then pioneered a social/religious structure that held them (and their descendants) together when most other societies were going belly up. No small accomplishment.

While scriptural accounts may idolize certain religious leaders, the Biblical story offers plenty of reasons to keep Moses off the proverbial pedestal. For one thing, Moses was as human as any of us. Though not of royal blood, he was reportedly raised as an Egyptian prince. His name probably derives from the Egyptian *meses,* meaning "son of." (*Ra*-meses, in case you forgot, means "Son of the Sun.") Trouble is, no one apparently knew who Moses was the son *of*. Either the father was unknown—scandal in the royal family?—or Moses really *was* pulled from a basket floating down the Nile and heralded as a gift from the gods.

Either way, the young prince is reported to have stumbled onto an Egyptian taskmaster who was beating a Hebrew workman. Outraged, Moses killed the taskmaster and was forced to flee to the Sinai peninsula. There he married, raised a family, and wrestled for years with the notion that he had some greater mission in life than herding sheep and hiding from the long arm of the Pharaoh. The internal debate probably sounded much like the voices we all hear when we run away from Who We Are. After all, it's so easy to take the comfortable route, to avoid the confrontation that finally puts everything on the line, that will either destroy us or raise us to greatness.

In Moses' case the inner voices won. Or perhaps it was those haunting visions of Hebrew bondage. Moses eventually returned to Egypt; and by using whatever royal leverage he still had (and/or taking advantage of a few natural disasters), he was able to snatch several thousand of his kinsmen from under Pharaoh's nose. Returning to the Sinai, he spent a full generation putting together the political organization and moral code necessary to forge the former slaves into a People.

His long-term goal, of course, was to re-establish his band of Wandering Hebrews alongside their cousins who had remained in Canaan. Moses no doubt drew on the political savvy he'd learned in Egypt's royal house, which must have included some exposure to the legal practices of other religions and cultures. The Code of Hammurabi, for example, was written five or six hundred years before the Ten Commandments, and contains many of the same principles if not the identical wording. Not that Moses meant to steal all the credit. But why re-invent the wheel?

The proclamation of a single, jealous God from whom the laws originated was more than a ploy to insure that they be obeyed. It was an insight into The Way Things Are, formulated in rich and compelling Faithspeak. Recognizing one God and no others emphasized that the laws of other gods were now superseded, and that the new laws applied equally to everyone. "Jealous" meant that the people had better take them damned seriously. Including Moses himself.

The Torah admits that even Moses grew a tad too arrogant and disobedient for his own good. More than once the Great Lawgiver-and-First-Prophet forgot that only God can create Law (with an upper-case "L,") and all a prophet can do is give voice to it. For a few such lapses, Moses was prevented from reaching the Promised Land he'd spent the better part of his life preparing for.

Which is to say three things. First, that the greatest human beings are still *human* beings, with flaws as well as strengths. Second, that the Power which moves humanity toward some kind of salvation still manages to work through human beings in spite of those flaws. And third, doing a lot of wonderful things does not entitle any human being to think too highly of himself, and whenever any of us forgets that, life has a way of setting us straight.

Revered by Christians and Muslims as well as Jews, Moses is one of only a handful of figures through whom the world has been truly transformed...

MUHAMMAD

...And Muhammad was another.

Like Moses, Muhammad inspired widespread change. Like Moses, he was both Lawgiver and Prophet. Like Moses, he was acknowledged as being fully human and not without his flaws.

Not that his human weaknesses prevented his being treated almost like a god. The name Muhammad, after all, is Arabic for "Praised One," a title Jews reserve for God alone. Nor does any other religion regard its founder quite so protectively as Islam. The words he spoke, the smallest detail about the way he lived, have all become primary components of the tradition. Testimonies of the "Companions"—the people who knew him best and lived alongside him—were eventually assembled into writings known as *Hadith*. This collection of remembered sayings and anecdotes about his daily practices is regarded as sacred scripture second only to the Qur'an in its authority.

Muhammad's early life wasn't all that remarkable. Employed as a camel-boy by a wealthy widow, he rose to become manager of her trading operation and eventually married her. During his travels, he encountered the many Christian and Jewish communities that had settled on the Arabian Peninsula in the sixth and seventh centuries, CE. In contrast to the paganism and tribal warfare rampant among his fellow Arabs, these communities must have seemed like oases of moral cohesion and spirituality. Muhammad became familiar with much of their folklore and traditions, and took to heart their concept of monotheism.

Later, with more time for leisure, he grew increasingly meditative. He finally became convinced that God had called him to be a messenger to his people. He began sharing his belief in a single, universal God (Allah) who had been revealed to him, and to whom complete submission was now required. And he warned of a coming Day of Judgment.

Muhammad's imagery and language drew heavily from both Christian and Jewish sources. In fact, hoping to win Jewish converts, he directed his early followers to face Jerusalem when reciting their prayers. The ploy failed. He thereupon ordered them to face Mecca, previously a center of idol-worship, and finally began winning large numbers of Arab converts by incorporating existing customs and rituals into his religious practices.

Which was hardly the first or last time theology would yield some ground to enhance its popularity. Some scholars claim that Christianity ceded much of its Jewish identity in order to accommodate the Faithspeak of first-century pagan Europe. Islam can be considered an amalgamation of Jewish theology and ethics, plus Christian charity and missionary zeal, translated into the Faithspeak of seventh-century Arabia. The incorporation of existing rituals was only "form." The revolutionary function in its message remained pretty much intact.

And that message, like the core of all great religious traditions, had the effect not only of civilizing the societies that embraced it, but of empowering individuals through a new and transformative relationship with Ultimate Reality. Muhammad's theme, in short, was about personal and communal salvation.

Unfortunately, like most movements dominated by one central figure, the fledgling religion of Islam was thrown into disarray soon after the leader's death. Power struggles and assassinations became common—though perhaps no more so than in Israel's royal house after Solomon, or during the great battles recorded in Hindu literature, or in the constant internecine warfare throughout Christian history.

It's almost as if people just don't get it. Or maybe they can't separate the message from the message-bearer, and when he's gone, *it's* gone.

God is great, Muhammad said. Respect one another. Take care of the poor and helpless. Pray and fast and do whatever it takes to keep your priorities in order, to keep what's good and true always in your thoughts. Live a decent life and you'll be rewarded.

Which is just as valid whether or not Muhammad said so. Or whether or not he's still around to keep his followers in line.

MUSIC

In a sense, all music is religious. Or at least spiritual.

Not because religion practically invented music as a way to dress up its rituals. And not because religious compositions get more airtime, world-wide, than American Idol. Music is spiritual because it epitomizes Faithspeak. It is a certified "language" that affects Who We Are on several different levels, most of them non-verbal.

No one doubts that a kind of non-verbal communication is going on when someone listens to a musical performance. Imagine, for instance, the audience at a United Nations benefit concert where Bach's "Brandenburg Concerto in G Major" is being played. Picture the assembled delegates from India, China, Morocco, Germany and Ethiopia, as well as a few guests from the mountains of New Guinea and Peru. Chances are, all of these culturally-diverse people are going through similar visceral responses as they listen to the music: Wonder and excitement as the orchestra interweaves and builds; a sense of serenity when the brass section backs off to leave the woodwinds or strings in charge of the melody; a growing uneasiness or even foreboding when the basses and pipe organ plumb the low notes, followed by relief and lightheartedness when the flutes take over. There are minor chords that create melancholy and uncertainty, major chords that inspire majesty and confidence; and an overall sensation, when the final crescendo fades, that one has undergone a more or less satisfying journey through some interior landscape, and for a while nothing else mattered.

This isn't intended to be a lesson in Music Appreciation 101. Maybe you prefer the Beach Boys to Bach, with vocals and good vibrations rather than symphonic splendor. The point is, here's a medium that affects human beings the world over without having to cross the threshold of rational intellect or spoken language. It comes through the ether, so to speak, unseen, like radio waves. It gets inside us, uplifts or depresses us, calms the savage beast or makes us want to get up and dance. It can provoke and inspire you to go back out there and give 'em hell, or simply take your mind off your troubles long enough to give it some rest.

Which is precisely how Faithspeak works. If there are any words at all, verbal content is secondary. The real message is the overall effect it has on you. Interpreting the Bible or Qur'an or Vedas literally—or the story of Jesus life and death—is something like studying the sheet music to Handel's "Messiah" instead of going to the concert. You can do it, of course. You might even get something out of it. But the real Messiah lies in the performance, and in your own interaction with it.

An old Hasidic adage has it that God invented music "so we could pray without words." Which is simply to say that the same center of our being that is affected by music can also *express* itself through music. *You* can perform, too. Learning to play an instrument is optional. Whistling or singing—even if it's only nonsense syllables like "la-la-la"—can be just as effective, if not more so. Hasidic music, like Greek and other folk forms, makes extensive use of la-la's and bim-bam's and yie-lie's, syllables that carry meaning not in what is sung but *how*. As if the feeling that produces the sonic vibrations is the message.

But why stop there? If music represents one class of vibrations that can communicate non-verbally, who's to say there aren't other unseen vibrations that may affect us? Maybe the so-called spiritual world is some kind of inaudible music that's playing in and around us all the time—a *Concerto in G Major* we could tune in if only we developed a sensitivity to it. In fact, one of the more recent versions of the Unified Field Theory, known to physicists as Superstring Theory, conceives of matter as the vibratory effects of mysterious "strings" (or just *one* string!) of energy that pervades the universe.

Perhaps music is just the tip of the iceberg. And the reason it seems to resonate with us is because it's the audible form of what turns out to be the very essence of the universe.

Or try this on for size: Music is not merely spiritual. It *is* spirit.

MYSTICISM

Let's start with the Greek root from which myth, mystery and mysticism derive. *Mystos,* which means "keeping silent," comes from *myein,* "to be closed," referring specifically to the lips or eyes, and therefore implying something that's unspoken (like a secret) or unseen (or hidden).

To describe an object as hidden is not to say something about the object itself, but about its *relationship* to someone. The police car hidden behind the billboard is the same police car whether it's just sitting there waiting for speeders, or it's chasing the red Corvette that just flew by doing ninety. "Hidden" is a description of the temporary relationship between the approaching Corvette and the police car. It couldn't be seen at first. But *whoops!*—now it can.

A "mystery" broadcast on TMC depends on some story element which is not yet known—the solution to a crime, say, or the explanation of an event—but will eventually become known as the plot unfolds. The solution or explanation has been there all along. "Mystery" simply alludes to the fact that it was hidden from the main characters and/or the viewers. At least until the final commercial.

The mystery cults prevalent in the Roman world during the first two or three centuries CE were labeled as such only because the wisdom they taught was hidden from the unsaved masses. It was even hidden from their own adherents until they'd undergone a lengthy period of instruction or passed an elaborate initiation rite.

In none of these examples does the word "mystery" refer to an inherent quality of things or ideas. It refers to something about *us*. If we "know," there's no mystery. If we *don't,* it's mysterious.

"Mysticism," in the strictest sense, is an attitude which admits that many of the really important things about life and Ultimate Reality are hidden from us. It's not that they can *never* be known or seen; it's just that the answers are a mystery to us, or they *seem* to be, at least for the moment. The person who reflects this attitude is called a "mystic."

Of course, if that were all there was to mysticism, the mystic would hardly be different from your average agnostic, who likewise admits that he "just doesn't know." For the mystic, however, not knowing is turned into a positive faith, a whole complex of attitudes in which the world is viewed through new eyes, where what isn't known can actually lead to other, more important ways of knowing.

For example, why is it that we don't know the answers to life's ultimate questions by now? The mystic would reply that the way humans ordinarily know things simply can't get at these ultimate truths. We can't know ultimate reality in the same way we know that 2+2=4, or that sulfate of ammonia makes grass green. The mystic would agree with the Eastern view that the physical world is a functional illusion, and what's behind the world is Something altogether different.

The mystic is also convinced that the languages we normally use to describe Ultimate Reality are functional, but illusory. The best our language can do is approximate, analogize, to merely *point* at truth. Scriptural accounts of angels or demons, of heaven and hell, visions of God, transfigurations and resurrections are more or less clumsy efforts at using our words to describe what is essentially beyond words. Not that we shouldn't keep trying. It's just that we must learn to see the deeper, wordless truths hidden in our words. Or under them.

So it is with religion. Mysticism has long recognized that religious concepts are only the flesh and bones that embody truth. Even the rules and regulations are only expressions of deeper truth. "Thou shalt not kill" and "Love your neighbor as yourself" are ways of breaking it down into digestible bites. But experiencing the "one-ness" of all people directly, through meditation or mystical insight, makes all those rules and regulations redundant. To comprehend this deeper reality is to already know that murder is wrong and loving one another is right.

Fortunately, mysticism is not beyond the abilities of ordinary people. Virtually everyone has had mystical experiences—moments that teach and transform us in ways we can't fully express. The father who witnesses the birth of his child. A group of noisy boy scouts hiking through the forest, who suddenly shush each other into silence and stand there transfixed by the utter stillness. The truth that comes out of such experiences can sometimes be worth all those rituals and sacred hymns and Sunday-morning sermons put together.

Which is why the genuine mystics of every religion and spiritual movement are often closer to one another in their faith than to members of their own tradition. While Catholics and Mormons may regard themselves as members of the One True Church, or fundamentalist Muslims as recipients of the only perfect revelation, mystics celebrate what makes *all* religions expressions of the same Reality. Even if that reality, for most people, continues to be hidden.

Because most people can't see behind that billboard... *yet*.

MYTH

More than one cynic has put down religion with the accusation that "It's all just a bunch of myths." What that cynic probably means by using the word "myths" is that the stories on which religions are based are nothing but primitive folklore. Or that they lack scientific accuracy. Or that they're outright fabrications and fairy tales.

But what the person has actually said (even if he doesn't know it), is that the stories are *full of hidden truth*.

Because a myth, by definition, is a story not meant to be taken at face value. It's a story that may look like a straightforward account of an event, or an explanation of how something happened. But it actually hides a deeper level of meaning—sometimes even for the people who tell the story over and over.

According to last century's champion of mythology, Joseph Campbell, myth is "the secret opening through which the inexhaustible energies of the cosmos pour into human cultural manifestation." Nice line. It's as if, when the storyteller weaves his tale, he can't help but unleash elements from the world of dreams, from deeper resources that motivate not only him, but us—elements that transcend the storyteller's private language and speak to his audience in a kind of universal symbolism.

Psychoanalyst Carl Jung called it the "collective unconscious," an internal, wordless language all people share because of the way the human mind works. And insofar as a story appeals to others, insofar as it becomes a part of a culture's tradition, it is almost certainly because that story possesses a power to tap into these unconscious elements. It connects with us on a level deeper than the verbal, delivering a message of importance that can change one's whole outlook.

Which happens to be a good description of Faithspeak.

Today, movies can perform this same cultural/religious function. After all, what is it that makes some movies and characters so popular? Was the 1990 epic, *Dances With Wolves,* just another entertaining diversion about white men versus the natives—or was it attempting to reconnect us all with that simpler, earth-oriented part of ourselves modern society is losing touch with?

In the scene where Dunbar makes friends with the wolf, was he merely trying to turn a wild animal into a house pet—or was he really acting out our efforts to recover the animal side of ourselves without which we are less than full human beings? Was Dunbar's capture by the soldiers (who promptly put him in chains) only the required Act Three plot-point leading to the movie's climax—or was it a graphic symbol for our struggles against the so-called forces of civilization, forces that are supposed to raise humanity to a higher level but only end up repressing and destroying our native (natural-at-birth) freedom and joy?

Dances With Wolves was only a film. It might have been based on real, historical incidents or entirely fabricated. Whether it's true or false by some objective standard isn't the point. The dynamic *behind* the story is what matters. And this story has the ring of truth because the outward plot activates those unconscious elements deep within us. It frames questions about the meaning of life; it tells us that something is wrong and needs to be made right. It shows us a Way forward.

Not literally—*please.* The movie isn't suggesting we all live in tepees and hunt buffalo and dance in a big circle when there's a drought. We mustn't make the same mistake as those who read scripture like it's a scientific or historical textbook. The story simply asks us to review Who We Are and Where We're Going. It reminds us we're on a Journey, as individuals and as a community.

Joseph Campbell and others have outlined a paradigm for this "mythic journey." It's a story structure most myths follow, that makes sacred scriptures "sacred," that gives the world's great books and films an enduring quality.

And it begins with a central character—let's call him or her our "hero"—who receives a "call to adventure," a challenge that forces our hero to do something because things simply can't go on the way they are. The hero (read: *us*) may ignore that call at first, but circumstances eventually force his/her hand. Suddenly there's no turning back. Our hero is plunged into uncharted territory and subjected to incredible physical and mental ordeals with no one around to help, and yet he's not entirely alone. Someone or something is watching over him. The universe itself, maybe. And the fate of the universe seems to hang on our hero's success, as if to say our own salvation and the world's salvation can't be separated.

What's discovered in this foreign, uncharted land—the golden fleece, perhaps, or the ruby slippers, the Wolf inside us or the Kingdom Within—is what eventually saves us. But not until the hero *brings back* this treasure. Because only when we apply this new discovery to our previous lives can we be genuinely transformed. And hopefully transform others by our example.

The power of myth is that it mirrors life. It shows us our selves and the resources to which we can connect. The answers may be hidden for a time. But they're there. Always have been, always will be.

And eventually circumstances will force us to go looking.

Notes

NAMASTE

One of the most beautiful greetings in any tradition, the word *namasté* is derived from two Sanskrit words meaning, literally, "I bow to you." It is usually delivered with palms pressed together over the heart, fingers pointing upward, followed by a slight but respectful bow.

Almost from the beginning, however, the "you" in this phrase was understood by Hindus to mean the divine essence within the person being greeted. What the speaker is therefore saying with this single word is more like the sentence, "I honor the divine in you." Or better, "The divine within me acknowledges the divine within you."

To take it even further, *namasté* reflects a faith. "We are more than this physical form," it proclaims. "Beneath this outer skin, we are more alike than not. Let's be together in this moment as incarnations of the holy spirit, not as contentious, self-centered mortals." *Namasté,* in short, is an appeal to our higher natures.

It is also a reminder that greetings are important. Because our initial interactions set the tone for what happens next. That's why *Shalom Alechum* or *Salaam Alekum*—"Peace be upon you"—is the traditional greeting for Jews and Muslims... and why the more familiar "Hello" is so emotionally barren and meaningless by contrast. "How are you?" at least conveys interest in the other person, even if the words are rarely intended or understood as an actual question.

Of course, *namasté* can also be uttered without feeling, as if it were little more than a verbal acknowledgement that another person has entered one's proximity. Which is why it might be better to speak the longer sentence it represents. Sometimes we need to hear all of those words in order to remember who we really are.

And then act accordingly.

NEW AGE / NEW THOUGHT

"New Age" is one more example of a name that's applied to a group or movement not by those within that group or movement, but by those who are criticizing or otherwise examining it. Usually from the outside.

It wasn't the first time outsiders were responsible for labeling a group or whole race of people. "Jew" was the term applied by foreigners to the natives (Hebrews) who lived in the Roman province of Judea, or whose ancestors came from Judea. The name was sometimes uttered with contempt, and sometimes with a begrudging admiration for the peoples' resilience.

"Christian" was first used by Greek observers of a certain upstart movement whose members believed in an Anointed One (i.e. *Christus*). "Muslim" was actually a derogatory term by which early followers of Muhammad were singled out by the local pagans as traitors to their own culture. Likewise Methodists, Mormons and Moonies. These and other names were all applied by outsiders or even enemies. They stuck.

But naming a group doesn't thereby turn that group into a cohesive community with a central leadership or even a common set of principles. Especially in the case of "New Age."

Reportedly coined by a social commentator because of its catchy, journalistic ring, New Age is at best an umbrella term covering a wide spectrum of groups and/or attitudes. If there is any single principle that unites them, it is simply the conviction that a pervasive revolution in human society (and human spirituality) is now underway, and *has* been for several decades. Whether or not this revolution is seen as a threat to existing traditions and power brokers determines whether New Age is considered the dawn of our salvation or the work of The Devil.

But even die-hard fundamentalists foresee the coming of a new age. In a sense there's no avoiding it. Within mere decades, humankind has gained the ability to blow itself up ten times over. Nuclear melt-down, nuclear war, nuclear winter... in an era where the same saber-rattling goes on within arm's reach of buttons that launch ballistic missiles, how much longer can we avoid catastrophe if we don't change? And if we don't destroy ourselves violently, we can still do it ecologically. Industrialization has built up chemical pollution, ozone depletion, and a global warming trend that can just as surely end life as we know it.

But another of New Age's convictions is its optimistic assertion that we *can* survive this crisis. Marilyn Ferguson's ground-breaking, 80s-era book, *The Aquarian Conspiracy,* was among the first to outline our path to survival, while reminding us that our efforts are not being orchestrated by any conscious human effort. The "conspiracy" lies in the very scheme of things. To use religious language, it's as if we're being "saved by grace." And many New Agers put it specifically in those terms.

In fact, contrary to what many fundamentalists think, New Age—or New Thought, to use the insiders term—is not at all anti-religious. Most groups within the New Age/New Thought umbrella admit that traditional religions have had their collective hands on The Truth all along. Maybe not in a literal sense, but in the way that counts most: By conceptualizing and exploiting the dynamics of transformation that lie hidden within the deeper dimensions of existence.

Of course, most institutional religions offer what they see as an exclusive means of personal transformation. Like "Accepting Jesus Christ as Lord and Savior." Or "Submitting to Allah." Or "Following the Eight-Fold Path." The New Spirituality doesn't deny for a moment that these systems can and *do* transform people's faith. But insofar as they do, it's because they trigger a mechanism that goes deeper than the specific language and symbolism of any one of them. New Thought therefore differs from other religions only by suggesting that we should acknowledge that deeper mechanism, and that we employ all the tools at our disposal to further refine it.

Many of these tools are already present within the ancient traditions. Positive thinking is one of the most universal. So are the power of visualization, altered states of consciousness and subliminal programming. The effects of music; of human touch; of experiences designed to reach the heart more than the intellect, that shake us up emotionally in order to ignite the engines of change—these are age-old, time-tested tools for personal transformation. New Thought is simply updating these tools in keeping with today's culture and scientific resources. It's Faithspeak at work.

Naturally, all this "work" has attracted its share of charlatans and what's come to be called "New Age froo-froo." Fast-buck artists ride the coattails of any revolution; and for awhile, magical objects, special potions and unproven techniques for healing were as common as snake oil in the Wild West. The collateral damage was enough to give the whole movement a bad name. Or at least send its supporters looking for a *new* name. But don't forget Jim Bakker and holy relics and the images of Jesus or Virgin Mary that appear on somebody's back door screen and attract droves of prayerful penitents. The same old silliness and trading on human credulity mocks Christianity and every other religion, too.

But the New Spirituality also has its own way of mirroring the timeless truths, its own diverse ways of connecting people with Ultimate Reality. And if that's so, the movement is here to stay.

No matter what name it currently goes by.

NIRVANA

Over the past thousand years, the English vocabulary has absorbed more words from foreign languages, traditions and cultures than any other vocabulary. By far. Problem is, those words can easily become separated from their original meanings.

Nirvana, for instance.

"Nirvana" is employed by some people to refer to a blissful, dreamy state similar to the one hippies were known for back in The Sixties, usually achieved through drugs or sex, or preferably both. The word is often spoken in ridicule, implying the loss of one's mental faculties. To say someone was "in Nirvana, man," is like saying "She's a real space cadet" or "That guy's obviously feeling no pain."

Those who know a bit more about the genuine meaning might use the word to suggest an ideal state or peak experience. "He's looking for Nirvana" would therefore imply a person's tendency to reject anything less than absolute perfection, or a kind of hopeless search for ultimate fulfillment.

Actually, the Hindu concept of Nirvana *does* imply blissfulness, and also "ultimate fulfillment." But it isn't a temporary state achievable by artificial means or even physical effort. It's the final reward for a lifetime (or lifetimes) of self-realization and spiritual purification—the state in which the refined soul need no longer be incarnated and is at last reabsorbed into The Absolute.

The way to Nirvana is through a much misunderstood process Buddhists call the "annihilation of the ego." Some New Thought teachers equate it with "becoming impersonal." Which doesn't mean treating other people coldly, or passing someone on the street without so much as a sidelong glance. What the process requires is an all-encompassing change in the concept of Who You Are. It requires a new frame of reference where an individual no longer puts himself at the center of everything, and in which personal identity is no longer dependent on one's body. It's as if you just *happen* to be a human male or female; you just *happen* to be living in this particular time or place. The essence of what you are is neither male nor female, black or white, rich or poor, or bound by the limits of Eastern Standard Time.

Not that your physical life is of no consequence. It's just that you truly see yourself as an "image of God," or else a tiny portion of God, whose primary goal in life is no longer merely doing whatever makes your particular body/mind comfortable and secure and self-satisfied. Your goal is to think and do whatever God/Divinity/The Absolute would think and do if He/They/It resided in your body.

In other words, you *become* Divinity. You think what It thinks, do what It would do, be what It would be. You "annihilate" your ego. You live as if life weren't so bloody personal. Along the way, your body will probably have its needs satisfied; after all, it's a valuable tool for this life. But suffering and sacrifice can now be taken in stride right along with joy and pleasure, because Divinity is in charge, not some puny little ego that once lived inside you. And the experience of that wider point of view is called "bliss." Which is as close to Nirvana as anybody can get while still in the flesh.

If you've caught on to the theme of this book by now, you'll see all kinds of analogies with other brands of Faithspeak. Bliss equals peace, equals Heaven on Earth, equals Shalom, equals wholeness. Jesus said that "All who lose themselves for my sake" will find themselves—a pretty clear description of annihilating one's ego. Evangelists describe it as being "baptized in the Holy Spirit." For the Jew it's living out the Law with loving-kindness. For the Muslim it's submission to Allah, the submerging of Who You Once Were into the Creator Who Always Was, Is and Will Be. The New Spirituality calls it "merging with Universal Mind."

George Bernard Shaw, hardly the most religious person who ever walked the earth, described much the same process. "This is the true joy in life," he wrote, "the being used for a purpose recognized by yourself as a mighty one; the being thoroughly worn out before you are thrown on the scrapheap; the being a force of nature instead of a selfish little clod of ailments and grievances, complaining that the world will not devote itself to making you happy…"

Sounds a lot like Nirvana, G.B.

And if Western religions insist that we have only one lifetime to achieve Nirvana—or, in their own terms, to "get to heaven"—we can take that as the spiritual kick-in-the-pants it is meant to be. Because it just might be possible to reach Nirvana this time around.

If we stop dreaming and start doing. If we don't go looking for Nirvana where it can't be found.

NOAH

Everybody knows the story of Noah and the Ark. It's as much a part of our popular culture as Santa Claus or Smokey Bear. Noah was that nice old man with a long white beard who loaded up his boat with one pair of every kind of animal—along with a few of his own relatives—so life on Earth could start all over again after The Flood. Noah is now immortalized in colorful posters, wallpaper for kids' nurseries, and terrible comedies featuring Steve Carrell.

But let's get serious. Noah, we are told, was a good man in a bad world. Relatively speaking, anyway. He certainly wasn't perfect himself. He got drunk, got naked, and basically engaged in many of the same unhealthy customs practiced by the very people God decided to wipe out with a few zillion acre-feet of rainfall. But beggars can't be choosers, and even God is forced to work with whoever's left in the bullpen.

But that's not why Noah is in this Lexicon. The reason Noah has been further immortalized on these pages is to provide a good excuse for asking the following question:

What religion was Noah?

He wasn't Jewish or Muslim, even though he's featured in the scriptures of those traditions. He certainly wasn't a born-again Christian. If anything, he was a dyed-in-the-wool pagan, with a generic set of rules for behavior and common decency which are now labeled the "Noahic Laws" and considered the minimum ethical standard for all human beings. Even Noah had a tough time living up to them.

And yet no Western religion would bar him from heaven. He's right up there alongside the best of 'em. But on what basis? Is there a double standard, or at least a different standard, on which people are judged before Christianity or Islam or some other religion comes along to set the rules? Or is there one standard, and every era tries to formulate and refine that standard as best they can?

Noah, it turns out, reflected some remarkable qualities that would earn brownie points in any religious tradition. Think back to the story. What Noah did, first of all, was listen to God—or if you prefer, to his "inner voice," to the part of him that was connected to some greater Reality. And what that voice advised him to do was absolutely crazy. At least everyone who knew him thought so. Because they saw things differently. They weren't open to the resources Noah relied on, so the storm clouds on the horizon weren't visible to them.

But Noah marched to a different beat, did what he believed was right in the face of all evidence to the contrary. He was the fool who, in every age, takes the ultimate risk, who lays everything on the line (including some things that don't even belong to him) and ends up the only one to stay afloat.

And does he say "I told you so" when everybody else goes under? No, he suffers their loss as if it was *his* loss. He wonders why he was chosen for the job, why no one else saw it coming. He questions whether he's really good enough to shoulder the burden of keeping civilization alive. And the best he can do, it turns out, is simply continue to be Who He Is and maybe even improve himself a little. If all else fails, he keeps the faith that somewhere in his chromosomes, or in his legacy, there's something that'll help the next generation do just a little better.

Which is as good as any religion has ever done.

NOSTRADAMUS

A French physician best known for the so-called prophecies he made in the mid-sixteenth century, Michel de Nostredame deserves mention on these pages mostly as a warning. Because his predictions, popularized over recent decades in books and documentaries, were constructed as a series of four-line poems (quatrains) using such vague language that most of them can be interpreted in any number of ways.

Much like passages in scripture.

We can't say with certainty that every line Nostradamus wrote pertained only to conditions and events in his own time—in the same way the Book of Revelation clearly referred to the early Christian era—or that the good doctor purposely couched his predictions in symbolism so that he would avoid the wrath of the local authorities. What *can* be said is that, similar to John's visions in the New Testament, symbolic language almost always leads to wildly differing interpretations that confuse and divide people rather than clarify and unite them. Worse, trying to ferret out hidden references to modern events while attending End Times seminars and weekly Bible courses on Revelation only end up heightening and misdirecting our fears, while squandering hours and days better spent doing the real work of religion.

The answers to our deepest questions don't hinge on the question of whether Nostradamus was referring to Hitler when he wrote "Hister," or to the World Trade Towers when he wrote about a "great collapse" of "twin brothers" in "the city of york." Neither is it worth more than a footnote to acknowledge the debate about the prophet Isaiah's line, "A virgin shall conceive," and whether the crucial word refers to a woman who's never had sexual intercourse or simply to a "young maiden."

Wordplay can be fun, like the New York Times crossword puzzle on a lazy Sunday morning. But let's not equate an amusing diversion with the larger questions whose answers might actually change our lives.

NOTES

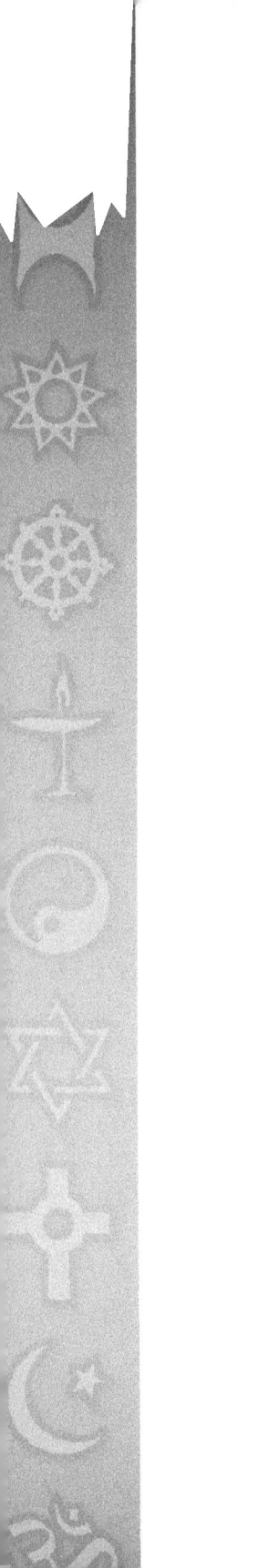

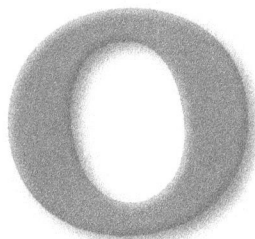

OBEDIENCE

Almost every religious tradition emphasizes strict obedience to institutional authority. Which is exactly why religion is such a turn-off to so many.

We have this *thing* against having to "obey," don't we? We imagine some angry parent pointing a finger and shouting, "Go to your room!" Obedience means going to your room when you broke that expensive vase on the coffee table after your mother told you to stop playing with the Frisbee indoors, and now you're going upstairs to sulk in silence and feel guilty for the rest of the night and maybe even miss *The Simpsons* on TV.

Or imagine that you really, *really* want that new Taylor Swift CD, but it's your little brother's birthday and you knuckle under and blow your whole week's allowance on some stupid present instead. Doing what you don't really want to do, but your dad says you'd better do it or else you won't be allowed to watch *The Simpson*'s season finale... is to be "obedient."

That's the common view. The distorted view. And parents, society and religion are usually responsible for it.

Obedience isn't about following orders. It's about acting in accordance with what we know or believe to be appropriate behavior. We obey traffic signs because we know the streets would be utter chaos without them. We obey the Law of Gravity by not jumping off ten-story buildings. We don't stick our hand on the stove-top burner, or play tag on the freeway, or go swimming with the sharks. We obey all kinds of written and unwritten rules without so much as a second thought because we already know what the consequences would be if we didn't.

It's when we *don't* know what the consequences would be that obedience gets a little tricky. Or when we're pretty sure, but we wish things could be otherwise. Or we think maybe we can beat the odds.

And the problem is, this behavioral grey area seems to cover most of the things we do. Or at least the things religion talks about. After all, it's pretty hard to "love your neighbor as yourself" when the guy's such a jerk. Plus, how do you know that treating him with respect and going out of your way to do nice things for him will eventually change his snotty attitude? How do you know that committing adultery will ruin your marriage and infect all your other relationships with dishonesty and mutual suspicion? How can any of us be expected to obey rules we don't know for sure are valid?

Religious traditions are like the salesman who knows you're having second thoughts but says, "Take my word for it... *trust* me." And at least for starters you do. Because tradition is the collected wisdom about what works and what doesn't. Enough other people have shown that loving your neighbor can work wonders. Enough other people have committed adultery—which is not to be confused with loving your neighbor—to know that it *rarely* works wonders. And all the wishing it were otherwise doesn't change that.

So if religions make such a big deal about obedience, it's because religious people are fairly certain what the consequences would be otherwise. And frankly, the facts tend to be on their side. Not because each and every rule in their rule book is necessarily valid. (Or at least valid today.) It's because, in general, societies that toss out all the rules tend to have very short lives. The same goes for individuals.

Obedience is a concept that can provide some much-needed perspective. It's one more reminder that human beings don't ultimately make the rules; that the universe doesn't revolve around our own private wants and needs; and that things like justice and mercy and love are not just nice ideas invented by gutless wimps in prayer shawls but are built into the mechanics of Ultimate Reality. That's the way things are. And if we act in accordance with "the way things are," our lives will tend to run a little more smoothly.

In Hebrew, the word for "obey" comes from the same root as the word "hear." As if to suggest that once you hear the truth, you'll act in accordance with it. Automatically.

But first we've got to listen.

ORIGINAL SIN

Look up "Original Sin" in most Bible dictionaries—even solid, upstanding, Evangelical ones—and you know what? It can't be found. Because nowhere in scripture is there any mention of it. Not in the Hebrew Bible. Not in the New Testament Gospels or the Epistles of Saint Paul. Nothing. Nada. Zip.

And yet it's presented to us as fundamental Christian theology. It's like the First Theorem in geometry. When Adam took that fateful bite from the "fruit of the tree of knowledge"—the proverbial apple given to Eve by the proverbial snake in the proverbial Garden of Eden—Adam supposedly stained the human race with a sin so deep and so permanent that nothing could wash it away.

Except, of course, for the blood of Jesus Christ, Savior of the World.

Which is why, when the concept of original sin was finally fleshed out hundreds of years after the death of Jesus, the Church embraced it as if it *were* scripture. It became the primary reason for our need to accept Christ's sacrificial death on the cross. No one else could make up for the abiding sinfulness we inherited from Adam. Left in the death-grip of Original Sin, human beings were depraved, disgusting, murderous, perverted, sex-crazed animals doomed to everlasting Hell.

Who the hell dreamed this up, anyway?

Answer: One Augustine of Hippo, later sainted by the Roman Catholic Church for the insightful book he authored, aptly named *The Confessions of Saint Augustine.* Today's soap operas would do well to take a lesson. Augustine, you see, was your basic hedonist during his early life. Having both wealth and leisure, he indulged in all the pleasures money could buy. Rich food, fancy clothes, loose women... *especially* loose women. Maybe the guy was insatiable for a time. But he also had a change of heart. After getting his fill of the good life, he realized (like The Buddha before him) how ultimately empty it was, and he promptly began searching for something to explain his previous, evil behavior.

Whereupon he invented Original Sin. Not that it excused his years of mindless partying. But there was something in the human heart, Augustine argued, that makes us all prone to evil. Despite our best intentions (and an uncanny ability to fool people into thinking we're Mr. or Ms. Goody Two-Shoes), we have a streak in us that's downright devilish.

And, by God, it must've originally begun with ol' Adam.

Okay—so the Jews never bought it. Muslims, many of whom take Adam as literally as today's Christian fundamentalists, don't buy it either. Even the Roman Catholic Church that first embraced it now finds the doctrine a little harsh, if not slightly embarrassing. A few radical theologians have suggested replacing it with a more positive concept they call "Original Blessing," preferring to accentuate the best in human nature rather than dwelling on the worst.

But with all that said—and admitting that Original Sin has become something of a public relations problem—Augustine of Hippo *had* hit on an important point. Because, damn it all, there is a streak in human nature that, if it isn't exactly evil, at least gives every one of us a heap o' trouble now and then.

And the fact is, it *is* inherited. Not from Adam but from a million-plus years of evolution. As a result, human beings now possess not only an amazing aptitude for higher level thinking and creativity, but a physical body that is every bit a part of the animal kingdom as lions and tigers and bears, oh my.

Anthropologists and biologists tell us that our bodies are ideally adapted to the evolutionary stage in which human beings roamed a relatively unpopulated earth in small hunter/gatherer bands, along with other animals that hunted *us*. Our emotional responses and instincts—and yes, humans do have instincts—are therefore matched to the demands of a more ancient, more primitive environment. Fight-or-flight was a daily survival skill for obvious reasons; and continuous breeding in not-necessarily-monogamous pairings was necessary to maintain the population. And with apologies to the politically-correct guardians of male/female equality, the sexes had evolved distinctly divergent roles.

All of which makes the modern-day human being more than a little schizophrenic. While major evolutionary changes take place over hundreds of centuries, human society utterly changed us in six or seven thousand years. Like the critical mass in a nuclear reaction, the human brain/mind reached a certain point, then exploded with creative energies that not only redesigned the face of the earth, but the lifestyle to which our physical bodies were once superbly adapted. Unfortunately, our more-advanced minds are still married to our less-advanced bodies. Both have needs. And for better or worse, they frequently conflict.

Augustine, bless his fifth-century soul, was simply trying to put into words this on-going conflict—a struggle science has only recently given us the tools to better understand. Original Sin, if we look on the concept as Faithspeak, is as good a name for it as any. And what it means is that all of us are carrying some heavy baggage from the moment we step through the turnstile. Whatever wonderful things human beings may be capable of, we also have an inherent potential for doing things society labels as "bad"—if only because our genetic programming was in place before polite society was. And now, like every notable religious thinker has said (in so many words), *We just gotta deal with it, darlin'*.

It turns out that one of best ways to deal with it (in so many words) is to become a "new creature." We do this by first acknowledging our sinful nature—our legacy from evolution, so to speak—then reaching out for whatever resources might help integrate that sinful streak or evolutionary legacy into Who We Are.

The good news is, those resources are already within us. The very minds that caused our estrangement from the physical roles for which we were designed, can now reconcile us. By tapping into a realm that is stronger than the purely physical—whether submitting to Allah, or to The Law, or by "accepting Christ" or "annihilating the ego" or "becoming clear"—each person can overcome the universal problems that go along with being human. And unless we *can* do that, we'll never be as fully human as we could. Or as fully divine.

Augustine, in his bumbling, stumbling way, was absolutely right.

ORTHODOX

"Orthodox" is another way of saying, as that old gospel toe-tapper puts it, "If it's good enough for granddad, it's good enough for me." It's also, cynically speaking, the notion that form is more important than substance. Or rather, that form *is* substance.

An orthodox religion is one that jealously preserves a specific form for the expression of its message. That form may include the words and language of its founder, the symbols and rituals as they were practiced from ancient times, the institutional organization and even the style of clothing worn by its priests. From a pair of Greek words meaning "true to opinion," the word "orthodox" is a linguistic label which denotes and assures authenticity. Like that little red tag on a pair of Levi's.

Admittedly, maintaining things as authentically as possible can provide a connection to the past that's almost palpable, a sense that the characters in all those dusty scriptures were more than figments of someone's imagination. Not to mention the fact that, once people start messing with tradition, it's difficult to know where to draw the line. For example, how much alteration of the original form can be allowed before the inherent meaning changes? Can you put Christianity on the tube like some late-night talk show—*heeeerrrrre's Jeezus!*—with interviews and gospel rock bands and commercial breaks (or regular pleas for financial support), and still deliver the same message?

If you accept one of the primary principles of this book, you already know that Faithspeak is as much about *how* something is said as *what*. It must follow, therefore, that the only way to keep the original message intact is to remain strictly orthodox, to maintain the form exactly as it was from the beginning. Right?

Wrong. Authentically, genuinely wrong.

Because if you accept another principle of Faithspeak, you'll remember that the context in which a message is delivered has a direct impact on how that message is heard by people. As society changes, as science develops new knowledge and new analogies for expressing ideas—in short, as our language and symbols evolve—the words and rituals of one century inevitably convey different meanings to the next. So by trying to preserve authenticity, orthodoxy can actually disconnect us from the original message. And the longer its original form remains the same, the more that message can be subverted or lose relevance.

The only way to preserve the truth, ironically, is to continually update the way it's presented.

To a point.

Notes

PACIFISM

Some people believe that human life is so inherently valuable that killing another human being, even in self-defense, would render one's own life no longer worth living. Better to let your life be taken than to take another's. Such is the position of radical pacifism. And the courage to do this—to die in spite of all your hopes and dreams and the family you'd leave behind—far surpasses that of any battlefield soldier charging enemy lines in a modified dune buggy mounted with a 50-caliber machine gun.

Some of those same pacifists will inevitably point to the New Testament story where Jesus asks his followers to "turn the other cheek" when insulted or attacked, as if Jesus was advising people to just stand there and take whatever pummeling the bad guys dish out, up to and including the punch that turns your lights out once and for all.

Others aren't so sure that's what Jesus meant. Judaism is not a pacifist religion, after all; and maybe this well-known Jewish rabbi was simply counseling "tactics." Perhaps he was advising followers not to be goaded into a confrontation whose conditions were being set by someone else. Wait for the right moment; don't let them draw you in with superficial blows designed to make you lose your cool and give them an excuse to respond with deadly force. Give them the shirt off your back if necessary. At least you'll survive to do battle on your terms when the time is right.

A persuasive argument. And certainly the manner in which Christian Presidents and church-going generals would interpret the story. But maybe there's some truth to both interpretations.

For example, Jesus must've had a pretty good sense of what his life was for. He talked about timing on several occasions: It's not time for this or that to happen; my "hour is not yet come." The final act of his life would be to die on the cross. And if a knife-wielding assassin had tried to slice his left jugular vein instead of slapping his left cheek, it's doubtful Jesus would've turned his right jugular too.

On the other hand, there's the argument that a willingness to turn the other cheek can prevent one from ever *having* to turn the other cheek. Or rarely having to. Letting people know in advance that you mean them no harm lessens the threat other people perceive, thereby reducing the overall atmosphere of confrontation.

And it isn't, as some cynics claim, that not hitting back can be an even more powerful way of "hitting back." As a symbol of Jesus' radical message of love, turning the other cheek expresses the belief that you recognize within your adversary the same divine spark you yourself possess. Standing there unflinchingly as your opponent raises his hand, staring into his eyes with the firm conviction that violence can't possibly solve anything, challenges his divinity to manifest itself.

It's almost a magnetic force. If I love you in a courageous, unexpected, entirely unwarranted way, you can't help but love me back. As violence feeds on itself, so does love. But violence can't change people; the losers in war rarely turn into peace-loving folk who promise to mind their own business and never bother anybody again.

Love *can*. It alone can literally transform not only individuals but nations.

Pacifism is what love looks like within the context of confrontation. Examples can be found in every tradition. The pacifist is the one who realizes somebody has to set the example, and has the courage to risk it. Like the song says, "Let there be peace on earth, and let it begin with me." The pacifist takes that tired cliché and makes it stunningly, transformingly real.

Come to think of it, maybe it *is* about tactics. And maybe someday more of us will actually try it.

PAGAN

From a Greek word meaning "to tend flocks," *pagan* was originally used to point to the simpler folk who populated the rural countryside. These, of course, were in contrast to the presumably more refined and more intelligent citizens to whom fell the greater responsibilities of government, priesthood, higher education and waging war. Like the Hebrew word *goyim,* which referred to everyone who wasn't Jewish, "pagan" became the Christian appellation for everyone who hadn't yet converted to the Roman Empire's new state religion. Or to those who *had* been given the chance to convert, but stubbornly refused to see the light.

It was the latter choice, especially, that turned the word into an epithet, dripping with judgment against a whole class of people supposedly ignorant enough or wicked enough to prefer their polytheism and their nature spirits to the Savior of the World. Ironically, scholarly research has shown how the suppression of pagan beliefs—an attachment to nature's cycles, a respect for the sometimes beneficent, sometimes scary forces behind the vagaries of life—were re-channeled into the festivals, saints and demons of Roman Catholicism. And maybe it's true, as scholars and psychologists have also suggested, that we are *all* pagans at heart, that we all need rituals and symbols to nourish this simpler, nature-connected part of ourselves.

Which explains why you'll find holy days in every religious tradition that celebrate changes in seasons, that commemorate times for planting and harvesting, that call for periods of both hunger (fasting) and consumption (feasting). It also explains why we have divinities who seek to save us, alongside equally-powerful devils seemingly hell-bent on our destruction. It's only natural. It's nature's dualistic, cyclical story. And the way we write our story's climax defines whether we think life is worth living, or it's all just a country lark.

PARABLE

The parable is one of the finest teaching tools ever invented. Jesus wasn't the first to use it, but he was awfully good at it. Ancient Greeks and Persians also used it effectively. The Hebrew Bible records several parables, one of which hit King David like a wagon-load of sheep manure when he realized it was about *him.* Jewish sages and rabbis used them to illustrate their talking points long before (and for centuries after) Jesus perfected the technique.

You've probably made up a few parables yourself. Basically it's a deceptively simple story told for the deeper meaning or message it contains. Whether it's true or "made up" isn't at issue. Somebody asks you a tough question, let's say. And instead of tackling the query head on, you invent a little story with a dramatic flair that answers the question in a way that may take a while to "get"; but once your listener *does* get it, he's less likely to forget.

It might be no more than a pointed analogy. "Hey, don't you miss when Desert Storm was on the news every night?" somebody asks. "Sure do," comes the reply, "an' I was really bummed when they took *The Sopranos* off the air, too."

Think about it.

Or it may take even more thought. "What's your opinion of the new middle-class tax cuts?" Answer: "A shot of Novocain helps before the dentist starts drilling."

Or someone asks you what the qualifications are for being a good neighbor. You reply that there was once a man walking along a road who was attacked by robbers and left for dead. A couple of other guys come along and find the victim bleeding on the side of the road. One is a deacon in his church and the other is on the City Council, and both shake their heads and hurry past. They've got appointments; they're late for important meetings; there's just no time to get involved, you see. And then someone comes along from the ramshackle housing development across the tracks, somebody you'd never invite over for dinner or even be seen with in public. But this social outcast stops and picks up the poor, dying victim, cleans up his wounds, gives him some new clothes and nurses him back to health.

About this time everyone who's listening starts to get the point. Who would *you* want for a neighbor? And what's better—a big shot reputation or a willingness to take time out from our busy lives and act like human beings made in the divine image?

And the point is, a good story always makes the point better than cold logic or a scholarly exposition of facts. Like Faithspeak, parables involve emotion as well as intellect. That's the way we learn; that's how we remember. The dictionary definitions of "good" and "neighbor" are lifeless and forgettable. The Parable of the Good Samaritan is a memorable drama. It can actually re-shape how we think and act.

Parables can also hide or reveal meaning. The best ones have more than one level, like a movie that can be appreciated for its action and mystery; and then, when you go out afterward for a hot fudge sundae and start talking it over, you realize there were all sorts of hidden messages. The movie was saying things you weren't aware of at the time.

Or maybe you decide the real story was altogether different from the surface-level plot. Much of this re-interpretation of the movie depends on what you bring to it, your own experience and knowledge, your hopes and dreams—or lack of them. Two people might watch the same movie and come away with two very different versions of what it was about.

Jesus admitted as much in describing his own teaching technique. "This is why I speak to them in parables," he said, "because in seeing they do not see, and hearing they do not hear..." And "...to you it has been given to know the secrets of the kingdom of heaven, but to them it has not been given." Some people can figure it out, some can't. Some just aren't ready for the truth yet.

A statement attributed to the Islamic poet Nasiri Khusraw is even more direct. "A prophet must always explain his teaching in similes," he wrote, "devised for the understanding of all grades of intelligence. Primitive people do not understand anything beyond this, but intelligent people will at once grasp the purpose of the simile."

There are many who think that is precisely why great stories are great, why scriptures become "scripture." They speak to us at whatever level we currently operate—primitive, advanced, or somewhere in between—each level valid, each offering insight to light our way.

Perhaps, as more than one theologian has suggested, the whole New Testament is an extended parable. "Does God really love the world?" someone asks. "Well," comes the reply, "there was once This Guy who planted a family in a Garden and then went away to watch from a distance while their descendents started screwing things up until he just couldn't stand it any longer. So He comes back and transforms himself into a little baby, and he grows up and..."

And...?

And how you interpret the rest of the parable, what it means in the context of your own life, depends on how that story connects with your understanding and experience, how you interact with it, and thus whether it has any power to shape you. Maybe into someone who's content simply to earn himself a big shot reputation. Or maybe into someone who takes time out from his busy life and acts like a human being made in the divine image.

PATH

It's hardly surprising that the word "path" has been as central to spirituality and religion as it has to travel and cartography. After all, its root meaning—"a way of going"—is rich with symbolic possibilities. That's no doubt why John's philosophical version of the Gospel labels Jesus as "The Way." And why a whole religious tradition, Taoism, goes by that very same name.

Since the Sixties, if not before, "finding your path" has been synonymous with discovering which spiritual practice best serves your specific needs and goals. And what's most important isn't so much whether you actually reach those goals or arrive at some predetermined destination; it's *how you get there.*

Some paths, for example, can be solitary ventures winding through the rocky, treacherous terrain of self-discovery. Others walk the straight-and-narrow highway of self-discipline and obedience. For many, it's a wider, well-paved avenue crowded with fellow pilgrims, where there are plenty of ups and downs but the route is well-established and the road signs prepare you for what's around the bend.

Admittedly, finding your path is far more difficult today than for past generations—at least in pluralistic societies where multiple paths are available and the well-paved avenue of a single tradition can't sweep you along, like it or not. Having what amounts to a religious smorgasbord presents unique challenges: How to weigh the truth claims of various traditions, for example; or how to see through religious language to the shared meanings behind them; whether to pick an existing tradition and commit oneself to its path alone, or select elements from several and fashion a practice that's custom-tailored to your needs—and your idiosyncrasies.

So many choices, so little time!

Of course, some decisions should be made before you even embark. Like what the Path is *for* in the first place, or what kind of person you hope to become while you're on the way.

It's tempting to take your time before you decide these things. But it's equally tempting to just get a move on. After all, once you start down one path, you can always take a detour and find another. Most paths intersect at various points along the way. And, as it turns out, almost all are headed in the same general direction.

PEACE

It ought to be clear by now that peace is far more than an absence of conflict or war. Neither is it merely a kind of undisturbed rest, as in "She was sleeping peacefully." The Hebrew word for "peace," *shalom,* implies wholeness. Likewise the Arabic *salaam,* or the Eastern concept of "bliss."

Peace is the condition in which the whole being is working at its optimum level. Peace is the condition wherein physical and spiritual elements are successfully integrated, working together toward some goal that gives meaning to existence, while providing the energy to meet any challenge.

Every religious tradition is designed to create, maintain and enhance this optimum condition—both inward and outward, individual and communal. Approaches differ, of course, just like all the various techniques for learning and refining your golf game. There's the basic handbook that talks about the "rules" of golf, and describes how to swing a club or which iron to use depending on distance and obstacles on the fairway. Then there's the video that shows you how a real pro does it, and you get inspired and buy yourself a new set of clubs and go out and practice and try to become *like* the pro.

There's also the advanced manual that asks you to concentrate on the "inner game," on developing and maintaining self-confidence. It might ask you to imagine yourself swinging your club smoothly and easily, or maybe to imagine yourself as the golf ball, arching gracefully toward the green while the cup draws you into itself. You become not only the golfer, but the ball, the course, and the whole bloomin' game.

All of these techniques can help you improve. Some of them overlap. Most are simply different ways of conceptualizing the game in order to produce the same outcome: To play golf to the best of your abilities, within the rules, while getting you to compete not so much against the other players in your foursome but against the course. The trees and sand-traps are there only to make it more interesting, to force you to focus on your skills, to hone them, to find the best way to reach the objective. Some days you've got just the right touch, and some days you don't; but when you do it's like everything just... *flows.*

Ironically, once it starts flowing, it's best not to analyze it too much. The wholeness you've achieved goes beyond words. It's that elusive unity of mind/body. It's peak performance. It's "the peace that surpasses all understanding." It's heaven on earth. It's bliss.

Forgive the sports analogy. Maybe it's because "parable" came up a couple of listings ago, and improving your golf game happens to make a good one. As a matter of fact, almost any sport does, as long as it's familiar enough to your audience.

And maybe the deeper meaning of this parable is that if we were only half as serious about our faiths as we are about golf—or skiing, or computer games, or our jobs—we just might achieve peace yet. In our lives. In our world.

PERFECT

The religious meaning of "perfect" has basically been trashed by holier-than-thou types who hold an inflated view of themselves and their religion, or by people who forget that doing the right thing is rarely easy. "Perfect," for these people, is a condition in which their human flaws and weaknesses have supposedly been washed away or otherwise removed. Which means those people are probably blind to their own faults because, as the saying goes, *Nobody's perfect.*

And yet Hindu literature acknowledges perfection as an achievable goal. Jesus was apparently serious when he said, "Be perfect, even as I am perfect." What gives?

To start with, try looking at the word as a *verb* instead of an adjective. "Perfect" (with the accent on the second syllable) is something you *do,* not something you are. The original Latin *perfectus,* after all, is composed of a suffix which means "to make," and a prefix which means "thoroughly." Perfect therefore implies doing a job as if you intend to finish it, working at it with the kind of attitude that says "anything worth doing is worth doing well." Whether or not you actually *do* finish, or whether or not you do it "well," is less important than *striving* to.

So when Jesus said "Be perfect" he wasn't telling followers that he expected them to start living flawlessly, or even that he wanted them to become flawless. He was simply saying, "Work hard; put your heart and mind into it—the way I am." Being perfect is a faith, an outlook on life, a commitment to refine your own personal attitudes and behavior as if it mattered more than anything, as if it was the most important project in your life. Because it is.

Which is also the Hindu understanding of perfection. It is the attitude that makes refining Who You Are the reason for your existence. Going to school, getting a job, finding a mate, raising a family, saving up for that bigger house or flashy new car or comfortable retirement—or deciding *not* to do these things—are all occasions to work on your Self, to do what the New Spirituality calls "soul-work."

In fact, whatever you are currently facing in life is part of a well-oiled Scheme to move you toward the full realization and expression of your divinity. The timing is not by accident. As Hinduism puts it, "The Lotus is unfolding as it must." Each petal opens as you complete another stage in your ongoing development.

Outward events are the tools for inner refinement. To be perfect is to know that.

PHILOSOPHY

When the word was originally cobbled together—from the Greek *philos* (love) and *sophia* (wisdom)—it pretty much encompassed every subject a person could have knowledge about. The study of religion was philosophy. Ethics or mathematics was a philosophy. All the fields of science were philosophies. So were metaphysics and logic and similar intellectual pursuits where reason alone could uncover truths about human existence.

Unfortunately, philosophy inevitably ran up against Mother Church, at which time the word was downgraded to imply "matters of opinion" or "speculation," in contrast to the revealed Truth confirmed by no less an authority than God Himself. Worse, philosophy also came to be considered a product of human vanity. To suppose that human thought could add anything significant to Church teaching was not only boastful, it was sinful enough to merit a few lashes, if not a good roasting on the vertical spit.

Today the word "philosophy" has become a kind of linguistic prefix for various subjects instead of the subjects themselves, as in The Philosophy of Religion or The Philosophy of Education, or The Philosophy of Star Trek. Used in this way, it stands for "the wisdom gleaned from" or "the collected thoughts about" whatever the subject happens to be. Genuine philosophy, however—literally "loving to be wise"—is less about specific subjects or compilations of wisdom than the process of acquiring it. Philosophy, in short, is something you *do*.

We are all philosophers insofar as we love learning about a certain subject, and our love leads to wisdom, and our wisdom leads to action, and our action becomes an expression of our love. And when that cycle continues for a lifetime, it's what some call salvation.

PILGRIMAGE

Narrowly defined, a pilgrimage is a journey to a sacred place for the purpose of spiritual reflection or "grounding" in the tradition. Understood as a metaphor for a deeper process, it's... well, if you've come this far in the book, you can probably write the definition for yourself.

Because we are *all* pilgrims, religious or not, having embarked on a journey that spans a lifetime, traveling a long and winding road to multiple places where we are given repeated opportunities to look back on our lives from another perspective, from "higher ground" perhaps, to consider what we've learned up to that point, and what we haven't learned but should.

For Muslims, the required pilgrimage (*Hajj*) is to Mecca—whether by camel or boat or Airbus 320—where subsequent, smaller pilgrimages include the "circumambulation" of the Ka'aba (*Tawaf*) and a trip to the nearby Hills of Mina to throw stones at Shaitan. For Jews, the recommended pilgrimage is back to the restored State of Israel to tour sites like the Western Wall (which is all that remains of the Jerusalem Temple), or the fortress of Masada (where Jewish rebels held off the Roman legions for the better part of a year), or the Valley of Elah (where David slew Goliath), perhaps joining in an archeological dig along the way.

Christians are advised to visit the Holy Land as well, and especially to walk the Via de la Rosa where Jesus carried his cross on the way to Golgotha. Other Christian pilgrimages are plentiful—among them the Camino de Santiago (Way of Saint James) from Spain to Portugal, featured in the Martin Sheen movie *The Way*, or a trip to the steps of Wittenberg Chapel where Martin Luther nailed his Ninety-Five Theses to the front door.

Hinduism boasts almost as many pilgrimages as there are gurus and gods, the completing of which could easily consume several lifetimes, much less leave time to reflect on a single life. Buddhist pilgrimages include visits to the sites where the Enlightened One was born, where he fasted under the bodhi tree or offered his most famous sermons, and finally where he entered *mahaparinirvana* (i.e. died).

Most Sikhs are content to visit only one site during their lifetime—

the Golden Temple in Amritsar, though other major temples throughout the world can substitute for this rather expensive trek to India's Punjab region. Baha'is "in good standing" may apply to visit the Baha'i World Center in Haifa, Israel, where a nine-day guided tour will bus the faithful to holy shrines commemorating the central figures in their history, as well as to the Baha'i burial grounds and the luxuriant gardens on Mount Carmel.

Pilgrimages need not be connected to religious figures or sacred history, however, even if they remain in some sense spiritual. Citizens of the U.S. and visitors from around the world now flock to the 9/11 Memorial where the World Trade Towers once stood, just as they've been drawn for decades to the marble monuments scattered throughout Washington, D.C., all the while treating these sites as if they were holy ground. Serious "thru-hikers" and ordinary nature-lovers follow all or part of the Pacific Crest Trail from California to Washington like their paragon John Muir did, on a holy quest to explore Mother Nature's many faces, if not their own character and inner resources.

And the common denominator in all these sacred treks is that they symbolize something important about our collective journeys through Life: Our dependence on the Earth; our connectedness to the past; our indebtedness to both the common and uncommon people who came before us... how the significance and sheer reality of their lives can suddenly hit us like a divine revelation just by walking the ground they walked on, seeing the geography they saw, touching the stones and mortar of the houses they inhabited... how all those people were likewise on spiritual pilgrimages in their own time just as we are now... and how, in the end, it was worth all the blood, sweat and tears they shed.

As we hope and pray it will be for us.

PLURALISM

No, this does *not* mean "Anything goes." Pluralism is not the notion that one religion works just as well as another. Nor is it the idea that there are no universal standards for judging the merits of any religious claim or concept, or that it's all a matter of personal taste and people should be allowed to believe whatever the heck they want.

What pluralism *is,* is the recognition that religious traditions (and ethnic differences) are only indirectly related to the kinds of behavior necessary for the functioning of a modern society. It is therefore possible to allow and even encourage a wide range of religious expression.

In other words, what people say they "believe" does not preclude them from getting along just fine, thanks. One person's claim that Jesus wasn't conceived through normal sexual relations doesn't prevent him from stopping when the traffic light turns red, or from enjoying egg-flower soup at a restaurant owned by someone who doesn't believe in Jesus at all. Your belief that God is a man in a white beard, or a force like gravity or a figment of someone's imagination, has almost nothing to do with your obeying the laws of the land and being a productive member of society.

Which leads to several possible conclusions, including: 1) Religious belief and tradition are irrelevant to human interaction; or 2) Religious traditions are relevant in theory, but most people ignore them or don't practice them, which makes them irrelevant for all practical purposes; or 3) Religious traditions are relevant, but not in the way most people think they are.

The premise of this book is compatible with #2, though conclusion #3 is best. Faithspeak asserts that religious traditions are toolkits for getting at truths that run deeper than the words by which people have attempted to formulate them. So what we may think are two widely different religious systems are only two different "languages" for discussing the same Ultimate Reality. The net effects on the people who speak those languages can often be identical.

It might be nice, of course, if everybody spoke the same language, because it would make communication so much easier, and people might be less inclined to mistake artificial differences for real ones. But pluralism is—or ought to be—based on one more conviction: We *need* those differences. More than ever, humankind needs a variety of spiritual languages to make Ultimate Reality accessible to everyone. Offering any single religion simply won't do. And not because one particular religion may not convey Truth as well as another. It's because Truth isn't conveyed through those particular words and symbols for certain people. For whatever reason, the Good News just can't reach them that way.

In a pluralistic society, however, there are alternatives. Those people can find some other language that speaks to their heart. They can still be made whole in another way, along another Path.

What's the best path to the mountaintop? For you, the one that gets you there. For him, the one that gets *him* there.

Ad infinitum.

POOR

Poverty is one of the basic motifs running throughout the world's sacred scriptures. In reading them we get the sense that poor people are everywhere; that hunger and homelessness have always been part of the human condition—even when much of society is getting along quite comfortably.

Hebrew prophetic writings, especially, pointed out the glaring inconsistency between the grinding poverty of some people and the inordinate wealth of others who were living in luxury. And who, even if they earned their wealth honestly, were in danger of losing it all by ignoring the suffering around them.

Not ignoring the poor is nearly always combined with some notion of Justice. It's almost as if poverty exists in order to force us to recognize our responsibility for one another, to put our own needs into a broader context. It's as if the homeless people we pass on the street are a direct challenge to Who We Are and why it's not *us* sleeping on the park bench instead of them.

The endless pages of Mosaic and Islamic laws detailing how we must provide support for widows and orphans and impoverished strangers are designed not merely to distribute resources more equitably—though that's certainly an admirable practice. Modern societies, from capitalist to communist, have all incorporated some variation on this duty to the poor. Not to mention the purely practical angle: People who have nothing, have nothing to lose. That's how revolutions start.

But there's a spiritual angle, too—one that's even more important. It's important partly because our spiritual health is enhanced by a "giving instinct" that encourages us to share some portion of what we have, thereby preventing us from becoming too selfish.

The deeper effect, however, lies in the constant reminder that we cannot define ourselves in outward terms. Who We Are isn't a matter of being a doctor or a migrant farm worker. Whether we live in a nice house or make enough money this year to afford that 10-day Mediterranean cruise isn't what saves us. In fact all these things can work *against* us by fueling the mistaken idea that material needs and desires are what life is about.

What's on the *inside,* so to speak, is our salvation: A sense of purpose; an open acceptance of the ups-and-downs life sends our way; an appreciation for other people, other views; an ability to listen, to be non-judgmental, to love. All of which are aspects of one's faith.

How we treat the poor, or react to *being* poor, offers a continuing opportunity to shape our faith and redefine ourselves. Whether we can stare unblinkingly into the face of poverty and come to grips with it, or turn away from it altogether, reflects how far we've come.

And maybe the fact that poverty just won't go away is a strong hint that there's much more work for us to do.

POWER

Simply put, power is "the ability to act."

This is not to be confused with the *source* of that ability—that is, the energy or authority that enables it—or the specific *uses* of power, like the ability to manipulate matter or control other people. It is simply the condition of being able to consciously choose to do something, and then *do* it.

Much of our life is spent learning how to wield power for either benefit or harm, deciding how much of it we should expend on ourselves versus others, not to mention discovering how much of it we "have" to begin with. Religious texts are filled with stories about such power struggles, using metaphors suited to their authors' time and place: Hebrew slaves vs. the Pharaoh's armies; the King of Kings vs. The Prince of Darkness; Arjuna and Krishna on the battlefield where the Pandavas and Kauravas prepare to fight to the death.

And the moral of the story isn't about military victories or who ends up on the throne. It's about giving up our power to others versus expanding our own innate ability to choose and act. It's about the fact, learned from human experience if not divine revelation, that some of our choices in the present will constrain our power in the future—bad habits and addictions, violence, turning a blind eye toward injustice, giving up freedom in exchange for security—while other choices tend to increase it. Like loving your neighbor as yourself, or acting with honesty and respect, or extending equal rights to *all* people, not just the ones you agree with or approve of.

Power is inherently neither good nor bad. But as mythology and sacred scripture remind us, it does tend to be self-limiting unless we use it wisely.

PRAISE

Prayer and praise are as related as their linguistic forms would suggest. Both are religious rituals. Both are directed toward some higher power. But whereas prayer is usually regarded as asking, praise is the act of acknowledging.

It acknowledges, first, that some Higher Power exists. There may always be some lingering doubts, yes; but every now and then it suddenly becomes so clear that you're compelled to make a little noise. "You—whoever or whatever you are—are really there! And to think I once considered myself the center of the universe!"

Praise may also acknowledge one's debt or dependence on that Higher Power. "Thanks for turning things around for me," you might gush. Or "Good lord, I couldn't have done it without you!" Not that this Power doesn't already know that, or that He/It is vain enough to need the acclaim and recognition we occasionally offer.

Actually, the expression of praise is more for our own benefit than anyone else's. To offer praise is to reaffirm that we are "in the loop" with divinity, so to speak. By recognizing that there are deeper currents moving below the surface, we open ourselves to the energy of that spiritual ocean. We become more attentive to the signs and resources other sailors might not see, better prepared for the inevitable storms.

Which inevitably gives the cynic one more opportunity to argue that praise is only a ploy used by superstitious fools to butter up their gods in hopes of winning favor. Like an apple for the teacher. Or a compliment on the boss's new hairpiece just before your next pay-raise comes up for review.

But what the teacher or the boss can't know for sure is whether the apple or the compliments are sincere, or merely strategically-placed bribes. Presumably the higher power *does* know. The deeper waters that buoy up the universe are also connected to the spiritual currents within each of us, and therefore nothing remains hidden. Not even the praise in our hearts we're too timid to express, or the praise we hold back because it seems so irrational or downright old-fashioned.

And yet, who's to say that your child-like wonder at the beauty of a rosebud, or your slack-jawed awe while watching a bevy of starlings as they swoop and reverse direction in utter unison, or the warmth that washes over you while in your lover's embrace... that these too aren't forms of praise?

PRAYER

It is one thing to acknowledge that you are in the divine "loop"—that is, connected to spiritual resources that can change your life for the better. It is something else to actually *use* that connection and make those changes. Or, in Faithspeak, to know "how to pray."

The full instructions would fill a book. Or a few thousand. Understanding when to pray, what to pray, and why you'd want to pray in the first place is one of the primary businesses of religion. Like meditation, prayer is often said to be what religion is *about.*

The usual definition revolves around the idea of "asking" God for something. The Latin word for prayer, *precari,* refers to making a "request." The Indian Sanskrit *prchati* means, literally, "he asks." No wonder most of us get a mental image of some ninth-century nobleman, decked out in his finest robes, kneeling before the throne as he humbly petitions the king for a favor: Help in resolving a legal matter, say, or a few hundred acres of royal land on which to build a nice hunting lodge.

This petitionary model, in fact, is why people still kneel or "bow down" or otherwise have the courtesy to "humble themselves" a bit before launching into their request. It's also why people put that request into *words,* speaking them aloud as if God is actually listening in the way His Royal Highness would.

Which is not to imply that talking out loud is the wrong approach. It's just that the words are not what the prayer *is.* And "hearing" them is not how God receives your request.

Look at it strictly from a numbers point of view. Let's say that, at any given moment, one-tenth of one percent of the world's population is actively praying. Obviously, a lot of people don't pray to begin with; and of those who do, odds are most of them are probably doing something else right now, like sleeping. One person praying for every thousand people seems a conservative enough figure. So out of seven billion people on planet, that means seven *million* people are praying to God (by whatever name) at this moment.

For the sake of argument, however, let's suppose that God only listens to *certain* people's prayers. Some fundamentalist Christians, for example, claim that God doesn't hear the prayers of Jews or Muslims. Some Muslims are convinced that many Christians and Hindus (and definitely pagans) are never heard. For whatever narrow, self-serving reason, let's pretend that only one-tenth of one percent of those seven million people who are currently praying are actually being "listened to" by God. That still leaves seven thousand voices simultaneously competing for God's attention. On planet Earth, anyway.

It won't help to reply that God can do anything, and even though we humans would be hard pressed to follow two or three conversations at the same time, seven thousand is no big deal for God. Because even if that's so, then it must follow that *how* God hears those clamoring voices is completely beyond anything in human experience. The notion of God hearing us in the same way human beings hear one another is merely a poetic analogy.

Most Eastern traditions avoid the need for such literal descriptions. God's "hearing us" is more like an automated process. It's as natural as atoms holding themselves together in the shape of objects, or transferring energy through the interactions of their electrons. It's a system of inter-communication that's built into the very nature of things.

After all, the spiritual resource that "listens" obviously doesn't function only in Arabic or Hebrew. Or in Sanskrit, Latin, the King's English or inner-city slang. And the mode of transmission isn't the vibrations of air generated by our vocal chords. It's what gives rise to those vibrations, or may even be left entirely unspoken. It's the whole complex of what's in our hearts, the willingness to open every layer of one's self to spiritual inspection and renewal. It's a direct linking with Ultimate Reality in a way that both defies verbal description and is beyond words.

Words can still play an important role, of course. Praying aloud may enable us to link with Ultimate Reality more easily, at least to start with, either by helping us shut out distractions or by giving our deepest feelings an acceptable outlet through which to reveal themselves. Psychologists have confirmed what sages have known for thousands of years: That simply talking about your feelings (a.k.a. "spilling your guts") not only relieves the terrible burden of secrecy, but often brings to consciousness feelings you never knew you had.

And even if no one else were listening, prayer would still be a worthwhile exercise. In giving voice to your hopes and dreams, your strengths and faults, you gain a valuable new perspective. A part of you hears these things as if they were someone else's problems. They become less personal, more separable from Who You Are. And since they are no longer so wrapped up in your private little ego, you can be more objective about them.

There is one other form of prayer where spoken words can help. Because sometimes it's not just our own voice we need to hear; it's the voices of other people. The kind of ritual prayers or responsive readings one hears at most worship services aren't so much designed to petition a particular divinity as to *bind members of the congregation to one another.* Public prayer promotes a sense of community. To hear other people recite the same words you're reciting—no matter what those words may be—is a deeply affecting symbol that "We are in this together" or "We are all equal before God."

And if New Age is on to anything, this prayerful solidarity is more than symbolic. Linking ourselves to other people may actually create a spiritual energy that can affect physical reality. Similar thoughts may amplify one another like electromagnetic waves intersecting. Public prayer puts everyone on the same wavelength, so to speak, producing a powerful mental resonance that can then be focused on some specific problem or need.

"Where two or three are gathered," Jesus said, "there I will be." As if to emphasize that, at least for the big things on the agenda, group effort is the key. Prayer circles capitalize on this same principle. And if the process generates results—directly or indirectly—it must work.

The thing about prayer is, most people don't give it *time* to work. Whatever its scientific underpinnings, praying appears to be a skill that takes time to develop. The fact that virtually anyone can learn to swim, and that certain natural laws can be exploited in order to do it increasingly well, doesn't mean that swimming comes easily. It takes effort and commitment and the overcoming of one's fears, not the least of which is the fear of looking like a fool until you get the hang of it.

And yet people *do* get the hang of it. They will also spend years developing a decent backhand in tennis, or perfecting their chip shot in golf, or working out on the rowing machine like galley slaves to keep their thighs from turning to cellulite. But after a couple of unanswered prayers, many folks decide the whole business is rubbish.

Well, some of it may be. Or it may be that not very many people have the necessary patience. Or that the particular form of prayer you tried couldn't reach down into your guts and bring about the desired results. Maybe that brand of Faithspeak was wrong for you.

Fortunately there are other brands, other "technologies" of prayer. And since prayer isn't primarily about talking or asking to begin with, we ought to feel encouraged to try another form. One of the strong points of the New Spirituality is making people aware of the alternatives. From chanting to silent meditation to focused breathing, from guided visualization to the recitation of positive affirmations—whatever it is that connects the deepest core of your being to the deepest resources within the universe, *that* is your form of prayer.

To some extent you're probably already connected whether you consider yourself religious or not. The longing in your heart, the wish that things could be different, or that rare, glorious glow when you wouldn't change a thing—all of these spiritual feelings have deeper roots than we think, roots that reach into the same soil which nourishes everyone and everything else.

Prayer says *Yes* to those roots, and to that soil. And if it asks for anything, it simply asks to keep growing.

PRIESTHOOD

A priest or priestess is the functionary of a religious institution authorized to perform its sacred rites. Especially those rites which mediate between the human and the divine.

In ancient times these were mostly sacrificial rites, designed to win the favor of the gods by giving them something humans considered especially valuable: A first-born child; an unblemished virgin; the still-beating heart of a defeated foe. When or wherever human sacrifice fell out of vogue, various animals were commonly substituted, making them the preferred agents of divine bribery instead.

The way the ritual was performed was critical. To the modern mind, it seems ludicrous that there could be any correct way to conduct a sacrifice, human or otherwise. Back then, however, not just anyone could be trusted to do the job. If proper form wasn't followed, the sacrifice might not only fail to please the gods, it could make them downright angry. Priests were the only ones trained to do the rites right.

Today, of course, the sacred rites have more to do with life-cycle events than ritual slaughter: Birth, baptism and burial; marriage, communion, blessings for special occasions; routine worship and communal prayers. And yet "priest" still has an ancient, almost primitive ring to it, bringing visions of stone altars and splattered blood and burning incense. That's why Muslims don't even *have* priests, and Protestants prefer to call them "ministers" or "pastors."

But what the idea of the priest stands for (apart from the archaic meaning), is that there are people who are better equipped to mediate for us, especially-qualified people we can call on to help us "win the gods' favor" or otherwise connect with divinity. The priest and priestess symbolize those who can assist us on our spiritual journeys, either because they've walked the path before us, or because they've developed a special relationship to The Divine that gives them unique insights and abilities. There's no shame in asking for a helping hand if you can't seem to do something yourself—mend a broken relationship, say, or take that next step in your career or spiritual life—and if someone else's experience can save us some grief, why not take advantage of it?

More often than not, the people with the most experience are older than we are, which is why "priest" comes from a Greek word meaning "old man." But priests are wherever you find them, no matter what age or sex. A priest is anyone who can help improve your relationship to Ultimate Reality, or shed some light when it's too dark to see.

Which isn't exactly a new idea. Ancient Israel was called by its prophets to be "a kingdom of priests" where one's everyday life was a sacrificial rite and every member of the community could mediate for anyone else because they were all equal before God. Early Christianity labeled itself "the priesthood of all believers" for essentially the same reason—and because *faith* is what demonstrates Who We Are, not some official title bestowed by some religious institution.

Even if that title happens to be "priest."

PROGRAMMING

Over the last century, the art of shaping human behavior has finally become a recognized science. Not so much because anyone is particularly good at it yet, but because we're at last beginning to use the tools of technology to figure out why we do the things we do.

Early psychologists and behaviorists like Pavlov and Skinner made incredible advancements by treating humans as complex machines. Our bodies became the organic equivalents of blueprints and gears and engines. Behavior could be reduced to the products of mechanistic factors: $X + Y = Z$. And by tracing all the X's and Y's of heredity and environment, we could accurately predict the Z's of behavior.

If being reduced to mechanical equations was demeaning to our humanity, there was also something useful and uplifting about it. Because if our Z's were undesirable according to some agreed-upon standard, tinkering with our X's and Y's might just transform them.

Admittedly this had already been going on for some time. Spanking your Neanderthal teenager after catching him sneaking out of the cave at night—or threatening your parishioners with the flames of hell for their sins—are more or less scientific methods for shaping future behavior. Rewarding a young warrior with an eagle's feather—and promising entrance to Heaven for a life of good deeds—also qualify as behavior modification techniques.

Some techniques, however, are less direct and immediate. Most of our behavior, in fact, evolves over years of exposure to a complex set of ideas and stories and real-life examples, as well as artificially created environments where these influences supposedly make more of an impact. Some of the process is planned, some of it accidental. The outcome for each of us is Who We Are Right Now.

But because we are largely unaware of what has gone into this process, and since we never agreed to it in the first place, most of Who We Are is not of our own making. Basically, we've been brainwashed. We are like prisoners who've been subjected to whispered messages while we're asleep, manipulated by external forces into saying and doing things we might not otherwise do. Or maybe we *are* machines, pre-wired for our roles, computer-programmed to follow a certain set of instructions. And just because we may be conscious of how we behave doesn't mean we actually control it.

The computer analogy is remarkably fitting. Our bodies, brains and genetic characteristics are the "hardware" and Read-Only Memory of our personal CPUs. Our family experiences and formal schooling, as well as the ongoing events in our lives, are the software and new data entry—the programming. But here's where our humanity re-enters the picture: At the very point we realize we have been programmed, by becoming aware that our Z's are products of X's and Y's that have been manufactured and input by other people and other forces, we can step outside of that process. We suddenly gain the power to become our own programmers. Or, in the words of Genesis, to "be as gods."

More important, not only can we start programming ourselves, we can't help but accept full responsibility for it from this point on. We can no longer use our past programming as an excuse. Welcoming this fact as an opportunity, as a decisive turning point in our lives, is the equivalent of being "born again." The slate is wiped clean; we can now redesign Who We Are, change everything we don't like about ourselves and strengthen everything we do.

No one is so naive as to think this will be easy. It's a long, arduous process of rewriting our programs, then testing and further refining the "output." Obviously, it's essential to find out what our personal hardware is to begin with—from its intrinsic capabilities and positive qualities (i.e. the Image of God within us), to its inherent weaknesses (Original Sin). And because every computer has a built-in language, we must learn how to access our specific Operating System, then input new data in a form (Faithspeak) it can both understand and be energized by.

Interestingly, as sophisticated as that computer might seem, its language is surprisingly simple. Like the binary math that runs on your company's IBM mainframe. Like yes's and no's. Do's and don'ts.

And sometimes our biggest hurdle is just accepting that.

PROPHET

If people made a list of the most commonly misunderstood words in the spiritual vocabulary, this word would be right there near the top.

Prophet—in Hebrew, *nabi*—does not imply some divine talent for crystal-ball gazing, fortune telling, or otherwise predicting the future. Prophet literally means "mouthpiece" and was used as a synonym for "spokesman."

The function of the prophet/spokesman was to put into words whatever the divine spirit wanted humans to hear. Muhammad is called The Prophet because Muslims believe his message is God's word for them. Moses was the Jews' first and greatest prophet because Mosaic Law seemed to have come straight from God. Ironically, Moses asked his brother Aaron to be *his* nabi/spokesman, since Aaron was so much better at public speaking.

Moses appointed Aaron to that position; Aaron didn't ask for it. And apparently most of the great prophets didn't go looking for their jobs either. When Isaiah felt the divine finger pointing his way, the first thing he did was ask how long his mission would take, like someone who'd rather be fishing. Jeremiah objected on the grounds that he was too young. Jonah simply ran away. And Amos denied being one because he knew prophets weren't exactly the most popular guys in town.

In fact, prophets were usually the kind of people you'd go across the street to avoid. Not that they all looked weird or smelled bad, though a few of them did. It was just that they didn't have a lot of nice things to say. Many of them went around condemning people for idol worship—that is, for wasting their time and energy on false gods and religious practices that were the spiritual equivalent of masturbation or visiting the local whorehouse. And they enjoyed using terms and illustrations that were at least as shocking as that last sentence, and usually more so.

They also raged against corruption in high places as well as in the lives of the common folk. They criticized the religious establishment for paying more attention to the letter of the law than to its spirit (just as Jesus would do), and especially for thinking that worship consisted of rituals rather than righteousness. Whether someone performs Temple sacrifices (or goes to church on Sunday), the prophets railed, is the last thing that matters. Justice... *justice* is what matters. Taking care of the poor and the sick is what matters. Loving-kindness is what matters, saith the Lord.

And then—maybe—some prophets might indulge in a little forecasting of the future. But not because of any divine hocus-pocus or a talent for reading tea leaves. Prophets were chosen (or felt themselves chosen) because they had a pretty good handle on human nature. They also understood *divine* nature. And they could often see when the two were on a collision course. Their predictions were more like warnings: "If you continue to do what you're doing, here's what's going to happen..." Just as today someone might warn, "If this country continues to ignore its homeless, if it continues spending money on border walls or glass cathedrals or new casinos instead of people, then we're all going to pay a terrible price. And the currency won't be in dollars."

It was all a matter of $X + Y = Z$, to borrow a line from the last entry. And whether or not Z actually came about was often the standard by which someone was labeled a genuine prophet/spokesperson, or his scrolls got tossed into the historical trash heap.

And therein lies the confusion between prophecy and predicting. Therein *also* lies the fact that most people don't know a prophet when they hear one, at least until after he's gone. Because what he said eventually turns out to be correct. Or it was something we needed to hear, even if we didn't appreciate hearing it at the time. It was, as the poet says, "a lover's quarrel."

After all, prophets don't usually appear to those who haven't made a commitment, who haven't yet tied the knot with divinity. They come to those who already profess a relationship with God, but who are in mortal danger of losing it. We're rarely happy with people who accuse us of failing to keep our commitments, or who point out that some of our new commitments conflict with old. We forget that our link with divinity is permanent only if we regularly renew our vows.

The prophet is the voice of Ultimate Reality calling us back to the relationship we once had, or to an even deeper, more lasting one. And the good news is, even if the voice is gone before we realize who was speaking, Who Was Speaking is still there. Still listening.

Now it's our turn to say a few words… preferably through action.

PROSELYTIZE

From a pair of Greek words meaning "he came to," proselytizing is the act (or art) of encouraging someone to come around to a certain predetermined conclusion or viewpoint, usually when that person currently holds a different one. The word, unfortunately, no longer has this ordinary, secular use. We wouldn't say, for example, that a Democrat was proselytized into joining the Republican Party, or that Copernicus proselytized fellow scientists into accepting his theory about the planets revolving around the sun—although, technically speaking, the term *does* apply here. Today's meaning is strictly religious.

And usually not in a good way.

The pair of Jehovah's Witnesses who ring your doorbell on Saturday mornings to ask whether you'd like to discuss the cover story in their latest *Watchtower* magazine have probably ruined more brunches than saved souls. The Catholic priests who built a string of missions from Mexico to Northern California while proselytizing the indigenous tribes not only ruined a few brunches but wiped out a whole culture and most of the native population in the process.

Things weren't much better back in the Old World. The spread of Islam wasn't achieved so much by an encouraging word as a curved sword. Popes who led their papal armies into battle to teach non-believers a lesson were hardly following the Sermon on the Mount. The Prince of Peace would be appalled at the Crusaders' campaigns to win back the Holy Land, or the tortures used by the Inquisition to bring heretics back to the One True Faith. Violence and mayhem were also popular in Jewish and Hindu scriptures, if not for the purpose of gaining converts then to simply wipe out the people who were trying to convert *them*.

And it wasn't meant to be this way. The Islamic equivalent of proselytizing, *Da'wah*, literally means to "invite to," in the sense of offering an opportunity for the curious to find out more about Islam; conversion wasn't the primary goal. A passage from the Qur'an reads, "Invite (everyone) to the way of your Lord (Allah) with beautiful preaching; and argue with them in ways that are best and most gracious." In short, arguing (i.e. providing a cogent argument) to attract a prospective convert was as heated as proselytizing was supposed to get. And if the argument wasn't won, neither was the proselyte.

Of course, that's a far cry from standard procedure throughout most of civilized history. Even in democracies where religious freedom is enshrined, the efforts of those who would proselytize others have ranged from merely annoying to relentless and criminal. Which explains why, over the last century, proselytizing has fallen out of favor and "evangelizing" has become the preferred catchword.

Not that the methods have changed much. The latter term simply sounds, well, more inviting. For one thing, the derivation of the word comes from "angel." For another, when you combine its meaning, "messenger," with its Greek prefix, which means "good," evangelizing basically implies being a good messenger. Or, in verb form, spreading the Good News. How can you argue with that?

You *can,* if you remember what Marshall McLuhan said, and what Madison Avenue admen know all too well: "The medium is the message." In other words, presenting the good news in a bad way is, quite simply, Bad News.

Perhaps *Star Trek*'s Captain Picard put it best. "Our only influence," he said, "is by example." Meaning that we should demonstrate our own highest ideals and aspirations through the way we live; that we should "be a light unto the nations," or at least to our neighbors. And if anyone should ask you how you've come to be such a beacon of light, such an angel of goodness, go ahead and tell them what works for you.

And then go on shining.

PROTESTANT

A protestant with a lower-case "p" is anyone who protests or rises up against something, or who aligns himself with someone else who protests. Protestant with a capital "P" refers to any member of the successive (or secessionist) Christian denominations that arose out of the political/spiritual protest movement called The Reformation.

What needed reforming was Christianity itself, or at least the for-profit corporation running the show throughout most of Western Europe at the time. The Holy Roman Church, it so happened, had begun to think of itself as the ultimate Authority in the world, rather than the God whom it represented. And with the power of the State firmly behind it, the Church was growing a little too dictatorial, corrupt, and, well... *rich*. Or maybe it had been that way all along, more or less, and people had simply learned to put up with it.

By the sixteenth century, however, the winds of change had begun to blow. After a certain Catholic priest named Martin Luther demanded a whole laundry list of Church reforms, there followed a fierce Papal gale, complete with thunder and lightning.

Most of the uproar had less to do with spiritual truth than institutional authority. And who controls it. And who else can have some. The Church had gone through similar power plays five hundred years earlier, resulting in the Great Schism between Rome and the Greek/Eastern Orthodox Church. Three centuries before that, a massive power struggle split the new religion of Islam into Sunni and Shiite factions. The royal houses of Israel likewise went their separate ways over a thousand years earlier, resulting in two versions of the Mosaic tradition: Samaritan and Judean. Hindus suffered much the same royal treatment—again, more as a result of who held the reigns than why.

Add "lust for power" to the Seven Deadly Sins, please.

Meanwhile, back in Christendom, a group of German princes filed a protest when the Roman Church tried to clamp down on Luther's reforms. They argued for greater freedom of conscience, proposing that individuals were "justified by faith" rather than by obedience to Mother Church. The upstart princes and their supporters were branded as "Protestants"—spoken with much the same slanderous sentiment as when Muslims were labeled "traitors"—and the label stuck. Eventually everyone who walked out on the Pope marched under the same banner.

Ironically, some of today's Catholic churches would probably be condemned as too revolutionary by the original Protestants. The early reforms were mild in comparison with how far the movement has gone ever since, though Catholic historians pretty much agree that institutional reforms were sorely needed. More importantly, both sides acknowledge that protest can be as healthy and necessary to religious tradition as it is for governments. The Protestant tradition, after all, was the opening salvo in a wider battle for human freedom that's still going on all over the world today—and in which Catholics, Jews, Muslims, Hindus and atheists are often more "Protestant" than many Protestants.

Which brings us back to the more generic, lower-case definition, one that can be found in every religious tradition. To repeat the line from the Qur'an, "No compulsion is there in religion." The point being that religious compulsion simply shouldn't exist. No tradition should be allowed to force its doctrines or its particular religious language on anyone, members or not. And yet people and institutions keep trying. So when that happens, the rest of us have not only a right but a *duty* to protest, to be protestants.

As much for their sake as for ours.

PROVIDENCE

Often used in eighteenth-century Deist literature in place of "God," Providence refers to the natural bias in the design and operation of the universe which tends to favor life, including ever more advanced forms that, on this planet, have now culminated in the human race.

From the Latin *pro* (for) and *vida* (life), Providence therefore points to the process whereby human needs are taken care of, in much the same way that rains satisfy the needs of flowers, forests and fauna. It's built into the system. It's "given." There may be dry spells, yes. Humans may even have a hand in prolonging the drought at times. But the rain will return, inevitably, naturally. We don't even need to ask for it.

Providence is also a kind of faith. It's the attitude that God/The Universe is basically *for* us, not against us; that our real inheritance is the Garden of Eden, not the Sahara Desert; that our destiny is to receive healing when we're sick, forgiveness when we've sinned, strength to overcome our addictions, and confidence to get back up after we fall.

It's the recurring theme in the scriptures of every tradition, and now, increasingly, in the findings of science. The universe *does* favor life, and *does* provide for it. If ink on parchment weren't enough, it's written in our DNA. It's written in the stars.

PSYCHOLOGY

Here's another word you won't find in the scriptures of pre-twentieth-century religious traditions. But the concept is there nevertheless.

Psyche, in Greek, literally means "breath." The term was generally used to talk about the soul or mind, or the principle of life itself. The suffix "ology," from the Greek *logos* (word) essentially stands for the phrase "the words that help us understand" a given subject, or "the theories and opinions" about it. *Voila!*—Psychology: The words, theories and opinions that enable us to understand the principles of life.

Religion has been the primary form of psychology for thousands of years. The prophets of every tradition were nothing if not psychologists, speaking in a language appropriate for their time and place. The fact that we now have all sorts of new technologies for understanding the human mind does not mean religion has now been rendered obsolete. The new technologies are simply carrying on the same enterprise.

True, those technologies may be able to analyze our behavior and motivations in ways our ancestors never imagined; they may speak in a language that sounds technical and up-to-date. But none of them can do any more than put the same principles of life under a more powerful microscope, principles psychology didn't invent, even if it *can* assist us in refining our understanding and application of them.

And what psychologists are discovering is that religious traditions have preserved insights into those principles that are as valid as ever, that can often be applied just as effectively as the most advanced psychiatric treatment programs. Because all the behavioral research, all the latest theories, all the mind-altering drugs, are worth only as much as their combined ability to sustain people while they search for some sense of purpose and meaning in their lives. And the ongoing journey toward that end is still best expressed in stories and symbols and simple human compassion. In the language of the heart. In Faithspeak.

If that doesn't sound sophisticated enough for all us amateur psychologists, maybe we should do what a real psychologist would do: Put it to the test.

PURGATORY

Purgatory is one of the remaining differences that separate Christian Catholics from Protestants, despite their rapprochement in recent decades. From the Latin *purigare,* meaning "to make pure," purgatory is considered by Catholics to be a kind of temporary holding cell for people who are mostly on The Straight and Narrow, but who aren't quite pure enough to get past the Heavenly Gates just yet.

Some Christians, both Catholic and Protestant, have suggested that *this life* is purgatory. Human existence, after all, seems to be a continuing cycle of getting dirty and then cleaning ourselves up. Others suggest that purgatory is as close as Christianity could come to the idea of reincarnation without stepping over the line. Because what purgatory implies is that, even if we're on the road to salvation, even when we've made a sincere commitment to God or Christ or Ultimate Reality, death might snatch us up before all the chains of our sins (read: *karma*) have been cast off. A single lifetime, in other words, is rarely enough.

But the good news is, the Powers-That-Be will give us however long it takes. Hindus and some New Agers tend to interpret "however long it takes" as requiring successive incarnations. Catholics figure one incarnation is enough to get the hang of it, but if further soul-work is required—and except for saints and a few exceptional people it always *is*—purgatory provides our one-stop, afterlife repair shop.

Even Protestants will admit that our souls continue to grow after we get to heaven, assuming we get there. For some, it's not out of the question that this growth may require an experience in another body, if that's what it takes for a particular spiritual lesson to sink in. Which amounts to reincarnation.

For that matter, most religious traditions at least tip their hats at the concept. Mormons, for instance, hold that our present human lives are based on our spiritual development in a previous angelic existence. Human birth is therefore already a kind of re-incarnation. Then, after death, we're assigned to one of several "levels" of heaven and placed into re-invigorated bodies that may as well be a *third* incarnation. And so on, all the way up the heavenly ladder toward godhood.

Jewish Kabbalah and Islamic Sufism hide references to previous and future lives in more mystical language. The Greek philosopher Socrates was more forthright, essentially arguing in favor of reincarnation in his theory on learning. We come to "know" things, he said, through a process of remembering what we already knew in an earlier existence. Unfortunately, Socrates was put to death for the crime of "subverting the common morality" through such teachings, so maybe he should have remembered to keep his mouth shut.

Openly espousing reincarnation has always been a little dangerous in the Western world. Purgatory is Christianity's back-door way of embracing at least the spiritual basis for it. Admittedly, all of us have a long way to go before we fully reflect the divine image within us. A hundred years is the blink of an eye, spiritually speaking—not to mention the fact that some people only get a fraction of that. A loving God, or a Reality in which justice is a part of the natural order, could hardly deny those people a second chance somewhere.

Even if it *is* in a temporary holding cell.

PURIFICATION

Forget the Victorian characterization of "purity," which brings to mind twenty-five-year-old virgins dressed in white saffron, who faint at the mention of sex and gasp at speech peppered with an occasional "hell" or "damn." Purity is simply the condition in which your relationships with other people, with the Powers-That-Be—and especially with your *self*—are in proper balance. Maybe they're not perfect; they're just as good as they can be considering the circumstances. And if they aren't, there are ways of fixing them.

The purification rites of ancient and modern religions are basically techniques for "fixing" our relationships. Many of these rites show an uncanny insight into human psychology and group dynamics. Ancient Hebrews, for example, knew that purity must begin with interpersonal harmony. If one member of the community were to injure another, physically or emotionally, that individual was first required to make amends with the other person face-to-face. Or at least try to. It wouldn't do to merely ask God's forgiveness.

Then again, wronging another person was usually a sign that one's relationship with God—or The Way Things Are—was also out of proper balance. Likewise the relationship with one's self. So getting right with *all* these relationships is a necessary start. Trouble is, admitting your need for improvement can imply that there was something bad or evil within you that caused your wrongdoing. As a result you may doubt your ability to *ever* improve, especially if there's any remaining residue from this evil.

As we should know by now, it is often these nagging doubts and sneaking suspicions that hold people back more than any residual evil or genuine personality defects. In fact your doubts and suspicions may be the *only* defects. To put it in Faithspeak, if you feel impure, you *are* impure.

The methods people have used to recover their sense of purity may seem downright weird. The most universal purification rite, immersion in water, is probably the least odd. Other rituals have included everything from sacrificing a goat to having yourself sprinkled with blood, from swinging a chicken over one's head to dipping a dove into a bowl of holy water before letting it fly off.

Clearly there is no direct, causal relationship between releasing a bird into the air and becoming "pure." Unless, that is, you *think* there is. Because the reverse of "If you feel impure, you *are* impure" is equally true: Namely, that if you think you've been purified, you *have* been purified. To the ancient Sumerians, those purple-robed priests certainly looked like they knew what they were doing around that sacrificial altar. If you happened to be alive around, say, 856 BCE, a few dismembered bullocks might do the trick for you, too.

And if you think visualizing a white light can protect you from evil forces, it just might. If you think rubbing Buddha's cast-bronze belly can bring good fortune, or the plastic crucifix over your bed will keep Satan from paying a visit, it probably will. How we think and feel about the world, whether it's objectively true or not, *does* affect reality.

An excellent analogy for this spiritual process can be found in contemporary studies into the problem of depression. In his book, *Learned Optimism,* psychologist Martin Seligman described experiments in which laboratory rats—and later, humans—were put into situations where they were intentionally made to feel helpless. No matter what the test subjects did or how hard they tried, they could not stop a certain event from happening, or finish some assigned task in the time allowed. As a result, most of them quickly lost energy and willpower. Human subjects almost invariably lost hope, blamed themselves personally for their supposed failures, and developed all the classic symptoms of depression that can end up contaminating one's entire life.

Another test group, however, was taught a set of mental techniques that transferred blame elsewhere and provided a sense that any setbacks would only be temporary. While members of this group felt equally helpless when put in the same experimental situation, they rarely lost their energy or will, and quickly bounced back from depression. It was all a matter of having the right attitude. Or, as some might say, of "keeping the faith."

Learned optimism is only one of the more recent technologies for purifying one's faith. The "Twelve Steps" of Alcoholics Anonymous and other addiction-kicking programs are similar forms of purification. Many times, of course, there are organic issues or deep-seated personality disorders at the core of our problems, and solutions are harder to come by. But sometimes it's the case that we are our own worst enemy, and our chains are only as real as we allow them to be. Religious traditions have always understood this implicitly. Their language and symbols are the only difference.

PURPOSE

There are only two people who can give you that genuine, gut-level feeling that life is worth living. Or that something is worth living for.

You... and *you*.

Of course, what makes life worthwhile for one person might not work for the next guy. And what gets you out of bed one morning may not work a year from now. In fact, what motivates you will change over the course of your lifetime—perhaps only a little, but more likely a lot. Either way, since no one else lives inside your skin but you, no one else can determine what is or isn't sufficient to keep you inside it.

The decision that *nothing* is sufficient is another name for suicide. (Whether you actually end up killing yourself is a separate issue.) And it's not uncommon for everyone to flirt with the idea once or twice. Not so much when life lets us down, but when it doesn't.

Because after getting that new twelve-speed mountain bike that was "all I ever wanted," or that dream date with the cute guy in third-period math, or a driver's license and the keys to Dad's Mustang, it finally dawns on most of us that something's still missing. There must be something more to life. What that "more" is, is our purpose.

For many people it never gets beyond the adult equivalent of the cute guy or Dad's Mustang: A husband or wife with a fashion-magazine figure; maybe a house in the 'burbs with a swimming pool, spa and high-speed internet; vacations in Aspen or Oahu and the good jobs to pay for them; influential friends and children who make us proud. Those whose purpose revolves around the fulfillment of primary physical drives like food, clothing, shelter and sex—or other external things—are usually labeled "materialists." Or in the extreme form, "hedonists."

Both of which are contrasted with the more spiritual person who knows that Dad's Mustang is just a flashy vehicle to get from one place to another; who knows that the best place to call home can't be found by driving there in a Mustang (or even a Mercedes) because it's not on a map and your on-board GPS doesn't know the coordinates.

Spiritual people, it turns out, are often former materialists who have already gone for the joyride in the flashy car and discovered little joy in it. Religious traditions abound with their stories. Moses was banished from the luxury of Egypt's royal palace, but he eventually found a wife and flock of sheep and the simple pleasures of a shepherd's life; and alas, that wasn't enough. Buddha inherited enough wealth to buy the most extravagant pleasures; but none could satisfy him. Muhammad married into wealth, then earned more than enough to kick back for the rest of his life; but that too wasn't sufficient. And Jesus was at least *offered* the whole world during his legendary encounter with Satan in the wilderness. Not only was it insufficient, the deal wasn't even worth considering. As he would later reflect on it, "What does it profit a man if he gains the whole world and loses his soul?"

Which is simply to agree with virtually every religious tradition before and since, that what makes life worth living doesn't come from the material world—from things we can touch and see and buy with money. Not that those things are altogether worthless. One of Jesus' other top-ten quotes, that "Man does not live by bread alone," presupposes certain material needs (like bread) that should be met... and met *first*.

But the universal agreement that materialism is not the answer must count for something. What's equally significant is that most sacred scriptures don't say what the answer *is*. There's a lot of finger-pointing going on, a lot of storytelling about historical people and legendary figures and prodigal sons who discover their own answers. Even today, the novels and films that continue to have the most public appeal are the familiar tales about people searching for personal meaning. But all of these stories fall flat if they get too specific, if they try to impose someone else's meaning-of-life on us.

Because our purpose is to find *our* purpose. And some people—if you can believe this—don't even *like* Mustangs.

QUEST

From the same Latin root that gives us the word "question," a quest is a project or journey during which the person(s) involved seek answers to one or more burning questions. Or at least they hope to amass evidence and experience that will help formulate answers at some later time.

Historically, most quests have involved travel. The Search for the Golden Fleece, for example, or Columbus' Voyages of Discovery, or NASA's exploration of Mars. But even in cases where the answer-seeker is confined to a sterile research lab, the metaphor of voyaging or exploring is still appropriate. Because the quest inevitably requires venturing into uncharted territory, sometimes with little information to go on and plenty at stake. And that, in turn, demands exceptional courage, the commitment of both resources and labor, and a willingness to accept failure and ridicule as well as success and acclaim.

Which means the quest is as much about exploring one*self*, one's internal territory, one's spirit, as the external world or the material issues that provided the original inspiration. And it is this spiritual element that makes "Quest" the appropriate term for what we're all engaged in, whether we're already committed to one religious tradition, or exploring several spiritual paths, or considering whether *any* language of faith can help light the way for us.

Life is a quest. Or as one of Unity's favorite study guides splashes across its cover, *The* Quest.

QUR'AN

The name of the book is often spelled "Koran" outside of this Lexicon. But the fact is, "Q" words don't exactly grow on trees. Besides, Qur'an is the more accurate transliteration of the Arabic.

For Muslims, the Holy Qur'an is the word of Allah/God as communicated to humanity through the angel Gabriel to the Prophet Muhammad. It is the culmination of a long chain of divine communications going all the way back to Adam—whom Muslims revere as the first prophet because he was the first person to whom God revealed himself, and Adam passed on the news.

God also revealed himself to Abraham and Moses and Solomon and Jesus, who are likewise acknowledged by Muslims as prophets, and whose Jewish and Christian followers are mentioned numerous times in the Qur'an as "The People of the Book." That Book—which can mean either the Hebrew Torah or The New Testament—represented two earlier accounts of God's revelation. Unfortunately, between the time those revelations were received and scribes finally wrote them down, God's word had become distorted and even corrupted.

The underlying message was accurate enough—that humankind's success and happiness derived from submission to the One God, and that a Day of Reckoning would someday separate the wheat from the chaff. But many of the details in those Books, the Qur'an insisted, were perverted by men who were either evil at heart or simply mistaken. Muhammad promised to get it right this time. The Qur'an would be the Final Revelation, the divine message heard loud and clear and then committed to parchment before anybody could alter one single letter.

Which is probably why Muslims are only too happy to stand back and watch as Jewish and Christian scholars analyze their scriptures; as they develop complex theories about the various documents that went into them, and how vast portions were embellished and rewritten in the process of putting them all together. But try to subject the Qur'an to the same kind of scholarly scrutiny and you'll probably run into a stone wall. If not the holy outrage of the "defenders of the faith," complete with violent protests and maybe a *fatwa* threatening your life.

Not that Muslims have never been known to question their most sacred text. On the contrary, major debates were held centuries ago on such issues as whether the Qur'an was "created" or existed eternally, and whether its words are to be taken as literal truth or metaphor. The written records of these debates sound surprisingly reminiscent of more recent arguments between Christian fundamentalists and liberal theologians. For example, when Allah is referred to in the Qur'an as having hands and eyes and a face, did the text really mean it in a factual sense? And if the Qur'an was eternal and uncreated, was it somehow floating around in the heavens before there were people around to read it, already cast in Arabic letters exactly as Muhammad would deliver it?

Islamic scholars of "the Middle Way" tried to compromise. Qur'anic references to God's human-like attributes are true, Al-Ashari suggested, but the divine hands and face are not the same as human ones. And yes, the Qur'an *is* the eternal Word of God, a scheme built into the very fabric of Ultimate Reality (to put it in today's terms). But the sounds and written symbols by which people have access to it are "created things."

And as students of comparative religion will admit, the Qur'an is a very *powerful* created thing. Whatever its theological content, its descriptions in the original Arabic are reported to be as vivid, poetic, tender and terrifying as anything ever written. It deserves its place among the world's most cherished writings for that reason alone. In the context of seventh-century Arabia, it was the very light of salvation. For hundreds of millions of people the world over, it still is. Or can be.

But any light that shines is valuable not in the beauty of the flame itself, or in the candle that fuels it, or in the ornately-carved candlestick that supports it. Its value lies in the illumination it provides.

Its value—just like that of every other holy book—lies in how clearly people can *see* by it.

And, as with every other holy book, the evaluation is ongoing.

RABBI

Usually translated as "teacher" because that term is less offensive to our egalitarian sensibilities, rabbi literally means "my master." Like the Hindu *guru*, it refers to someone who has mastered the spiritual disciplines and knowledge passed down by tradition. In the case of the Hebrew rabbi, the disciplines and knowledge are based on Mosaic Law, the writings of the Prophets, and the transcriptions of oral tradition—not only in terms of what those texts literally say, but what they *imply*, and what difference that makes in our daily lives.

Of course, there was always room for interpretation. Numerous schools formed around specific interpretations of the Law, or the personal appeal of the sages who were doing the interpreting. In a sense, addressing someone by the title "my master" was to choose sides, to agree with the views of one school or teacher over another.

Those who called Jesus "rabbi" were publicly aligning themselves with what has come to be called the "prophetic interpretation of scripture," in which there was greater focus on the poor and oppressed. Justice was the primary theme; love was the outward sign of having learned it.

For that reason, rabbi can also be translated as "example." As can guru. The fact is, some people are well ahead of us in our spiritual journeys. The mastery they've achieved is demonstrated not so much in their ability to quote chapter and verse, but in the application of their knowledge to daily life. Their actions exemplify the tradition.

To acknowledge a rabbi is not some medieval act of subservience. It is simply to admit that we have much to learn from the lives of others. There are hundreds of spiritual advisors and fallen evangelists whose motto seems to be "Do as I say, not as I do." When you find one where "do" is equal to (or greater than) "say," chances are you've stumbled onto the genuine article.

RAINBOW

Symbol of God's/Allah's covenant with Noah (i.e. humankind) in both the Hebrew Bible and Qur'an, the rainbow has been adopted by numerous organizations—and designers of nursery-room wallpaper—ever since. If only because it's so colorful and compact.

Forget the fact that the ancient Hebrews had no clue the rainbow was a natural phenomena caused by the refraction of light through distant raindrops. To them it was a miraculous, breathtaking tapestry of color that could only have been orchestrated by a divine hand. The image was also associated with something beneficial and not that common in the mid-east: *rain*. And yet, rare as the rainbow was, it showed up often enough to act as a regular reminder. A company logo could hardly do better.

But unlike a company's logo, the rainbow couldn't be trademarked. It was subsequently conscripted to serve as a generic symbol indicating better times ahead, as a banner for racial and cultural diversity, and for a certain lifestyle orthodox religions continue to rail against.

The rainbow's come a long way, baby.

It can also symbolize not just social diversity and divine covenants, but the mysterious forces that turn something as seemingly immaterial as light into what appears to be a physical object; that can transform what's unseen into what's visible; that hints at levels of existence behind the material world, as rich with diversity and texture as the five dimensions we can experience directly. And even if we end up explaining them scientifically, just as we can the rainbow, they're still as miraculous and breathtaking as they were before we knew better.

RAMADAN

Let's say that every year, as a way to focus on our physical and spiritual well-being, we all agreed to give up certain bad habits and ordinary human indulgences (including eating and drinking!) between dawn and sundown, for one entire month. Let's say the month we agreed to observe this daily, daylight ritual was September.

Ramadan, then, would be the equivalent of September. In Islamic tradition, it's simply the name of the month during which this spiritual cleansing takes place. However, as a consequence of the Arabic lunar calendar—which the tradition neglects to adjust every few years to stay in sync with the solar calendar—Ramadan retrogrades through all four seasons over the course of 32-33 years. This makes one's daily fast a relatively easy eight hours in winter, and a grueling sixteen or more hours during the summer. Ramadan may not require the almost super-human twenty-four hour fast practiced by orthodox Jews; but the 28-29 straight days of the Muslim observance more than make up for it.

As in all fasts, the deeper purpose is not so much about proving one's commitment to tradition or obedience to the God who prescribed it. It's about consciously (re)exerting control over one's physical urges and materialistic desires. Sadly, secular society has pretty much relieved its constituents of this take-control incentive. Quite the contrary. The Western media's twenty-four-seven barrage of consumer advertising, with every TV spot or website banner designed to whet our appetites for new material possessions and sensual experiences, promotes an increasing abandonment of self-control and personal discipline.

Except in those who must resist their body's urges and material desires because, well, they have no other choice.

Many in Western society, especially where the disparity between rich and poor continues to grow, are forced to go without food or basic necessities for lack of money or other resources. Which means that what may look like fasting is actually the spectre of poverty.

And that's where Ramadan and its spiritual cousins have a secondary purpose: To pool the wealth not spent during one's fast so it can be given to those in need. Ramadan therefore rises above a merely personal discipline to a communal effort for assisting the poor.

The *Eid al Fitr*—the feast marking the end of the Muslim's month-long fast—symbolizes this redistribution of wealth in a Christmas-like practice of festive meals and gift-giving. Much like the commercialization of Christmas, however, the tradition can sometimes have more to do with bestowing our largesse on family and friends than on those who are less fortunate.

How much richer we'd all be by regularly practicing the discipline to give a little less to ourselves and those we know, so we might give a little more to those we don't.

RAPTURE

Sorry, End-Time enthusiasts and Book of Revelation readers: The Rapture is a term never explicitly used or described in the Bible. Rather, it's a concept inferred from a few lines of New Testament text with the same kind of wild-eyed excitement that can turn a quatrain from Nostradamus into a crystal clear prediction of the events of 9/11.

While commentators have struggled for centuries with the notion that Christ's followers would be "seized" or "carried away" (Latin *raptus*) before or during his Second Coming, the formal concept of The Rapture was a product of Puritan preachers and popular authors beginning in the late 1700s. Basically, the idea was that loyal and deserving believers, whether departed or living, will escape the chaos and destruction of the Antichrist's reign on Earth by being swept up "in the clouds." Or, in other words, transported directly from earth to heaven.

As a consequence—and as envisioned in such novels as the popular *Left Behind* series—buses and airplanes would suddenly lose their drivers and pilots. The special guest on tonight's 700 Club would vanish into thin air. Desks in the offices of Focus on the Family and Oral Roberts University's lecture hall would be vacated in the blink of an eye... as would a large number of seats on the Republican side of the aisle in State Assemblies all across the U.S., thereby leaving Democrats with a ruling majority for the first time in years. Except that the ruling Antichrist will have already abolished democracy.

But we kid. It's just that The Rapture isn't what Christianity is coming to. Or was ever about. It makes mediocre fiction at best, saves no souls, inspires no one to practice the loving-kindness and compassion that Jesus taught. Worse, it co-opts one of the better words in our spiritual vocabulary.

"Rapture," properly understood, is the experience celebrated by the mystics of all religions. It's the bliss of being "seized" by the divine, the all-consuming *ananda* of the Hindu and St. Teresa's passionate soul-union with her savior. It is the Sufi's total immersion in movement and music that reflects the rhythms of the divine order. It is the Hasidic Jew's prayerful ecstasy and the cosmic consciousness of the Buddhist's *Samadhi*. Sexual union can provide a small taste of it on occasion.

Rapture is just too good a word to let a anyone hijack it. Maybe if there were a good reason, yes. But let's not get carried away here.

REALIZATION

To realize is to "make real," to bring something into existence. To "realize" is therefore to create. To create is to realize.

Despite the fact that "real" is derived from the Latin/Sanskrit words meaning "thing" or "property," the term doesn't refer only to solid objects, like a chair or a building. A thought is also real, even if nobody's ever seen one. A smile is real, though it's no more than the way a person's lips turn up. A beautiful sunset is no less real because it's a collection of "subjective appearances."

All of which is simply to say that there are various ways of being real—and ways of realizing. The carpenter can realize a chair, the builder an office tower; and both can realize their construction objectives. An organization called Self-Realization Fellowship recommends that we realize our *selves,* a life-long process of creation in which we make real the fullest expression of our own divinity. Hopefully we can *all* realize that people have different ways of symbolizing and talking about Ultimate Reality—which is nothing like a chair or a building or a self, because it was already real before anyone realized it.

These are not mere word games. There is a mysterious connection between what is real and what we realize. The ordinary definition of "realization," that sudden flash of "Oh yeah, *now* I get it!" may turn out to be more than a kind of mental correspondence between What Is and what we have just come to know. Our realizations can literally change the world around us.

The New Age slogan that we can "create our own reality"—which seems absurd or even sacrilegious when you first hear it—may actually hold the key to our personal growth and salvation. Not that we can snap our fingers and create hundred dollar bills, or walk on water, or say the words, "Let there be light" and the sun suddenly turns itself on. But we *can* develop a frame of mind or attitude—or faith—that makes certain beneficial events more likely to happen than others.

Psychologists tell us that if we dwell on our shortcomings or think of ourselves as "bad," we tend to become involved in situations where our shortcomings and supposed "badness" are more likely to reveal themselves. On the other hand, if we recognize and celebrate our potential for doing (and being) good—or, in religious language, if we believe we're created in the divine image—we tend to find situations in which our inherent goodness will be expressed and rewarded. Our lives become self-fulfilling prophecies. We *do* create our own reality.

But to do it intentionally and not by accident, we need a plan. Or at least a mental picture of who we'd like to become, if only to help us measure our progress: A person who's kind and loving, say; who has a sense of connectedness to the universe; a person who can face adversity without falling apart; who enjoys other people as well as his/her solitude; whose life's work offers personal fulfillment and service, and who can be satisfied with whatever level of prosperity that work happens to provide. Whoever your "ideal you" is, stop for a few moments and mentally picture it. Go ahead... *picture* it.

Now go about creating that person, trusting you can do it even if you don't always know how. Prayer and meditation, programming and religion (by whatever name), can certainly assist you in that process. In fact, whether we call on those resources or not, we are automatically realizing some kind of "self" already. Unfortunately, that self is often one we wouldn't consciously choose. But precisely by becoming conscious of it, we also become capable of choosing a new one.

And that's a major realization in itself.

RECONCILIATION

To bring two things together—people, ideas, religions, whatever—is to "reconcile" them.

That doesn't mean making them "the same." Fitting two pieces of a jigsaw puzzle together is, in a way, reconciling them. But if the two pieces were identical in shape they probably wouldn't fit. So it's often the differences that lead to genuine reconciliation, not the similarities.

In fact, like jigsaw pieces fitting together to form a larger picture, the process of reconciliation is a kind of addition in which the sum becomes greater than its parts. Not in the sense that one-plus-one equals three or four, or ten. It's where one-plus-one equals *one*. Except in this case, the "one" belongs in another category. It's a new creation.

No wonder reconciliation is such a pervasive theme in religion. And it's more than the usual notion that God wants sinners to admit their mistakes and "come back" to him, like an unfaithful husband who begs forgiveness, or a prodigal son who returns home for good. The fact is, the husband or the son who genuinely puts the past behind him becomes a new person in a new relationship. Something exists now that never existed before.

The Hindu practice of Yoga is the reconciliation of body and spirit. In balancing both elements, the human being is no longer merely an intelligent animal driven by bodily instincts, nor a disembodied soul living in some divine realm of pure thought. Yoga integrates body and mind into a working partnership that not only combines the best of both, but is so much more powerful and productive it becomes a completely new creature.

Christianity's Saint Paul described much the same thing, using "Christ" to symbolize the reconciliation between man and God, flesh and spirit. The process of Self-Realization is also a kind of reconciliation. The Muslim's submission to Allah is the first step toward it. And the Jewish *shalom* refers to the wholeness which is its product.

Most of us have some concept of this wholeness, perhaps because we've experienced it, but more likely because we deep-down know it's been missing from our lives. Stories of reconciliation are popular because they show us how things might be if only we could "get it all together." Charles Dickens' *A Christmas Carol* illustrates the reconciliation of past and present that can lead to a new life (rebirth) rather than death. *Dances With Wolves* portrays the reconciliation of a man with the core self we surrender by becoming "civilized." Similarly, Robert Bly's Wildman and the feminist's "goddess" are gender-specific means of reconciling society's artificial roles with what nature intended us to be.

Cinderella-type stories, *The Wizard of Oz* or *It's a Wonderful Life*—these and other mythic tales exemplify the small and great conflicts that can re-create Who We Are. And not through some Rambo-like destruction of evil, but by embracing the opposites, by bringing all the pieces of our jigsaw-puzzle lives into a working partnership: Our successes *and* our failures, strengths *and* weaknesses, past and present, mind and body, individual and community.

To reconcile these opposites means more than learning to tolerate them or becoming resigned to them. The word "reconcile" begins with "recon," meaning "to look around," to *see*. To see things *differently*. All too often what we view as opposites are really a lock and a key. Or that inevitable piece of the jigsaw that doesn't seem to fit anywhere until there's only one hole left to fill. And now that ugly duckling, that one seemingly worthless, overlooked, out-of-place piece ends up being what finally completes the whole picture.

RECOVERY

A term commonly heard in today's mental health departments and 12-Step programs, "recovery" is the achievement or experience of having overcome a major impediment in one's life. As when the drug addict kicks his habit. Or when a married couple or dysfunctional family repairs its relationships and harmony is restored. Or when the sinner not only finds forgiveness but has changed his ways.

But as most sinners will attest, recovery is only rarely a one-time achievement. For most of us, it's an ongoing process. More often than not it involves falling back into the old patterns and destructive behaviors we thought we'd beaten, only to face the same uphill battle again. Even for those who seem to be in the clear, recovery is the understanding that we could easily relapse if we let down our guard, if we weren't vigilant to the snares and warning signs, if we didn't know any better. Which, hopefully, we do now.

Whether we're religious or not, we need to give traditional religions credit for embodying an understanding of damaged psyches and destructive behavior, and for using the imagery, language and psychology of the times to inspire healing. The fact that religions are still thriving right alongside mental health departments and modern psychology is a measure of their effectiveness. Not to mention that 12-Step programs have achieved their success largely by modeling themselves after the recovery process embedded in religious practice.

If Christianity makes a big deal out of "being saved," it's only because recovery is essentially what our lives are about. If Islam labels the struggle within each of us as the Greater Jihad, it is only to remind us where the real battleground lies. And if pure Buddhism strips away all deities and devotions in order to focus on eight practical rules of righteous living, it's merely to say that behind all the symbolism and stories of other traditions is a Path toward wholeness that's built into the very landscape of Ultimate Reality.

And that it's within our power to learn it, to *use* it. And be reborn.

REDEMPTION

Back in the 1950s and 60s, many retail stores and gas stations offered what were called "Bonus Stamp" promotions. (To remember this, you must be *very old*.) Whenever you'd purchase an item from a participating retailer, you would be rewarded with an appropriate number of S&H Green Stamps, or the classier Blue Chip Stamps. After saving up a certain quantity and pasting them into the little books provided by the sponsoring companies, you could turn in your stamps at their redemption center and pick out a free gift or prize from their master catalog. The more stamps you accumulated, the more valuable the prize.

Redemption, religiously speaking, is something like a Bonus Stamp Promotion. Except that what we collect are the hard knocks and sacrifices and lessons of everyday life. And the free gift is our own salvation.

Christianity didn't invent redemption. A thousand years earlier, God (Yahweh) had been worshipped as Redeemer of Israel. Muslims declare that they are redeemed by Allah. In Hinduism, the transmigrating soul is essentially redeemed through its absorption into the Absolute.

The common motif behind the concept of redemption is the unhappy fact that life can be a real pain. As communities or countries, we are often subjected to natural disasters or the ravages of war. As individuals we suffer the slings and arrows of economic misfortune and physical illness and personal attacks by mean-spirited people. And then there's the ongoing temptation to lie or cheat on your income taxes or give in to that casual affair that "won't really hurt anybody" but always does. We are the walking wounded. The pain and suffering of our lives is written across our shoulders like oozing, half-healed lash marks.

But at the heart of redemption is the assurance that each of those lash marks counts. They are the proverbial dues we pay to join The Club, the sign of having run the gauntlet before becoming a full-fledged Warrior of the Spirit. And it's not merely that these experiences make you "sadder but wiser"; those are life's lesser Bonus Stamp prizes. The evidence of true redemption is that you're not only wiser, but in some unfathomable way... *happier.*

This deeper transformation rarely occurs as just one more event in a routine sequence of events. There is usually some "outside" force involved, some unexpected or improbable conjunction of coincidences, some utterly explosive flash of illumination that seems to come out of the blue and put everything into perspective. Whatever it is, it's as if you've bridged that unbridgeable Chasm, connected with The Way It Is, merged with the primal forces of the universe. And every one of those wounds you've collected suddenly seems to have had a purpose. Every scar, every bruise is an insight, a lesson learned, a purple heart. And not one of them would you give up. Not one.

Which explains why religious traditions celebrate this realignment of one's whole outlook in such dramatic, forceful terms. It often *is* a One-Time-Only Event. It's not something you can plan, or do to yourself. And it doesn't necessarily happen to everybody. But when it does—hallelujah, sister!

Meanwhile the rest of us go on collecting stamps, patiently pasting them into our little books. And maybe it's enough to know that each one is worth something, that every single event in our life has redeeming value even if we don't know what it is yet, or whether we'll have time to save up for the biggest prize in the catalog.

And if "sadder but wiser" is the best we can do for the time being, that too is okay.

REINCARNATION

If the verb "incarnate" means to take on a body, to *re*-incarnate means to take on a body *again.* Most Eastern religions assume without question that the essence of each individual—the soul or atman—will take on a body again and again in a long series of human (and sometimes sub-human) lives until at last it is perfected. Or, in Western terms, "saved."

The fact is, throughout the history of both the East and the West, more people have believed in reincarnation than haven't. Which doesn't make it true, of course, since for millennia most people also thought the Earth was flat as a chessboard. But what makes the concept of reincarnation attractive even today is its underlying message that life is ultimately a spiritual journey.

It's not this materialistic rat race we've allowed ourselves to get sucked into. Neither is it about buying the two-story Cape Cod in Sag Harbor or sending the kids to Harvard. It's not even about dedicating your life to serving humanity—though that's often the by-product of a more advanced soul. Life, rather, is a process of refining ourselves in accordance with some spiritual end-game, in light of the Image of God within us, in hopes of achieving at-one-ment with the divine All. It's what Hindus call *moksha.* And it's the same ultimate goal we all share.

Something similar to this ideal is envisioned by virtually every religious tradition and self-help movement on the planet. Yet it seems the height of folly, or simple conceit, to think we can reach this goal in a single lifetime. Or that the child born into abject poverty, surrounded by crime and drugs and despair, or who's destined to die by the age of eight because of some birth defect or terrorist's gunshot, has the same opportunity as everyone else.

Reincarnation not only presupposes a fine sense of fairness and equity in the Scheme of Things, it also implies an unsurpassed depth of divine love. Because, in the end, *everybody* gets saved. It may take a thousand lifetimes, or ten thousand lifetimes, but nobody ultimately fails The Course.

And there are other things reincarnation has going for it. One is simply those weird flashes of familiarity that tell us we've "been here before" even when we know we haven't. Or the feeling that something we're doing for the first time is really more like getting back on a bicycle after several years and still being able to pedal around like a pro. Admittedly these moments of *deja vu* can often be explained. Then again, sometimes not.

Equally interesting are the experiments which suggest that many (or most?) people—Hindu, Christian or atheist—can remember one or more past lives while under deep hypnosis. Frequently, events in these former existences turn out to be the cause of specific fears or character traits one has in *this* life. Nothing else can adequately explain them.

What reincarnation *doesn't* have going for it is a good explanation for our failure to remember all the lessons we supposedly learned during those past lives. Or why we don't have any recollection of ourselves *between* lives, when we're presumably going through the kind of review process portrayed in Albert Brooks' classic film, *Defending Your Life.*

And, by the way, the scientific data about people remembering past lives under hypnosis isn't all that convincing anyway. What may be happening is that people are merely tapping into psychic data banks, some kind of mental or spiritual reservoir where everyone's lives are somehow recorded for posterity. This alternative may be just as weird, yes. But it's not reincarnation.

The perennial problem with reincarnation is its tendency to instill a sense of resignation in people, a better-luck-next-time attitude, a pervasive feeling that things don't matter quite so much because, after all, we'll get there eventually. What's another fifty, sixty years when countless lifetimes still lay ahead? There's nothing like Western theology's "you-only-go-around-once" attitude to get us off our bloomin' arses.

But the idea of reincarnation never precludes the possibility that *this* life is the one destined to produce our big breakthrough. There's work to be done every time we go around. We can make more work for ourselves next time, or we can make things a helluva lot easier. It's always up to us. Each of our choices has important consequences.

Reincarnation may be no harder to swallow than the idea of waking up to find ourselves standing in line at the Pearly Gates—or someplace where the climate is much warmer. Or not waking up at all. Part of the excitement comes from not knowing. Part of it comes from knowing that, whatever comes next, doing the best we can in the here-and-now certainly can't hurt our chances.

RELATIVITY

Two kinds.

The first—let's call it "relativ-*ism*"—is the kind many religious leaders consider The Root of All Evil. According to this view, there are no Absolutes. Everything is relative. Moral laws that work for one society and time period are not necessarily appropriate for another. It is wrong, the relativist would say, to impose our value judgments on ancient cultures, or on present-day societies whose rules and regulations may differ from ours.

Of course, "Everything is relative" turns out to be an Absolute itself—one that happens to be self-contradicting. Like the paradox, "This statement is false." If the statement is false, it must be true. If it's true, it's false.

Actually, relativism doesn't claim there are no absolutes or ultimate truths. What it proposes is that any given truth may express itself in a variety of ways. Or more accurately, that societies (and individuals) may understand that truth in a variety of ways, more or less clearly.

It is therefore wrong to impose our value judgments on other cultures (assuming we have consistent values to impose) not because their values are just fine, thank you, and nothing we might say could benefit them. It's because we could probably benefit from each other. After all, what the so-called Absolutes really are is often discovered only by comparing how two different cultures understand and apply them in their own unique context and environment. If we experience only one "expression" of moral or spiritual truth, we often mistake the form it takes with the truth itself. Like reading the King James version of the New Testament and concluding that Jesus spoke English as eloquently as Shakespeare did.

If anything, relativism is simply a tool that allows us to better expose the real truth, in the same way a comparative religions class can help uncover the spiritual realities all of them are struggling to describe. Of course these deeper truths won't automatically become clear even then. In fact, the second kind of "relativity"—the one that pertains to physics—is a perfect illustration.

Scientifically speaking, "relativity" refers to the relationship between space, time, matter, energy and gravity. It was an early Twentieth-Century attempt to describe how the universe operates, and how all these concepts and forces are inter-related. And it worked—better than any previous theory, at least. But it also entailed a few conclusions that seemed to contradict our ordinary ways of describing things: Like light rays that are "bent" when they travel around a massive object; or empty space that is somehow "curved" by matter; not to mention the ludicrous notion that people who travel at enormous speeds operate on a slower time frame relative to a stationary observer, and time actually *stops* at the speed of light.

What kind of a crock is this?

Planck's Constant, Heisenberg's Principle, Schrödinger's Equation and Feynman's Diagrams—these and other explanatory tools paint a picture of a universe that's even more absurd and farther removed from our ordinary experience than Einstein's Theory of Relativity. And yet, despite their imperfections, they are collectively giving us a more and more detailed understanding of the ultimate laws and realities behind ordinary experience than we've ever had before. And... they *work.*

True, most people don't give a hoot about Heisenberg or Schrödinger or the Theory of Relativity. The point is, subatomic reality is so far removed from normal things like trees and cars and human anatomy—even though, without it, none of these things would exist—that it defies understanding. To discuss the latest scientific theories, as one physicist put it, requires going through "four levels of increasing abstraction." All we can possibly do under these conditions is to symbolize, to draw parallels, to point; to use ordinary language, knowing that what we're talking about is completely beyond the ordinary; and then to apply our present level of knowledge as best we can and see how it works.

Think about that last sentence. Relative to religion.

RELIGION

Shorthand for "how to get there from here."

Or as the spiritual pharmacist might say, it's the prescription for creating Who You Ought to Be, starting with Who You Are Now, assuming the two are different. In the unlikely event they're the same, it's the prescription for keeping things that way.

The words "God" and "Christ" and "salvation" are not all that essential to religion. But what those words *point* to—the realities and resources Faithspeak more or less crudely describes—are essential. Otherwise you probably *can't* get there from here.

Then again, nothing is ever this simple. For the more detailed explanation of "religion," see Part One of this book.

REPENTENCE

Don't be put off by the antiquated sound of this word. Repentance is an activity everybody engages in, whether die-hard believer or card-carrying atheist. Like turning right at the next corner instead of left.

Actually, to "repent" *is* a kind of turning. Or rather, a turning *away*. What we're turning away from is usually some aspect of ourselves we want to change, like a personality trait that gets us into trouble, or a bad habit we'd like to break. And, as habits go, we often keep doing it long after we realize it's bad for us. It may even seem impossible to stop.

The word "repent," in fact, assumes that things have probably been going on much too long already. The Latin root *pentir* means "to be sorry," and the prefix *re* means "again." Repenting therefore implies that we're sorry—again—because we keep doing the same damn thing over and over and it's way past time to do something about it.

What we must "do about it" is take control. The trouble is, once our behavioral programs are set in motion during childhood, it's easier to proceed along the path of least resistance. Even if it occasionally leads right off the cliff. Or straight to hell, if you prefer more dramatic language. To break our habits, nothing less than a conscious choice must be made. Being sorry is a start, but it must be combined with a decision not to repeat the behavior, and then to turn away from it, to give a good yank on the steering wheel of our lives.

"Just say no" isn't strong enough. You've got to get physical. The way to stop drinking is to literally turn away when someone offers that cocktail, or when you catch yourself reaching for the bottle. The way to break the habit of staring at photos of naked ladies is to physically turn away from those images. The way to stop lusting after fast cars or the newest gadget or the latest fashions is to turn away from the magazine ads and TV commercials and website banners that brainwash us into thinking we can't live without these things. It's a matter of breaking into our usual response patterns, of demonstrating in some concrete way that you're serious, that it's possible to turn in a new direction after all.

Of course, in turning away from one thing, we can't avoid turning toward something else; and it helps to be clear about what that "something else" *is*. Often it's simply your mental picture of a new-and-improved "You" who's finally taking the initiative, happily waving off the gin-and-tonic, or walking past the news rack with this month's Bump-and-Grind magazine, or flipping the channel to PBS instead of the Home Shopping Channel. It could also be visualizing some role-model to provide inspiration and accountability: Mary, Jesus, Krishna, Buddha; your best friend or favorite teacher; a Higher Self or Guiding Light.

People who are forced to battle serious mental problems or addictions can be the most dramatic (and inspiring) examples of this process. It's no coincidence that those who survive it—and literal survival is often at stake—almost always become more spiritual. Their concept of Self may radically change. They begin to see themselves as more connected to other people, to deeper forces. Some of us will do little more than battle the chocolate demon, or the annual temptation to fudge the numbers on our 1040s. But even in these seemingly minor skirmishes, our lives are on the line. Practicing our turning-away skills on the minor stuff can develop into the ingrained habit that wins the major battles.

Like practicing U-turns on a quiet residential street to prepare you for those busy downtown intersections, where the red-light district lies ahead and you were only intending to stop at Home Depot.

RESURRECTION

The verb "resurrect" literally means "to raise again." The boxer who gets up after being knocked down, the South after the Civil War, the legendary phoenix rising from the ashes—all these are examples of resurrection. Or being resurrected.

There are some Christians who are perfectly happy with only this much: The notion that we can get up after being knocked down; the assurance that when all seems lost, there's still enough within us to start over, and even to thrive again; the conviction that, at the very heart of things, there is a natural process able to turn our worst defeat into victory. The Gospel account of Jesus is certainly a moving portrayal of this theme, and the question of whether or not he actually walked away from his rock tomb is intriguing but irrelevant.

Which isn't the case for most Christians. For them, Resurrection with a capital "R" refers to what they see as a certifiable historical event. Jesus died on the cross one Friday afternoon and rose from the grave on Sunday morning, walking and talking just as free-and-easy as the Thursday before. *Easier,* really, because the hard part was over. He'd survived the worst his opponents could throw at him. And his "rising again" is our assurance that the same victory is in store for us.

Namely, resurrection with a small "r." The grave, in short, is not the end. If we mind our P's and Q's, or X's and Y's—or, in some traditions, even if we *don't* mind them—we will rise again after our earthly lives and continue our existence elsewhere.

What that existence may *be* is never precisely defined in scripture, and thus subject to debate. One of the major causes for debate hinges on whether we get back the same physical body we owned in our mortal life or some kind of holographic copy that's no longer subject to physical limitations. Or maybe we're reduced to whatever our "soul" is—some kind of spiritual essence that requires neither a flesh-and-bone replica nor a holographic one.

If nothing else, such debates are a good excuse to think about what it is that makes each of us *us.* Some religious traditions, however, won't settle for anything less than the same physical equipment we had before death, though in a somewhat enhanced or "incorruptible" condition. Ancient Babylonians, Jews of the Second Temple era, as well as today's Orthodox Jews, Muslims, Mormons, Jehovah's Witnesses and fundamentalist Christians all favor what's called "bodily resurrection."

The age of that resurrected body, of course, is still ripe for speculation. Is there some ideal prime-of-life we'll return to after death? Twenty-one, perhaps, or thirty-something? What if you never reached that age during your earthly lifetime? Or what if you're an aborted fetus, in which case you never had much of a body to begin with?

Assuming you're old enough to know about sex, will you keep your reproductive organs after being resurrected? Why or why not? And will the scores of 1960s thalidomide babies finally get the arms or legs they never grew the first time around?

Maybe we're getting lost in the details. Maybe trying to picture it too precisely and settle all these issues beforehand says more about our own doubts and fears than the reality to which all these religions are pointing. And what they're pointing at is more than the notion that we can "live on" by virtue of the ongoing impact our lives will continue to make, or in the chromosomes of our children and grandchildren.

"Resurrection" embodies the hope that an afterlife must be in some sense *material.* Or at least as real as the material world, as complex and amazing as that is. And if we can't entertain at least the possibility that Who We Are "rises again"—somehow, in some form—then maybe our concept of reality isn't as free and easy as it might be.

REVELATION

The ordinary meaning of the word is remarkably like the religious one. Maybe there's *no* difference.

Almost everyone has had a revelation or two. Not the little hunch that later turns out to be true, mind you, or the little voice that whispers its opinion on whether some action is right or wrong. A revelation is an experience or collection of experiences that permanently alters your attitude about something or someone. Or that alters your whole outlook on life, usually by changing the way you see yourself.

An example of the first kind is the statement, "I thought he loved me, but he was only using me!" An example of the second: "You know what?—I'm not such a bad person after all!"

What characterizes these revelations is that they are not something you deduce by a process of careful reasoning—even if thinking about it for a while might have produced the same conclusion. Instead, the conclusion is presented to your conscious mind like a message written on one of those portable whiteboards. Suddenly somebody wheels it around and there it is in red, felt-pen letters—the wide-tip kind. Because it's bold and unambiguous. You don't doubt what it says. In fact, a revelation usually comes with a sense of utter conviction that simply thinking about it can never produce.

The human mind, after all, has a number of mechanisms for making judgments and coming to conclusions, only one of which depends on logic. Trusting our inner, intuitive processes is something we sophisticated, modern types are rarely comfortable with. Revelation occurs when that inner knowing breaks through in spite of us, sometimes when we're least expecting it. Like a gift that's unwrapped and ready to use. Batteries included.

There is something decidedly "religious" even about this ordinary kind of revelation. Maybe because it *does* have the power to change Who We Are. Having a sudden flash that life is good, or that someone loves us, or that no matter what happens everything's gonna be just fine—all of these convictions shape our attitudes. They are components of faith. And it is that connection to faith which specifically defines religious revelation.

The Torah is said to be revelation. Likewise the Qur'an and various Hindu scriptures. Not because the author sat down with pen and parchment and transcribed whatever the divinity dictated; but because they (or their followers) were convinced that their writings could change people's faith, and that the message came from a reservoir of wisdom beyond human reason.

It was as if God had spoken to them. And when the prophets of these traditions said something like "Thus saith the Lord," it symbolized their complete conviction that what they were saying to us is what God *would have said* if only He or It could speak with human lips.

Even Buddha, who reportedly did not believe in a God, received his enlightenment as a sudden, faith-changing revelation from some deeper source. It might have been no more than his unconscious mind. Sitting under that banyan tree day and night while he reflected on his life may have provided the raw materials for the Eightfold Path that finally came to him in a flash of insight. Or maybe his mind *did* connect with some level of reality that is normally inaccessible, a kind of divine data bank that comes bursting into awareness under certain conditions. Maybe it's the same level of reality that breaks into our awareness at times, and the only difference between our revelations and those of Buddha or Muhammad or Moses is that we think they apply only to us. The prophets, on the other hand, take it a step further. "What works for me," they seemed to be saying, "might work for you, too."

Which is partly true, at least. Whatever fulfills your needs and shapes your faith for the better may indeed help someone else. The problem, as usual, is that people continue to mistake form for substance.

Is the real revelation that everyone on earth should turn toward Mecca and pray five times daily—or that turning our attention toward The Divine on a regular basis will give us all a broader perspective and unite us as one human community? Is the real revelation that mixing meat and milk products is a desecration of divine Law, or that we can desecrate our*selves* if we don't exercise care over what we take into our bodies and how we prepare it?

It's hardly surprising that the idea of revelation has been abused throughout history. Not only have the followers of some prophets felt so strongly about a certain revelation that they punished or even killed those who failed to accept it, but some laws have been certified as "revelation" strictly as a ploy to enforce obedience. It's the oldest trick in the book. Tell someone "God says so" and debate comes to a screeching halt. Insofar as we're willing to believe that some religious leader has a direct pipeline to heaven—whether it's the Pope or the Ayatollah or Sophia the Palm Reader—we're at the mercy of *their* revelation rather than our own. And what really comes to a screeching halt is our own spiritual growth.

Fortunately, we all have access to the same reservoir of wisdom as Popes and palm readers. The genuine prophets are only dramatizing what we can do for ourselves. What we already do for ourselves.

What we could do *more* of, if we'd only leave the channels open.

RICHES

One of the interesting by-products of modern society is known as "the checkbook mentality." It's the notion that money can solve everything. After all, money can buy food, clothing and shelter, as well as vacations, entertainment and companionship. It can even buy the vote of a senator, or maybe the senate seat itself. Problems can be handled the same way: Write a check. Declining school performance, crime, drug abuse, joblessness, homelessness, *hope*lessness—if only we were rich enough, we could spend all of our problems away.

Cow manure.

The combined testimony of religious traditions, both old and new, is that there is nothing as valuable, nothing as effective, as faith. Specifically, the kind of personal faith that can handle the bad along with the good, that sees one's self in proper relationship to other people and to some Ultimate Reality that gives meaning to one's life. No checkbook can buy this faith; no checking account is flush enough to accomplish what this faith can achieve. Whoever has it solves all the other problems for himself. Whoever can nurture it in others helps *them* solve those same problems for themselves.

Which is why every religion, in so many words, speaks out against "laying up earthly treasures" and recommends the kind of riches that pay real dividends. Bliss, eternal life, redemption and salvation are just fancy words for the jackpot. And missionaries—however guided or *mis*guided—are simply those who want to share the wealth.

RITUAL

Another by-product of modern life is a general dislike for ritual. Especially *religious* ritual. The dislike is understandable, even if unfortunate.

And one of the reasons for it is simply that, in a pluralistic society, there are so many different rituals, in so many different languages and theological frameworks. Learning what they all mean amounts to a full-time job. People have enough trouble learning what their *own* rituals mean.

Of course, some people don't make the effort to do even that. Because they're so weird, right? They don't make any sense. What does sprinkling water on a baby's head, or carrying the Torah up and down the aisle, or marching around the Ka'aba seven times, have to do with anything? Why do we need these rituals, anyway?

You already know: Because the shortest route to a person's heart is not always through the written or spoken word. Ritual is heavy-duty, hard-core, high-octane Faithspeak.

In study after study, behavioral scientists have shown that the judgments we make about what other people say are only partially dependent on their words. Over sixty percent of our reaction to someone's message, in fact, is based on body language. Tone of voice and context account for another thirty percent; and less than ten percent relates to what's called "rational content." Sorry, professor: Communication is only remotely a left-brain, logical enterprise.

Take the ritual of shaking hands. For our ancestors who frequently encountered tribes with different spoken languages, holding out one's hands in greeting, palms up, was a non-verbal sign that you were carrying no weapon and thus had no intention of doing harm. Taking the other person's empty hand in yours was a sign not only that you shared his intention, but you were each giving your pledge not to do anything "underhanded." A hearty handshake signaled a desire to be friends. Add an embrace or a kiss on the cheek and prospects were even brighter.

Most of our rituals, religious or otherwise, are connected in similar ways to some form of primal symbolism. Sprinkling water on a baby's head wasn't just a crazy idea some priest hatched after drinking a little too much sacramental wine. The ritual has roots as old as the handshake and as ancient as the connection between an expectant mother's breaking water and giving birth. It's not even necessary to know what the connection *is* exactly, just that there's something in us which resonates, some unconscious transaction that symbolically unites us with the elemental, life-giving forces of the universe.

Ritual, in short, is the symbolic "acting out" designed to evoke life-affirming responses. It is body language. It is tone and context; and it only indirectly involves conscious, rational analysis. Rituals break open our protective shells, cut through the layers of excuses and rationalizations and speak to our hearts precisely because they *are* so weird and because they *don't* always make sense. And the only fair way to judge those rituals is to look at what effect they have on us. Because what a ritual means is what it *does*.

There is one other characteristic of ritual worth noting. Because another thing ritual does is repeat itself—over and over. Catholics are given Communion at every Mass. Jews recite the same prayers in virtually the same order every Sabbath. Muslims prostrate themselves five times a day, every day. The same root word that gives us "arithmetic" is what gives us "ritual." It's all about numbers. Repetition. The more the better. Do it again. And again.

Someday maybe the message will finally sink in.

SABBATH

Literally "to stop working." To rest. Inning over. You deserve a break today. Even God figured it was time to clock out after six straight days of hard labor.

The Romans thought the Jews were deadbeats for wasting one entire day every week. Not that the Romans didn't throw an occasional Festival to lighten the load. But mostly it was work, work, work. Compared to ancient Rome, or at least Rome's blue-collar workers, the Puritan ethic was a picnic on the village green.

Even before the Torah, the Hebrews had other ideas. Life in the desert was definitely no picnic. Resting from one's daily chores each night was barely enough. Taking a full day off now and then was the only way to prevent terminal burn-out.

Since time was already divided into four seven-day weeks per month based on the lunar cycle, one day in seven seemed fitting. Then Genesis and Exodus hit the newsstands and made it official. God was quoted as saying, "Remember the Sabbath, to keep it holy." It was therefore not only acceptable to rest on Saturday, it was now a religious obligation. (And yes, the Sabbath was a Saturday affair, since it happened to coincide with the Roman empire's Saturn's Day, not its Sun's Day.)

How to "keep it holy" was a separate issue. For centuries it was enough simply to not work. Later, when Assyrian invaders packed up Judah's leading citizens and hauled them off to Babylon, the Jewish captives instituted formal meetings on the Sabbath. Reading from the Torah and the Prophets held them together as a community and a culture, and thereby prevented assimilation.

New rituals evolved, traditions were started; and after their release, the former captives took the whole routine back to Judah. Even when the Temple was rebuilt and the priestly functions re-established, people continued to meet in local houses for Torah readings and ritual. Daily, if possible; every Sabbath at a minimum. After all, reading scripture was one of the few activities that wasn't considered work.

By the time of Jesus, keeping the Sabbath holy had turned into a major source of squabbling. For some Jewish factions the Sabbath was a very formal, highly regimented affair whose obligations seemed (at least to others) more like work than plowing fields or otherwise earning a living. Jesus was one of several critics who argued that the original purpose had been lost in all the rules and regulations and group coercion. Maybe it had.

Still, the idea of spending one day a week feeding one's soul rather than pursuing another silver shekel was admirable. Christians adopted the practice, but chose the Sun's Day to observe it. Muslims did likewise, though their observance (on Friday) is primarily for congregational prayer and a public address. Abstaining from work all day long is not required.

For the Orthodox Jew, though, not working is still obligatory. In fact for all Jews, and all Christians, the Sabbath is still the single most important religious institution. More important than Christmas or Easter, Passover or the Day of Atonement, it is the focal point for the entire calendar. Because it is the one day each week for putting our lives in perspective; for reaffirming what we believe, or what we're *trying* to believe, despite having made the same dumb mistakes we did last week. The Sabbath affirms that life is a learning process. And while the best way to learn about life is to just go out and *live* it, it's also essential to call a regular time-out to analyze how things are going.

In a sense the Sabbath *is* coercive. For people wrapped up in jobs and appointment-book social lives, being forced to rest can be a real lifesaver. The temptation is always to become consumed by what we do for our daily bread, by our roles as mother or father, by what other people expect of us. So the ancient Hebrews were right. Without drawing the line somewhere, without getting out of the trenches now and then, we inevitably burn out or become robots, lifelessly going through the motions. We lose touch with our divinity. We forget Who We Are.

Which is why the Sabbath is worthwhile even for those who don't attend church or synagogue or the neighborhood mosque. Pick a day: Sunday, Wednesday, *any* day will do as long as you do it regularly. Take the whole day off, all twenty-four hours of it. Read something. Or let your mind wander while the ice melts in your tumbler of tea. Invite a friend over, but don't talk about work. Take a child to the zoo. Sit by a stream, or climb a hill and gaze at the scenery. Or your navel. Reward yourself for making it through the last six days.

Keep on doing it and your whole outlook will change. Guaranteed.

SACRAMENT

There are moments... and then there are moments.

Sometimes what happens is like a window into another dimension. All at once you're aware of something deeper, something more meaningful going on than what outward appearances tell you. And that one moment, that one act, one event, becomes a symbol for *all* those moments and acts and events.

The Christian Church identified the occasions when some of these special moments were most likely to occur and called them "the Sacraments." The ritual of Communion was one such occasion. Baptism was another. Others include the affirming of one's religious tradition (called Confirmation); the act of confessing your sins (Penance); getting married to someone, or to Mother Church (Matrimony and Ordination, respectively); or when a person dies (described as Extreme Unction). All of these experiences hold the promise for witnessing not just an isolated event, but one of the major themes of Life Itself.

Of course it doesn't always happen. Fact is, it rarely happens, because so much depends on our frame of mind. And we often go through the institutional form of these events in a mechanical, I-know-what-to-expect fashion that shuts off spiritual insight instead of enhancing it.

But sometimes the deeper levels *do* break through... when the four-year-old ring-bearer at the wedding drops the groom's ring and it bounces down the chancery steps and rolls under the first pew and you realize that life is just like that, and all the ceremony and pageantry can't protect us from the fact that stuff happens, and we're just ordinary folks doing the best we can. Or when a sleeping infant wakes up in the middle of her baptism, sucks air and breaks into an ear-splitting wail that mirrors the first moments out of the womb and seems to say, "I don't understand this, it's all so new, just keep holding me until I have a chance to get my bearings."

Or being there when your father is finally taken off the respirator, and his chest heaves a few more times, and the glazed eyes never quite shut even when the breathing stops, and you know he wasn't seeing anything anyway, that he'd left his body days ago and for all you know he's watching the same scene right there alongside you and your brothers, holding you as you all hold each other, and that it's okay, it's life and there's more to it than we'll ever, ever know on this side of The Veil.

No church can limit the number or forms of sacramental moments. Nor is Christianity the only context for them. Those moments of merging with Something Deeper are the domain of Baha'i, Muslim, Hindu and atheist alike, and as common as the events we experience every day. Like watching your child fall off her bike, whimper a little and climb right back on. Or standing around helplessly as your cat gives birth to four healthy kittens, and a fifth one dies. Or listening to the crickets at night, or the sound your lover makes at the peak of ecstasy. Or feeling your unborn baby turn placental somersaults while you place your palm on your wife's impossibly stretched abdomen; then, twenty years later, watching your little baby drive off to college.

Or saying just the right thing, right when it was needed.

And the beauty of it is, the more those moments happen—the more we *let* them happen—the more they keep happening. The gaps between them begin to close. The occasional sacramental moment becomes a string of sacraments, which in turn becomes the continuum called Life. Even the pain, even the tears are sacramental. Our whole outlook changes. Labels like Christian or Buddhist or agnostic lose meaning because it is this larger Faith that now shapes you.

It's like the story about the teacher who is eventually surpassed by his student. Religious traditions can point to a few of the more common sacraments; they can tell us to be alert for other gaps in the Veil where the divine dimension may come shining through. But when we learn, when we start to notice for ourselves, the best those religions can do is stand back and let that divine Light reveal itself in its countless ways, and maybe offer a few hallelujahs from the sidelines.

For just as giving birth is a sacrament, so is letting go.

SACRIFICE

This is one of those primal symbols, the practice of which is completely out of place in modern society, yet still resonates with something deep inside us.

Not that we should go out and erect stone altars on the hilltops like our distant ancestors did, stretch out a struggling, year-old lamb, then sink a carving knife from stem to stern and sprinkle its blood all over the place before setting it on fire. We don't live in the same world. Most of us don't raise lambs or bullocks or barley, so bringing them to the Temple and watching them turned into smoke doesn't mean anything to us. Or else it means something primitive and blood-thirsty.

But let's look at it from our ancestors' point of view and see what it meant to them.

Let's say you live in Canaan and you *do* have a nice flock of lambs. You're aware the success of your flock is not altogether under your control. Such factors as the availability of good grazing, the possibility of attacks by predators or raiders from other tribes, the fertility of the rams and ewes, the absence of disease—all these elements are reportedly under the control of the local divinity. That divinity is something like the king or caliph or Caesar, only more powerful.

And the way to secure his continued blessings and protection is in the same royal fashion. You bring him gifts as a token of your affection; you make peace offerings should you ever fall from grace. The "first fruits" from your orchard would be appropriate, or the first-born of your flock—the Grade A products that would've brought in the biggest bucks on the open market. Whatever tangible things you treasure most for yourself is what most impresses the Powers-That-Be.

Trouble is, the local divinity is not as tangible as the gift you're planning to give him. The only way to send him a few sheaves of your newly-harvested wheat is to burn them and let him inhale the smoke. The only way to make a present of that first-born calf is to send its life back from where it came. And just as "sweat" represents the idea of work to people today, blood symbolized "life" to our ancestors. Shedding it, sprinkling it, or being washed in it (which certain European cults specialized in), openly acknowledged that the animal's life was *our* life, that the divinity owns not only what is most important to us, but *us*.

This is pretty advanced theology when viewed in context. But it was also specific to cultures where shedding blood and funeral pyres were already familiar images. People slaughtered the animals they ate for dinner that night. They burned fields and saw the stubble of their crops returned to the soil. They sometimes saw loved ones die and turned into ashes, too. That was the language of their life and times.

It is not ours.

But what it *stands for* has analogies in our lives today. We are probably as aware as our ancestors that our lives are not fully under our control. We don't ultimately make the rules any more than they did. There is still some greater Reality we must try to understand and in some sense obey. And we must continue to relate to it in a way that allows us to maintain its favor. The question is, *How?*

Certainly not by ignoring it. In some manner appropriate to our time and place, we must openly acknowledge that the things we treasure most are dependent on this Reality. If we fail to declare that dependence, chances are we value our money and possessions more than the Reality that supports their existence. Which means our priorities are skewed. And our lives can't help but suffer.

But it is not enough to admit our dependence in words, to merely *say* it. We know in our guts when we're only giving lip service. So it's essential to send our inner selves (read: our subconscious) a message affirming that our priorities are now in order. That message must be in Faithspeak—something that goes straight to our hearts, that involves emotion; something with a visceral exclamation point.

To deflower a marketing motto, "Say it with sacrifice." Make a sacrificial offering. Give up something.

So, then: What are the things we treasure so much that giving them up would make a big enough impression on ourselves? Since blood is no longer acceptable, offering our time and labor to a charitable organization might do. Skipping a meal once a week and giving the unused food to someone who's hungry can also make a tangible impact. Donating our material possessions to the needy is another possibility—not just last year's outdated sportswear or the CD player with the remote that no longer works, but something you'd actually use if you kept it.

But sacrifice can also involve less tangible things, like "experiences" or "life's simple pleasures." Catholic priests give up marriage and family. Jews give up the enjoyment of certain foods, including lobster with melted butter or a nice ham-on-rye. The devout Muslim will not only skip the ham-on-rye but the taste of a cold margarita on a hot summer night. These are also sacrifices of a sort.

And who knows? Maybe, as the ancients believed, giving up something—whether tangible or *in*tangible—really does have a kind of pump-priming effect. New Agers and Christian fundamentalists share the notion that giving generously of one's money and possessions initiates a cycle whereby the more you give, the more you receive. It's as if giving something away creates a vacuum that draws in more of the same.

Or maybe Ultimate Reality is always on the lookout for people through whom it can pour out its infinite resources; and once someone gives the handle a few good pumps, the supply just keeps on flowing, keeps on replenishing itself, keeps on replenishing *us*.

Like the blood in our veins.

SAINT

The cynical view (even if there is some truth to it) is that saints are the human counterparts to all those deities the Greeks and Romans gave up when Christianity took over. In place of Hermes or Hera, the common folk could now pray to Saint Christopher or Saint Agnes. And do so all the more easily because saints were as human as they were.

The saints could also continue to intercede on their behalf, just like the old gods did, appealing to the Higher Powers for specific blessings or help with their personal affairs. Some saints even developed a specialty, the way attorneys tend to focus on a certain type of litigation. One saint became associated with the needs of travelers, another with marital problems, another with animal husbandry. These are known as "patron saints."

Hindus, with more human-like gods and devas than you can shake a stick at, had already assigned divine specialists to virtually every area of life. To question whether these divinities existed was both unnecessary and self-defeating. With the proper ritual (or *puja*), help was always an offering or incense-perfumed prayer away.

And the fact is, help *is* close at hand. Ultimate Reality *does* provide built-in resources for humans with special needs. To say it's "all in the mind" makes it no less effective. The very idea of a "sympathetic listener" or imaginary companion with whom you can share your innermost secrets somehow opens a healing channel between your conscious mind and your subconscious. Or, put another way, the emotions released in conversation with some compassionate "other" connects your inner being to that spiritual reservoir from which new insights and energies come. Patron saints and imaginary helpmates are simply the

Faithspeak that sparks this deeper-level connection.

But the fact that the Catholic Church has an elaborate procedure for recognizing and confirming saints emphasizes that not just any helpmate will do. For example, we wouldn't expect to gain much from someone who is merely a duplicate of our present self, who has no more of a handle on our problems than we do; who might even confirm our baser instincts and end up making matters worse. Our helpmate must draw out our own divine image and set an example of humanity at its best. That's why they're called "saints"—literally, those who are "set apart" to be our examples.

Which brings us to the more common understanding of the word. Not the goody two-shoes definition, but the ordinary saint who rolls up his-or-her sleeves and gets involved in the real world and still manages to shine. Or the person who's not above an occasional bout of looneyness, like knocking over the tables in the Temple courtyard or talking to the animals when nobody's looking; yet whose life stands for something, whose sense of connection with a deeper reality somehow makes "all things possible."

Saints are the everyday heroes and heroines, the Christs, Buddhas and Muhammads found in our workplaces and on our streets. They're the Mother Theresas and Albert Schweitzers, or the guy on the next block who works like hell to keep the local gang-leader in school and finds him a job and turns his life around because there's a divine image in him, too, if only someone will help unveil it.

Saints are those who unveil *us*. Sometimes it takes a real person or a religious figure to do it. But sometimes all it takes is ourselves. Even if it means putting the words in our own hearts on someone else's imaginary lips.

SALVATION

It's a process. And a goal. It's every concept in this Lexicon, every experience in life taken together, working toward a wholeness we can only dimly imagine. It is a universal human enterprise, not the exclusive domain of Christians or Jews, Buddhists or Muslims, New Agers or secular humanists—even though all of these traditions and groups have specific ways of talking about it.

And what they are talking about is what they all share, what lies *behind* the words, even if they'll tell you otherwise. It's a journey we're all engaged in—even now—and which, in ordinary language, goes something like this:

Whether we're born rich or poor, brown-eyed or blue, intelligent or not, we're all pretty much in the same boat. True, taking care of the physical necessities of life is a struggle, and some come out better than others. But the real struggle takes place on another, deeper level. Here, material wealth and intelligence provide no automatic advantage. And while the particular body each of us lives in may differ from others, we are all endowed with the same inner resources that can lead to more fulfilled, more satisfying lives.

Unfortunately, discovering those resources and learning how to use them is a difficult, life-long campaign. In fact, *that* is the struggle.

Fortunately, there are also "outside" resources. After all, *we* didn't create the world. We didn't make the rules. And therefore whatever brought the world and the rules into being—and continues to maintain them—must have an existence independent of us. If we could live in accordance with that "whatever," if we could more fully connect or harmonize with that larger reality (or let's say *Ultimate* Reality), then our lives might be less of a struggle.

The good news is that this Reality seems to be as serious about connecting with us as we are with *it.* Through an infinite variety of circumstances and interactions with other people, we are inevitably pushed not only toward the same questions about Who We Are and Why We're Here, but the same basic answers. While these answers have been written down by groups of people throughout history based on their collective experience and their particular framework for understanding, an individual's salvation does not depend on living in accordance with those answers. It depends on living in accordance with the Reality which those answers more or less accurately describe.

Read those last two sentences until they sink in.

Or think of it this way: We don't finally learn that two-plus-two equals four because someone tells us, or because we read it in a book. We learn it when our own experience confirms that two-plus-two *does* equal four, because that's just the way it is, that's the reality and we finally "get it." We also get it because when we apply that rule, we can keep our checkbooks balanced. If, instead, we'd been taught that two-plus-two equals five, reality would have brought us back to four sooner or later. Or else we'd have learned that the word "five" meant the concept that lies behind what everybody else understands as "four."

What religion has to do with salvation is hidden in that last paragraph, in case you didn't notice.

Of course there are lots of two-plus-two-equals-four's to be learned. Learning them all is an ongoing process, the bottom line of which is how it affects your life—not necessarily in terms of outward circumstances, but in the way you experience it and interact with it. In your faith.

To sum up, salvation is the shaping of our faiths toward some ideal expression of ourselves. No one else can do that for us. No one else can tell us if or when we've achieved it, or how far along The Path we've come. In some sense it involves the reconciliation of everything in our individual and collective lives. It involves bridging the gap between what limits us and what expands us, between What We Are and What We *Can Be*. Other words in this Lexicon describe some of the mechanics of the process, or where we are in the process right now, or where we hope to be at the end of it. But these are only useful words. Like "Two plus two equals four." They point; they help us focus on what we need to learn.

And sometimes they keep us from making more dumb mistakes until we finally "get it."

SATAN

It has always been tempting to symbolize evil by dressing it in quasi-human form, just as beneficial forces are characterized as angels, saints and Olympia-style gods. In this way we can imagine good and evil in more concrete terms. We can represent the push-pull of those forces like the proverbial devil and angel perched atop either shoulder. "Go ahead—who's gonna know?" whispers the one with horns. "Don't listen," warns the winged one. "And besides, *you'll* know!"

Satan, according to tradition, is the incarnation of the worst instincts and capabilities within our humanity, as Christ embodies the best. Not that he started out that way. Ancient Hebrews knew Satan simply as "The Adversary"; that's what the name means in both Hebrew and Arabic. No more than a folksy story-telling gimmick in early literature, Satan was originally portrayed as a kind of professional snoop, ferreting out people's sins and reporting them back to God.

As his literary character developed over the centuries, Satan began actively tempting people into sin instead of just spying on them, like a news reporter goading a rioter into breaking that store window so he'll have some good video for the Eleven O'clock News or his YouTube page. Eventually, because the protagonist of every great story requires a strong antagonist, Satan evolved into the Adversary of God Himself, continually opposing and thwarting the Divine Plan for salvation.

And what makes Satan so good at his job, literarily speaking, is that he knows what God's plans *are,* almost down to the last detail. Worse, he knows what makes humans tick. He knows our weaknesses. He knows the price point at which each of us will sell our souls. Satan, after all, was once a Son of God himself. He was there when the blueprints were drawn. But like Lucifer—or rather, because his identity had now *merged* with Lucifer—he figured he could do better. Whereupon he started a revolt and took a chunk of the Heavenly Kingdom along with him.

Not coincidentally, the full characterization of Satan from petty stool-pigeon to the Incarnation of Evil came only after Judah's defeat by the Assyrians and the abduction of many Jews to Babylon. Assyria's religion, it so happens, featured a theology based on a great cosmological battle between the forces of Light and the forces of Darkness. It was a persuasive framework for looking at what was going on in the world at the time, especially after what the Jews had just suffered.

Those who returned to Judah carried that world-view with them. By the time of Jesus, a minor literary character had been elevated into the Sole Cause of Everything Wrong with the World. Which also redefined the duties of the long-awaited Messiah, for some Jews at least. It was now no longer enough to merely cast off the yoke of foreign oppression. The Messiah had to overthrow Satan and his Evil Kingdom as well.

Whether Jews (and Jesus) took this Evil-Kingdom-slash-Forces-of-Darkness stuff literally, or merely as a handy way to dramatize current events, is still a subject of scholarly discussion. Certainly the Jews were capable of writing and speaking in symbolic language, of understanding that they were communicating in Faithspeak—or even in a kind of secret dialect. The Hebrew books of Ezekiel and Daniel, not to mention Christianity's wildly visionary book of Revelation, are regarded by most Biblical scholars as vehicles for discussing the events of their time in what they call "coded language."

On the other hand, to label all this as Faithspeak is not to deny what lies behind these words and stories. Admitting that Satan is only a device for conceptualizing the forces of evil doesn't for a moment deny that forces of evil do exist in some sense. Our own divine image can get buried in "lusts of the flesh"—or at least in the pursuit of material things and sensual pleasures that may not be good for us. Something *does* whisper in our ears in our weaker moments, enticing us to be less than we can be, tempting us to accept short-term satisfaction instead of long-term fulfillment, to "do evil" even when we're trying our hardest to be good. It's as if there's a malevolent conspiracy by some Great Schemer who takes delight in seeing our best efforts go down the porcelain pony. That's how we *feel,* anyway.

But even proponents of a literal Satan agree that God could punch his lights out if He wanted to. Which means that He must *not* want to, at least for now. And that means Satan must be part of the Divine Plan. The forces of evil exist for a purpose.

Maybe it's because the soldier of Darkness who finally sees the Light often becomes more passionate about being good than the person who's never been tempted. Or maybe it's because having an adversary forces us to choose, and that choice shapes Who We Are; it shapes our faith. That's the role Satan still plays in the historic Abrahamic traditions of Judaism, Christianity and Islam. The idea behind Satan is the realization that we can't sit on the sidelines forever. We can't straddle the fence, remain uncommitted, stay undecided. We must join the Companions of the Right, or the Companions of the Left.

As the singer James Taylor puts it, "Have you waded in and been to Hell, or will you lie upon the sofa?" Are you gonna put up your dukes, or sleep through another round? In other words, you need a mountain to climb. When the going gets tough, the tough get going. Adversity brings out the best in people. Adversity builds character.

The *Adversary* builds character.

SAVE

In Hebrew, the word usually translated as "saved"—*yashau*—literally means "to be expanded."

The implications are both physical and spiritual. Being saved implies freedom, the condition of not being physically confined or enslaved. In a wider sense it also means to be healthy and prosperous enough to meet your basic survival needs. Otherwise you'd still be enslaved.

On a mental/spiritual level, it implies a new awareness of ourselves, a new sense of possibilities, of room to grow. To be saved is to realize that we needn't be held back by our own past, that we can rise above Who We Are at this particular moment. We can discover a whole new aspect of Self not defined merely by our evolution as animals in a physical environment, with material needs demanding material solutions. Instead we become connected to a deeper reality behind the world we see and touch. We become "expanded."

Recognizing this at a gut level—whether inside or outside of a religious context—can change our lives. Because we're suddenly aware that we've begun a journey, and there's no turning back. It's not that we're perfect, or that we've "arrived," or even that we're moving forward all the time. It's just that we know we're on the way and that everything we do affects our progress.

One more thought: When you're working on your laptop, it's a good practice to hit a specific combination of keys every so often and save your work on your hard drive, or to an external disk. You thereby record it in a more permanent fashion so that if the power goes down, or some glitch in the program trashes your working file, you haven't lost everything. You can recover.

To be saved, in the spiritual sense, is to confirm what you've learned on your journey toward salvation. The more often, the better. So even if the power fails, or what you're working on at the moment gets trashed, you haven't lost everything.

You can recover.

SCIENCE

There are five primary lines of communication connecting the average human being to the world. Through sight. Through touch. By tasting it, smelling it, or hearing it.

None of these sensory faculties is remotely like the others. (Okay—tasting and smelling, maybe.) But try to describe how something sounds by what it feels like, or what something smells like based on its looks, and you're bound to fail. Language simply won't bridge the gap between different types of perception. You'll never really know how a kiwi fruit tastes from even the most detailed description of its visual appearance. And that's assuming you have experience with visual information to begin with. Because unless you can see, language involving color, brightness and perspective won't make sense anyway.

Imagine a dolphin describing to a human what it's like to "sonarize" an approaching shark through a hundred yards of murky seawater, and somehow pick up his own reflected signals amidst those of fellow dolphins who are sonarizing the same shark. Not to mention how it is that those signals mean "shark" as opposed to a dolphin or a scuba diver, or an outcropping of coral? How are reflected sound waves turned into useful information, and what does that information "look like" or "feel like" to the dolphin?

For that matter, how do light waves bouncing off tables or chairs or movie screens get translated into electrical charges in our brains, and then end up as the mental copies of tables or chairs or moving images that we "see"?

And are we ever going to talk about science here or what?

We *have* been. Every time the word "how" came up. Questions that start with "How" are what science specializes in. Not just "How do we see?" or "How do birds fly?" but how we go about finding answers to those questions in the first place. And how do we test or verify those answers to make sure they're correct or otherwise consistent with reality. Which is what we call The Scientific Method.

All the correct answers and the methods by which we found those answers, put together, are what we call "knowledge." The word "science," after all, comes from the Latin *scientia,* which means "knowing." Knowing about the physical world is what science does best. In that domain, in fact, it is without peer.

Not that everything science tells us is guaranteed to be 100-percent reliable and true. Just look at a typical science textbook from the 1930s. Or even the 1980s. Science is full of hypotheses that have since been disproven—canals on Mars, anyone?—and others that have yet to be proven or disproven because the process of verification is still going on.

But a method that admits its own limitations and attacks the fallacies in its own theories shouldn't be taken as a sign of weakness. And a certain other field of knowledge that presumes to compete with science—even as it clings to a view of the physical universe written long before humans had the scientific tools to investigate it—can only end up destroying its own credibility.

Picture, if you will, the holy fathers of the Church Tribunal, dressed in their taffeta gowns and sanctimonious scowls, sitting across from Galileo, insisting that the poor, misguided astronomer was headed for the fires of Hell unless he recanted his blasphemous theory that the planets actually revolved around the sun! For behold, the Bible hath spoken otherwise!

But the Bible—or the Qur'an, or the I Ching and the Ramayanas—are not science books. They view the world through different senses. It's as if science perceives the universe through the eyes, and religion through touch. Both provide useful information. Both provide sensory data about different aspects of reality. They even communicate with our brains in a different sensory language. But those perceptions are not thereby incompatible. They are each valid within their own domain, and together they give us a more complete picture of the "totality of reality" than we would have otherwise.

And just as the way something looks doesn't convey how it tastes or smells, science can tell us *how* to do something, but not always how to do it responsibly. Or whether we should be doing it at all.

The so-called conflict between science and religion is like a conversation between people who are trying to hear with their eyes and see with their ears. The organs work fine. The owners have just forgotten what they're for.

SCRIPTURE

For many people, the word "scripture" already has two strikes against it. The very sound of it seems outmoded and archaic, like "thou" and "thine" and "Verily, he saith." It brings up images of brittle parchment, inscribed with fading ink and fanciful text whose meaning and relevance is likewise brittle and fading, or that can be preserved only by keeping it in some climate-controlled vault, away from the real world.

Actually, "scripture" *is* an archaic word recalling a time when all records and documents were written by hand. *Scribere* is Latin for the act of writing; *scriptum* refers to the product, (usually in the form of a parchment scroll); and *scriptorium* was the ancient equivalent of a modern pressroom.

Since paper wasn't exactly cheap at the time and inscribing it required lots of time and talent—and because not that many people could read anyway—information had to be fairly important before it was written down. The most common documents were therefore business contracts and deeds to property, peace treaties and royal decrees, and the accounts of major military battles. The collected laws, traditions, religious observances and historical records of various peoples were also committed to paper. Usually after a weeding out process that took place over several generations of oral transmission.

Examples of religious documents include the Hebrew Bible (comprised of the Torah, writings of the prophets, and collected "wisdom literature")... the Holy Bible of Christianity (which combines the Hebrew Bible with a "New" Testament and, in some circles, what's known as The Apocrypha)... the Holy Qur'an of Islam, (complemented by the Acts of the Messenger and the Hadith)... the early Vedic writings of Hinduism (most notably the Upanishads), plus the Great Epics (featuring the Ramayana and Mahabharata, from which the Bhagavad-gita or "Celestial Song" was excerpted), as well as the more mystical Yoga.

Of course we mustn't forget the Tao-Teh-King of Taoism, the three Pitakas of Buddhism, or the Avesta of Zoroastrianism. And if we add to these the hundreds of writings from long-dead traditions, obscure sects and off-shoots of the major traditions (like the group that produced the Dead Sea Scrolls)... along with more recent texts like the Book of Mormon, the commentaries of Baha'u'llah, and the self-help handbook that laid the groundwork for Scientology, you'll have enough religious literature to stock several dozen libraries.

Technically, most of these historical and religious documents can be labeled as "scripture" simply by virtue of their having been painstakingly written and re-written by hand over the centuries. What the term has generally come to imply, however, are only religious writings; and more specifically, only those writings that are regarded as the basis for their respective religious traditions. Whether they're written on a scroll in Sanskrit or Old English, or printed in 10-point Helvetica in a paperback book, no longer matters.

Of course, certain members of certain traditions regard only *their* writings as scripture, and the others merely as "religious documents." But this, again, reflects the mistaken view that limits truth and meaning to only one language or symbolic expression. There is no reason why someone couldn't collect all the religious writings mentioned above, package them as a set and call the entire collection The Holy Scriptures.

The Judeo-Christian scriptures, in fact, are just such a diverse collection of books, each one with a different symbolic motif, a different world-view, as well as a different scope, message and purpose. Inconsistencies abound, and are usually explained away as only *seeming* to be that way. The overall theme of the collection, it's claimed, is humankind's need for salvation, and how to find it.

But the same might be said for a compendium of scriptures gathered from every tradition. The inconsistencies only seem that way. And the overall theme is our salvation, and how we may find it.

SECOND COMING

If at first you don't succeed, try, try again.

Once is never enough.

Jesus is coming again.

The first is an aphorism, the second a book title, the third is Faithspeak. All of them express in one pithy sentence the universal sentiment that nothing is ever easy, and the first attempt at anything is rarely successful. Especially the things that matter most. Changing the world, or changing our*selves,* is hard enough even when we've seen The Light, even after we've supposedly gotten the message.

The problem is, we hardly ever get the message the first time we hear it. Jesus couldn't have made it any clearer when he said that we're all headed for the dumpster if we don't fix things; and even though the resources for fixing them are as close as your own solar plexus, it's typical of humans to simply accuse someone else for what's wrong and let them hang. Which is why Jesus himself ended up on the cross.

So things never did get fixed, at least the way most Jews (and even the early Christians) expected. Sometime after his crucifixion, rumors began to circulate that Jesus would "come again" to finish the job and finally establish the Kingdom of God "on earth as it is in heaven." Many believers practically camped out on their rooftops, hoping to catch sight of his glorious "coming in the clouds," like members of some modern-day cult might run off to the mountains (or Waco, Texas) to await the end of the world.

As decades passed, however, a more formal concept of his Second Coming began to replace rumors of Jesus' imminent return. After all, no one really knew the exact schedule. It could be tomorrow or next week, or the next millennium. Or maybe 1914 (as Seventh-Day Adventists once believed), or the year 2032.

Whatever the date, the promise of a Second Coming is Faithspeak for the fact that the work of personal and communal salvation is still not finished, but will be someday... hopefully. That expectation is at the heart of every religious tradition. If we missed the boat on its maiden voyage, don't worry, there's another one heading upriver.

But what to do in the meantime, while we're all waiting, is another matter. And here's where attitudes—faiths—can differ.

One version of waiting would have us all standing around at the docks, twiddling our thumbs while we scan the horizon for any sign of the approaching ship. (And getting each other all worked up whenever we'd mistake a distant white-cap for a sail or puff of steam.) Another version of waiting is the kind associated with being a waiter or waitress at a restaurant. The only "standing around" going on is the kind that actively looks for the next opportunity to serve one's patrons. Most of the time is spent "waiting on tables," taking orders and serving meals.

Most religions agree that if we wait in this more active way, the next ship arrives sooner. Paradoxically, we speed up the schedule precisely by ignoring it, by not hanging all our hopes and dreams on the boat's arrival, and simply going on with our lives as if it's not even coming. Christianity admits as much by saying that we must prepare the world for the Savior's return before he'll actually come. Judaism proclaims that we hasten the Messianic Era by striving to complete the Creation God started. Hinduism is the most direct when it tells us bluntly that we're on our own; don't expect divinity to do the work for you.

And you know what? If we really *do* work at it instead of twiddling our collective thumbs, the boat that arrives is *us*—first on a personal level, then as a wider community. The Second Coming is when *we* arrive, when we all figure out or "come around to" the message we didn't understand the first time. Maybe it's not the one we thought it was, but the one hidden below the words and symbols, the one that unites us rather than divides us, that says we are all Sons and Daughters of the What Is.

So come on—quit standing around! Get to work for a change.

SECULAR

Before the word gained its current status as an adjective, "Secular" was the title given to a cleric who was ordained by the early church for work "in the world." The Secular, as he was called, dealt with the everyday affairs of the diocese to which he was assigned, including such diverse tasks as routine building maintenance, dealing with the local peasantry and distributing food to the poor. Officiating at Mass or reading from the holy books, administering baptisms, last rites and other church sacraments—these were responsibilities reserved for the priesthood.

Over the decades, church officials realized some of the priestly duties could be handled just as well by ordinary church members or "laymen." Which is probably when "secular" began its transition into a lowly adjective, and was increasingly used to describe all things worldly, whether church-related or outside its domain (i.e. *pro fanum*).

The irony here is that the Church's foundational figure, Jesus of Nazareth, would almost certainly have preferred that his followers focus precisely on that outside, more worldly work, not on the supposedly superior activities that went on inside the gold-embellished, icon-laden walls of a sanctuary. A second irony is that, in the primitive church—as in more ancient cultures—there simply was no division between what we now call "secular" and "religious." Life was made of one cloth, so to speak, interwoven equally with the profane and the sacred, with obedience to civil authority and devotion to the divine. Participation in the mundane world of industry and family was just another expression of one's religious responsibilities.

Of course, as the world's religion-saturated societies continued to clash with one another, often violently, the masses became increasingly convinced that conditions would improve if only civil authority and divine authority were kept separate, if the police and military powers of the State could be removed from all the competing religious factions that inevitably abused those powers. True, history's so-called religious wars were usually more about political or economic issues; but appealing to religion was always the best way to whip up popular support.

Dividing human activities into what we now consider the "sacred" and the "secular" became the only lasting method—in the West, at least—for ending that ongoing strife. The solution was legally enshrined in the U.S. Constitution's "Establishment Clause" and similar laws elsewhere, all of which effectively prohibited any one religion from enforcing its will on everybody else. The contemporary understanding of "secular," in short, is almost wholly an outcome of the centuries of violence and terror foisted on the masses by those who called themselves religious.

And the third irony here is that, as we learn more about what faith and religion really are, the sacred and secular begin to dissolve back into one another just as they were in ancient times. Even if the reasons have changed. And hopefully because *we* have changed.

SELF-HELP

The same year Charles Darwin launched all the uproar over Evolution with his book, *Origin of the Species,* another British author by the genial name of Samuel Smiles published his own best-seller entitled *Self-Help.* Translated into nearly two-dozen languages, Smiles' masterpiece set the stage for a whole new genre of periodicals and handbooks based on the premise that people are quite capable of doing lots of things for themselves, tank ya veddy mooch, many of which they'd ceded over recent centuries to social programs and government. Sadly, many people had now come to depend on those institutions, or even become enslaved by them. And since Smiles believed that individuals have ultimate power, it was their own bloody fault. Self-Help was the solution.

While planting your own vegetable garden and rebuilding your classic car are among today's most popular self-help subjects, books featuring do-it-yourself spiritual practices and techniques for the feeding and caring of your soul are not uncommon. People can read, after all, and don't need cantors or imams to chant from the scriptures to know what they say. Nor, in countries where a Bill of Rights is enshrined and the Common Man is equal to royalty, do people need priests to stand in for them, or conduct the rituals designed to nurture their faith.

Thus saith Self-Help.

And there *is* much we can do for ourselves (and our Self), certainly. But having said that, there's also much we can do in tandem with others, in a spiritual community, that can make things so much easier. We can let a book be our guide and guru, allow our private meditations to substitute for the call-and-response of a reading in church. But something qualitatively different happens when we *hear* words rather than read them. Something unique occurs when somebody shows us how to fix a carburetor instead of handing us a repair manual. Something almost sacred takes place when we stand up from our folding chairs and admit our drinking problem in the company of other alcoholics—something that does not, or maybe cannot, happen if we try to go it alone.

We are social animals. We are organically programmed for certain kinds of nurturing only others can give, for developmental stages where group interaction facilitates our progress and isolation hinders it.

It's no coincidence that the word "self" has meaning only in relationship to others.

SEMINARY

A seminary—from the Latin *seminarium,* meaning "garden" or "nursery"—is an institution of learning wherein people plant the seeds from which their life's mission will grow. In the typical seminary, people discover how tradition and scripture can shape Who They Are, what their relationship to Ultimate Reality is, and how to serve other people while also serving their own best interests.

We are all, every one of us, enrolled.

SENTIENCE

All life is sentient to the extent that it can sense the world around it, whether through the eyes, ears and other sense organs common to members of the animal kingdom, or through the photosynthetic cells and other receptors of the plant world. Space scientists and *Star Trek* characters generally restrict sentient life to creatures capable of "critical thinking," similar to what human beings allegedly do, although their physical forms may differ.

In Buddhism, sentient beings are the ordinary humans who perceive life solely through their material senses. Such people have a limited, distorted view of the world, in which they (and all other life forms) seem separate from one another, confined to their earthly bodies, and have no understanding of the One Mind that unites them all. Humans, therefore, are essentially no different from other living things for whom sense receptors are their primary (if not exclusive) connection to the world, even if they do have the capacity to rise above this limited perspective on occasion.

For our purposes, it is "consciousness" that distinguishes humanity from other sentient life. Paradoxically, this kind of awareness is rooted in a sense of one's separateness. But it can also give rise, under certain conditions, to a profound experience of unity with other humans, other life forms, and ultimately with the universe.

These "certain conditions" may include the communal rituals of traditional religion, or one's private reflections on a good book, or the impact of a loving relationship that brings our defensive walls crashing down. A mystical experience can accomplish the same thing. Like watching the moon rise over Bridalveil Falls and the light edges over the granite ridge above it, catching the spray coming off the water just so, and suddenly there's no separate "you" looking at the Falls, only a oneness with All That Is which comes less as a divine revelation than a simple acceptance of what has always been.

And, for all you know, may always be.

SERVICE

It's no surprise that many Protestants describe their Sunday-morning main event not simply as "worship," but as a worship *service*. Take it as a gentle reminder, Pastor Graham might say, that putting oneself in proper relationship to God is only Step One. The point of it all, once you've stepped from the pew, is to go out and serve.

Portrayed through the metaphor of kings and their loyal subjects—or sometimes masters and servants—"service" is understood not only as a duty to some higher authority, but as a responsibility to be relished. Because we are not just interchangeable automatons or dime-a-dozen drones. Each of us has specific gifts and passions. The idea of service is not merely about doing something that's useful and beneficial to others. It's about discovering and performing a function within the larger community that's designed just for you.

This unique mission makes each of us different, while at the same time enfolding us all into the progressively larger entity we become one with. Which is why—and not just for Protestants—service is the path to salvation.

SEX

In case you hadn't noticed before you cracked open this lexicon, religious traditions have had a lot to say about sex over the centuries. If you *have* noticed, chances are you already know that much of what they say is, well... troubling. Or maybe, let's say, disapproving.

Okay—*appalling*.

For one thing, participating in an act designed by God (or the gods) to insure the continuation of the species is bound to unleash nature's most primal forces. Anything that powerful can't help but have significant consequences, not the least of which is the manufacture of another human being.

Sex also inevitably involves our relationships—the autoerotic and homoerotic kinds included. One of the major concerns of religion is whether sex builds bridges between people or pushes them apart. And much of what we assume is religion's negativity toward sex is simply the conviction, after centuries of experience, that certain uses of sex are far more likely to divide people than unite them.

Hopping in bed with the neighbor's wife isn't bad because *sex* is bad. It's because relationships can be permanently damaged as a result. An hour of presumed pleasure can change not only the course of one life, but the lives of at least three others. Or ten others, or twenty. And all those Thou-Shalt-Not's and threats of Hellfire are heaped on the faithful only to convey the fact that, for many sexual behaviors, the probability of the positive effects outweighing the bad is pretty damn doubtful. There's no guarantee those behaviors will end up harming your life, mind you. But as Dirty Harry would say, it's better if you "Don't even think about it."

And maybe that's exactly the point: Sex isn't something we normally *can* think about. Not that we should just give in to it. Not that we shouldn't attempt to analyze our sexual practices and our relationships and come to some rational conclusions about the subject. But the fact is, the ultimate meaning of sex lies below the level of logical thought. Sex symbolizes. It conveys messages even as it answers biological needs. Sex is a body-oriented form of Faithspeak, directed not only at those we may share it with, but at ourselves.

For instance, what are you saying to yourself when hormones continually dictate your choice of activities? Or if you continually repress those hormonal urges? To whom are you actually "making love" if you go through the motions with one person while you're thinking about another? What message do we send by sharing sex with anyone who happens to be agreeable and claims to be free of any sexually-transmitted diseases? Or by not even caring about those diseases?

What if we prefer the kind of sex that involves only one person and a magazine or an X-rated website? What can it mean to our relationships and our views of other people when we evaluate them by certain physical endowments rather than the character of the person to whom they belong? Can we see past the facade to the person inside? Can we see the divine image beneath our *own* sexuality, revealed in our body language, our own sexual practices?

We have no choice. Our sexual acts are an open book, behavioral print-outs of Who We Are. They reveal to our own hearts, even more so than to others, whether we're tender or insensitive; whether we're concerned for another's needs as much as our own; whether we're comfortable in our body or embarrassed by it; whether we're truly "making love" or simply riding off on a fantasy and it hardly matters whose flesh is rubbing against ours. Sex, in short, is an expression of how we view the world and therefore, by definition, a testimony to our faith.

But we can also *listen* to that testimony and respond in kind. By changing our sexual behavior, we can send new messages to our hearts. We can use sex as one more means by which to shape our faith, to heal and transform Who We Are. And because it has such primal power behind it, it can often affect us as nothing else can.

Maybe that's why religious traditions harp on it, sometimes to their own detriment. The potential for changing us is *that* great. The new life it creates is only rarely another's. Most of the time it is our own.

SHAMANISM

Let this be a reminder that many of our modern religious traditions and esoteric philosophies were born out of ideas and practices that can be traced back to the Ice Age, if not beyond, and continue even to this day.

It didn't require much intelligence for early humans to notice that some members of the tribe seemed to have a greater understanding of how things worked than the average hunter-gatherer. The title of "shaman," possibly from the proto-Sanskrit word *s'ramana*—but also thought to be a Central Asian word meaning "to leap up and dance"—was conferred on that person who could somehow enlist nature spirits or other superhuman powers to benefit his or her tribe. Whether by dance or chants, medicinal plants or prophetic dreams, enlisting these powers was vital for healing injuries, for determining when to sow crops or go on the hunt, for deciding which members of the tribe were best suited for particular tasks, and for telling people's fortunes.

All of these functions became the basis for the medicine man of tribal societies, and later for the priestly class within larger communities and nation-states. The special knowledge required might be learned through personal experience or an apprenticeship of sorts, but was more often handed down through family lineage. Hence the Kohanim and Levites of Hebrew tradition, or the Mullahs and Brahmans and Borgia Popes for whom spiritual leadership was more a matter of birthright than merit. At least until people realized that performance was the measure of one's gift, not one's bloodline.

For the shaman, performance was everything. If the current one couldn't heal consistently, or the crops failed for several years in a row—and if he couldn't successfully blame those failures on an escalation in demonic activity or the evil-doers in their midst—he was sent packing.

And if all this sounds vaguely familiar, it *should*. Shamanism is still practiced across the globe, and not just among our remaining indigenous societies or neo-Pagan revivalists. Shamanism survives wherever people place responsibility for their fortunes and their souls on others who are presumed to have superior knowledge of how things work, who are anointed or permitted to manage their material or spiritual affairs when they should be taking on that responsibility themselves.

There are times and places where having a shaman might be excusable, even productive. There are times and places where it isn't.

SHARIA

One of those Culture Wars code-words some Christians employ to stir up fear and militancy against Muslims, Sharia (*Shari'ah*) might as well be an abbreviation for the claim that "Islam is out to enslave you!"

Alright, maybe that's overstating the case. The problem is, for many Christians—as well as Jews, Hindus, Buddhists, and millions of Muslims who now enjoy life in Western countries—Sharia has come to represent their worst perceptions about Islam. Like the Arabic words *fatwa* or *jihad*, Sharia is considered symptomatic of a repressive and regressive legal code fit for a desert-based tribal society, where one's hand is cut off for stealing, lashes are prescribed for petty crimes, women are turned into non-persons by being imprisoned within *burqas*, and capital punishment is levied not only for murder, but for slandering the Prophet or questioning the Qur'an. And, oh yeah... also for preserving the honor of a female rape victim while sparing her male rapist.

Admittedly, Sharia can seem pretty severe. But history demonstrates that other legal systems could be equally harsh, especially where chaos prevailed or the very existence of a society was at stake. Not one of the stereotypical Sharia laws publicized by fear-mongers hasn't been enforced at various times, to a greater or lesser extent, in other cultures.

And fortunately, Sharia is specifically designed to evolve over time. Like Jewish *Halacha,* the regulations governing the religious community require its leaders to take into account changing economic and social conditions, as well as current science and psychology. Sharia also demands an awareness of what the holy text meant to believers in the place and time when those texts were written... and therefore how they must be *re*-interpreted for today.

Jews had a head start at such reinterpretation, as witnessed in the Talmud's multiple takes on the Bible's most important passages. The same process has been carried on by rabbinical assemblies ever since. Christians were especially handy at reinterpretation, too, as evidenced by differences in the Gospels themselves and the many heresies eventually stamped out by Mother Church, some of which were reawakened during the Enlightenment after torture and burning at the stake fell out of favor.

Ironically, the fact that Islam is undergoing its own modern-day Enlightenment is demonstrated by the same kind of fundamentalist fury seen when the Protestant Revolution was met by a regressive Counter-Revolution spearheaded by Church zealots and self-appointed preservers of orthodoxy. It's a phase, a stage in every religion's development, even if it is tragic and often bloody. And still going on.

In democratic societies, Sharia law (or Jewish Halacha, for that matter) is imposed only on those who have already agreed to accept it, and only where it does not conflict with the legal rights and protections given to all citizens in the larger society. Where state law trumps religious law, it's often because the latter hasn't understood Higher Law correctly, or hasn't evolved in accordance with science and psychology and other advances in human understanding.

Then again, the opposite has also been the case. Witness how long it took, historically speaking, to abolish slavery. Or to extend equal rights to women and minorities. Sometimes The State gets it wrong, too.

But that's why there's separation of Church and State, and the Balance of Powers. Also Yoga, in which balance and power are a daily regimen. If the union of body, mind and spirit isn't exactly a matter of law, it's surely the goal.

And as human understanding continues to advance, we're beginning to learn that having a goal often works better than having a law.

SIKH

The name means "lion" or "warrior" in Punjabi (as does *Ari* in Hebrew). Depending on whom you ask, or which biography you read, the Sikh tradition began as a warrior caste within Hinduism to protect India from the increasing incursions of Muslim invaders; or else it grew out of a movement within the Hindu tradition that arose in opposition to India's caste system, based on a belief in the equality of all people under the lordship of a single God.

Either way, the founding of the tradition is credited to Guru Nanak, who lived in the 15th Century CE and reportedly traveled through China, India, and all the way to Mecca in search of spiritual truth. Nanak was followed by nine more Gurus who spent their lives doing pretty much what their founder did, not only exploring other religions but researching the most beneficial practices for living simultaneously in both the spiritual and material worlds.

In the process, elements of Buddhism, Islam, Jainism, and the more monotheistic aspects of Hinduism found their way into Sikh tradition. The tenth Guru, Gobind Singh, declared that the holy book, the *Granth Sahib*—originally compiled by the fifth Guru—would henceforth be the Sikh's ultimate authority on earth and, in fact, would be known as the "final Guru" in their line of succession.

In place of Islam's Five Pillars, the Granth serves up "The Five K's" as its articles of faith, all of which name items worn by male Sikhs. (How this male orientation accords with a belief in the equality of all people is problematic.) The first "K," *Kesh,* refers to men's hair, which must be left uncut to indicate the perfection of God's creation, and is wound up in the turban that immediately identifies observant members of the faith. *Khanga,* the second, denotes the wooden comb worn in men's hair, which is used twice a day and symbolizes cleanliness and order.

The third "K," *Kara,* refers to the metal band encircling the Sikh male's wrist, thereby reminding him of his link to the tradition, as well as the belief that life is never-ending. Wrist-bands, rings and circles of various kinds are a common motif in most religions, it so happens, and carry much the same meaning.

The *Kachera* is a shorts-like garment worn day and night—even during bathing by some—usually as underwear but sometimes as an outer-garment. The kachera not only symbolizes the Sikh's readiness for battle at any moment (i.e. he already has his pants on!), but supposedly acts as a caution against lustful thoughts.

The *Kirpan* has been a subject of much controversy, if only because it is now considered a concealed weapon in Western societies. Worn by all Sikh men and male youths, this short, curved dagger may only be used in self-defense or to protect others. It symbolizes the Sikh belief that each member of a community is responsible for its overall safety and welfare, and one must never assume that lending a hand or intervening to stop an injustice is someone *else's* business.

In several notable lawsuits, non-Sikh parents have understandably objected to the practice of knives being carried around by children on their grade-school and junior-high campuses. Sikh defendants have usually (though not always) prevailed on grounds of religious freedom; but only after conceding that a plastic or rubber replica of the kirpan could still convey its symbolic meaning.

Unfortunately, back in India, the Five K's and other Sikh practices had long ago become just as objectionable to the Hindu majority as the Islamic invaders they were originally mobilized to fight. Sikhs became progressively more segregated and isolated within the northern area of India known as The Punjab. Cultural and territorial conflicts have continued into modern times, partly aggravated by the same kind of ethnic cleansing that brought about the subdivision of India into West and East Pakistan (now Bangladesh).

Though a more or less peaceful truce has now settled over the region, decades of turmoil led many Sikhs to emigrate, especially to the United States where they rapidly assumed their place among its most productive and successful citizens. Despite that success, conversion to Sikhism will continue to be a tough sell outside of India, owing to its strict discipline, all-inclusive lifestyle, and the seeming difficulty separating religion from ethnicity.

It's the same problem that plagues any religious tradition whose geographic and ethnic roots remain so central to its practice. Overcoming that barrier is a challenge for its leaders, but also a strong motivation for them to explore ways of universalizing the tradition's appeal.

SIN

Don't think of it as something you commit against God. Think of it as something you do to yourself.

No one would deny that our actions affect other people. We can help others or we can hurt them. One approach is positive, productive; the other negative, destructive. But the same is true for ourselves. Our thoughts and actions can also affect *us*. Some of these thoughts and actions promote our own growth and happiness; others destroy our inner harmony and stunt our personal development.

"Sin" is the word most religious traditions use to label those things we do that affect us in negative ways. The Greek word for it is *amartia—*

literally "missing the mark"—the same word an archer might use if his arrow missed its target. Other words sometimes used interchangeably with sin are "transgression," which conveys a sense of having broken the law; "error," which implies "straying from the path" in a way that may or may not be deliberate; "wickedness," which *is* a deliberate act, or even a conscious rejection of what the perpetrator knows is right; and "iniquity," which is also a kind of personal commitment to doing evil.

As the last two words reveal, sin can refer not only to an individual act, but to the mental or spiritual condition which leads someone to act in a negative way. It is the one-word description of an attitude—again, a *faith*—that tends to generate and direct destructive behavior, toward ourselves as much as others. We are all "living in sin" to the extent that our own faiths require major adjustments (or wholesale transformation) in order to overcome that behavior. And it is in this generic, we-still-have-work-to-do sense that all of us can be labeled as "sinners."

Unfortunately, the word "sin" is rarely understood in so generic a fashion. It's practically inseparable from the narrow definitions used by specific religions or the long lists of Thou-Shalt-Not's drummed into us in Sunday School or the madrassa. The concept has also been corrupted by institutions that have used it as a tool for manipulation.

Churches, religions, monarchies and modern cults have often enhanced their power over subjects' lives by defining sin in self-serving ways. For one thing, making people feel bad about themselves—sometimes even for things they should feel good about—can be an effective method for making them more dependent on the institution's particular brand of salvation. And of course, the only way to avoid "the wages of sin" is to remain an obedient, dues-paying member.

But the fact that the concept of sin has been misused is no reason to dismiss it outright. At its best, the word is a necessary reminder that we can always be just a little better than we are now—or maybe a whole lot better. Sin is Faithspeak for the fact that what we do *matters;* and specifically, that the bad things we do, or the negative attitudes we maintain, have an insidious, corrosive effect on our lives. We can't commit some harmful act, or harbor resentment or hate, and expect to go merrily on our way. These things will catch up to us. We can't outrun their effects for long because they have karma. Like rocks in our shoes or the proverbial monkey on our backs, sins must be dealt with before we can comfortably resume our spiritual journeys.

And yet some people will go on with rocks in their shoes until they build up such thick calluses that they can't feel them anymore. An extreme case of calluses is what Christianity calls the "unforgivable sin," the sin against the Holy Spirit. It's a condition described in virtually every religion, where someone who once felt the glimmerings of his own divinity no longer can.

Most of us, fortunately, still have at least an occasional glimmer—those little tugs on our heartstrings, the quasi-mystical experiences when some larger Reality lowers its veil, the feelings of empathy that bind our own good to the good of others. But we often fight those feelings, refuse to act on them, resist them so long that they no longer affect us. In which case we become immune. Emotionally dead. Life would be hell but for the fact that, in this condition, we usually don't even know it.

It needn't be that way. People can be taught to listen to their hearts, to leave the channel open to that source of divinity within them. According to many theologians, expressing our divinity is really more natural and human than demonstrating what miserable sinners we are. Trouble is, in trying to institutionalize the whole process, our natural, inborn Image of God gets buried under layers of complex terminology and theology, and religious obligations that can hinder our spiritual journeys as much as those dang rocks in our shoes.

And that is *truly* missing the mark.

SOUL

The ancient understanding of this term is pretty straightforward. Ages ago, a "soul" was defined as any animated being or living entity. The word referred to the totality of that entity—the physical body along with whatever animated it. And it wasn't just that people (along with cattle and frogs and cockroaches) had souls. They *were* souls. To be an organism infused with the "breath of life" was to be a soul.

The word therefore operated as a pre-scientific means of dividing the animate world from the inanimate. An animate being was no less created by whoever or whatever created everything else. It was simply endowed with an extra attribute, the same thing every other animate being was endowed with: A soul.

While the earliest Hebrews couldn't imagine that this something extra was separable from the being it happened to animate, the Greeks and the Hindus could. The Greek words *psyche* and *pneuma,* for example, pointed to a kind of animating force or principle that was independent of the creature it inhabited. Not that this force started out as a "person," like a ghost with its own thoughts and feelings. It was simply the energy that, when put into a body, *became* a person. When that force was referred to generically, it was "pneuma." When it was referred to as it individualized itself in a particular body, it was "psyche."

Along with this sense of personal identity, psyche also carried with it a kind of built-in mental health index. Some psyches could be judged as healthy and productive; others less so, or not at all. (The study of our psyches, unhealthy ones especially, is obviously where psychology got its name.) But there was no automatic assumption that the psyche survived bodily death—at least as far as the ancient Greeks were concerned. The fact that you could talk about it as a separate entity had nothing to do with it being immortal any more than talking about our bodies (or trees or houses) means they'll exist forever.

The Hindu *atman,* on the other hand, *did* imply this. It combined the Greek psyche with an ability to exist independently of the body, though its purpose was to incarnate successively until bodies were no longer needed for its spiritual education and refinement. That process might take thousands of years, or hundreds of thousands of years, until its final absorption into the Absolute.

For modern Christianity, and to some extent contemporary Judaism and Islam, the soul is basically the Hindu atman minus the idea of reincarnation. The soul is that irreducible part of us which we identify as our Self. It is the unique collection of personal qualities that defines Who We Are—not in terms of our bodies, but in terms of our faith: Our geniality or aggressiveness, benevolence or selfishness; our compassion, joy, optimism and commitment to improve ourselves, or lack of these.

There is also a kind of primal awareness of our own existence, usually referred to as "self-consciousness," that is implicit in the concept of soul. Theoretically, even if another person had exactly the same personal qualities, this subjective sense of *I Am*—this locus of awareness that no one else can experience or they would *be* us—would remain.

It's not necessary to be religious in order to buy into this concept. Take away the question of immortality and "soul" is simply a convenient word for pointing at that core of individual identity, at whatever it is that makes each of us a separate, unique person.

But because we *can* imagine this identity outside of a particular body, we can also imagine it existing independently of bodies in general. And here's where all the religious implications can kick in. In fact, things often get downright crazy at this point. About as crazy as the

Theory of Relativity, or the "personalities" of a quark.
Or robots on Mars. (See next entry.)

SPIRIT

If "soul" refers to the essence of personal identity, "spirit" is the stuff it's made of. That is, if it's made of *any*thing.

After all, what is a thought made of? If we can describe the mechanics of mental processes and measure the electrical exchanges across specific synapses in the cells of our brains when a thought occurs, is that what a thought *is?* Brain cells and electrical charges?

To quote our favorite nay-sayer: *Not!*

Thought is a kind of experience a person has when those physical things happen. The two are clearly related, but it's not altogether certain whether the physical events produce the experience of thought, or they're the effects, or both the thought and the physical effects result from still another phenomenon.

The connection is even more inexplicable when you consider the after-death experiences thousands of people have now reported. In dozens of medically-documented cases, the brain activity of a patient appears to have utterly ceased; and yet, upon being revived, the patient reports visions and experiences and thoughts that should have registered on an electro-encephalogram, but didn't.

And then there are dreams. Ordinary, garden-variety dreams. Dreams that occur so commonly that people rarely stop to consider how truly amazing they are. Because the experience of a dream can feel as genuine and sensually complex as waking reality. Under hypnosis, people can recall dreams as clearly as real events. They can describe details and objects both inside and outside their direct field of vision, remember how things tasted and felt to the touch, as well as subjective feelings like sadness, elation or love. So while a person might be lying in a bed in Boston, they would swear they were frolicking on a beach in Barbados, or being chased through the forest by fire-breathing dragons.

Maybe they really *were* somewhere else. Not their body, of course, but the identity at the core of their being. Most of our distant ancestors were convinced of this. There was another, deeper level of reality, they believed, connected with the physical world but not identical to it nor restricted to its limitations. And it was no less real. This level is commonly known as the world of spirit, as distinct from the physical world of matter. And dreams, among other things, can take us there.

Ironically, some of the best evidence for this other reality comes from contemporary science. For one thing, the most hard-headed physicist finds it impossible to describe the ultimate building blocks of matter without resorting to an almost spiritual conception of reality. For another, science is giving us some wonderful models for conceptualizing spirit.

Consider, for instance, robots. Not the ones that weld parts together on an automotive assembly line or solder circuit boards into computers. More like the kind envisioned in those classic sci-fi movies back in the Fifties. The ideal robot would basically be an electronic/mechanical reproduction of the human body, complete with the ability to sense its surroundings in multiple ways, to transport itself no matter what the terrain, and to manipulate objects by using appendages similar to ours. It would also be able to energize and revitalize itself when necessary.

Now imagine such a robot walking around on another planet—Mars, say—while being controlled by a NASA scientist in some cubicle at the Jet Propulsion Lab in Pasadena. Let's picture the controller/scientist (who no doubt grew up playing video games) wearing a set of stereoscopic goggles that enable him to see through the robot's "eyes," and headphones that allow him to hear sounds (or at least radio transmissions). Let's add some kind of tactile sensory devices by which the robot could move around in the environment and handle objects, and to adjust temperature and energy levels as our bodies do. In short, we'll hook up our Earth-based scientist in such a way that his own senses are fully integrated with his mechanical counterpart on Mars on a one-to-one basis. Oh, and let's pretend there's no time delay when sending or receiving data. (If you've read about the "quantum entanglement" of electrons that respond to one another instantaneously, no matter how far apart they're separated in space, this isn't so far-fetched.)

Under this scenario the scientist would essentially *become* that robot walking around on Mars. As tests with virtual reality already suggest, human subjects often lose connection with their own biological bodies after a period of adjustment. Our NASA scientist's identity and point of view (and even his purpose) could very well merge so completely with the robot and the Martian environment that he would likely forget what and where he really is. Until, that is, he's somehow brought back to his Earth-based reality. Which would probably come as a shock.

For an even more compelling version of this thought experiment, rent the movie, *Avatar,* preferably in 3D. The Bruce Willis flick, *Surrogates,* also works... but just barely.

So, assuming you can imagine this scenario—or you've already seen *Avatar*—you may catch a glimpse of what the words "soul" and "spirit" might be pointing at. Because the robot in the story (or the sinuous alien form Jake Sully intermittently inhabits in *Avatar*) represents our own human bodies. Our soul, then, is the sense of personal identity we retain, which just happens to be integrated with our earthly bodies in this particular lifetime. But maybe we haven't been "brought back" yet. And, like our experience during dreams, we tend to forget that we're actually fast asleep in our comfy, queen-size bed in Boston.

And "spirit"? What's that word pointing at?

Spirit is the stuff thoughts are made of, the immaterial "material" that supports the soul, like the unseen electromagnetic waves that connect the scientist to the robot, or Jake Sully to his Na'vi incarnation. It's the unknown, maybe unknowable, concentration of energy or Mind or Consciousness that is somehow "hooked up" to this physical world.

The non-material soul may be in another place entirely, as separate and distinct as Pasadena's JPL and the Elysium Planitia on Mars. Or perhaps it's no "place" at all because it's outside of space and time, it's beyond the physical world, and the only thing that really matters is that it's connected.

Either way, just as the scientist (soul) can act through the robot (body) to manipulate and affect the Martian environment, that otherworldly environment can also manipulate and affect *him;* it can teach him things. More crucially, the robot's interactions with *other* robots can teach him things. And one of the lessons he might learn is that, at the core of these other robots, hiding "inside" their equipment, beneath all the shiny chrome plating and size 38-D visual enhancer units, is some essence which is really no different from whatever *he* is.

The message of virtually all religious traditions and movements is that it is possible to draw energy and wisdom and love directly from this other, spiritual realm in a way that makes our material existence operate more smoothly. Obviously, if what we are "in essence" is the same kind of stuff as that which underlies the whole universe, then we have a more direct connection to that resource—and potentially more power to affect the physical world—than we normally assume.

This view of spirit as some kind of non-physical resource is very close to our ordinary use of that word. We talk about the "indomitable spirit" of human beings; the "spiritedness" of a particular person or a race horse. We might say our daughter's volleyball team "is full of spirit," and that the crowd watching them got "caught up in the spirit." There's the "Christmas Spirit" and the "spirit of giving" and the "Spirit of '76." All of these imply a certain energy, an *aliveness*—something that feels almost as if an outside force has taken over, one that exerts control over us even as it makes us feel more alive and "in control" than ever before.

Much like getting a breath of pure oxygen can invigorate you when you're exhausted.

"Spirit" or *spiritus,* it so happens, is the Latin word for "breath." As a religious concept, it symbolizes whatever it is that makes us alive, that animates and invigorates this self-conscious entity called a "soul." It is no more necessary to know what that animating stuff actually *is,* than it's necessary to know what bodies are made of before you can start walking and talking.

But think how much more you might be capable of if you *did* know.

SPIRITUAL

In the second episode of the original *Star Wars* trilogy, Yoda, the diminutive Jedi Master, lectures young Luke Skywalker after he once again fails to learn an important lesson. "You are not this crude matter," Yoda says, poking Luke's shoulder. "A luminous being you are."

It's a great line—one most religions try to convey in their own fashion, sometimes crudely. A line that can change one's faith.

In the film, the statement was meant to encourage Luke to look at the world in a new way. "Don't be fooled by your human form," Yoda was saying. "You have powers that go beyond what hands and feet or bone and muscle can do... powers that transcend the boundaries of the ordinary physical world." And the point was, before Luke could unleash those deeper powers, he first had to accept his "luminous being-ness." He needed to expand his frame of reference. His faith had to grow.

To be "spiritual" is to have a different—expanded—frame of reference. Specifically it is a frame of reference which acknowledges that What We Are, ultimately, is more than this "crude flesh"; that what animates and re-purposes our physical lives comes from another, more illuminating dimension.

This level is so profoundly different that it may seem downright other-worldly—even though it's as commonplace as light, as natural as the concentrations of swirling energy that form and transform matter. Or that vibrate in and around us all the time like electromagnetic waves, passing through walls and turning into sounds and images when our hi-def TVs are turned on.

Spirituality is the frame of reference in which our outward lives are the TV reality shows we help produce and play essential roles in. Tuning to the proper channel, improving the reception, and getting the color and sound just right can make all the difference.

STEWARDSHIP

Here's another term that hasn't gotten much good press lately.

For one thing, the word "stewardship" has been much maligned by all those fund-raising committees and well-meaning volunteers who visit church-members' homes and make them feel guilty for not pledging more money toward the new stained-glass windows or the pastor's retirement fund. For too many of us, stewardship has come to mean our religious institution's hand in our pockets.

Which is maybe one percent of it.

From ancient times until the last century or so, the "steward" was a fairly common position within prosperous families. A steward was a rather high-level servant—sometimes indentured, sometimes paid—who supervised the family's affairs while the master went off and did whatever masters do. The steward usually had autonomy to make business decisions, to invest the family's money, and to manage the other servants or employees of the household. The steward did not thereby *own* the property or funds entrusted to his care. He merely supervised it as wisely as he knew how.

Actually, "merely" doesn't give the position enough credit. Because the steward could conceivably blow the family fortune, or increase it many times over. A steward who performed well could expect a nice fat bonus from his master, from a share of the profits to the honor of being allowed to continue as steward. One who did poorly—or merely "broke even"—could expect to lose his job. Or worse.

As master/servant relationships go, the concept of "the steward" has a certain resonance even today. After all, we aren't the masters in this existence. We didn't create the family fortune (i.e. the earth and everything in it). Even the things we *did* create are only transformations and re-combinations of what already existed.

What we seem to be in the wider scheme of things are stewards. We are entrusted with someone else's property, and we have inherited the responsibility of using it wisely. In Western religion, God reportedly gives humankind "dominion" over the earth, meaning two things: First, that it is God who does the giving, and therefore retains ultimate authority; and secondly, that dominion is not the same as ownership. It's a management position, and it can be taken away if we can't, well, *manage*.

Eastern religion takes a similar stand, with a slightly different spin. In both Hindu and Buddhist traditions, ownership of material things is an illusion. If our very bodies are only on temporary loan, how can we expect to own real estate or diamond necklaces? In fact, Buddhism says, it is our possessions that cause us the most pain. We struggle to earn them, worry about keeping them, and fear for our comfort if we lose them. Better to remain unattached.

The Native American view is just as bold. Even the things we make for ourselves don't entitle us to permanent property rights. More like a temporary use permit. The bow fashioned by Blue Elk for buffalo hunting is still essentially the branch he found on the ground. And because the branch was not permitted to decay back into the ground where it fell, Blue Elk must repay the Earth. In other words, stewardship requires knowing what the natural cycles are, and keeping them in balance. What you take out, you must somehow put back in. And, according to native tradition, we must live as if people seven generations into the future are depending on what we do today. Pretty strong stuff.

Stewardship has recently taken on this kind of environmentalist connotation. It is deeply concerned with our relationship to the Earth's resources, with keeping things in balance. It is even more concerned with the realization that the demands of modern technology can utterly consume those resources and leave behind nothing but a toxic wasteland and uncontrolled climate change for future generations to deal with. Preventing that outcome requires an almost religious fervor. Or at least a change in faith.

It so happens that stewardship *is* a kind of faith. It is the mind-set whereby each individual sees himself as an integral part of the cycle of giving and taking. It calls for a thoughtful re-prioritizing of physical needs in which we decide how much we really require to live, and what we'll do with any excess we are blessed with.

Such decisions are best made beforehand since it's always tempting to simply accommodate one's lifestyle to any increase in prosperity; to go out and buy that 60-inch big-screen or opt for the gas-guzzling SUV when we find a few extra C-notes in our pockets. The marketplace would dearly love to show you exactly how to spend all that extra money you made last month. Plus the money you hope to make next month.

And while you're out spending it, someone else goes hungry. And another baby dies for lack of medical care. And an army vet who can't seem to find his way back to a normal life huddles in a downtown doorway trying to stay warm on a cold winter's night.

STOICISM

Here's a term to file under the heading, "Ain't nothin' new under the sun, man."

Stoicism, according to the history books, was the Greek religion-slash-philosophy which taught that the highest good was to "live naturally." Human beings were meant to live in harmony with the laws of nature. Man-made laws were artificial, repressive, and often unhealthy.

Sound like an early version of the fabled Flower Children? Not quite.

Since the essence of nature was Reason, how we ought to live and what goals we ought to pursue could best be determined by applying logic, by coldly examining the "will of the universe" and following its dictates. Which sounds more like the flowering of the Enlightenment.

Actually, Stoics did share the same enlightened optimism of the seventeenth and eighteenth centuries: If we could all just *be reasonable,* if we could only stop letting our emotions get in the way—or stop showing our emotions altogether—things would run so much more smoothly.

If we could only be more like Mr. Spock.

For Stoics (unlike their fellow Greeks of 300 BCE), the idea of God or "the gods" was simply unreasonable. Divinity had no separate existence in the same way a potter is separate from the pot he makes. Divinity was an inherent component of everything—the stars, the earth, the wind, and us. Stoicism was therefore much like Buddhism in its "*un*-theology." Unfortunately the tradition lacked a central, larger-than-life teacher like Buddha to give it some sense of humanity.

In fact, what finally killed Stoicism as a religion was its failure to acknowledge that our emotions are just as natural as anything else in nature. Emotions result from natural law, too. Bringing them under control in some fashion is certainly a worthy objective in life. But it is less reasonable to ignore them than to make them our allies; *more* reasonable to enlist them in pursuit of all those goals we've logically set for ourselves, to use our emotions as a complement to our reason.

Maybe Faithspeak is the science of doing just that.

STORIES

Stories are among the best examples of Faithspeak. Stories are vehicles that can be used to make coldly logical points—and without which those coldly logical points might never get made. Or at least made with enough emotional impact to make any real difference.

For example, one person can advise another that adultery is bad. Or he can weave a story in which a married man becomes involved in a seemingly no-strings-attached affair that unexpectedly escalates into a web of deceit and destruction like 1987's *Fatal Attraction*... or any number of similar tales from David and Bathsheba to Bill and Monica.

Someone else can try to convince us through logical argument that the universe values each human being as a unique, priceless component in the greater Scheme of Things, and that everything we do conspires to make us increasingly better expressions of Universal Love. Or he can tell the story of a Supreme Being who incarnates as a human, and grows up to feel such sympathy for his fellow beings that he takes the blame for everything they've ever done wrong and then dies in their place so they might have a little more time to get things right.

Bare explanations can sometimes be enough to change someone's mind. But intellectual conviction is rarely enough to change that person's behavior. Knowing that smoking is bad for you isn't enough. To quit, you'll need to enroll in one of those programs that literally makes you sick of it; or you look through a microscope at the decaying, carbon-coated lungs of a two-pack-a-day smoker who just died of lung cancer. You see and *feel* something. What you see and feel is the message.

Stories can give us this kind of intentional experience. They let us crawl inside someone else's skin, see things through their eyes, or perhaps simply watch as an objective observer. The more our senses are drawn in, the greater the impact. The more visceral our response, the more that experience—and its message—sinks in.

Which is a mixed blessing if ever there was one. Because it raises two important issues:

The first revolves around the fact that we should pay more attention to the stories we read or watch on our screens. Stories, after all, are a kind of subtle programming. As much as we may dislike the idea of censors trying to impose their moral values on us, they are driven by the truth that what we see and hear *does* affect us. Bikini-clad women in TV commercials sell more than cars or Carl's Jr. hamburgers. Movies that feature graphic violence and killing-as-entertainment deliver more than two hours of pulse-pounding escapism. Media watchdogs like the once-infamous Reverend Wildmon or the "thought police" of totalitarian regimes are only acting on their conviction that stories have the power to transform faiths.

On the other hand, *how* those stories affect our faiths may not be as cut-and-dried as the moral censors claim. Stories with graphic violence may show us how futile and self-destructive that violence is. Far from promoting it, they may *prevent* it—if the message is unambiguous. Other stories of violence can have a cathartic effect, releasing pent-up hostility under controlled conditions, making it less likely to be acted out. By pulling certain stories from the airwaves and bookshelves, censors may actually produce the very effects they seek to eliminate. It takes more than a sense of self-righteousness to judge what the message of a story really is, and to declare it unfit for public consumption.

Not to mention the fact that, by the censor's own standards, many of the stories in the Bible, the Qur'an and the Hindu scriptures deserve to be banned. And there's also the question of tactics—of the possible damage done to the kind of free expression democracy requires, and Faithspeak requires.

All of which implies, secondly, that experience and reason still play the central role in analyzing and selecting our stories. Through reason, we can make choices. We can choose to switch the channel. We can choose to read or not read any book, depending on whether we have reason to believe it will nourish us or poison us. We can choose to watch those movies whose messages encourage the kind of faith we desire, knowing that, in choosing them, we choose ourselves.

SUBLIMINAL

From the roots *sub* (below) and *limin* (limit), "subliminal" refers to that which lies below the limitations or boundaries of our normal awareness. Sometimes used interchangeably with "subconscious," it points to the mental processes we need not exert conscious control over, or are no longer required to think about, in order to function.

And thankfully so. It'd be pretty tiresome to consciously "will" each breath we take, or every beat of our heart, or to decide on the placement of each footfall as we go out for our morning jog. Trouble is, sometimes our subconscious takes over processes we *should* be thinking about. Like snacking on junk food whenever we sit down to watch TV. Or having a second or third double IPA after a stressful day at work.

Or judging other people by their sexual attractiveness or race. Or buying a new coat or new Cadillac even when we don't need one. Or facing new experiences with a sense of foreboding rather than excitement. Or shaking someone's hand in preference to a friendly embrace.

All of these are unthinking actions or reactions learned subliminally—through childhood experiences or the power of suggestion or the allure of advertising, or the dozen dozen influences that affect us under the radar and without our consent, yet often have a greater impact on our behavior than the conscious choices we make. To repeat: Our attitudes, our faith, is largely shaped before we're old enough to accept responsibility for it, much less realize what it is.

But the silver lining is that we can also use subliminal influences on ourselves. By associating with people who possess the kind of personal attributes we'd like to have. By practicing rituals we may not understand or even enjoy, but have a track record for producing the desired results. By learning how the media works its subtle magic and avoiding music and TV shows that damage our psyches. And by countering the thousand-odd sales pitches we are exposed to every day with our own repeated affirmations that we already have more than we need.

Unless we don't.

And that's where *conscious* planning comes into play.

SUBMISSION

There's submission... and—you got it—there's *submission*.

One kind enslaves, diminishes and destroys, even as it supposedly frees people. Another kind liberates, expands and creates, even as it appears to restrict and constrain them.

The paradox is that submission to an authority can be a kind of freedom. By subjecting oneself to an all-inclusive code of behavior, an individual can be released from the burden of making his own choices and value judgments. It's no longer necessary to think for yourself, or even to accept responsibility for your actions. If one has submitted to the Third Reich, then the killing of Jews, Gypsies and homosexuals can be carried out without question or remorse. If you submit completely to an ayatollah or Chairman or gang leader, your life becomes an extension of theirs; and what you lose in autonomy, you gain by being part of someone or something that's more important than your pitiful self.

For many people the effect is like removing the proverbial weight from one's shoulders. Another effect, of course, is the message that Who You Are as a person doesn't really matter. You have no individual worth, nothing unique to contribute because you can be replaced by any other empty-headed robot. And you probably *will* be, just as soon as you've completed whatever task someone else has assigned for you.

Progressive societies therefore have a right to be suspicious of submission, even if it *is* a knee-jerk reaction. Because properly understood, submission simply means *to accept What Is.* Not the "what is" of artificial rules and regulations established by some power elite or religious authority, and often used to crush individual autonomy. The genuine What Is is "the way things are" and the way things *can be.*

Ironically, submitting to this Reality, including its limits as well as its creative possibilities, is a source of great power. For one thing, it keeps us from walking off those ten-story buildings and hurting ourselves. What's more, the very laws that apply to people falling off ten-story buildings can also help them soar like eagles. The same Law of Gravity that pulls us down holds space stations up. It also flings planetary probes like slingshots across the solar system. So what at first might appear to enslave us ends up empowering us. And that awareness becomes a defining characteristic of our faith.

One religious tradition regards this latter aspect of faith as so crucial that its Arabic name is synonymous with it. The trick, naturally, is determining what to submit *to,* of separating What Is from what others *tell* us it is. And until we decide for ourselves, the best we can do is to keep searching, to keep the lines open, to keep comparing notes with our fellow searchers and *not* submit to anything just because someone else says we should.

Genuine submission is a conscious, positive, intentional act. Not a shrug-of-the-shoulders surrender, but a what-can-I-do-now commitment to find one's purpose, and spend one's life fulfilling it.

SUFFERING

For all the shared meanings behind religious traditions, and despite the often-heard claim that Buddhism can blend with almost any other spiritual practice, here is one critical difference.

Suffering, *dukkha* in Sanskrit, was thought by Buddha to be the fundamental feature of human existence. Built into nature itself, suffering is pervasive and unavoidable, not merely for the ignorant poor—among whom it was so visible and shocking to the future Enlightened One—but even for the intellectually gifted and wealthy.

Seeing no other solution, Buddha's spiritual cure-all was Liberation. Which means alleviating one's mental anguish by essentially learning not to care so much for the things that generated those feelings; by refocusing instead on the "right" things; and by the quiet acceptance of the idea that life will go on like this forever, one lifetime after another, until such time as you are fully fit to exit the cycle of *samsara*.

Western theology wasn't about to take all this misery lying down. Yes, there was suffering—plenty enough to go around, in fact. But in the concept of Salvation lies the certainty that something purposeful is at work, that suffering was meant to be a catalyst for producing something positive and wonderful, that sacrifice and death were precursors to abundance and life.

And hey—Buddha's own experience proved that very point, didn't it? So maybe the followers of Buddha missed the teaching embodied in his life: To accept suffering in the same way Jesus accepted that the poor would always be among us; and then to use that realization as motivation to change things. Suffer, then overcome. Grieve, but get past it. Experience darkness so you can get on with enlightenment. Die to the past that you might live from this day forward.

Maybe *that's* what was built into nature.

SUPERSTITION

A word that originally pointed to any belief in what was beyond rational understanding or logical proof, "superstition" is now used more in the sense of believing in something that is flatly irrational and illogical, or can actually be *dis*proven.

Like ghosts, for example. Or leprechauns, chupacabras or Bigfoot.

Demons with wings and pointy tails, perhaps. Monsters hiding under the bed, or in Loch Ness. Guardian angels. Good luck, or bad luck. Plane crashes that always come in threes. Betting all your chips on red-seven on July seventh. Or betting that the world's entire computer grid would crash on December 31, 2000, or that the world itself will be destroyed on December 24, 2013, or whatever the latest end-of-the-world prediction happens to be.

This is not to say there aren't human experiences or natural phenomena that might understandably generate a superstition. Are there unexplained events that lead people to believe in ghosts and guardian angels? No doubt. But getting from the mystery to the explanation usually involves a pretty big leap, and usually says more about the believer than the belief itself.

People seem to need their superstitions, and will happily admit that many of them are unfounded and downright silly. Trying to understand *why* amounts to a course in popular psychology. Or, for the atheist, a course in comparative religions.

Maybe it'd be a worthwhile exercise for all of us to define the line between superstition and sincere belief. And what makes the difference.

SWASTIKA

Why on Earth, our Jewish friends might ask, is the word for this Nazi symbol, this trademark for terror, listed in a book intended to increase religious understanding?

Because the swastika wasn't originally a Nazi symbol, for one thing. And because the design was meant to promote religious understanding. Or at least a religious idea.

As the Yin-Yang symbolizes the dualism of nature, of male and female, the swastika once stood for the four elements out of which nature was thought to be composed: Earth, Air, Water and Fire. At the center of this pinwheel of intermixing elements is *us*—the perfect combination, nature's highest achievement, the divine incarnation. And aside from its deeper meaning, a row of small swastikas made for an attractive border in rock carvings and Indian blankets.

What's not to like?

The Nazis, unfortunately, liked the design too. And despite their failed efforts to engineer a super-race and purge the world of "lesser" races, the swastika soon devolved into a symbol for political and ethnic hatreds, and for unspeakable atrocities and mass murder. Which is why the swastika is also a symbol for taking a perfectly good thing and corrupting or co-opting it. Just as white bigots did with a Southern battle flag. Just as a pope did when he carried the cross while leading soldiers into battle. Just as another army of zealots has been doing lately to a whole religion by misquoting and misusing its sacred text to justify depravities from murder to sexual enslavement, from wanton demolition of priceless antiquities to the destruction of entire communities and cultures.

It's too late to recover the positive, or at least benign, swastika used for spiritual reflection and decoration centuries ago. But we *can* rescue the symbols and practices that still provide spiritual nourishment for millions of people from the small minority who never learned what they truly mean.

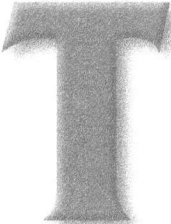

TAO

Literally, "The Way" in Chinese—partly in the sense of "the way things are" (i.e. Ultimate Reality and how it works), and partly in the sense of "the way to live" (the proper path, the lifestyle that leads to personal fulfillment or salvation).

Taoism, pronounced *Dow*-ism, was envisioned by its founder, Lao-tse, as a deeply intellectual religion, or better yet a philosophy, without gods, prayers, priests or sacrifices. The *Tao-Teh-King*, the Taoist equivalent of the Bible or Qur'an, presents Lao-tse's teachings regarding the universe, why it exists and how humankind ought to live according to its Way. Only by acknowledging The Way, by submitting oneself to its ebb and flow in the nature of things, could the individual blossom and thrive.

Taoism advocated purity, gentleness and simplicity. It also inspired an attitude of openness and spontaneity that might allow the universe to express itself through the individual in surprising, creative ways. And, five hundred years before Christianity, Taoism taught that people should not counter violence with more violence, anger with anger, or an eye for an eye. "Recompense injury with kindness," Lao-tse said.

Which was as difficult for his Chinese followers as it was for the disciples of a Jewish rabbi who said to "Turn the other cheek" and "Love your enemies." Yet both these teachers were absolutely convinced that, built into the very foundations of the universe, the only antidote for evil was to respond with goodness. Do what your enemies least expect: Be kind to them; *love* them. That, for Lao-tse, was the only Way.

It was almost inevitable that The Way would become institutionalized and corrupted. The Tao, described by one of Lao-tse's disciples as "the formless source of all form; the inaudible source of all sound; the invisible origin of all sight," was eventually turned into a pantheon of spirits who inhabited nature and who could be individually addressed through prayers. Ironically, Lao-tse himself was looked upon as a divinity in whose service a priesthood was formed—along with a whole compendium of magical rites and sacrificial offerings.

It wouldn't be the only time a spiritual teacher's vision would end up being obscured by his own followers. Some people just can't seem to see The Way any other way.

TAROT

Probably derived from the Arabic word *taraha,* meaning "to keep out," Tarot (pronounced *tare-oh*) is the centuries-old practice of fortune-telling employed by a select few who are trained in its arts, and must be kept out of ordinary people's hands. Or kept out of a community that regards it as evil and demonic.

Fortune-telling, however, is only one aspect of Tarot. Used by a skilled practitioner, the images in its deck of seventy-eight cards can reportedly help to evaluate the events and experiences a client is dealing with, then predict their consequences and suggest solutions. This *de facto* pre-psychology counseling service is accomplished by first focusing on a picture that summarizes the client's current dilemma or concern, after which alternative responses and possible outcomes can be explored as additional cards/pictures are dealt.

One can only imagine the abuses a dishonest Tarot practitioner might foist on the gullible. That's certainly one reason why this and other forms of fortune-telling were outlawed in many communities and whole religious traditions. One can also imagine the leap of faith required to believe that the order in a deck of cards can magically arrange itself to reflect the issues and options exactly suited to what's happening in the life of the person the Tarot reader is analyzing.

And it's this supposition of magic, this apparent need to enlist dark forces and secret powers to make Tarot work, that provides further justification for banning the practice, or even burning its practitioners at the stake. (Ironic that one of the Tarot cards actually shows a victim lashed to a stake as flames engulf him.) Then again, the manipulation of a Muslim's prayer beads while praying, or the chanting of ten Hail Mary's to absolve sins, or the sprinkling of baptismal water on a baby's forehead, can seem just as hocus-pocus to an outsider as the reading of a Tarot card.

Let's admit it: Some things we "keep out" because we can't understand how they work. Some things we keep out because we *do*.

TEMPTATION

Another quirk of alphabetical coincidence: This word and the next represent two of the most powerful methods by which Ultimate Reality shapes Who We Are. Or, in ordinary language, they're two of the best ways to build character.

The first half of this dynamic duo can be defined as "an enticement to do something bad." Like cheating on our 1040s because the odds of being caught are so slim. Or taking one drink too many because someone else is picking up the tab. Or accepting a job that gives us a bigger paycheck instead of greater fulfillment. All of these are occasions for expressing a weaker, more short-sighted, more materialistic aspect of ourselves precisely at a stage in our development when we could finally be growing out of it.

If we *do* express that weaker aspect, if we fail to "resist temptation," we reinforce the hold of the physical realm over our lives. We increase negative karma. Or, in more dramatic terms, we "fall deeper into sin." If, however, we overcome the temptation, if we "yield not," we reinforce our spiritual strength. We demonstrate our self-control, an ability to chart our own course in life rather than drift wherever the wind blows.

Temptation, after all, assumes we have a destination. That destination is our own salvation, or at least the realization of our highest potential. A temptation, then, is an offer to take a detour, to step backward or perhaps get blown completely off course. Most of those who've weathered the stormy seas report that temptations are really a sign of spiritual advancement. The fact that we recognize a temptation when we see one shows that we're ready for the challenge, ready for the next stage in our personal development. And if life seems to throw temptations our way in bunches—and it's uncanny how it does—it's as if the whole universe is saying, "You can do it! You can *beat* this thing! Come on, one more try... just one!"

It's not another obstacle on the Journey. It's another *chance*.

TEST

Here's the second part: Whereas temptation is an opportunity to grow spiritually by not doing something bad, a test is an opportunity to advance by doing something good.

There are at least as many potential tests in the world as temptations. Unfortunately, they're harder to identify. It takes initiative to be "tested." A certain situation arises, let's say, that requires us to do something. We must choose a course of action from numerous possibilities, and then we must act.

Failure to act when we should—not necessarily failing to do the right thing but doing nothing at all—is as damaging to our spiritual health as yielding to temptation. We become more and more callous, or, as some scriptures describe it, "hard-hearted." We look the other way, refuse to get involved, shut out that still small voice that calls us to get up from our easy chairs. According to the famous parable, the Good Samaritan passed the test. The other guys only passed by.

Which is simply to point out (again) that what we do, regardless of what we say or think, is what we truly believe. The opportunity to do something is a "test" of our beliefs.

Try this sometime: Write down what you think you believe, or what you'd *like* to believe. Then, after each item, write down what it would take to demonstrate—to prove without any shadow of a doubt—that you do, in fact, believe it. What act or series of actions would convince you? What would convince other people? Or perhaps God?

Whatever those actions may be, those are your "tests" for each specific belief. Make a chart of them. Keep score. Look for opportunities to be tested. If you don't pass with flying colors, reward yourself for the smallest improvements you can manage. Figure out how to do better next time. Get advice or assistance if you need it.

Shakespeare wrote that "All the world's a stage." In other words, *life* is a stage. Religion says that life is a series of tests. In the first scenario we're actors; in the second, students. Actually, we're both: We're students of acting.

The curtain's up, Mac.

THEOCRACY

If you believe in God, and you believe that God has ultimate control of the universe in general and human history in particular, you are living in a Theocracy right now. (Greek *theos*:god plus *kratia*:rule.)

Historically speaking, theocracy refers to government by the gods, or God, or human-god hybrids like Egypt's pharaohs or the pre-WWII emperors of Japan. During Europe's Middle Ages, it was enough to be a mere mortal who was ordained or appointed by God, usually with the generous assistance (or acquiescence) of the Church. The government's laws were therefore pretty much in keeping with the Law and ordinances written in the Bible and duly interpreted by Church authorities. This model followed that of the ancient Hebrews, whose kings from David to Herod were ordained and advised by its priesthood.

Today, Islamists (in contrast to the average Muslim) are the only members of a religious tradition who still seriously advocate for a worldwide theocracy, where God/Allah is king, and a kingdom/Caliphate his earthly government. Sharia law would prevail, as delivered in the Qur'an and interpreted by, well, whoever instills the most fear and ends up with the most power.

Theocracy in today's world is therefore unattainable, untenable and unthinkable. Except the kind in the first paragraph, where it doesn't matter who believes it, or who on Earth ends up with the most power.

THEOSOPHY

If you believe in God, and you believe in the ultimate truths about God as reflected in the universe in general and human history in particular, you are a Theosophist right now. (Greek *theos*:god plus *sophia*:wisdom.)

And if you didn't notice that the paragraph you just read is constructed exactly like the first paragraph in the previous listing... okay, you're right; it's not important.

Narrowly defined, Theosophy is the name of the movement founded in 1875 by the beloved—or else notorious—Madame Blavatsky. (Actress Shirley MacLaine may have known M.B. in one of her many past lives; but that's not important, either.) Over the decades Blavatsky's "Theosophical Society" had become a repository for, and disseminator of, what is variously known as The Perennial Philosophy or The Wisdom Religion. This systematic collection now reportedly encompasses all of the wisdom about God or The Divine that has been taught by sages and saints, spiritual masters and mahatmas, since the beginning of recorded history. Though largely *outside* the confines of institutional religion.

Which doesn't mean Christianity, Hinduism, Islam and all the rest don't contain wisdom about The Divine. Traditional religions are also expressions of this same wisdom, with institutional trappings and police powers added for good measure. Or, as a Theosophist would contend, *not* for good measure.

This book is an expression of a Theosophist insofar as its author supports the view that there are common, deeper truths behind the world's religions—again, the Mother Tongue from which the specific dialects are derived—and that a perennial wisdom exists which humankind has been collecting and practicing from the beginning of history. Determining what counts as "wisdom," however, is not only a project for our beloved/notorious Madame Blavatsky.

It's yours, too.

TIME

What?—you didn't know "time" was a religious term? It's high time you knew, then.

As a matter of fact, time has been as important a concept to religious traditions as it has for science or history. Not so much as a framework for locating events or keeping the trolleys on schedule. Time, for our ancestors, wasn't some theoretical continuum of moments stretching from the past into the future, like some grandfather clock ticking away. It was thought about more in terms of specific intervals during which something had to be done. The night watch, for instance. The season for sowing or reaping. Market day. The pre-dawn period when first prayers are recited.

Or the temporal space between birth and death.

That, for religion, is perhaps the most fundamental time. It was the most important interval during which something had to be done. Between birth and death one's karma had to be purified by performance of positive acts. One's soul had to be saved by accepting Jesus or submitting to Allah. Or in less religious terms, it was when everyone was supposed to find their special calling, their unique purpose in life, and spend the rest of their days doing what they were meant to do.

Of course, unlike the interval between dawn and dusk, or one season and the next, the space between birth and death was never fully known in advance. How many days you'd spend sojourning on Planet Earth might be pre-arranged by the Head Travel Agent, but as far as you knew the tour could be canceled without prior notice.

Which is merely to point out that time isn't something to be wasted. Doing "frivolous" things like playing card games and standing around chatting idly are still forbidden in some religious traditions. Not so much because these activities are bad in themselves, but because they pass the time without getting anything done.

Like pouring water out of a canteen you need for a journey across the desert. All too often, in the midst of the hot, dusty crossing, you come to realize there's only so much water left, and many more miles to go. And the sun-bleached bones of previous travelers along the way aren't exactly reassuring.

TOLERANCE

For several hundred years running, from the late 8th through 14th centuries CE, a period now described as Islam's Golden Age brought relative peace and prosperity to a vast swath of the known world. Having consolidated their governance from Spain and Morocco across Northern Africa to India and beyond, Muslim caliphs felt sufficiently at ease to allow a surprisingly wide diversity of social and intellectual pursuits. Science and medicine flourished as a result. Increasing commerce encouraged relationships and cooperation from east to west, bringing new innovations and knowledge. And profits.

And while Christians were persecuting Jews all over Europe, and the

Papal states were at war with each other and with the heretics among them, the Caliphate protected its Jews and Christians (and even Hindus and Buddhists) as long as they paid their taxes on time. Scholars and philosophers whose views sometimes contradicted Islamic orthodoxy were respected and even subsidized for their writings and research. Muhammad, after all, had advised followers to "Pursue knowledge, even unto China." The Qur'an was revered as true, certainly; but its truth lay deeper than mere words, and could also be found within the texts and religious practices of people all across the globe—which, by the way, the world was known to be, in contrast to the flat Earth most Europeans still believed in.

Not that social strife and political abuses disappeared altogether. Infidels (properly defined) were sometimes put to death. The hands of thieves were summarily chopped off under Sharia law, and power grabs were occasioned by assassinations and internecine intrigues. Nor, today, would any more than a small fraction of people trade their freedoms and cultural identities for a return to that Age, golden as it seemed.

But that period nevertheless remains an historical watershed, with after-effects that included no less than Europe's Age of Enlightenment and the Rise of the Common Man. It was also a centuries-long lesson that tolerance pays big dividends; that when people feel free to think "outside the box" or outside the Party Line, the resulting innovation and scientific progress benefits everyone. It also confirmed that when people know who they are—from their ethnic roots to their sexual identity—the presence of people who are different offers no real threat; and that religious affiliation is far less important than the character (faith) displayed in one's interactions with other people and the world at large.

The hope of all religions, and all humanist philosophies, is that somewhere along our collective spiritual journeys, we will eventually arrive at this crucial realization. Tolerance is the personal and communal practice of giving one another the time and space—within limits, of course—to get there. And as Golden Ages throughout history have progressively shown us, we *are* getting there.

TONGUES

"Speaking in tongues," to roll out the complete phrase, is one of those theological tempests in a teapot. It's the kind of minor religious issue that somehow manages to get blown out of proportion, and ends up causing divisions and sectarian off-shoots, and sometimes just plain shooting.

How many angels can dance on the head of a pin? Was the mother of Jesus a virgin in the sense of being sexually untouched or, as Hebrew scholars understand the word, simply a "young maiden"? Was Adam a real human being or only a fictional character?

Are our lives really *changed* by the answers?

The Christian debate over "tongues" concerns whether that word simply means "languages," or whether it refers to a specific language understood only by the Holy Spirit but uttered by human lips under certain conditions. The latter notion, called *glossalalia*, involves a trance-like state similar to that of a medium who is possessed by the spirit of a dead person, or the New Age "channeler" who provides vocal chords for entities from other dimensions. The difference, however, is that the human who speaks in tongues is channeling the third person of the Christian Trinity, and the language is distinctly *not* human. Those who practice glossalalia believe it is "the divine tongue." Others believe it's clearly jibberish.

What's clear is that *something* is going on. Anthropologists and psychologists admit that human beings can, in fact, enter a paranormal state of consciousness induced by religious fervor, in which ordinary speech patterns become altered. Claiming that God has taken over one's voice box is certainly one way of explaining it. The practice of purposely inducing this state isn't limited to Christianity, and seems to have been around in Europe, Africa and the Middle East long before Paul allegedly referred to it in his Epistles. Glossalalia supporters point to what Paul calls the "gift of tongues" and conclude that it must therefore be a valid part of the Christian tradition.

But was Paul actually referring to *this* practice? Opponents (including most Biblical scholars) think not. When it wasn't being used literally, the word "tongue" was employed by scriptural authors as a synonym for "language." And when people were reportedly speaking in tongues during the Jewish harvest festival (the Christian Pentecost), it was merely to say that many different languages were being spoken. Representatives of numerous cultures and traditions were present—Syrian, Aramaic, Hebrew, Greek, Roman and Egyptian—and yet all were hearing the stories of Jesus in their own native language. The "gift of tongues" was simply the talent some people had for translating the stories into the listener's language. To Paul, the ability to translate was a special gift, just like the ability to preach or heal or write. Or comprehend the truth.

Which doesn't necessarily invalidate glossalalia. Nor does the explanation that glossolalia is caused by a kind of short-circuiting of the brain's speech function. It may be, in ecstatic trances, that the syllables in words get rearranged, repeated and recombined so that a statement like "For God so loved the world" comes out "Solala gotha foworla dor." Or words to that effect.

Maybe the important thing to know about speaking in tongues is exactly that: Its *effect;* what the practice symbolizes to the people who experience it, either directly or by watching another person do it.

Because what it symbolizes is the fact that normal human speech is not the only way to communicate. Or rather that it's one of the *least* important ways. Communication is a mysterious process involving our entire being. The human spirit has its own language, which only sounds like jibberish sometimes because we're trying to hear it with our intellect and our reason. Perhaps we ought to try listening with our hearts now and then—to hear the emotion, see the passion; to feel the vibrations and energy beneath the words; to acknowledge that there's a whole other dimension within us that longs to be addressed and liberated.

That dimension is so alien to our carefully-controlled, scientific sensibilities that it scares many of us. But it's there. It is somehow connected to the core of our being, to what various traditions call our divinity or higher self or Holy Spirit. And it sometimes takes an obscure, even primitive religious ritual to remind us.

TRADITION

From the Latin *tradere,* meaning "to deliver," tradition refers to the collected stories, wisdom and rituals which are essentially packaged and delivered to us by those who've lived in the past, sometimes centuries or even millennia ago. This is contrasted with the stories and other things we discover from our own experiences in the present, even if others have already learned it and could've told us so if only we'd asked.

Tradition has the advantage of being, in some sense, demonstrably true or valuable over a long time span, and by large numbers of people. Our own experience has the advantage of being immediate and convincing, and not dependent on what someone else says, should we happen to ask.

FaithSpeak—this book—uses the phrase "religious tradition" or "traditional religion" to point to the world's major religions, or to the prepackaged, institutional style of a specific religion. This is contrasted with the kind of religion cobbled together by oneself from various sources, put into practice and demonstrated as true or valuable through one's own experience, even if others have already learned the same thing, and could've helped us learn it all the more easily if only we'd asked.

TRANSCENDENCE

Don't let the sheer magnitude of this word throw you. Or the fact that, around the turn of the Millennium, it became one of the favorite buzzwords not only for mainline preachers but New Age gurus and authors of self-help books. To the point it's now become almost meaningless.

Or maybe it means several things.

As a verb, it simply means "to climb beyond" or "climb out of." Transcendence is what happens when someone climbs out of the lousy condition or state of mind they used to be in, into a new and presumably better one. A person who grows up in poverty but develops some skill that eventually makes him wealthy is said to "transcend" his background. A woman who breaks through male prejudice to become a steelworker or Supreme Court justice transcends sexual stereotypes. A New Age devotee who has an out-of-body experience during meditation and then witnesses events in some distant location transcends normal waking reality.

In each of these cases, there is an assumption of customary limits that restrict people or create specific expectations. A child whose parents are dependent on welfare can be expected to live on the public dole when he, too, becomes an adult. A woman in a male-dominated culture is expected to "keep her place," and may even be punished if she rebels. We all have certain expectations about physical reality based on ordinary experience, which inevitably limits what we can do. Or what we *think* we can do.

So another aspect of transcendence is the "climbing out of" our previous ways of thinking. Before we're able to transcend something outwardly, we must shake off those inward, culturally-imposed or *self*-imposed limitations and expectations. We must change our attitude.

Transcendence is therefore a noun as well, referring to both a mental state in which one no longer accepts previous limitations, and the condition of living in accordance with that new attitude. Your outward conditions may not immediately change as a result; and there's no guarantee you'll actually rise above the limitations you've decided not to accept. But your point of view has changed. Your sense of what's possible has expanded, and thus your sense of Who You Are. As some would say, "The world is as you perceive it." And since you now perceive it differently, it *is* different.

Maybe that statement doesn't sound as radical as it's meant to be. Because the world isn't different merely because we look at it in a fresh way. The physical world can change in a *physical* way, the New Spirituality asserts, literally conforming itself to the attitudes we have about it. Maybe one single person can't affect it. But maybe two or three people can. Or five hundred, or five million.

That's why all religious traditions emphasize communal prayer, why "the spirit moves" when large crowds gather in common cause. Some of the more recent theories about physical reality and human consciousness lend scientific credence to this view, to the extent that if we were all convinced we could fly, we probably *could* fly. Or at least levitate. To paraphrase Jesus, if only we had the faith to move mountains, we could all be landscape designers.

And if you don't buy that, let's just say there are certain limitations you have yet to transcend.

So get out your hiking boots. Go climb a rock.

TRINITY

The story is told about a certain theology professor who gave his students a lecture on the Christian concept of The Trinity. After he'd finished he asked them: "Now, is that clear?" When some of the students answered *Yes,* he shook his head sadly. "Then you don't understand."

In other words, the concept of the Trinity *can't* be understood—by theologians, much less divinity students. It can only be accepted or rejected. Or ignored.

According to Christian tradition, The Holy Trinity is the fullest picture of God that humans can hope to comprehend. Even if, ironically, humans can never fully comprehend it. It is an image that simultaneously envisions God as a Father, a Son, and a Holy Spirit.

The Father, the so-called "first person" of The Trinity, is the entity responsible for creation. Or else the aspect of the Godhead we associate with creation. Or perhaps the divine reality behind the physical universe and everything that exists.

The Son is the "second person" who, it just so happens, was the historical Jesus of Nazareth proclaimed by Christians to be the Messiah or Christ, the Savior of the World. Or else the aspect of God that incarnates in humanity and just so happens to be the only force that can save us from our own destruction. Or perhaps the divinity (or Image of God) which already exists within us.

The Holy Spirit, the "third person," is also known by several other names including Holy Ghost, The Comforter, and Counselor. This is probably the most mysterious of the three, a kind of behind-the-scenes Power working in both the physical universe and the human heart, calling us to acknowledge our own divinity and to be transformed by it. Or else...

Or else whatever we can't fit into the first two aspects of God, we lump together, call it "Holy Spirit" and leave it at that.

Divine trinities and triads, it so happens, are fairly common among the world's religious traditions. Perhaps it's because there's something basically solid and balanced about them. The physical world can be visualized in three dimensions. Four-legged stools often wobble; three-legged ones don't. A single event is a fluke; two events is a coincidence; three events prove the rule. Trios are familiar, natural, reassuring.

Other theological trios include the Brahma/Vishnu/Shiva of Hinduism, combining the forces of creation, preservation and destruction. Ther's also the *Trikaya* of Buddhism, composed of the impersonal Body of Essence of Being behind the world of things; which in turn manifests as the Body of Spiritual Bliss, a redemptive Holy Spirit-like force; and the Body of Earthly Forms, which manifests in all earthly redeemers (including The Buddha). There is even the triad of the Yin-Yang—which most people assume stands for the duality of existence, but really represents the collection of all opposite forces together with their union: Spirit, flesh, and the unity of both; good, evil, and the unity in which there is neither; past, future, and their unity in the Eternal now.

These Trinities, of course, are no less incomprehensible than the Christian one. All of them are efforts to explain Ultimate Reality by dissecting it into its major components, while acknowledging that they are all really the same in essence. How they can seem separable and yet not be—or how they can be Three while really being One—is, as Church patriarchs conveniently labeled it, the Supreme Mystery.

Maybe that admission is a clue. The Trinity as Mystery: The Mystery out there *beyond* us; the Mystery walking *among* us; and the Mystery working *within* us. One great, big Mystery of Life, and three ways of relating to it.

Now, surely that's clear, isn't it?

TRUTH

The modern understanding of truth is virtually absent in most sacred texts until quite late, historically speaking. Truth as we know it was a Greek concept, originally a philosophical proposition which held that something could exist—a scientific law, say, or an historical event—apart from what anyone thought about it, or whether they thought about it at all. What happened during the creation of the universe happened regardless of what contemporary cosmology may hypothesize. The laws and forces that govern nature are whatever they are, whether we've managed to figure them out or not. What is, *is*. What is, is The Truth.

And knowing the truth, as both Christianity and Greek Gnosticism put it, will "set you free." Knowing the What Is, instead of depending on the philosophies and religions and thought-control systems designed to keep the masses in their place, is the only real freedom.

Naturally, how people come to know the truth is always an issue. A certain Roman Procurator's query to the would-be Messiah is informative. "What is the truth?" Pontius Pilate asks Jesus. The narrative records no answer. Not because there *is* no answer, but because truth can't be coughed up like some concise, one- or two-liner on the back of a Trivial Pursuit game card.

In fact truth can't really be put into words at all, not in any final form. Having a series of words in proper order isn't the same as having the truth. The real truth lies *behind* the words. And the best anyone can do is witness to it in their behavior and in their lives, and then let other people discover and incorporate it into *their* lives when they're ready. Jesus must have realized, as Pilate stood there waiting for a response like the host of Family Feud with fifteen seconds left on the clock, that Pilate wasn't ready for it.

Jewish tradition relates a similar story that pre-dates the Christian one, in which a cynical Roman soldier reportedly confronts a rabbi and asks him to distill the truth of the Torah while standing on one foot.

Unlike Jesus, who stood before Pilate in silence, the Jewish rabbi took his best shot. "What is hateful to you," he replied, "do not do to another. That is the whole of the Torah. The rest is only commentary."

Most people who retell this tale leave it at that point. So did this Lexicon in the entry on "Charity." But the real story doesn't end there. The rabbi adds one more thing—the most important thing, really—before the surprised soldier turns away. "Now go and learn it," he says.

Which is simply to restate the point that any one-shot answer, or magic formula, or article of faith, is simplistic and hollow unless we do something about it—unless we learn it by studying it and applying it and making it a part of Who We Are. To genuinely know the truth is to embody it, to incarnate it, to *be* it.

This is The Truth behind the goal of becoming Sons and Daughters of God, or becoming "Bar Mitzvah" (Son of the Commandment). It is the meaning of submission to Allah or "annihilating one's ego." And while the Pilate in us may ask for an easy answer, the God in us remains silent, knowing that it remains for us to learn it in our own way.

And in our own good time.

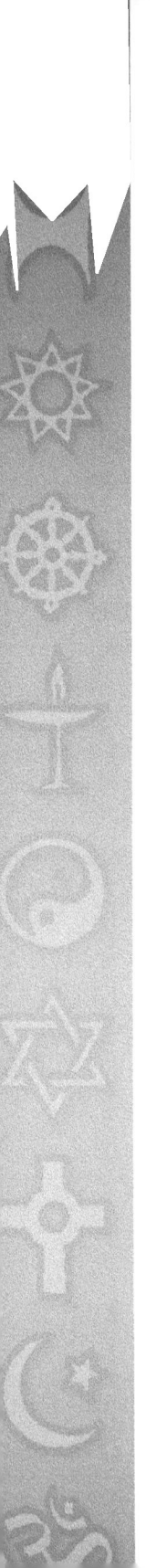

ULTIMATE REALITY

Take the concept of "God"...

...And then take away what you think you know about it, including what you've been taught by your religious tradition and your Philosophy 101 teacher and your best friend's brother who's a card-carrying atheist and just won't stop trying to convince you there's no such thing.

Now imagine that there *is* such a thing, or at least that there's some deeper Truth or Reality that people have pointed at for thousands of years whenever they've used the word "God." Realize that no matter what your religious tradition claims to know about the subject, or what your philosophy teacher or your best friend's brother may tell you—or even what this Lexicon says— none of it ultimately changes what that deeper Truth or Reality actually *is*.

Let the words "Ultimate Reality" stand for That Which Actually Is, no matter what anybody claims or says or thinks, or has ever written about it.

And then move on.

UNITY

In a word, "one-ness."

It's a tough concept to get across, but religious traditions and governments keep on trying. Even our dimes and dollars say it: *E Pluribus Unum.* Out of many, One.

It is a statement about Ultimate Reality, and about Who We Are. Or at least Who We Ought to Be. The wisdom of the ages suggests that, despite all appearances to the contrary, everything is designed to work together. Death and destruction are the flip side of birth and creation. Winter is preparation for spring. Evil is only a potential force for good that's been tragically misdirected. And if the human community could only operate as smoothly and harmoniously as the natural seasons and cycles, our existence would be Paradise.

Faithspeak, inevitably, was called upon to make the case. As human beings began to grasp the essential harmony of the universe, the divinities they imagined likewise became increasingly united. The nature spirits of early cultures were subsumed under a supreme ruler. All those bickering Greek gods were gathered into an extended family with Zeus as its leader. The monotheism of Jewish tradition was distilled into a doctrine that implied a unification of previous gods (or conceptions of God). Christianity's Holy Trinity plainly admits that the supreme Reality, while seemingly separable, is really One. And Hinduism has long recognized that the countless faces of divinity are ultimately reducible to one God/Truth/Absolute.

While most of us never get beyond an incomplete portrait of God—a profile view, perhaps, or maybe a close-up of the forehead or jawline or left temple—the full picture is there if only we can put all the pieces together.

The deeper message of unity, however, is that it's not necessary for each of us, individually, to put all the pieces together. It's nice if we do, of course; but it's more important to realize that, even if we see only a limited piece of the picture, even if we have only one talent, or we've accomplished only one decent thing in our whole lifetime, that one element is still an essential part of a greater whole.

Unity doesn't imply sameness; it isn't the notion that we should all become alike. In fact unity requires diversity, just as a community requires different people doing different things. Unity, in short, is the conviction that it is precisely through our differences that we finally become One.

And, not coincidentally, it's the name of a denomination calling itself "Practical Christianity" that subscribes to all of the above.

UTOPIA

Coined by Sir Thomas More as the title of a book he published in 1516, *Utopia* combines the Greek word *ou*, meaning "no" or "not," with *topos*, meaning "place" or "location." Utopia therefore literally means "no place." Or, in street slang, "Ain't never gonna happen, bro."

The utopian communities envisioned by 19th-Century social philosophers and Transcendentalists like Henry David Thoreau, in which everyone was supposedly equal and life's necessities were available to all, were simply unsustainable. The experimental Essene community at Qumran could never live up to its ideal of an observant, orthodox Jewish life unsullied by a corrupt Temple priesthood and the Hellenizing influences of the Roman occupation. The so-called Islamic State's idealized Caliphate was a disaster before its first beheading. The American Dream is still a nightmare for many, if only because some people still believe black lives don't matter, and if other people live in poverty it's only because they're not working hard enough. Even the Garden of Eden didn't last, because knowledge can be used for evil as well as good, and the more we know, the more potential there is for evil.

That doesn't mean we shouldn't continue to hold on to our visions for such an ideal place—or to *any* ideal, for that matter—even though we may never achieve it. Having a vision is more about striving than achieving. The Kingdom of God is a goal, not a location.

Which brings us to a kind of Zen Buddhist interpretation where "no place," like the concept of "No Mind," is actually our objective. It's where we no longer think of "place" as either an external or internal reality. It's the condition where your needs are as important as mine, where "yours" and "mine" are irrelevant distinctions to begin with.

And yes, it ain't never gonna happen this side of heaven. But it's a worthy exercise to try and visualize it... to see where that takes you.

To see where that takes "you."

VIDUI

From a Hebrew verb variously translated as "to reaveal" or "to acknowledge," a Vidui (*Vidj-wee*) is a kind of deathbed confession Jews are encouraged to recite if they feel their demise may be imminent. The words can be recited by the person who is facing death, or, if requested, by another on his or her behalf.

Like prayers recited on the Jewish Day of Atonement, the Vidui doesn't so much plead with God for forgiveness; rather, it asks one's fellow human beings to forgive any wrongs committed against them, while forgiving others for the wrongs committed against oneself. Each form of the Vidui—of which there are several—traditionally concludes with the *Sh'ma,* Judaism's proclamation of the Oneness of God, whose words are ideally the last ones on the dying person's lips.

Mirroring the Buddhist belief that the circumstances surrounding one's death set the stage for his/her next incarnation, Vidui reflects the same end-of-life hopes we all share: That our preparations for Whatever Comes Next will tie up any loose ends that may remain, console those whom we are leaving behind, and otherwise bring some sense of closure to the disjointed, disorganized, imperfectly-acted dramas that are our lives. And whose final scenes may unfold at any moment, often unexpectedly.

The Vidui serves as a reminder that it's never too early to begin thinking about what we'd like to say to others before we die, even if—or *especially* if—we never get the chance to say it.

VIRGIN BIRTH

Author Frederick Buechner probably summarized it best several decades ago: "Life is complicated enough," he wrote, "without confusing theology and gynecology."

Which may be a kinder and gentler way of saying, *What the heck difference does it make?*

The thing is, the Christian notion of the Virgin Birth *does* make a difference to millions of people. For the fundamentalist, the issue (as always) hinges on whether we're going to take the Bible literally or not. The New Testament says—or seems to say—that the mother of Jesus was not impregnated by her husband-to-be, Joseph, nor by any other human male. She was sexually unsullied at the time, and therefore, by the modern definition, a "virgin." And yet there she was, a mother-to-be all the same.

To get clinical about it, Mary supplied the ovum, the Holy Spirit supplied the sperm, and the end product was the Babe in the Manger. And if you don't accept that, the Christian fundamentalist will insist, you can't believe *anything* the Bible says.

Literalism, again, is one lens through which to read the Bible. And certainly a forceful way to emphasize how very, very important its broader message is.

On the other hand, stories of virgin births were being told all over the ancient map, most of which pre-dated Jesus. From Attis to Mithra, from Osiris to Zoraster, holy men and gods (and even a Caesar or two) were said to have been conceived in their mothers' wombs without fatherly fertilization. Considering the competition, the story of the latest Savior could hardly begin with routine human reproduction.

But the *non*-literal content is the real story of the virgin birth. Because what the story beautifully symbolizes is the idea that bringing a Son of God into the world—that is, attempting to mirror the Image of God in one's own life—is not a strictly biological process. If the ingredients are two parts flesh, the results are less than divine. The seed of the Holy Spirit must be planted in our wombs, or hearts or guts. Human instinct and flesh must be balanced by equal parts sacredness and soul. On this earth-bound plane at least, it takes both: A unity of seeming opposites. A unity without which there is no real salvation.

We're familiar enough with how evil takes root. Through child abuse and gun violence. Through a failure to provide role models and experiences that promote a sense of self-worth and direction. So when goodness appears in history, or in the life of someone we know, it's almost like a gift from heaven. It's as if such a life couldn't have come about without a dose of divine intervention, without God Himself coupling with the fairest maiden Earth has to offer.

Which is simply to admit that we're not very good at sowing the seeds of peace and harmony on our own. We may be able to conceive it intellectually. We're just having trouble getting past the flesh part.

VISUALIZATION

Most of us have witnessed a puppy sleeping, seemingly immersed in a dream, legs twitching as if he's chasing a cat or being chased by some bigger dog. So here's the question: Is the dog actually dreaming? Is he somehow picturing himself in pursuit, or being pursued—or maybe plowing through water or mud the way we experience that nightmare where we're trying to get someplace but we can hardly move our legs?

The short answer is *No.* Though we like to project human attributes and abilities on our animal friends, dogs don't dream as humans do. The life-like images we humans "see" in our sleep state, and especially the symbolic overlays we attach to them, are a by-product of a more advanced intelligence that also produces what we call "mind."

Somehow related to the mental images in our dreams are the visions we can create consciously, in our waking state—of a loved one, say, or a place we've been, or that sleek new Tesla we saw in a commercial between the Six O'clock News and a re-run of The Big Bang Theory. This uniquely-human ability is called "visualization," and under normal circumstances the resulting images aren't so much created as *re*-created, or reassembled from our memories.

Taking it one step further, *creative* visualization refers to our ability to imagine places we've never been before or which don't yet exist, or perhaps to envision the person we'd like to be, doing things we've never done before and living the life we'd like to lead. Exercising this ability for the purpose of producing actual changes in the real world, or in ourselves, is a hallmark of the New Thought movement and contemporary spiritual practices like "guided meditation." And yet this discipline is probably as ancient as dreaming, and why that word has always been used as a synonym for what we now call "visualization."

After all, just as remembered images can bring back strong emotions, *created* images can produce the emotional energy to inspire one's efforts to change the world. The same mechanism explains why prayer can be effective, if only by inspiring us to do the work we think we're asking our divinities to do for us.

But another question arises: Can creative visualization—or prayer, or guided meditation—create or enlist some kind of divine energy that is beyond our own emotions, independent of our own physical effort, and produce real changes to our four-dimensional, material world?

Most world religions are certain of it. Many "spiritual-but-not-religious" people are likewise convinced. And if the scientific evidence isn't in yet, neither has science ruled it out—especially in view of the relationships between matter and consciousness we can already prove.

In the meantime, even if creative visualization were no more efficacious than inspiring us to change things in a material way, that would be miraculous enough. And worth including in our religious toolbox.

VOCATION

Religious traditions not only affirm the necessity of work, but the honor and dignity of it. Moses was a simple shepherd, Jesus a carpenter, Muhammad a camel-driver. And while Buddha never had to work a day in his life, at least he came to realize that money is one of the least meaningful rewards for doing it.

Still, the need to be rewarded *some*how for what you do—and to do something for which you are rewarded—is as basic as the need for food, clothing and shelter. Because it helps define Who We Are. It shapes our sense of worth, of having a purpose in life, of making a difference. As counselors in drug rehabilitation programs can attest, only three things can permanently overcome someone's addiction: Finding God, falling in love... or becoming involved in rewarding work. Work is that powerful.

So it's not surprising that work should also be a major concern for religion. It's a matter of faith. The word "work," in fact, comes from the Latin *vocare*, which means "calling"—and which implies that what you do for a living is what you are *called* to do by God or Ultimate Reality. Just as Lancelot obediently answered the call of King Arthur, when you hear The Voice you take the job.

Today, choosing one's vocation still requires a good sense of hearing. But what we're listening for is not so much someone *else's* voice. It's the one inside us, which often sounds so far away it may *seem* like someone else's. And what makes it even harder to hear are the dozens of other voices conflicting and competing with it.

We all know what those other voices are. The ones that shout to us from magazine ads and TV commercials, that tell us what products we need in order to be fulfilled, thereby pushing us into jobs whose only justification is to help us pay for all those "necessary" products. Then there are the voices that want to buy our time and talents without employing our minds. Or that ask us to work for something contrary to our principles, or to sell out to security, or to do what is "expected."

The notion of having a vocation, as distinct from a job, is simply to remind us that listening to those other voices can be ultimately self-defeating. Because each of us harbors a subconscious awareness of the unique talents and skills we possess, the kinds of activities that will lead to genuine fulfillment. To suppress that awareness, to ignore our own inner voice, is to kill part of our selves. To do work that you hate, as Kahlil Gibran put it, is to "bake a bitter bread that feeds but half man's hunger." But working at something you love, he went on, "is to weave a cloth with threads drawn from your heart."

Which doesn't necessarily mean that our hearts are calling us on some glorious mission to save the world or end famine in Africa, or to discover a cure for cancer. In fact one of the other implications of "vocation" is that we may be called to do something quite humble. Our King or Queen of Hearts may summon us to the throne room only to assign us the mission of being a forklift driver or a waitress, a dental assistant or a teacher's aide.

Often our own egotistical pride turns out to be one of those other voices that prevents us from hearing our real calling. A desire for greatness doesn't require public visibility or fame. And an awakened spiritual awareness doesn't always mean you're being called to the ministry, either—perhaps only that your vocation should minister in some way to the needs of others.

Actually, the word "vocare" *does* imply a sense of ministry, of work that serves other peoples' needs even as it serves your own. It is the ideal intersection of what the world needs and what only you can give.

Or maybe it comes down to this bit of word-play: Do what you are *called* to do. Do what you are called to *do*. Do what *you* are called to do.

VODOU/VOODOO

Today this seemingly-spooky tradition is associated mainly with the island nation of Haiti. But the practice has roots in millennia-old African traditions and, indeed, in the pre-technological mindset from which nearly all the world's religions emerged. Haiti is simply one of its last remaining sanctuaries.

Some anthropologists point out, with tongues only partially in cheek, that the population of Haiti is 70% Catholic, 30% Protestant... and 100% Vodou. Which is simply to say that the practices are more cultural than religious, and now exist side-by-side with the belief systems taught by the priests and preachers who descended upon Haiti to eradicate them.

Contrary to Hollywood horror films, Vodou is not primarily about demon possession or poking needles into hand-made dolls that represent one's enemies. Certainly there is this darker side, just as most religions harbor tenets and texts followers interpret as divine permission to heap punishment on non-believers. But the central story in Vodou is about a beneficent universe whose creator god, even though distant, can still be approached through any of several spiritual intermediaries. Called *Lwa*, these helpful spirits are capable of bestowing health, wealth and other rewards in exchange for the worshippers' devotion.

Like Hinduism's pantheon of gods, each *Lwa* has a distinct personality and graphic representation (*Ve've'*). A few are admittedly frightful. Many require that a priest (*oungan*) or priestess (*mambo*) be "mounted" in order to channel their pronouncements, not unlike the early Hebrew prophets who drove themselves into ecstatic trances before they could speak on behalf of Yahweh.

The most beloved *Lwa*, however, are not so much frenetic and fearsome as serene and maternal. Queen of this more motherly approach is *Erzulie Dantor*, depicted in paintings and clay figurines in a pose reminiscent of the Virgin Mary, complete with a benevolent smile as she lovingly cradles an infant son against her breast.

The tragedy of Vodou lies not so much in its primitive view of the universe and rituals critics describe as satanic. Rather, it results from the unfortunate notion that believers must beguile the spirits for any benefits and blessings they may receive, instead of inspiring them to undertake the hard work of personal and communal betterment that might save Haiti from its worst-in-the-West living conditions.

Do resources exist outside our normal sensory awareness that certain spiritual practices may be able to summon for our benefit? Arguably so. But it's no coincidence that one of the Bible's most quoted texts is, "The Lord helps those who help themselves."

VOID

If you haven't already formed this impression from our previous references to Buddhism, let's be clear about it: Several of that tradition's core teachings are as esoteric and wildly metaphysical as they come. "Void" is one such teaching.

Essentially, Void refers to the Buddhist understanding of reality as a kind of apparition, having no more substance than a reflection in a mirror, or the glimmer of moonlight on water. (The latter is an oft-used metaphor.) There is no such thing as an independent object or event, only the infinite, unknowable, inter-related phenomenal "field" that produces the illusions of matter and time.

Which isn't so crazy, given the scientific evidence that everything we see, touch, hear, smell and taste are merely the sensory representations of energy fields vibrating in certain patterns and combinations, at certain levels of excitement. And the words used in that very explanation are equally illusory... verbal pointers we employ to wrap our minds around this supreme mystery.

Much like the way we use religious words to grasp another set of mysteries, or, as some would say, the very same Mystery.

In the beginning, Genesis says, there was only a Void. Emptiness. Nothingness. Buddhism would heartily agree. Most other scriptures say something similar. And then something came from nothing. Even if it was only words, or The Word, or a Way to mentally deconstruct our illusions and find meaning in them.

And to make all of it, for lack of a better word, *matter.*

WAR

The sacred texts of every religious tradition are bristling with armed conflict. Joshua fought the battle of Jericho. Arjuna (with Krishna at his side) meets his ruthless enemies, the Kauravas, in one of many epic battles repeated throughout Hindu literature. From Mattathias to Muhammad, skirmishes and sieges and all-out wars are reported in the same gory detail CNN splashes across our screens today.

And how could it be otherwise? Any history of the human race would be incomplete without a demonstration of the violence and atrocities of which we are capable. One of those atrocities relates to the fact that the losing side almost always gets pegged as The Bad Guys. The fact that "our side" uses the same grisly methods for solving disputes as they do (except that our methods were apparently more effective) is glossed over.

Even Christianity's "Love your enemies" and Taoism's "Return violence with kindness" were only temporary aberrations. The Chinese warlords who brought along their priests saw to that. The Popes who led their troops into battle saw to it, too, as well as the Christian Crusaders who wiped out whole Jewish communities on their merry way to the Holy Land so they could slaughter Muslims. Scriptures have often turned their respective divinities into cheerleaders for death and destruction. It's one thing to justify war as a kind of necessary evil; it's another thing to enshrine it as a religious duty. Either way it's an ugly legacy.

But the fact is, it is *our* legacy. We must own it. Like acknowledging our evolutionary roots in the animal kingdom, we must admit to what humanity has done in the past no less than what it can achieve in the future. Scriptural war stories are only showing us ourselves.

The battles recounted in religious traditions are also symbolic of the ongoing conflict between Good and Evil. So let's try reading between the lines, shall we? Forget for a moment that El Cid and his Moorish enemies both believed God was on their side, and that their tales of glory and victory came at the expense of the other. What makes the tales meaningful today is their message that our lives inevitably involve struggle, that our beliefs can sometimes run us straight into our opponent's wheelhouse. We can retreat or surrender to the resistance we encounter, or we can stand up for our principles and charge ahead despite all that. Whatever our choice, lives hang in the balance.

The primary meaning of Holy War or Jihad, you'll recall, is not about armed conflict with the neighboring tribe or the infidel who forsakes his religion. The Greater Jihad is the battle we all fight for control of our *selves*. Will our souls be plundered and carried away by purely physical pleasures and materialism, by what's expedient, by short-sighted self-interest? Or will we submit to that higher authority which binds our individual good to others—even to those we call enemies—and unites our minds and bodies in common pursuit of spiritual fulfillment?

The overcoming of one's fears, the passionate commitment, the risking of one's very life in the course of this interior Jihad finds a dramatic analogy in the courage and strength of the warrior. His sword and shield symbolize the ruthlessness we must have in rooting out the evil in our own hearts. The horse and chariot become the Law and Truth that give us a fighting chance, if not an edge over our spiritual adversary. And having other warriors on our side represents the fact that we're all in this together; we're not out there on the battlefield alone.

Stories of defeat only emphasize what the stakes are. Victories are statements that the struggle is winnable, and that the effort will ultimately be rewarded. In most scriptures, there are moral lessons in both winning and losing, not the least of which is that sometimes winning *is* losing, and losing is winning.

In fact, all things considered, it's too bad war makes such a good analogy for life's struggles. Maybe if we could expunge war from our collective scriptures and history books, we could eliminate it as a viable option today. Think of it: What would happen if we had no template for resolving disputes through violence? What if all the swords in literature were replaced by plowshares, and spears with pruning hooks? If human beings had absolutely no racial awareness of ever resorting to armed aggression in the past, might not war be unthinkable in the future?

Not on your proton torpedo, Captain Kirk.

War is Faithspeak for "the evil that men do," and *keep* doing, almost as if we're genetically programmed that way. And until men and women come to grips with it, the scriptural stories (and the live reports on CNN) remind us that our transformation is far from complete.

WICCA

From the Indo-European *weik,* meaning "sacred, holy," Wicca is the more formal name for the nature-oriented religion that's as old as our Paleolithic ancestors, and which sees the Earth (Gaia/Mother Nature) as one of its two primary deities. Unlike the equally ancient Shamanism, however, which restricted control of nature's animistic forces to a select few practitioners, Wicca is far more democratic in the sense that all (or most) of its tribal group members were given access to its ways.

That's one of the reasons why, as other religions became more formalized and their rituals confined to a priestly class, Wiccans were increasingly ostracized. Wiccan practices, now pejoratively labeled as "Witchcraft"—after all, any ol' witch could perform the rites, not just the authorized agents—were not only considered "wicked," but outlawed under penalty of death.

It's an interesting commentary on human progress that our more primitive forebears were often denigrated (and in some cases hunted to extinction) for their honest efforts to cope with life's spiritual questions, using their best understanding at the time, along with symbols that carried special meaning for them. Ironically, some of those primitive symbols still carry profound meaning, despite great advancements in knowledge and science.

And if you thought those last two sentences apply only to Wicca, think again.

WITNESS

Most of us think of the term in a rather legalistic fashion. A witness is someone who testifies in a court of law that an event did or didn't happen, or that a certain person was or wasn't at the scene of a crime. The witness can say this because he was there; he knows. In Old English, the word for "knowledge" is *witnes*. (Yes, without the final "s.") That on-the-scene knowledge is then used as evidence by the defense or prosecution to demonstrate the truth of some proposition, to prove their case.

In religious tradition, a "witness" can be any form of evidence, spoken or silent, human or otherwise, that demonstrates the truth or proves someone's case. A companion of Muhammad who was actually with him when he was alive is obviously a witness to the events of his time and to the statements he made. The blind person whose "eyes were opened" (whether literally or figuratively) is a witness to Jesus' healing power, just as the withered fig tree was witness to his destructive capabilities. (What?—you didn't know Jesus had a mean streak?) In a more symbolic way, the changed lives of Buddha's disciples were witness to the truth and efficacy of his Eightfold Path. Forgiveness or charity witnesses to the power of love. The mountains witness to God's majesty, the rainbow to his promise.

Of course, in most religious traditions a single witness isn't enough. Jewish law required at least three. And even then the reliability of the witnesses had to be confirmed by supporting evidence. A witness in a legal dispute, after all, might have a vested interest in the outcome that could color his judgment. Or he may flat-out lie, or simply be mistaken. What's more, testimony given as evidence for one claim may eventually prove something entirely different by the time all the relevant facts are in. Jumping to conclusions is no more advisable in religion than it is in court. In either case, what someone merely *says* is never decisive. Talk is cheap.

The most powerful definition of "witness," religiously speaking, is what a person *does*. Our actions witness to what we believe, to what our faith really is. Labeling ourselves as a Christian or Muslim (or even as an atheist) doesn't make us so. Declaring through some spoken article of faith that we believe in love or justice or peace-on-earth isn't proof we truly hold these sentiments. We need evidence, witnesses. Three at least; more would be preferable. Our daily lives are the courtroom, our actions our best defense.

And if that's so, the case against many of us looks pretty bad. Our only hope is that the jury won't jump to any conclusions before they've heard from all the witnesses. Maybe there's still time to go out and find some. Or *do* some.

WORD

Having just sung the virtues of actions over words, let us pause to remember that words sometimes *are* actions. Or at least they can inspire actions.

The Hebrew word *dabar,* in fact, can mean either "word" or "deed." Words often lead to deeds, and deeds are a kind of spoken word. Flip sides of the same coin.

The right word, or combination of words, sometimes has the power to motivate us when nothing else will. They can push a button in our brains, complete a circuit that may finally jolt us into actually doing something. We are susceptible to the power of words precisely because words are the symbols by which we think, at least consciously. Thinking and doing go together. Doing "witnesses" to Who We Are. Our words become flesh. We live out our words.

Which is why we go on searching for the right ones. The Word of God is shorthand for any collection of words that can convey to us How Things Are and therefore how we ought to live. If any particular Word of God doesn't happen to push our particular buttons, another one might. The mistake is to stop searching, stop listening.

Even when we think we've heard the last word.

WORSHIP

The Old English *weorthscipe* meant "worthiness." The word (noun) denoted the condition of having worth, of possessing value or importance.

Various people were sometimes addressed by the title "Your Worthiness"—or, in shortened form, "Your Worship." And here's an instance where a word is also an action (verb). Because in calling someone "Your Worship" you were openly acknowledging that person's value and importance. The title implied a recognition of your dependence on him or her, as well as your submission to their authority. Saying it was doing it.

This act of acknowledgement eventually evolved into the action verb "worship." The word was applied to any act that recognized the greater worth of someone or something, whether through a spoken affirmation or some kind of ritual. Like bowing one's head to the queen, or prostrating oneself on the temple steps.

The kinds of activities that go on in temples and churches are the most obvious examples of worship—the recognition through song, prayer and other rituals of the value of some higher power or Ultimate Reality. But people may also acknowledge the superior value (at least for them) of things like money or the human body, or sex or science, or the literal interpretation of scripture. By all manner of spoken and unspoken acts, people can and do worship these things as well.

For the most part, though, worship has come to refer only to those acts that express spiritual values. And the purpose of those acts is not to make us feel better (although they often do), or to give us a break from the hassles of daily life (although they certainly can). Their purpose is simply and solely to recognize and affirm that which is of greatest worth. By whatever name.

This activity is a two-way street. It's an ongoing dynamic, a daily interchange between Who We Are and Ultimate Reality during which our increased awareness of what's truly worthwhile affects what we do, and what we do reaffirms what's worthwhile. This kind of worship doesn't end at 11:30 on Sunday morning after the benediction, or when we rise from our knees after evening prayers. It isn't restricted to sanctuaries or tent meetings or the red-rock cliffs of Sedona. *Living* is worship.

How we earn a salary, spending an hour or two a month stocking groceries at the food bank... helping an old man find his car in the mall parking lot, giving a child encouragement or a smile... donating sixty bucks to charity instead of spending it on dinner and a show... taking care of your own health, giving your lover or friend (or even a total stranger) sixty minutes of your undivided attention and really, *really* listening—these are the most compelling demonstrations of worth. So too is yelling at your child, or ignoring the bag lady pushing all her worldly possessions down the street in a shopping cart, or spending $10,000 on a diamond-studded Rolex while people starve in Yemen.

Which is why we go back on Saturday or Sunday or Wednesday nights for those preplanned events we call worship services. Because in the midst of the daily grind we all too often forget what things are really worth. We need help to remember what's of greatest importance. To re-value our lives. And in the process ourselves.

Notes

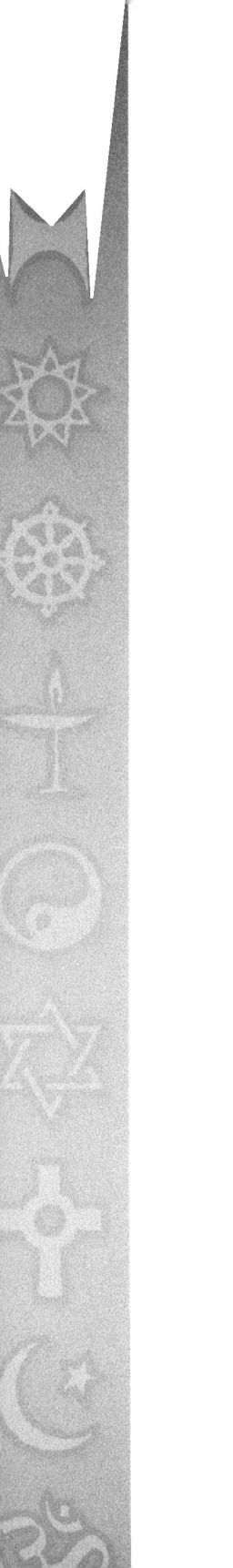

XEROGRAPHY

It's not that the author of this Lexicon is desperate to find any word that begins with an "X." Xerography really *does* have something to do with religion. And not just because the church bulletin may still be run off on your trusty Xerox copy machine.

One of the jobs of Faithspeak is to continually search for new and useful analogies for conveying the eternal truths. Computers and robots turn out to be excellent models for understanding abstract concepts like mind, soul, and body. But an even more difficult concept to get across is how the so-called material world "manifests itself" from, and interacts with, the spiritual dimension. Even supposing there *were* these two separate dimensions, how would the process work?

Enter the lowly Xerox machine. Or whatever brand-name copier or four-in-one machine you may prefer.

And by the way, "lowly" is hardly a fair description. The process of xerography is as amazing a technological feat as you'll find. What happens, basically, is that the image on an original document is converted through light into an electrostatic charge on a metal drum. That electrical information attracts a powdery black substance (toner) which, under heat and pressure, is then fused onto a blank sheet of paper to create an exact replica of the original.

If a Xerox machine could have been transported back into, say, the fourteenth century, someone watching this process might well have concluded that the machine contained a spirit. Or worse, a demon. It was the *demon* that transformed the original into an apparition of itself, probably by use of black magic. The operator of the Xerox machine would thereupon be accused of witchcraft and promptly burned at the stake. Along with his demon-possessed box.

The point here isn't that our fourteenth century friend just wasn't ready for the technology of the future, that it probably scared the hell out of him and he was only interpreting what he saw in terms he was familiar with. (Though all of that may be true.) The point is that one thing or "reality"—namely, the replica that was made, which we can now see and touch and read as if it were the original—can be created from another reality that seems so different to whoever is watching that it might as well have come from another dimension.

The fact that there was an original, material thing from which our duplicate was copied isn't the issue. We could just as easily have built our analogy around a fax machine or an ink-jet printer or even a TV screen. The lesson is that what all these devices produce, at some point during the process of producing them, was nothing more than an invisible electrical field or magnetic pattern or wave phenomenon.

In fact, in the case of the ink-jet, what ends up as a page of text was never a material thing to begin with. It originated in the author's mind as he was sitting at his computer or thumbing away on his iPhone. It was input through the electrolytic impulses within the nerves of his fingers, conveyed through the electrical signals of a keyboard and translated through binary digital language into temporary magnetic patterns on a memory chip, and then into the somewhat more permanent magnetic patterns on a hard drive or flash card. Each of these steps is barely comprehensible even to those who designed this process. But out comes the page of text anyway.

So let's imagine the electrostatic charges in our Xerox machine (or the magnetic patterns on a computer drive) as the "spiritual" dimension. The type on the printed page would be the "material." Fortunately for us, even after our page has "materialized," we can still use other material objects to change it. For example, we can brush a little white-out fluid over the smudges and misspelled words, then slip the paper into an old-fashioned typewriter and make corrections or additions.

In like fashion we can apply purely material solutions to other material problems in our lives. We can treat diseases with medicines. We can repair dented fenders and broken axles with Bondo and welding torches. We can hammer and dig and manipulate physical reality in all sorts of totally physical ways.

But what if we could go back to the Xerox machine and change the electrostatic charges before they're transformed into a printed page? What if we could manipulate *that* reality in order to fix the copy that's about to come out, or at least the next one after that? To assume this is possible is no more inconceivable than to accept what happens during the process of xerography itself.

To the fourteenth century mind-set, the Xerox machine would have been magic, sorcery, demonic. But only because no one had figured out the technology yet. Nobody had the vaguest notion, the mental building blocks to even think about it. They didn't have a conceptual model for imagining the possibilities.

Stop reading for a moment. Close your eyes. Imagine the possibilities.

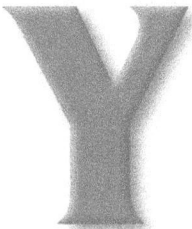

YES

In the field of mass marketing, there are several words that have special power to motivate people to purchase a product. Most of Madison Avenue's Top Ten marketing words haven't changed over the last fifty years. The word "you," for example, has always been near the top of the list. "New" is also right up there, or some variation like "Fresh" or "Improved." Other power words include "save," "love" and "younger." These words work because they grab our attention and push our emotional hot buttons. They connect with primal drives or instincts. They answer a need.

But of all these power words, nothing grabs, pushes, connects or answers our needs like "Yes."

YES!

Think how many times we've heard the word "No" in our lives. No, you can't go out and play. No, you can't have a cookie, or a new Barbie Doll, or a new car or pay raise. No, no, *NO*—until it's not merely the most common response to our requests, but a continuous refrain in the litany of our lives.

It doesn't matter that the denials may be justified. The word "No," for most of us, has come to symbolize the notion of denial itself, that our lives are continually corralled by limits and restrictions, defined by what we *can't* do instead of what we can. Worse, the phrase "No you can't" becomes synonymous with "You're not worth it."

"Yes" is the single word that turns this negative faith upside down. Yes means you *are* worth something. Yes means the glass is half full, not half empty. Yes is permission to try again, the freedom to become who you're meant to be.

Not that limits no longer apply. You still can't step off that ten-story building; but you can take up hang-gliding. You can't have sex with every attractive person you meet (or even the ones who say they're willing); but you *can* re-channel that same physical energy into doing things for others that can be far more gratifying. There are probably ten things you can do for each thing you can't; and even the things you supposedly can't do you probably *could* do if only you made up your mind to. Or you had a little help doing. And many times—incredibly, astoundingly often, in fact—the only help you need is the permission you give yourself by overcoming the No deep down in your soul by substituting Yes.

This kind of self-empowerment is almost a religion in itself. Its banner has been carried by mystics from the Sufis of Islam to the Hasidim of Jewish tradition. It has been endorsed by history's greatest religious figures. Promoters of positive thinking populate the bookracks and video shelves. The New Spirituality has taken it on as a primary theme, and TV evangelists have jumped on the bandwagon by offering free gold-plated "Yes You Can!" lapel pins from their studio pulpits. For only a small donation, of course.

The fact that it's suddenly in vogue, that "Yes" *sells,* makes it no less true. In a profound way it's one of those eternal truths. Religious traditions have been saying Yes to us all along, even if the Thou-Shalt-Not's keep getting all the publicity.

Maybe "Yes" is the image of God.

YOGA

Most of us think of it as an Eastern discipline that combines various postures, stretches and breathing exercises designed to help reduce the stresses of modern life, while promoting the body's flexibility and overall health. Which it is... in part.

The fact that this "part" belongs to a larger body of Hindu traditions is why many fundamentalist Christian denominations sought to ban its practice. And why, since their members have made it clear they want to continue enjoying yoga's health benefits, some of those denominations have attempted to invent their own religiously-sanctioned version under another name.

From a Sanskrit word meaning "to unite," Hindu-based Yoga seeks to unify an individual's body/mind—one's lower self—with the state of Pure Consciousness. The result not only brings bliss into one's earthly life, but the final unification that ends the cycle of death and rebirth.

There are six primary branches, each focusing on a different discipline for achieving that goal. These include: *Bhakti* yoga, which concentrates on one's devotional life; *Hatha* yoga, where the focus is on health and agility (this is the branch most Westerners mistakenly consider a synonym for "yoga"); *Jnana* yoga, which sees wisdom as the path to unity; *Karma* yoga, in which duty and action are central; *Kundalini* yoga, where one's inner spirit is the focus; and *Mantra* yoga, which employs chants and sounds in the quest to achieve higher consciousness.

Not one of these disciplines can't be found, in some form or other, in the stories, rituals and daily practices of the world's other great religions or denominations.

Including the ones that ban yoga altogether.

ZEUS

As the word "God" is to gods, Zeus is to *deus* (or deva or deity). Zeus, however, never grew out of his role as the blustering leader of all those lesser gods into an all-powerful, one-and-only, take-it-or-leave-it Absolute, as happened with the chief gods of many other historic cultures. The Greeks and Romans loved their pantheon of anthropomorphic gods too much. And while Zeus was allowed to be father of the divine family, he could sometimes be tricked like an ordinary mortal. He plowed other fields, sexually speaking, even though he was married to Hera; and he showed a whole range of human emotions and weaknesses that clouded and restricted his powers, just like they do ours.

Perhaps more than any culture's Top God, Zeus was a reflection of our inherent humanity more than our potential divinity. Rather than setting an example of the best and brightest, he was pretty much a down-to-earth dude, even if he did exhibit a few superhuman talents.

There's ample evidence to suggest he didn't start out that way. The root meaning of his name, after all, comes from a word meaning "brilliant" or "shining one." Zeus may have been a divinity of high moral standards in his theological youth, a luminous role model, a light to draw followers upward toward those elevated Olympian peaks. But as the centuries wore on and the stories and fables about him were further embellished, the masses took away his luster by bringing him down to their level. His increasingly human habits kept him within easy reach, made him more understandable, comfortable. And less threatening to the status quo.

There's a fine line between keeping our images of divinity accessible, and putting on such a human-like face that they lose their inspirational ability to bring out our best. Zeus is an example of crossing over the line. *Way* over.

Not that the Greek philosophers and intelligentsia ever believed in Zeus anyway. At least not literally. Zeus, Apollo, Aphrodite and all the others were convenient handles for talking about the workings of divinity, or at least the mysterious workings behind our everyday world, while maintaining a linguistic connection to tradition. It was a visual language; it was Faithspeak.

When St. Paul finally came along on his missionary journeys and told the Greeks that their gods were phony, he was basically telling the masses that the language of their tradition didn't work anymore. Like Zeus, their particular brand of Faithspeak had lost meaning and power. It was tired and uninspiring. It could no longer transform people's hearts. In short, it was out of touch with Ultimate Reality. The language of Christianity was far better, Paul said.

For all intents and purposes, it *was*. And the Greeks were the first to admit it.

ZODIAC

From a Greek word meaning "animals," the Zodiac comprises the twelve constellations (i.e. visible star formations) in which ancient people imagined the shapes of other living creatures, as people today might see animals and objects in the shapes of passing clouds.

Throughout the centuries these constellations—which are generally found along the same celestial plane as the sun and planets—took on a variety of symbolic meanings. In the Greco-Roman mystery religions, for example, they represented the sequence of spiritual tests required for a candidate's initiation. In astrology, the star patterns recalled the human patterns or "signs" for twelve different personality types. As often happens, a pseudo-science developed around this growing body of esoteric knowledge, in which people's birth dates relegated them to one star sign or other, and from which their future lives could then be "divined" or otherwise foretold.

In effect, a person's fate (and faith) was determined by the stars. And it's easy to see why this notion remains so popular today, even for people who adhere to a religious tradition, or who admit to reading Sydney Omarr's daily horoscope more for entertainment than guidance. Because astrology reflects our gut feeling that our lives are ultimately under the control of some greater power. True, people can still make choices. But the final outcome is written in the stars.

And there's a genuine sense of freedom, a wondrous, weight-off-our-shoulders release from responsibility, that flows from this belief. After all, sometimes our best efforts can seem like beating our heads against the proverbial wall, while at other times everything seems to go our way without us having to lift a finger. "In the stars" is simply another way of saying "It's God's will." Both are phrases we've been conditioned to accept as explanations, even though they don't technically explain anything.

But, hey—Life is a mystery. Sometimes there *is* no explanation. Or at least it seems that way. All we can do is shrug our collective shoulders or throw up our hands and flat-out admit we often have little to say about what happens during our lives, good or bad.

At least "written in the stars" keeps us looking up.

ZOROASTRIANISM

While Zeus and the other Greek gods are now remembered primarily as the literary leads in a body of ancient myth and legend, not all ancient religious languages have become obsolete. Depending on the richness of the tradition and its flexibility for conveying What Is, the same old words may still be the best.

Zoroastrianism still exists—and elements of that religion live on in many other traditions—because it still conveys meaning. For some people its words are still "the best."

The name comes from its founder, Zoroaster—or, according to some translators, Zarathustra. (Remember the opening theme in the sci-fi classic, *2001: A Space Odyssey?* This is the guy in the title.) A spiritual activist who lived in Persia during the seventh century BCE, Zoroaster made quite a splash in the local tabloids, reportedly being born through an immaculate conception (read: virgin birth), then going on to preach that salvation could be attained by joining the Forces of Good in their battle against the Forces of Evil.

There was no spiritual neutrality, Zoroaster warned. As a consequence of which side you chose and the deeds that flowed from your choice, you would eventually be judged worthy of Paradise or else condemned to the eternal punishments of Hell. The goal of mortal life was therefore *to actively fight evil*—a theme articulated clearly for perhaps the first time in history.

The supreme judge and Lord of Wisdom, representing the spirit of Good, was known as Ahura Mazda. He was assisted by Mithras, originally conceived as pure Light, but later humanized as a savior-god born of yet another virgin—this one impregnated in a lake of Zoroaster's semen. (Who said immaculate conception had to be pretty?) The spirit of Evil, by contrast, was embodied in Ahriman, who assisted in spreading moral and physical decay among humans through the idols and gods of the past.

If much of this sounds familiar, it should. If the Jewish captivity in Babylon, their eventual release by Cyrus of Persia, and the sweeping changes that subsequently took place not only in Jewish theology but in Greek, Christian and Islamic thought—if all these so-called coincidences now seem less than coincidental, they *should*. Because Zoroastrianism laid the groundwork for most of the Faithspeak that came to characterize Western religious tradition. Even if Zoroastrianism itself is hardly the thriving tradition it once was.

Does all this cross-pollination diminish the uniqueness and credibility of its Western descendants? Not at all. Insofar as the basic themes and symbols of Zoroastrianism stuck, it was because they conveyed essential truths about reality, about who or what the ultimate powers of the universe are, and how humans should interact with them.

In fact, it is through the study of *all* religions, past and present, that we finally begin to catch sight of the Ultimate Reality beyond them. In their similarities and differences, in what these religions are saying and doing, the dynamic of faith begins to peek out from behind the specific words and symbols being used. Like the testimony of three witnesses in a court of law, their combined evidence begins to confirm and clarify not what those people *say* the truth is, but what the truth really *is*.

And sometimes, when we look deeply into another tradition—whether Zoroastrianism or any other—the language of our own religion opens up in surprising new ways, taking on deeper meaning, unveiling more to us than ever before. No longer can we mouth the same words or go through the same rituals with the same routine dispassion. We suddenly get an inkling of the great and amazing things going on around us and through us. We realize (along with Shakespeare) that there are far, far more things in heaven and earth, dear Horatio, than are dreamt of in your philosophy. Or anybody *else's* philosophy. Or all of humanity's philosophies and religions and sciences put together.

Behold the awesome, infinite, now-you-see-it, now-you-don't Mystery of the What Is.

Behold the equally awesome Mystery of What We Are.

And watch the space between them grow smaller and smaller as we continue our mission to understand them both.

About the Author 493

Author Interview 494

Other Books by Mark Haskett 497

Pages for Reader's Notes* 498

*Additional pages for notes may be
found on pages 57, 187, 265,
317, 327, 335 and 477.

About the Author

MARK HASKETT *is a working artist, writer and musician, and has been a student of philosophy and religion for most of his adult life. He has authored articles, novels and non-fiction books, each of which invites his readers to explore the deeper dimensions of everyday life that provide meaning and enhance mutual understanding. For more on his other books, please turn to page 497.*

Active in his local interfaith community, Mark is a frequent guest speaker and moderator on matters of practical faith and spirituality. He occasionally tours with his "Song of The Prophet" concert/service drawn from Kahlil Gibran's poetic masterwork, THE PROPHET.

Mark lives with his wife Nancy in California's Central Valley, and may be contacted directly by going to: www.IFMedia.org/Feedback.

IF Media: *You've referred to FaithSpeak as your most important work. Why?*

Mark: Well, let me first say that "important" is an adjective best left to readers and literary critics. But I *do* hope the book will have an impact on the way people think about faith and religion, both their own and others.'

And that includes all of us, because, as you argue in your opening chapters, everybody has a faith, and everybody has a religion.

Mark: Exactly. Even so-called non-believers and atheists. Most of us simply aren't aware of what the two really are.

You spend the majority of the book's Part One defending your use of the terms "faith" and "religion." Can you summarize your argument for us?

Mark: James W. Fowler summarized it over three decades ago in his book, *Stages of Faith*. In addition to Kahlil Gibran's *The Prophet,* Fowler's book was one of the most significant revelations on my spiritual journey. Based on his thesis and the work of other psychologists before him, I use the word "religion" to point to the collected rituals, stories and organizing principles all of us employ, consciously or not, to shape Who We Are. Our "faith," on the other hand, is the collection of personal characteristics that describe Who We Are at any one point in time. Faith refers to the way we think, what motivates us, and most importantly, how we behave… what we *do*. The first is a process, the second a product.

And that distinction is important because…?

Mark: Because it forces us to pay attention not to what people call themselves or what tradition they may align themselves with, but on the kind of people they are. We can't—or at least shouldn't—form relationships or judge people on the basis of whether they claim to be Christians or Muslims, Hindus or Humanists. What matters is how they act, the "content of one's character," as Martin Luther King put it. A person's friendliness or suspicion of others, for example. Their tendency to demonstrate generosity or selfishness, loving-kindness or intolerance... these are all personal qualities.

And that leads to your claim that a Buddhist, a Baptist and an atheist can share the same basic "faith," all the while belonging to very different religious traditions.

Mark: It's not a claim. It's a fact we can observe in our lives every single day. It's also a clue that what shapes our faith—Who We Are—isn't just our religion, or even *primarily* religion. We're products of the larger culture we live in and the events we experience in our lives, especially during childhood. And once we realize the kind of person we are and how we've become that way, it becomes our responsibility to take the leading role in that ongoing faith-shaping process, hopefully toward a progressively-better version of Who We Can Be, and in that way we essentially "redeem" ourselves.

A word that makes a nice transition to what is by far the largest portion of your book... the Lexicon.

Mark: Right. Because if we accept this new understanding of faith and religion—or at least we go along with it for the sake of argument [*laughs*]—we now have the obligation to reconsider religious terms like "redeem" or "redemption" for what they are: Parts of a language designed specifically for faith-shaping, with deeper meanings that are shared by other traditions, too, and can often be expressed through ordinary secular words. Although, to give religion its due, I also argue that there are things religious language is able to communicate that secular words aren't as good at.

So you're not just religion-bashing here, as some of our fundamentalist friends might allege. Or apologizing for religion, as an atheist reader might see it.

Mark: Not at all. And I'd hope that, before people on either end of the spectrum send me their comments, they read my

Lexicon entries on "Fundamentalism" and "Atheist"—and remember that religion in the traditional sense can still play a vital role in our lives. Not in the manner where religious authorities impose it on their followers as many have tried to do for thousands of years, but in the sense that we can apply it *on ourselves* to refine and improve Who We Are.

So is that what motivates your interfaith work?

Mark: I guess it does help explain my ongoing involvement. I continue to believe that people all across the religious spectrum hold far more in common than not. Likewise those who identify as religious and those who don't. In a sense, *FaithSpeak* is a handbook for finding common ground.

What you've called "The Mother Tongue" behind humanity's religious dialects…?

Mark: Look, words are only mental constructs for pointing at meanings. We too often make the mistake that words which sound and look different point to different things.

But your Lexicon isn't merely an attempt to uncover the shared meanings behind the words. Or re-defining the religious words we use.

Mark: Like I admit in Part One, some words in the Lexicon are basically excuses for me to talk about the wider issues in our religious and spiritual journeys, from this new perspective. But it's not like I'm claiming to have the last word, either. More like starting a discussion. Or continuing a conversation that probably began in the reader's mind long before he or she picked up my book. And if there's ever a *FaithSpeak Two*, it'll probably be inspired by my readers' responses, and whether this new way of looking at faith has produced any positive results… in their personal lives or in their communities, or maybe even the wider world.

And that could be, well… important.

Mark: [*laughs*] Your word, not mine.

ALSO BY MARK

In Mark's latest novel, **GREATER MIRACLES**, Gabriel Woods is on the run because of the miraculous power he wields but doesn't want. When he chances upon Lane D'Arcy, an enigmatic beauty who appears immune to his "gift," Gabriel suddenly dreams of having a normal life again. A looming strike at the munitions plant in Lane's half-Anglo, half-Native American hometown soon gets in the way, as does a police chief determined to uncover his secret.

The timeless wisdom of Kahlil Gibran's poetic masterwork, THE PROPHET, is showcased in these insightful reflections on 101 of its most compelling passages. Divided into nine more universal themes that underlie Gibran's original 26 "counsels," **A DEEPER SONG** infuses the full breadth of human experience with fresh meaning and renewed significance.

When evangelist Jimmy Talbot opens a new Gospel-themed casino in downtown Las Vegas to resurrect his ministry, estranged half-brother Levi is unwillingly assigned to lead an investigation into both the bomb threat and string of grisly murders connected to it. Doubling as a crime novel and a social commentary, **CALVARY CASINO** is ultimately a page-turning parable on the subject of reconciliation and redemption.

Whether you're a devoted fan of Star Trek® or not, you'll find a treasury of inspiration and insight in **BOLDLY GOING ON YOUR INNER VOYAGE**. Each daily reading begins with a quotation from one of the franchise's diverse and fascinating cast of characters, then offers thoughtful meditations and practical affirmations on themes ranging from Inner Conflict to Inner Resources, from Accepting Oneself to Serving Others.

For longer synopses and author interviews relating to Mark's books, please visit our website at: www.IFMedia.org/IFBooks.

FAITHSPEAK

Notes

FAITHSPEAK

Notes

www.ingramcontent.com/pod-product-compliance
Lightning Source LLC
Chambersburg PA
CBHW070524090426
42735CB00013B/2861